Professional Review Guide
for the CCA Examination
2017 Edition

Patricia J. Schnering, RHIA, CCS

Lauralyn Kavanaugh-Burke, DrPH, RHIA, CHES, CHTS-IM

Marissa Lajaunie, MBA, RHIA

Shelley C. Safian, PhD, RHIA, CCS-P, COC, CPC-I,
AHIMA-Approved ICD-10-CM/PCS Trainer

Debra W. Cook, MAEd, RHIA

Australia • Brazil • Japan • Korea • Mexico • Singapore • Spain • United Kingdom • United States

Professional Review Guide for the CCA Examination, 2017 Edition
Patricia J. Schnering, RHIA, CCS

SVP, GM Skills & Global Product Management: Jonathan Lau

Product Director: Matthew Seeley

Product Team Manager: Stephen Smith

Senior Director, Development: Marah Bellegarde

Senior Content Development Manager: Juliet Steiner

Content Developer: Kaitlin Schlicht

Product Assistant: Mark Turner

Vice President, Marketing Services: Jennifer Ann Baker

Marketing Manager: Jonathan Sheehan

Marketing Coordinator: Andrew Ouimet

Senior Production Director: Wendy Troeger

Production Director: Andrew Crouth

Senior Content Project Manager: Kara A. DiCaterino

Art Director: Angela Sheehan

Cover image(s):
© Galyna Andrushko/Shutterstock.com

For product information and technology assistance, contact us at
Cengage Learning Customer & Sales Support,
1-800-354-9706

For permission to use material from this text or product, submit all requests online at **www.cengage.com/permissions.**

Further permissions questions can be e-mailed to
permissionrequest@cengage.com

Library of Congress Control Number: 2016961570

ISBN: 978-1-305-95654-4

Cengage Learning
20 Channel Center Street
Boston, MA 02210
USA

Cengage Learning is a leading provider of customized learning solutions with employees residing in nearly 40 different countries and sales in more than 125 countries around the world. Find your local representative at **www.cengage.com.**

Cengage Learning products are represented in Canada by Nelson Education, Ltd.

To learn more about Cengage Learning, visit **www.cengage.com**

Purchase any of our products at your local college store or at our preferred online store **www.cengagebrain.com**

Notice to the Reader

Printed in the United States of America
Print Number: 01   Print Year: 2017

ABOUT THE AUTHORS

Patricia J. Schnering, RHIA, CCS

Patricia J. Schnering was the founder of PRG Publishing, Inc. and Professional Review Guides, Inc. She works as an author and editor for PRG products. Mrs. Schnering is a 1995 graduate of the Health Information Management program at St. Petersburg College in St. Petersburg, Florida, and received her RHIT certification in 1995. In 1998, she was certified as a CCS, and in 1999 she received her RHIA certification. Her education includes a bachelor's degree from the University of South Florida in Tampa, Florida, with a major in Business Administration. Since 1993, her work in Health Information Services includes supervisory positions, as an HIM consultant and as an adjunct HIM instructor at St. Petersburg College. She was the recipient of the Florida Health Information Management Association (FHIMA) Literary Award in 2000 and 2006.

Marissa Lajaunie, MBA, RHIA

Marissa Lajaunie is currently an Associate Professor in the Health Information Management Program at the University of Louisiana at Lafayette. She obtained a Bachelor of Science degree in Health Information Management and a Master of Business Administration. She has also been a Registered Health Information Administrator since 2009. Mrs. Lajaunie teaches several courses, including Medical Terminology, Healthcare Statistics, Quality Improvement, Management Internship, and Concepts in Healthcare Delivery.

Prior to teaching, Mrs. Lajaunie held a management position at an inpatient psychiatric facility where she was responsible for the overall leadership and operation of the facility's services, departments, and functions.

Mrs. Lajaunie is currently a member of the American Health Information Management Association and the Louisiana Health Information Management Association, and is President of the Southwest District of the Louisiana Health Information Management Association.

Lauralyn Kavanaugh-Burke, DrPH, RHIA, CHES, CHTS-IM

After receiving a BS degree in Medical Record Administration with a minor in biology from York College of Pennsylvania, Dr. Burke worked in several hospitals in Virginia and Maryland in various management positions, including DRG Analyst, Assistant Director, and Director of the Medical Record/Health Information departments. During this time, her interest in pathophysiology intensified after working with several physicians in their research endeavors. She started teaching at an associate's degree Health Information Technology (HIT) program at Fairmont State College in West Virginia where she was able to strengthen her anatomy and pathophysiology skills, not only instructing HIT students, but also working with the medical laboratory and veterinary technology programs there. This position gave her the chance to complete her MS degree in Community Health Education from West Virginia University, which perfectly blended health information management and education. She achieved her Certified Health Education Specialist (CHES) credential shortly afterward. She then moved back to Pennsylvania and returned to the hospital arena as a DRG and coding consultant. Dr. Burke had the opportunity to teach at her alma mater and lay the foundation for an associate's degree program in HIT at a local community college.

Subsequent to relocating to Florida, she became a faculty member at Florida A&M University's BS degree program in Health Informatics & Information Management Division. She continued her pursuit of more training in pathophysiology, and soon after received her Doctor of Public Health (DrPH) with a concentration in epidemiology from Florida A&M University. Dr. Burke's main areas of interest are in disaster preparedness for hospitals, and bioterrorism and infectious diseases. She recently achieved certification as a Health Information Technology Implementation Manager (CHTS-IM) after completing her HITECH training through Santa Fe College.

Shelley C. Safian, PhD, RHIA, CCS-P, COC, CPC-I, AHIMA-Approved ICD-10-CM/PCS Trainer
Dr. Shelley C. Safian has been teaching Health Care Administration, Health Information Management, and Medical Billing and Coding, both onsite and online, for more than a decade. She writes several articles each year on various aspects of coding. In addition, she is the author of six textbooks, including *Essentials of Health Care Compliance* published by Cengage Learning.

Dr. Safian is entering her fourth year as the Chair of the Continuing Education committee for FHIMA (Florida Health Information Management Association). In the past, she has served on several committees and practice councils on the national, state, and local levels of Health Information Management Associations.

Debra W. Cook, MAEd, RHIA
Debra W. Cook is a graduate of the Medical Record Administration and the Adult Education programs at East Carolina University in Greenville, North Carolina. Her HIM experience includes 5 years in acute health care practice in a variety of positions, such as management, utilization management, coding, and consulting. She also has over 24 years' experience in HIM education at Alderson-Broaddus College and Marshall University in West Virginia, and Catawba Valley Community College (CVCC) in Hickory, North Carolina. Currently, she is the Department Head of Health Information Technology at CVCC and Director of the Workforce Development Program for Electronic Record Specialists. In addition to this, she serves on the Panel of Accreditation Reviewers for the Commission of Health Informatics and Information Management Education.

ACKNOWLEDGMENTS

First and foremost, I would like to express my gratitude to all of the authors who have worked on the educational materials PRG Publishing has produced. They are seasoned professionals and excellent educators. They inspire me to work harder to produce better products. Each of these educators presents a facet of HIM practice necessary to view the HIM arena as a whole.

I thoroughly enjoy working with the authors. They are experts in the HIM field. They go all out to keep the quality of HIM education at an increasingly higher level. The superb quality of work they produce keeps me motivated. It is a pleasure to be able to call them friends and professional peers.

The Cengage Learning family has been extremely patient and helpful in guiding me through the publishing system. Thank you all very much!

I want to especially thank Kaitlin Schlicht my Content Developer for Health Care at Cengage. She is magnificent at catching glitches and errors. She has the organizational skills to help keep the books on track. I couldn't ask for a better person to work with on the PRG books.

My thanks would not be complete without acknowledging all the HIM/HIT educators and students who support our efforts by purchasing PRG Publishing products.

My reward is knowing that the materials you study here may assist you in preparing for the challenge of the examination. Thank you for the letters and words of encouragement.

I wish you the very best now and throughout your career.

Until we meet....

Patricia J. Schnering, RHIA, CCS

PJSPRG@AOL.COM

TABLE OF CONTENTS

Introduction

Patricia J. Schnering, RHIA, CCS

INTRODUCTION TO THE PROFESSIONAL REVIEW GUIDE FOR THE CCA EXAMINATION

This examination review guide represents a renewed effort to provide materials for health information management (HIM) students and professionals preparing for the Certified Coding Associate (CCA) examination for entry-level coders. In reviewing the results of past examinations, we found that it would be beneficial for examination candidates to have additional practice in answering multiple-choice questions. We have selected questions to cover the broad topic of HIM categories necessary for sitting for the CCA Certification Examination. Researching the questions and cases as you study should increase your knowledge such that, when you encounter similar questions, you can arrive at the correct answer. We believe that this review material will jog your memory and build on information you have already gained through your education and professional experiences. This book provides you with a mix of coding questions to both increase your coding skills and provide you with testing that mimics the exam format.

The questions in this examination review guide are based on the broad competencies listed in the AHIMA Candidate Handbook for the CCA Examination. Review the latest candidate information and handbook when preparing for the exam. It can be found on AHIMA's website (http://www.AHIMA.org).

The beginning of this book offers suggestions for studying and test-taking strategies and a coding review section. The following chapters contain multiple-choice questions covering the competencies for the exam. Then there is a quiz with 35 multiple-choice questions and a mock examination containing 100 multiple-choice questions. The backmatter of the book contains appendices with information on pharmacology and laboratory testing. Table I-1 displays the major content areas of this book by section.

Table I-1 Chapter Contents for the Professional Review Guide for the CCA Examination	
Content Areas	Number of Questions
Study Strategies	N/A
Coding Review	N/A
Health Data Content and Standards	75
Medical Sciences	176
Classification Systems and Secondary Data Sources	87
ICD-10-CM/PCS Coding	203
CPT Coding	217
Medical Billing and Reimbursement Systems	130
CCA Mock Quiz	35
Mock Examination Multiple Choice Questions	100
Appendix A: Pharmacology	N/A
Appendix B: Laboratory Testing	N/A
Appendix C: ICD-10-CM Official Guidelines for Coding and Reporting, Effective October 1, 2016	N/A
Total Questions	1023

ABOUT THE COMPETENCIES FOR THE CCA EXAMINATION

We suggest that you start by examining the competencies for the Certified Coding Associate. The Domains and Task Statement Competencies were created to reflect the entry-level competencies for HIM professional practice. A detailed copy of the entry-level competencies is provided in the AHIMA Candidate Handbook Examination.

It is the responsibility of the American Health Information Management Association's (AHIMA) Commission on Certification for Health Informatics and Information Management (CCHIIM) to assess what job tasks are frequently executed by newly certified practitioners. In addition, the CCHIIM determines the job tasks that are critical to entry-level practice—in other words, which job tasks, if done incorrectly, could create a negative impact. The task statements are also referred to as the test specifications.

The process of identifying those critical job functions was accomplished by conducting a job analysis. The objective was to determine how entry-level practice is evolving and to develop the test specifications and a certification examination to correspond with changes that are occurring in the field. The data that were collected as a result of this research provided the essential elements that were necessary to establish the test specifications for the certifying exam. The CCHIIM is responsible for developing and administering the certification examination and determining the eligibility of applicants to write the exam.

The entry-level task statements for the Certified Coding Associate from the AHIMA Certification are grouped into six domains:

☑ Clinical Classification Systems
☑ Reimbursement Methodologies
☑ Health Records and Data Content
☑ Compliance
☑ Information Technologies
☑ Confidentiality and Privacy

These six domains are divided further into task statements. See the Candidate Handbook for a complete listing of the task statements.

Weights for each domain are assigned. Each weight correlates to the degree of emphasis, or importance, given to each domain as it relates to the health information practice. Table I-2 displays the weights that were assigned to each of the domains.

Table I-2 CCA Examination Content with Percentage of Questions by Domain	
Domain	Percentage of Exam
Domain 1: Clinical Classification Systems	30–34%
Domain 2: Reimbursement Methodologies	21–25%
Domain 3: Health Records and Data Content	13–17%
Domain 4: Compliance	12–16%
Domain 5: Information Technology	6–10%
Domain 6: Confidentiality and Privacy	6–10%
TOTAL	100%

Source: AHIMA Candidate Handbook for the CCA Examination. Reminder: Monitor AHIMA's website for updates on the testing information.

Although we have no way of knowing exactly what questions will be on the examination, the authors have tried to cover the competencies and content areas as comprehensively as possible. Researching the questions as you study should expand your knowledge such that, should you encounter similar questions, you can arrive at the correct answer. We believe this review material will serve to help you build on information you have already gained through your experience and education.

Crosswalks between the competencies for the CCA Certification Examination and the questions in the chapters are provided in Table I-3. In addition to the competencies, the questions are written in three cognitive levels of testing, which are explained on the next page.

Table I-3 Crosswalk of the CCA Examination Competencies to Chapters							
	Domains						
Chapter	1	2	3	4	5	6	Total
Health Data Content and Standards	6	3	49	4	11	2	75
Medical Science	176	0	0	0	0	0	176
Classification Systems and Secondary Data Sources	61	1	6	7	12	0	87
ICD-10-CM/PCS Coding	203	0	0	0	0	0	203
CPT Coding	217	0	0	0	0	0	217
Medical Billing and Reimbursement Systems	39	76	1	6	7	1	130
Mock Quiz	35	0	0	0	0	0	35
Mock Examination	71	11	9	2	5	2	100
Total Questions	808	91	65	19	35	5	1023

The key to success on the exam is a thorough knowledge of coding, which can only be achieved through extensive use of and familiarity with the code books. Having to use the code books to answer questions will help increase your speed in the use of both coding books.

This book is only one of many tools available to you to prepare. Use a variety of review methodologies (multiple-choice questions, case studies, review of theory, mock exams, etc.) as an effective means of reviewing. These tools can help prepare you for the challenge of the CCA coding exam.

In the following chapters, there are a myriad of suggested resources.

ABOUT THE COGNITIVE LEVELS OF TESTING FOR THE CCA EXAMINATION

The examination questions test your knowledge on three cognitive levels:

- Recall (RE)
- Application (AP)
- Analysis (AN)

The recall level tests your memory of basic facts, such as being able to identify terms, methods, and procedures. The application level tests your ability to interpret data and information, to be able to apply concepts and principles, to recognize relationships among data, and to calculate mathematical problems. The analysis level measures your ability to solve specific problems by evaluating, comparing, and selecting appropriate solutions for action and to evaluate information and perform multiple calculations to assemble various elements into a total picture. There are sample questions provided on the AHIMA website (http://www.AHIMA.org), so that you can experience the testing situation.

The general format of the exam is primarily designed to engage your problem-solving and critical thinking skills. These types of questions require you to translate and apply what you have learned as well as interpret information.

CCA EXAMINATION CONTENTS

The CCA examination is in a computer-based format. Carefully read the latest Candidate Handbook for the CCA Examination and continue to monitor AHIMA's website to look for updated information on the examination format. The handbook is available for downloading in PDF format on the AHIMA website (http://www.AHIMA.org).

The CCA examination has 100 questions (90 questions scored and 10 that are not scored for the exam). The 90 scored questions are the basis for scoring your examination. The 10 unscored questions on the CCA examination are used in obtaining statistical information to help in the construction of questions for future examinations. These 10 questions will not be identified in the exam, nor will they count toward the examination pass/fail score.

Pass rates for the CCA examination for 2013 through 2015 are shown in Table I-4.

Table I-4 CCA Certification Examination Pass Rates for First-Time Test Takers (2013–2015)			
Year	Number of Exam Takers	Pass Rate	Total Credentials Awarded
2015	2,250	60%	1,343
2014	2,241	60.5%	1,357
2013	2,381	63%	1,499

Examination pass rates are based on the calendar year (January 1 through December 31).
Source: http://www.ahima.org

ADDITIONAL INSIGHTS ABOUT THE CCA EXAMINATION

1. **Computerized testing.** You will be able to review questions on the computer screen to check your answers before you close the exam file on the computer.

2. **On-screen information.** Any additional information needed to complete the questions will be provided on the screen in the testing software.

3. **Medical sciences.** These questions tend to be interspersed throughout the other topic categories. Medical terminology, pathophysiology, and anatomy and physiology are part of the general knowledge base for health information management, coding, and reimbursement.

4. **National exam.** Keep in mind that this is a national examination. Concentrate on federal legislation, statutes, and legal issues that would be appropriate nationally in all 50 states.

5. **Be prepared to shift gears quickly throughout the exam.** Questions on the examinations are scrambled and change topics from question to question. Therefore, you may have a health care data question, followed by a coding question, followed by a reimbursement question, etc.

6. **You will need to bring your ICD-10-CM and ICD-10-PCS coding books and the AMA CPT-4 coding book to the test. AHIMA has a list of allowable code books in the Candidate Guide.** It is necessary that the entry-level coding practitioner be adept at using code books. Although some questions are in a narrative form and any necessary codes and/or code narratives will be supplied in the answer options on the computer screen for you to choose from, you will need to use your code books to answer other questions or verify the answer you choose. Practicing coding using your coding books will help increase your speed in finding the codes. Remember, the test is timed. The faster you code, the more time you have to choose your answers. It may be the difference in being able to successfully complete the examination in the time allotted.

7. **Review the latest candidate handbook.** The AHIMA Candidate Handbook for the CCA Examination contains information on the exam, how to apply for the examination, what to bring, and other pertinent information you need.

8. *Make sure that you have the necessary items for admission for testing.* You will need to bring your Authorization to Test (ATT), two forms of identification (one with your photograph), and your coding books. Verify that you have correct versions of the coding books. *Candidates that do no present the correct versions of codebooks will forfeit their exam fees.*

PROFESSIONAL REVIEW GUIDE ONLINE FOR THE CCA EXAMINATION, 2017

Instant Access Code (IAC) ISBN: 978-1-305-95666-7
Printed Access Code (PAC) ISBN: 978-1-305-95668-1

Available as an additional purchase, Professional Review Guide Online for the CCA Examination, 2017 offers you the content from this book in a digital format. Create customized exams, set time limits, and see answer feedback with this online quizzing software.

Features include:
- All of the quizzes and mock exams available in this book, customizable by subject area or domain.
- Immediate feedback options by subject area and competency for better self-assessment.

For instructors:
- The ability to track student and class progress by domain or subject area in real-time for better classroom focus.
- Excel™ exporting feature for gradebooks.

Visit www.cengage.com or contact your sales representative for more information.

I. Examination Study Strategies and Resources

Patricia J. Schnering, RHIA, CCS

FORMAT OF THE EXAMINATION

The multiple-choice questions developed for the examinations are based on specifications currently referred to as domains and task statements. A complete copy of these entry-level specifications is provided in the AHIMA Candidate Handbook. The handbook is available for downloading in PDF format from the AHIMA website (http://www.AHIMA.org).

The general format of the exam is primarily designed to engage your problem-solving and critical thinking skills. These types of questions require you to translate what you have learned and apply it to a situation. There are sample questions provided on the AHIMA website (http://www.AHIMA.org), so that you can experience the testing situation.

How to Use This Book

We suggest you answer the multiple-choice questions in the review section of the book before taking the mock examination. It will give you a baseline to begin your CCA examination preparation. Your strengths and weaknesses will become more apparent, allowing you to plan your study time more effectively and focus on your problem areas.

After working through the review questions, take the mock examination. It will provide you an opportunity to assess your speed in answering multiple-choice questions.

STUDY STRATEGIES

BEGIN BY BUILDING YOUR STUDY STRATEGIES

First, you must get organized
You must be deliberate about making sure that you develop and stick to a regular study routine. Find a place where you can study, either at home or at the library.

How you schedule your study time during the week is an individual decision. However, we recommend that you avoid all-nighters and other unreasonably long study sessions. The last thing you want to do is burn yourself out by working too long and too hard at one time. Try to do a little bit at a time, and maintain a steady pace that is manageable for you.

Second, develop your individual study program
Write the exam topics and subjects in a list. Outline the chapters in your coding textbooks, and review the sections in your code books. Pinpoint your weakest subjects. Pause at each chapter outline and recall basic points. Do you draw a blank, recall them more or less, or do you feel comfortable with your recall? By using this approach, you can see where you stand.

Then, weigh the importance of each subject
How are the topics emphasized in the examination competencies, textbooks, professional journal articles, coding guidelines, and coding books? Take a look at the top MS-DRGs and APCs. Try to pick out concepts that would make good examination questions.

Personalize your list
Avoid trying to make a head-on attack by giving equal time and attention to all topics. Use the outline you have made to identify your weakest topics. Determine which topics you believe will require a significant amount of study time and which will only require a brief review. Some experts suggest that you begin your plan with your strongest topics and concentrate on your weaknesses as you get closer to your exam date. That way they will be fresh in your mind. Reorganize your list of the topics in the order that you plan to study them.

Use your list

Your list will give you a clear mental picture of what you need to do and will keep you on track. There are three additional advantages to a list.

1. It builds your morale as you steadily cross off items that you have completed, and you can monitor your progress.
2. Glancing back at the list from time to time serves to reassure you that you are on target.
3. You can readily see that you are applying your time and effort where they are most needed.

Keep the list conspicuously in view. Carefully plan your pre-exam study time and stick to your plan.

Design a 10-week study program

Make your study process a systematic review of all topic categories, followed by achieving mastery of strategically selected subjects within the topic categories. To facilitate this effort, we recommend that you design a 10-week study program. You should plan on spending an average of 10–12 hours per week studying. The idea is to study smart, not to bulldoze through tons of material in a haphazard way.

Schedule study time

You have to be deliberate about making sure that you develop and stick to a regular study routine. Find a place where you can study, either at home or at the library. How you schedule your study time during the week is an individual decision. However, we recommend that you avoid all-nighters and other unreasonably long study sessions. The last thing you want to do is burn yourself out by working too long and too hard at one time. Try to do a little bit at a time and maintain a steady pace that is manageable for you.

Consider a study group

Everyone has his or her own particular study style. Some people prefer to study alone; others work best in a group. Regardless of your preference, we strongly recommend that you take advantage of group study at least some of the time. Studying with others can prove very helpful when working through your weakest areas. Each member of the study team will bring strengths and weaknesses to the table, and all can benefit from the collaboration. So, even if you are a solitary learner, you may occasionally want to work with a group for those topics you find more challenging. If you do not have easy access to a study group for the examination, you may want to study with other HIM professionals over the Internet. The AHIMA Communities of Practice (CoP) on the Internet is an excellent avenue to find others who are in the same position.

Increase your endurance

Preparing for a major exam is similar to preparing for a marathon athletic event. The time allotted for the CCA examination is 2 hours. One suggestion is to use your study process to slowly build up your concentration time until you can focus your energy for the appropriate period. This is like the runner who begins jogging for 30 minutes and builds up to 1 hour, then 1½ hours, and so on, and gradually increases the endurance time to meet the demands of the race. Try this strategy; it could work for you!

Go to the exam like a trained and disciplined runner going to a marathon event!

A SUMMARY OF TIPS FOR ORGANIZING YOUR TIME AND MATERIALS

1. **Make a list of exam topics.**
   Review the major topic categories and determine what your areas of strength are and what areas are in need of improvement.

2. **Focus on your weaknesses.**
   Using the list, identify your weaknesses. It's natural to spend time on the areas where you feel confident. However, it's important to spend more time and energy studying your areas of weakness. Remember, every question counts toward that passing score!

3. **Set up a realistic study schedule.**
   Refer to the sample schedule provided in this book and customize it to meet your needs. Consider having a study group that meets regularly.

4. **Organize and review all of the following items:**
   a. The latest AHIMA Candidate Handbook for the Examination
   b. Official Coding Guidelines for Inpatient and Outpatient
   c. Coding textbooks and any coding course syllabi, outlines, class notes, and tests
   d. Coding books
   e. *CPT Assistant* from the past 3–4 years
   f. Professional journal articles on documentation, reimbursement, and coding issues
   g. List of pertinent websites for research and review

5. **Organize and enter valuable coding information directly into your code books.**

   You will not be allowed to have loose materials in your books. However, information that is permanently attached or written into the code book is acceptable.

6. **Practice taking timed tests.**

   One of the best ways to study for an examination is to take tests. Practice answering questions and working coding cases as much as possible. Time yourself so that you become accustomed to taking, on the average, less than 1 minute per each multiple-choice question. Work with your watch in front of you.

7. **MANDATORY! Read the certification guide.**

   Carefully read the information and instructions in the latest AHIMA Candidate Guide for the Certified Coding Associate. If anything in the Certification Guide is unclear, seek assistance from AHIMA. You are held accountable for the important information, deadlines, and instructions addressed in this material.

SAMPLE STUDY SCHEDULE

Week 1   Review your resources for domains and tasks relating to:
             Health Data Content, Requirements and Standards
             Information and Communications Technologies
             Privacy, Confidentiality, Legal, and Ethical Issues
Work on the questions in the Health Data chapter in this book.

Week 2   Review your resources for medical sciences:
             Medical Terminology
             Anatomy and Physiology
             Pathophysiology (disease process and pharmacology)
Review Appendix A and Appendix B in this book.
Work on the questions in the Medical Science chapter in this book.

Week 3   Review your resources for regulatory requirements for health information.
             Work on the questions in the Classification Systems and Secondary Data Sources chapter in this book.

Week 4   Review your Billing and Reimbursement resources.
             Work on the questions in the Billing and Reimbursement chapter in this book.

Week 5   Review your ICD-10-CM/PCS coding resources, including:
             ICD-10-CM/PCS Inpatient Coding Guidelines
             ICD-10-CM/PCS Outpatient Coding Guidelines
Read the ICD-10-CM/PCS section in the Coding Review provided in the front of this book.
Begin working on the questions in the ICD-10-CM/PCS Coding chapter in the book.

Week 6   Continue your review and work on the ICD-10-CM/PCS Coding chapter.
             Work on areas in which you have weaknesses.

Week 7   Review your resources on CPT/HCPCS Coding.
             Read the CPT section in the Coding Review provided in the front of this book.
             Begin working on the questions in the CPT chapter in this book.

Week 8   Continue to review CPT/HCPCS Coding materials.
             Finish working on the questions in the CPT chapter in this book.
             Work on areas in which you have weaknesses in CPT.

Week 9   Work on the questions in the Mock Quiz.
             Take the Mock Examination in the back of this book.

Week 10   Do an overall review of areas in which you feel you have weaknesses.

STUDY RESOURCES

Don't spend time trying to memorize something you do not understand. The main issue is to understand the materials, so you can use the knowledge in a practical way. Search for additional information that will help make the subject clear to you. There are four basic sources of information: books, people, educational programs/colleges, and Internet resources.

Books and Other Written Resources

➢ A different textbook may use another style of presentation that you are more receptive to and may be all you need to gain a better insight into the subject. It can offer a fresh point of view, provide relief from boredom, and encourage critical thinking in the process of comparing the texts. There are a variety of books and workbooks available to use in studying for your coding certification.

➢ Periodical literature in the field provides well-written articles that may open up the subject to you and turn your study into an adventure in learning. AHIMA publishes authoritative and insightful information on every aspect of coding. In addition to the ongoing coding articles in the *Journal of AHIMA*, *Advance for Health Information Professionals* has a special series of articles called "CCS Prep!" Although this column is written specifically for those preparing to sit for the CCS examination, you will find that they will also apply to you. The journal *For the Record* has articles on coding in each issue. Sometimes an article can help put the subject material into practical perspective and pull it together so that you gain a deeper understanding. Don't forget to use *Coding Clinics* and *CPT Assistant* to refresh your memory and learn more about specific coding guidelines. Journals will help you keep updated on new information on coding issues that may be incorporated into the exams.

➢ Take advantage of the local college library by using reserved materials specifically set aside for HIM student study purposes.

Your HIM Community

➢ Interaction with others can be truly beneficial in keeping you motivated and on track.

➢ Professional contacts can also be helpful in your study effort. Most people in our field are eager to share their knowledge and are flattered by appeals for information. Schedule a conference with the director of the HIM/Coding program at your local college. These educators may have current information and resources you are not aware of. Talking to those who have recently taken the examination can also be of great assistance.

➢ Collaborating with other test applicants can reveal fresh viewpoints, stimulate thought by disagreement, or at least let you see that you are not alone in your quest. Organize study groups and set aside specific times to work together. This interaction can be truly beneficial in keeping you motivated and on task.

Classes, Workshops, Seminars, and Coding Teleconferences

These can present opportunities to learn and review the subject matter in a new light and to keep you updated on changes. Take advantage of any coding review sessions available in your area.

Internet Resources

➤ Use the Internet to connect with others who are preparing for the examination. In this dynamic, changing environment, the most up-to-date materials may not be available in a book. Don't overlook the power of AHIMA's website. The AHIMA online resources are extensive and quite easy to access at www.ahima.org. In addition, the Communities of Practice (CoPs) are a phenomenal source of contact with HIM professionals and other students preparing for the examination on a myriad of subjects. AHIMA is available online for members. You may find other examination applicants to work with by using e-mail.

➤ There are innumerable resources for coding and reimbursement on the Internet. **Just be aware that you may want to verify the information, as it is only as good as the source.**

Some Suggested Study Resources

1. **Mandatory:** AHIMA Candidate Handbook for the CCA Examination
2. **Mandatory:** *ICD-10-CM Code Book* (refer to instructions from AHIMA for the appropriate version)
3. **Mandatory:** "Official ICD-10-CM/PCS Guidelines for Coding and Reporting" is available online at http://www.cdc.gov/nchs/icd /icd10.htm
4. *Coding Clinic* issues for ICD-10-CM/PCS
5. **Mandatory:** AMA CPT Code Book (refer to instructions from AHIMA for the appropriate version)
6. *HCPCS Level II Code Book* (refer to instructions from AHIMA for the appropriate version)
7. "Documentation Guidelines for Evaluation and Management Services," *CPT Assistant* (May 1997) as well as other *CPT Assistant* issues
8. Professional journal articles on coding
   Journal of AHIMA
   Advance for Health Information Professionals
   For the Record
9. Medical dictionaries (check for the latest edition)
10. Coding classes, seminars, workshop notes, and tests
11. Study groups or partners
12. On-the-job experience
13. Examination review sessions
14. Review books written for CCA examination
15. Various online computer resources. For online coding practice sites as well as those for information and Internet interaction with others, visit the following examples:
    MANDATORY: http://www.AHIMA.org
    http://www.cms.hhs.gov
    http://www.hospitalconnect.com
16. HIM textbooks and class textbooks: There is a large variety of textbooks for HIM and coding available on the market. Both Cengage Learning (www.cengage.com) and AHIMA (www.ahima.org) have a variety of HIM products. For example, see the partial listing of books available through Cengage Learning.

Those resources marked **MANDATORY** are essential for you to have in order to prepare for the examination.

Contact Information for Resources for the CCA Examinations

ICD-10-CM/PCS Code Book with October 2016 updates
Optum360, 2525 Lake Park Blvd., Salt Lake City, UT 84120; Phone: 1-800-464-3649, option 1; Website: www.optum360.com

Official ICD-10-CM/PCS Guidelines for Coding and Reporting
Central Office on ICD-10-CM/PCS of the American Hospital Association (AHA); Phone: (312) 422-3000 or it can be accessed online at the website for National Center for Health Statistics (NCHS) http://www.cdc.gov/nchs

Coding Clinic for ICD-10-CM/PCS
American Hospital Association; Phone: (312) 422-3000

CPT Code Book 2017
American Medical Association (AMA); Phone: (800) 621-8335; Fax: (312) 464-5600

HCPCS II Code Book 2017 Edition
American Medical Association; Phone: (800) 621-8335

AMA CPT Assistant
American Medical Association; Phone: (800) 621-8335; Fax: (312) 464-5600
Documentation Guidelines for E & M Coding
Published May 1995 and revised November 1997 by American Medical Association (AMA) and Centers for Medicare and Medicaid Services (CMS).
Printed in the *CPT Assistant* May 1997 and November 1997.

Centers for Medicare and Medicaid Services
Website: http://www.cms.hhs.gov/

AHIMA has developed a series of HIM and coding resources.
To place an order: call (800) 335-5535
For additional resources and information about the coding certification examinations, visit the AHIMA website at http://www.ahima.org

Optum360 has an array of coding, reimbursement, and compliance products. Phone: 1-800-464-3649, option 1. Visit its website at https://www.optumcoding.com/

Cengage Learning has a multitude of HIM products. In addition, it has partnered with Optum360 so that you can order your Optum360 resources through Cengage Learning.
For a complete list, contact:
Cengage Learning, Inc., 10650 Toebben Drive, Independence, KY 41051
Website: http://www.cengagebrain.com
Phone: (800) 354-9706

The following is a partial listing of Cengage products for Health Information.
3-2-1 Code It! (6th Edition)
Green, Michelle A.
A Guide to Health Insurance Billing (4th Edition)
Moisio, Marie A.
Basic Allied Health Statistics and Analysis (4th Edition)
Koch, G.
Case Studies for Health Information Management (2nd Edition)
McCuen, Charlotte; Sayles, Nanette; and Schnering, Patricia

Comparative Health Information Management (4th Edition)
  Peden, Ann
Essentials of Health Information Management Principles and Practices (3rd Edition)
  Bowie, Mary Jo and Green, Michelle A.
Essentials of Healthcare Compliance
  Safian, Shelly
Guide to Coding Compliance
  Becker, Joanne M.
Health Services Research Methods (2nd Edition)
  Shi, L.
Legal and Ethical Aspects of Health Information Management (4th Edition)
  McWay, Dana C.
Medical Coding 101 (2nd Edition)
  Clack, Crystal and Renfroe, Linda
Medical Terminology for Insurance and Coding
  Moisio, Marie A.
Today's Health Information Management: An Integrated Approach (2nd Edition)
  McWay, Dana C.
Understanding Health Insurance: A Guide to Billing and Reimbursement (13th Edition)
  Green, Michelle A.
Understanding Hospital Coding and Billing: A Worktext (3rd Edition)
  Diamond, Marsha S.
Understanding ICD-10-CM/PCS: A Worktext (3rd Edition)
  Bowie, Mary Jo
Understanding Medical Coding: A Comprehensive Guide (4th Edition)
  Johnson, Sandra L. and Linker, Robin
Understanding Current Procedural Terminology and HCPCS Coding Systems (5th Edition)
  Bowie, Mary Jo
Using the Electronic Health Record in the Healthcare Provider Practice (4th Edition)
  Eichenwald-Maki, Shirley and Petterson, Bonnie

For additional information on these Health Information resources, visit Cengage Learning at **www.cengage.com.**

THE DAY BEFORE AND THE MORNING OF THE EXAM

1. **Know the exam location.** Take a practice drive. If necessary, spend the night before the examination in a hotel or motel near the exam test site if it is a great distance from your home.

2. **Avoid studying the night before the exam.** Last-minute studying tends to increase your anxiety level. However, you may want to allocate a small amount of time to review any information that you feel you must look at one more time.

3. **Organize in advance all the materials you need to take with you to the exam.** Review the candidate handbook carefully and be sure to have all the items that are required, especially the admission card and proof of identity and your code books.

4. **Get a good night's sleep.** Taking a 4-hour test with little rest the night before may prevent you from having the energy and stamina you need to complete the exam.

5. **Have a healthy meal before your exam.** Four hours is a long time to go on an empty stomach. Try to eat a nutritious meal, for instance, cereal and fruit, bagel and fruit or juice, or a meal with protein such as cheese and crackers or eggs and toast. You need something to give you energy to keep going. Take a healthy snack bar to munch on if you get hungry and need to take a short break at the testing center.

6. **Dress comfortably.** Plan for possible variations in room temperature. Dressing in layers may prove helpful.

7. **Arrive early.** Allow yourself plenty of time so that you arrive at the test site early.

TAKING THE EXAMINATION

You have stuck to your study schedule and have conditioned yourself to be in the best physical and mental shape possible. Now comes the "moment of truth": the examination pops up on the screen before your eyes. Every paratrooper knows that in addition to having a parachute, one must know how to open it. You have mastered the major topics; you have the parachute. Now, you need to utilize good test-taking techniques to apply the knowledge you have gained; open the parachute!

1. **Taking the practice test.** Prior to starting the exam, you will be given a chance to practice taking an examination on the computer. Time will be allotted for this practice test. However, you may quit the practice test and begin the actual exam when you are comfortable with the computerized testing process.

2. **Read all directions and questions carefully.** Try to avoid reading too much into the questions. Be sensible and practical in your interpretation. Read ALL of the possible answers, because the first one that looks good may not be the best one.

3. **Scan the screen quickly for general question format.** Like the marathon runner, pace yourself for the distance. A good rule of thumb is 1–1.5 minutes per question. You may wish to keep the timer displayed on the computer to check your schedule throughout the exam. For example, at question 30, about 1½ hour will have elapsed, etc.

4. **Coming back to questions.** Some people answer all questions that they are certain of first, and then go back through the exam a second time to answer any questions they were uncertain about. Others prefer not to skip questions, but make their best choice on encountering each question and go on. Both can be good approaches. Choose the one that works best for you. You can "mark" questions that you have left unanswered and/or those questions you may want to review. Before you sign off of the exam or run out of time, you will have the ability to go back to those questions for a final review.

5. **Answer all the questions.** There are no penalties for guessing, but not choosing an answer is definitely a wrong answer.

6. **Process of elimination.** Use deductive reasoning and the process of elimination to arrive at the most correct answer. Some questions may have more than one correct answer. You will be asked to select the "best" possible answer based on the information presented.

7. **Determine what is being asked.** If the question is written in a scenario format, first identify the question being asked and then review the entire question for the information needed to determine the correct answer.

8. **Use all the time available to recheck your answers.** However, avoid changing your answers unless you are absolutely certain it is necessary. Second-guessing yourself often results in a wrong answer.

9. **Getting your score.** A huge advantage to taking the computerized exam is that before you leave the testing center, you will be able to get your final test score instead of having to wait up to 6 weeks to receive the score by mail.

AFTER THE EXAM

Our advice is to reclaim your life and focus on your career. One good way to start is to plan a special reward for yourself at some point immediately following or shortly after the exam. Schedule a family vacation or a relaxing weekend getaway. Just find some way of being good to yourself. You certainly deserve it! You have worked hard, so relish your success.

II. Coding Review

Patricia Schnering, RHIA, CCS

Marissa Lajaunie, MBA, RHIA

Shelley C. Safian, PhD, RHIA, CCS-P, COC, CPC-I,

AHIMA-Approved ICD-10-CM/PCS Trainer

HEALTH RECORD CODING REVIEW: CODING PROCESS

Fine-tune your coding skills by seeking complete documentation and selecting the most detailed codes.

1. Assess the case by performing a quick review of the record's demographic information and the first few lines of the History and Physical.

2. Get an overview of key reports because they contain valuable detailed information.
   A. The <u>discharge summary</u> sums up the patient's hospital course and confirms conditions or complications. In ambulatory records, look at the final progress note and/or discharge instructions.
   B. Review the <u>physician orders</u> for treatment protocols. The orders may indicate chronic or acute conditions for which the patient is receiving treatment.
   C. Review the <u>history and physical</u> to complete the clinical picture. Social and family history, as well as past and present illnesses, may have clinical implications.
   D. Read the <u>progress notes</u> to track the course of hospitalization or outpatient treatment. These provide information concerning daily status, reactions, or postoperative complications.
   E. Study the <u>operative reports</u>. Additional procedures may be identified in the body of the operative report.

3. Check all data from clinical reports.
   A. <u>Laboratory</u> reports may show evidence of conditions such as anemia, renal failure, infections, and metabolic imbalances.
   B. <u>Radiology</u> reports may confirm diagnosis of pneumonia, COPD, CHF, degenerative joint diseases, and traumatic injuries.
   C. <u>Medication Administration Reports (MARs)</u> indicate all drugs that were administered to the patient. Look for documentation of diagnoses elsewhere in the medical record to correlate with each drug. If uncertain why a medication was administered, query the physician.
   D. <u>Respiratory therapy notes</u> document the use of mechanical ventilation and describe severity of respiratory disorders.
   E. <u>Physical therapy</u> reports detail useful information for coding musculoskeletal dysfunctions.
   F. <u>Dietary</u> reports describe nutritional deficiencies (e.g., malnutrition).
   G. <u>Speech pathology</u> reports give information on dysphasia, aphasia, and other speech-related conditions.
   H. <u>Pathology</u> reports are essential for accurate coding of conditions where excised tissue has been submitted for interpretation.

4. Perform a coding evaluation.
   A. Establish the principal diagnosis and formulate secondary diagnoses codes.
   B. Exclude all conditions not relevant to the case. Abnormal lab and X-ray findings and previous conditions having no effect on current management of the patient are not coded.

5. Take time to review and refine your coding.
   A. Review all diagnoses and procedures to confirm the selections of appropriate principal and secondary diagnoses and all procedure codes.
   B. For inpatient records, determine if each diagnosis was present on admission (POA) to adequately identify the POA indicator.
   C. Refine code assignments, where necessary, to make changes to more accurately classify the diagnoses and procedure codes selected.

Sample 10-Step Inpatient ICD-10-CM Coding Process
1. **Locate Patient's Gender, Age, and Discharge Date.**
2. **Locate Discharge Status (Disposition). Some examples include:** 　**01:** Home 　**02:** Short-term hospital 　**03:** Skilled nursing facility 　**04:** Facility providing custodial or supportive care 　**05:** Cancer or child hospital 　**06:** Home health services 　**07:** Against medical advice 　**20:** Expired 　**30:** Still a patient 　**61:** Swing bed 　**62:** Inpatient rehab facility or distinct rehab unit 　**63:** Long-term care hospital 　**65:** Psychiatric hospital or distinct psych unit 　**66:** Critical access hospital
3. **List consultants** as you go through the consults. **Write down pertinent diagnoses** (histories and present illnesses).
4. **Locate and list all procedures.** Review description of each procedure performed.
5. **Go through the physician orders and medication administration orders.** This is where you will find drugs ordered and administered. Make sure that you look for the diagnosis that corresponds with each medication. If not, query the physician.
6. **Read the H&P, ER record, and progress notes.** **Write down all diagnoses that meet criteria for principal and secondary diagnoses:** If a diagnosis is ruled out, just cross it off the list.
7. **Select the Principal Diagnosis.** UHDDS Definition: The condition established *after study* to be chiefly responsible for occasioning the admission of the patient to the hospital for care.
8. **Select Other Diagnoses and indicate whether each was present on admission (POA) or not.** UHDDS Definition: All conditions that coexist at the time of admission, develop subsequently, or affect the treatment received and/or the length of stay. Diagnoses that relate to an earlier episode of care that have no bearing on the current hospital stay are to be excluded. **Complication** UHDDS Definition: A condition arising during hospitalization, which increases the patient's length of stay by 1 day in 75% of cases. **Comorbidity** UHDDS Definition: Condition present at admission, in addition to the principal diagnosis, which increases the patient's length of stay by 1 day in 75% of cases.

Sample 10-Step Inpatient ICD-10-CM Coding Process (continued)

	For reporting purposes, the definition of "other diagnoses" is interpreted as additional conditions that affect patient care in terms of requiring: • clinical evaluation • therapeutic treatment • diagnostic procedures • extended length of hospital stay • increased nursing care and/or monitoring
9.	**Principal Procedure** UHDDS Definition: One performed for definitive treatment (rather than performed for diagnostic or exploratory purposes) or one that was necessary to care for a complication. If two or more procedures appear to meet the definition, then the one most closely related to the principal diagnosis should be selected as the principal procedure.
10.	**Other Procedures** UHDDS Definition for significant procedures: One that meets any of the following conditions: is surgical in nature, carries an anesthetic risk, carries a procedural risk, or requires specialized training.

SOME ADDITIONAL TIPS FOR CODING

1. When a patient is admitted with or develops a condition during his or her stay, look to see if there is documentation to differentiate if the complication is acute, chronic, or both acute and chronic.

2. When a patient presents with or develops infectious conditions, seek documentation of any positive cultures (urine, wound, sputum, blood) pertaining to that condition. If the positive cultures are available for that condition (e.g., sepsis due to *Pseudomonas*), it will help in being more specific in coding the diagnoses and may increase reimbursement in some cases. For example, in a case of pneumonia due to *Pseudomonas*, the MS-DRG may increase considerably. According to coding guidelines, if the culture is not documented, even though present in laboratory reports, the condition is to be coded as unspecified, which can affect reimbursement.
Examples: sepsis, cellulitis, UTI, pneumonia.

3. If a condition is due to surgery, ask the physician to verify and document that it is due to the procedure. If the patient has been discharged, and you are not sure but believe it was due to the procedure, seek verification that it is possibly due to the procedure by querying the physician.

4. If the patient had outpatient surgery for removal of a lesion, look for documentation of the size of the lesion that may have been removed. It should be documented in the operative report.
The American Medical Association's publication, *CPT Assistant* (issues from Fall 1995 and August 2000) states, "Since the physician can make an accurate measurement of the lesion(s) at the time of the excision, the size of the lesion should be documented in the OP (operative) report. A pathology report is likely to contain a less accurate measurement due to the shrinking of the specimen or the fact that the specimen may be fragmented."
Reimbursement is based on the diameter of the lesion(s). Even 1 millimeter (mm) off in the diameter calculation can mean fewer dollars for the hospital and the physician. The documentation in the record ensures appropriate reimbursement.

5. Look for documentation in the final diagnoses in the discharge summary for clarification or to differentiate whether specific conditions are currently present, or if the patient only has a history of the condition.
Examples:
   1. Acute CVA versus history of CVA
   2. Current drug or alcohol abuse versus history of drug or alcohol abuse
   3. Current neoplasm being treated versus history of malignancy

6. Verify if a condition is a manifestation of an existing condition.
Example: CRF secondary to DM or CRF due to HTN

7. Look for documentation of conditions that are secondary to previous conditions.
Examples:
   1. Quadriplegia due to fall
   2. Dysphagia due to previous CVA

ICD-10-CM OUTPATIENT/AMBULATORY CODING GUIDELINES

Note: This is a brief overview. ICD-10-CM codes are used for diagnoses. CPT codes are used for procedures for billing purposes.

1. Documentation should include specific diagnoses as well as symptoms, problems, and reasons for visits.

2. First-listed diagnosis is listed first with other codes following.

3. Chronic diseases may be coded as long as the patient receives treatment.

4. Code all documented conditions that coexist at the time of the visit and are treated or affect treatment. History codes may be used if they impact treatment.

5. Diagnosis coding for Diagnostic Services: Code the diagnosis chiefly responsible for the service. Secondary codes may follow.

   Instructions to Determine the Reason for the Test: The referring physicians are required to provide diagnostic information to the testing entity at the time the test is ordered. All diagnostic tests "must be ordered by the physician who is treating the beneficiary." An order by the physician may include the following forms of communication:
   1. A written document signed by the treating physician/practitioner, which is hand delivered, mailed, or faxed to the testing facility.
   2. A telephone call by the treating physician/practitioner or his or her office to the testing facility.
   3. An electronic mail by the treating physician or practitioner or his or her office to the testing facility.
   Note: Telephone orders must be documented by both the treating physician or practitioner office and the testing facility.
   If the interpreting physician does not have diagnostic information as to the reason for the test, and the referring physician is unavailable, it is appropriate to obtain the information directly from the patient or patient's medical record. Attempt to confirm any information obtained from the patient by contacting the referring physician.

6. Diagnosis coding for Therapeutic Services: Code the diagnosis chiefly responsible for the service. Secondary codes may follow.

7. Diagnosis coding for Ambulatory Surgery: Code the diagnosis for which surgery was done. Use the postoperative diagnosis if it is available and more specific.

COMMONLY MISSED COMPLICATIONS AND COMORBIDITIES (CCS)

Depending on the patient's principal diagnosis, this list of commonly missed complications and comorbidities (CCs) and major complications and comorbidities (MCCs) may or may not help the MS-DRG when documented and coded. If any of these conditions are being managed while the patient is being hospitalized, it may change the MS-DRG to a higher paying one. Some MS-DRGs will not change even if these are present. The MS-DRG may or may not change if the patient has a major procedure performed. Some of these conditions may be considered CCs, while others may be considered Major CCs.

Acidosis
Alcoholism acute/chronic
Alkalosis
Anemia due to blood loss, acute/chronic (e.g., from GI bleed, or surgery)
Angina pectoris (stable or unstable angina)
Atrial fibrillation/flutter
Atelectasis
Cachexia
Cardiogenic shock
Cardiomyopathy
Cellulitis
CHF
Combination of both acidosis/alkalosis
COPD
Decubitus ulcer
Dehydration (volume depletion)
Diabetes: If DM is uncontrolled (type 1 or 2)
Electrolyte imbalance
Hematuria
Hematemesis
Hypertension (HTN) accelerated or malignant HTN only qualifies (not uncontrolled, hypertensive urgency or hypertensive crisis)
Hypertensive heart disease with CHF
Hyponatremia ($\downarrow$ Na)
Hypernatremia ($\uparrow$ Na)
Hypochloremia ($\downarrow$ Cl)
Hyperchloremia ($\uparrow$ Cl)
Hyperpotassemia ($\uparrow$ K)
Malnutrition
Melena
Pleural effusion (especially if it has to be treated by a procedure, e.g., thoracentesis)
Pneumonia
Pneumothorax
Postoperative complications
Renal failure, acute or chronic (not renal insufficiency)
Respiratory failure
Septicemia
Urinary retention
UTI (e.g., urosepsis): If urosepsis is documented, it will be coded as a UTI unless otherwise specified.

Note: This is not an all-inclusive listing of possible complications and comorbidities.

SOME AREAS OF SPECIAL INTEREST WHEN CODING WITH ICD-10-CM

Adhesions
- When minor adhesions are present, but do not cause symptoms or increase the difficulty of an operative procedure, coding a diagnosis of adhesions and a lysis procedure is inappropriate.
- When adhesions are dense or strong or create problems during a surgical procedure, it is appropriate to code both the diagnosis of adhesions and the operative procedure to lyse the adhesions.

Anemia
- The coder must distinguish between chronic blood loss anemia and acute blood loss anemia because the two conditions are assigned to different category codes.
- Acute blood loss anemia occurring after surgery may or may not be a complication of surgery.
- The physician must clearly identify postoperative anemia as a complication of the surgery in order to use the complication code.
- Depending on the primary reason for admission, anemia of chronic disease can be used as the principal diagnosis (if the reason for admit is to treat the anemia) or as the secondary diagnosis.
- When assigning code D63.1(anemia in chronic kidney disease), also assign a code from category N18 (chronic kidney disease) to identify the stage of chronic kidney disease.

Asthma
- Acute exacerbation of asthma is increased severity of asthma symptoms, such as wheezing and shortness of breath.
- Terms suggesting status asthmaticus include intractable asthma, refractory asthma, severe intractable wheezing, and airway obstruction not relieved by medication. It is a life-threatening complication that requires emergency care.
- The coder must not assume status asthmaticus is present. The physician must document the condition in order to code it.

Body Mass Index (BMI)
- The code(s) for body mass index should only be reported as secondary diagnoses and must meet the definition of a reportable additional diagnosis.
- Documentation from clinicians (such as dieticians) may be used for code assignment as long as the physician has documented the diagnosis of obesity.
- If there is conflicting documentation, query the attending physician.

Burns
- When coding multiple burns, assign separate codes for each site and sequence the burn with the highest degree first.
- When coding burns of the same site with varying degrees, code only the highest degree.
- Necrosis of burned skin is coded as a nonhealing burn. Nonhealing burns are coded as acute burns.

Cellulitis
- Coders must not assume that documentation of redness at the edges of a wound represents cellulitis. Rely on physician documentation of cellulitis.
- Coding of cellulitis with an injury or burn requires one code for the injury and one for the cellulitis. Sequencing will depend on the circumstances of admission.

- When the patient is seen primarily for treating the original injury, sequence that code first. When the patient is seen primarily for treatment of the cellulitis, the code for cellulitis is the principal diagnosis.

Complications

- When coding complications of surgical and medical care, if the code fully describes the condition, no additional code is necessary. If it does not fully describe the condition, an additional code should be assigned. Codes for medical and surgical care are found within the body system chapters.

Congenital Anomalies

- Congenital anomaly codes have been assigned to categories Q00–Q99 and may be used for a principal or secondary diagnosis.
- When there is a code that identifies the congenital anomaly, do not assign additional codes for the inherent manifestations. Do assign additional codes for manifestations that are not an inherent component.
- For the birth admission, category Z38 is still the principal diagnosis followed by any congenital anomaly code (Q00–Q99).
- Codes from Chapter 17, Congenital Anomalies, can be reported for patients of any age. Many congenital anomalies do not manifest any symptoms until much later in life.

Diabetes Mellitus

- When the type of diabetes mellitus is not documented, code it as type 2.
- Diabetes with a manifestation or complication requires documentation of a causal relationship to be coded. Assign as many codes from the diabetes category as needed to identify all associated conditions.
- Even if the patient is using insulin, it does not necessarily mean that the patient is type 1.
- Most patients with type 1 diabetes develop the condition before reaching puberty. That is why type 1 diabetes mellitus is also referred to as juvenile diabetes.
- For type 2 patients who routinely use insulin, code (long-term, current use of insulin) should also be assigned. Do not use this code if the patient receives insulin to temporarily bring a type 2 patient's blood sugar under control.
- An underdose of insulin due to an insulin pump failure should be assigned T85.614 (breakdown [mechanical complications] of insulin pump) with a 7th character to report the encounter as the principal diagnosis code, followed by a code from categories E08–E13.
- When the patient has an insulin pump malfunction resulting in an overdose of insulin, assign a code from the T85 category as the principal diagnosis code with an additional code of T38.3- (poisoning by insulin and antidiabetic agents). Also code the appropriate diabetes mellitus code from E08–E13.
- Use codes from category E08 (secondary diabetes mellitus) to identify diabetes caused by another condition or event. Category code E08 is listed first followed by the code for the associated condition.
- The patient may be admitted for treatment of the secondary diabetes or one of its associated conditions OR for treatment of the condition causing the secondary diabetes. Code the primary reason for the encounter as the principal diagnosis, which will be a code from category E08 followed by the code for the associated condition or a code for the cause of the secondary diabetes.
- Assign code E89.1 for post-pancreatectomy hyperglycemia or E13.- for diabetes mellitus postpancreatectomy. Code first Z90.410 for acquired total absence of the pancreas or Z90.411 for acquired partial absence of pancreas. Also code any diabetic manifestations.

Dysplasia of the Vulva and Cervix

- A diagnosis of cervical intraepithelial neoplasia (CIN) III or vulvar intraepithelial neoplasia (VIN) III is classified as carcinoma in situ of the site.
- A diagnosis of CIN III or VIN III is made only on the basis of pathological evaluation of tissue.

Elevated Blood Pressure vs. Hypertension

- A diagnosis of high or elevated blood pressure without a firm diagnosis of hypertension is reported using code R03.0.
- This code is never assigned on the basis of a review of blood pressure readings; the physician must document elevated blood pressure/hypertension.

Fracture

- Traumatic fractures are coded as long as the patient is receiving active treatment.
- Subsequent care of traumatic fractures are coded to the acute fracture code with the appropriate 7th character. Aftercare Z-codes should not be reported for aftercare of traumatic fractures.
- An open fracture is one in which there is communication with the bone. The following terms indicate open fracture: compound, infected, missile, puncture, and with foreign body.
- A closed fracture does not produce an open wound. Some types of closed fractures are impacted, comminuted, depressed, elevated, greenstick, spiral, and simple.
- When a fracture is not identified as open or closed, the code for a closed fracture is used.
- Internal fixation devices include screws, pins, rods, staples, and plates.
- External fixation devices include casts, splints, and traction device (Kirschner wire) (Steinman pin).

Gastrointestinal Hemorrhage

- Patients may be admitted for an endoscopy after a history of GI bleeding. It is acceptable to use a code for GI hemorrhage even if there is no hemorrhage noted on the current encounter.

Hematuria

- Blood in the urine discovered on a urinalysis is not coded as hematuria but as R82.3, Hemoglobinuria.
- Hematuria following a urinary procedure is not considered a postoperative complication.

Human Immunodeficiency Virus (HIV)

- Documentation of HIV infection as "suspected," "possible," "likely," or "questionable": physician must be queried for clarification. Code only confirmed cases of HIV infection. Confirmation does not require documentation of positive test results for HIV. A physician's documentation is sufficient.
- B20: Patients with symptomatic HIV disease or AIDS. If HIV test results are positive and the patient has symptoms. Patients with known diagnosis of HIV-related illness should be coded to B20 on every subsequent admission.
- Z21: Patients with physician-documented asymptomatic HIV infection who have never had an HIV-related illness. If HIV results are positive and the patient is without symptoms. Do not use this code if the term "AIDS" is used or if the patient is being treated for HIV-related conditions. In these cases, use code B20.
- Patients previously diagnosed with HIV-related illness (B20) should never be assigned Z21.
- Z11.4: Patient seen to determine his or her HIV status (screening).
- Patients admitted with an HIV-related condition are assigned code B20 as the principal diagnosis followed by additional diagnosis codes for all reported HIV-related conditions.

- Patients admitted for a condition unrelated to the HIV (such as traumatic injury) are assigned the code for the unrelated condition as the principal diagnosis, then code B20.
- When an obstetric patient has the HIV infection, a code from subcategory O98.7 is sequenced first with either code B20 (symptomatic) or Z21 (asymptomatic) used as an additional code.

Hypertension
- Hypertensive heart disease I11. Physician must document causal relationship between hypertension and heart disease that is stated as "due to hypertension" or implied by documenting "hypertensive." Use an additional code from category I50 to identify the type of heart failure, if present. If the heart disease is stated as occurring "with hypertension," do not assume a cause-and-effect relationship and code it separately.
- Hypertensive chronic kidney disease I12-. ICD-10-CM assumes a causal relationship between hypertension and chronic kidney disease. There is no causal relationship with acute renal failure. Use an additional code from category N18 to identify the stage of CKD.
- Hypertensive heart and chronic kidney disease I13.0-. Physician must document causal relationship with the heart disease, but you may assume a causal relationship with chronic kidney disease. Assign an additional code for category I50 to identify the type of heart failure, if present. More than one code for category I50 may be assigned if the patient has systolic or diastolic failure and congestive heart failure. Use an additional code from category N18 to identify the stage of CKD.

Injuries
- Superficial injuries (e.g., abrasions, contusions) are not coded when there are more severe injuries of the same site.

Mechanical Ventilation
- Codes for intubation or tracheostomy should also be assigned.
- It is possible for a patient to be placed back on mechanical ventilation, thus necessitating two codes for mechanical ventilation on the same admission.

Methicillin-Resistant Staphylococcus aureus (MRSA)
- To code a current infection due to MRSA when that infection does not have a combination code that includes MRSA, code the infection first, and then add code A49.02; B95.62 (MRSA).
- Use code Z22.321 for MSSA (Methicillin-Susceptible *Staphylococcus aureus*) colonization.
- Use code Z22.322 for MRSA (Methicillin-Resistant *Staphylococcus aureus*) colonization.
- Use code Z22.31; Z22.39 for other types of *Staphylococcus* colonization.

Myocardial Infarction (MI)
- An MI that is documented as acute or with a duration of 4 weeks or less is coded to category I21, Acute MI.
- When a patient has a subsequent infarction at the time of the encounter for the original infarction, both the initial and the subsequent AMI should be reported with codes from categories I21.- and I22.-
- Subcategory codes I21.0–I21.2 are used for "ST elevation MI" (STEMI).
- Subcategory I21.4 is used for "non-ST elevation MI" (NSTEMI) and nontransmural MI.
- If only STEMI or transmural MI without the documentation of the site, query the physician.
- If an AMI is documented as transmural or subendocardial, but the site is provided, it is still coded as subendocardial AMI.
- If STEMI converts to an NSTEMI due to thrombolytic therapy, it is still coded as STEMI.

Neoplasms

- Neoplasms are listed in the Alphabetic Index in two ways:
  - The Table of Neoplasms provides code numbers for neoplasms by anatomic site. For each site, there are six possible code numbers according to whether the behavior of the neoplasm is malignant primary, malignant secondary, malignant in situ, benign, of uncertain behavior, or of unspecified nature.
  - Histological terms for neoplasms (e.g., adenoma, adenocarcinoma, and sarcoma) are listed as main terms in the appropriate alphabetic sequence and are usually followed by a cross reference to the neoplasm table.
- In sequencing neoplasms, when the treatment is directed toward the malignancy, then the malignancy of that site is designated as the principal diagnosis, unless the patient is admitted for one of the reasons listed next.
- When the patient has a primary neoplasm with metastasis and the treatment is directed toward the secondary site only, the secondary site is sequenced as the principal diagnosis.
- When a patient is admitted solely for chemotherapy, immunotherapy, or radiation therapy, a code from category Z51 (Z51.0, Z51.1) is used for the principal diagnosis with the malignant neoplasm coded as an additional diagnosis.
- Codes from category Z85 are used when the primary neoplasm is totally eradicated and the patient is no longer having treatment and there is no evidence of any existing primary malignancy. Codes from category Z85 can be listed only as an additional code, not as a principal diagnosis. If extension, invasion, or metastasis is mentioned, code secondary malignant neoplasm to that site as the principal diagnosis.
- When a patient is admitted for pain management associated with the malignancy, code G89.3 as the principal diagnosis followed by the appropriate code for the malignancy. When a patient is admitted for management of the malignancy, code the malignancy as the principal diagnosis with code G89.3 as an additional code.
- When admission/encounter is for management of an anemia associated with the malignancy, and the treatment is only for anemia, the appropriate code for the malignancy is sequenced as the principal or first-listed diagnosis followed by the appropriate code for the anemia (such as code D63.0, Anemia in neoplastic disease).
- When a patient is admitted for management of dehydration associated with the malignancy or the therapy, or both, and only the dehydration is being treated (intravenous rehydration), the dehydration is sequenced first, followed by the code(s) for the malignancy.
- If the patient is admitted for surgical removal of a neoplasm followed by chemotherapy or radiation therapy, code the neoplasm (primary or secondary) as the principal diagnosis.
- If the patient has anemia associated with chemotherapy, immunotherapy, or radiotherapy and the only treatment is for the anemia, code anemia due to antineoplastic chemotherapy, and then code the neoplasm as an additional code.
- If the patient is admitted for chemotherapy, immunotherapy, or radiation therapy and then complications occur (such as uncontrolled nausea and vomiting or dehydration); assign the appropriate code for chemotherapy, immunotherapy, or radiation therapy as the principal diagnosis followed by any codes for the complications.
- If the primary reason for admission is to determine the context of the malignancy or for a procedure, even though chemotherapy or radiotherapy is administered, code the malignancy (primary and secondary site) as the principal diagnosis.
- When a malignant neoplasm is associated with a transplanted organ, assign a code from category T86 (complications of transplanted organ), followed by code C80.2 (malignant neoplasm associated with transplanted organ) followed by a code for the specific malignancy.

Newborn

- Newborn (perinatal) codes P00–P96 are never used on the maternal record.
- The perinatal period is defined as before birth through the 28th day following birth.
- A code from category Z38.0 is assigned as the principal diagnosis for any live birth.
- Other diagnoses may be coded for significant conditions noted after birth as secondary diagnoses.
- Insignificant or transient conditions that resolve without treatment are not coded.
- Assign codes from subcategories P00–P04 for evaluation of newborns and infants for suspected condition not found, is used when a healthy baby is evaluated for a suspected condition that proves to not exist. These codes are used when the baby exhibits no signs or symptoms.

Obstetrics

- Chapter 15 codes are only used on the maternal record, even if a fetal condition complicates the pregnancy.
- Chapter 15 codes take sequencing precedence over other chapter codes, which may be assigned to provide further specificity as needed.
- The postpartum period begins immediately after delivery and continues for 6 weeks after delivery.
- The peripartum period is defined as the last month of pregnancy to 5 months.
- Codes from Chapter 15 can continue to be used after the 6-week period if the doctor documents that it is pregnancy related.
- When the mother delivers outside the hospital prior to admission and no complications are documented, code Z39.0 (postpartum care and examination immediately after delivery) as the principal diagnosis. If there are complications, the complications would be coded instead. Do not code a delivery diagnosis code because she delivered prior to admission.
- Principal diagnosis is determined by the circumstances of the encounter or admission.
- Complications: Any condition that occurs during pregnancy, childbirth, or the puerperium is considered to be a complication unless the physician specifically documents otherwise.
- A code from category Z37 is assigned as an additional code to indicate the outcome of delivery on the maternal chart. Z37 codes are not to be used on subsequent records or on the newborn record.
- Code O80, normal delivery, is used only when a delivery is perfectly normal and results in a single live birth. No abnormalities of labor or delivery or postpartum conditions can be present; therefore, there can be no additional code from Chapter 15. Z38.0-, single liveborn, is the only outcome of delivery code appropriate for use with O80.
- Z-codes from category Z34 are used when no obstetric complications are present and should not be used with any codes from Chapter 15.
- When the fetal condition is responsible for modifying the management of the mother (requires diagnostic studies or additional observation, special care, or termination of pregnancy), use codes from categories O35 and O36. The mere fact that the condition exists does not justify assigning a code from categories O35 and O36.
- When in utero surgery is performed on the fetus, assign codes from category O35. No code from Chapter 16 (the perinatal codes) should be used on the mother's record to identify fetal conditions.
- Patients with an HIV-related illness during pregnancy, childbirth, or the puerperium should have codes O98.7- and B20.
- Patients with asymptomatic HIV infection status during pregnancy, childbirth, or the puerperium should have codes O98.7- and Z21.
- Patients with diabetes during pregnancy, childbirth, or puerperium should have codes O24 and categories E08–E13. Also code Z79.4 (long-term, current use of insulin), if the diabetes is being treated with insulin.

Pain

- Use a code from category G89 in addition to other codes to provide more detail about whether the pain is acute, chronic, or neoplasm-related.
- If pain is not specified as acute or chronic, do not assign a code from category G89 except for postthoracotomy pain, postoperative pain, neoplasm-related pain, or central pain syndrome.
- A code from subcategories G89.1 and G89.2 should not be used if the underlying diagnosis is known unless the primary reason for admission is pain control.
- A code from category G89 can be the principal or first-listed diagnosis code when pain control or management is the reason for the admission or encounter. Code the underlying cause of the pain as an additional diagnosis.
- When a patient is admitted for a procedure for purposes of treating the underlying condition (e.g., spinal fusion), code the underlying condition (e.g., spinal stenosis) as the principal diagnosis. Do not code the pain from category G89.
- When a patient is admitted for the insertion of a neurostimulator for pain control, assign the code for pain as the principal diagnosis.
- If the patient is admitted primarily for a procedure to treat the underlying condition and a neurostimulator is inserted for pain, code the underlying condition as the principal diagnosis, followed by a code for the pain.
- If a code describes the site of the pain, but does not indicate whether the type of pain is acute or chronic (category G89), use two codes (one for the site and one for the type, such as procedural, due to trauma, etc.). If the admission is for pain control, assign category code G89 (acute or chronic) as the principal diagnosis. If the admission is not for pain control and a related definitive diagnosis is not documented, assign the code for the specific site of the pain as the principal diagnosis.
- Routine or expected postoperative pain immediately after surgery should not be coded.
- Postoperative pain not associated with a specific postoperative complication is coded using the appropriate code in category G89.
- Postoperative pain can be listed as the principal diagnosis when the reason for admission is pain control.

Pleural Effusion

- Pleural effusion is almost always integral to the underlying condition and therefore is usually not coded.
- When the effusion is addressed and treated separately, it can be coded.
- Pleural effusion noted only on an X-ray is not coded.

Pneumonia

- There are many combination codes that describe the pneumonia and the infecting organism.
- In some situations, the pneumonia is a manifestation of an underlying condition. In this situation, two codes are needed—one for the underlying condition and the other for the pneumonia.
- Lobar pneumonia does not refer to the lobe of the lung that is affected. It is a particular type of pneumonia.
- Gram-negative pneumonias are much more difficult to treat than gram-positive pneumonias. If the findings suggest a gram-negative pneumonia, and it is not documented as such, query the physician.
- Signs of gram-negative pneumonia include: worsening of cough, dyspnea, fever, purulent sputum, elevated leukocyte count, and patchy infiltrate on chest X-ray.
- When the physician has documented Ventilator Associated Pneumonia (VAP), use code J95.851. The physician must document that the pneumonia is attributed to the ventilator.
- Add an additional code to identify the organism associated with the VAP. Do not assign an additional code from categories J12–J18 to identify the type of pneumonia.

Postoperative Complications

- Physician must document that a condition is a complication of the procedure before assigning a complication code.
- "Expected" conditions occur in the immediate post-op period. These are not reported unless they exceed the usual post-op period and meet the criteria for reporting as an additional diagnosis.

Pressure Ulcers

- When the patient has multiple pressure ulcers at different sites and each is at different stages, code each of the sites and each of the different stages.
- When the patient has pressure ulcers documented as "healed," no code is assigned.
- When the patient has pressure ulcers documented as "healing," code the site(s) and the stage(s).
- When the patient has a pressure ulcer at one stage at the time of admission, but then it progresses to a higher stage, assign the code for the highest stage.

Pulmonary Edema

- Pulmonary edema can be cardiogenic or noncardiogenic.
- Pulmonary edema is a manifestation of heart failure and, as such, is included in heart failure, hypertension, or rheumatic heart disease. Therefore, it is not coded separately.
- Noncardiogenic acute pulmonary edema occurs in the absence of heart failure or other heart disease.

Respiratory Failure (Acute)

- Careful review of the medical record is required for the coding and sequencing of acute respiratory failure. If it meets the definition of principal diagnosis, it is coded as such. If it does not, it is coded as a secondary diagnosis.
- When a patient is admitted with acute respiratory failure and another acute condition, the principal diagnosis will depend on the individual patient's condition and the chief (main) reason that caused the admission of the patient to the hospital.

Septicemia

- A diagnosis of bacteremia R78.81 refers to the presence of bacteria in the bloodstream following a relatively minor injury or infection.
- Septicemia and sepsis are often used to mean the same thing, but they have two distinct and separate meanings.
- Septicemia is a systemic condition associated with pathogenic microorganisms or toxins in the blood (such as bacteria, viruses, fungi, or other organisms). Most septicemias are classified to category A40 and A41. Additional codes are assigned for any manifestations, if present.
- Negative blood cultures do not preclude a diagnosis of septicemia or sepsis. Query the physician.
- A code for septicemia is used only when the physician documents a diagnosis of septicemia.
- Urosepsis is not a condition that is classified in ICD-10-CM. A physician query should be initiated for clarification of the condition under treatment.
- Systemic Inflammatory Response Syndrome (SIRS) refers to the systemic response to infection, trauma, burns, or other insult (such as cancer) with symptoms (such as fever, tachycardia, tachypnea, and leukocytosis).
- When a patient has SIRS with no subsequent infection, and is a result of a noninfectious disease (such as trauma, cancer, or pancreatitis), code the noninfectious disease first, and then code R65.10 or R65.11. If an acute organ dysfunction is documented, code that also.

- Sepsis generally refers to SIRS due to infection.
- Severe sepsis generally refers to sepsis with associated acute organ dysfunction.
- If sepsis or severe sepsis is present on admission and meets the definition of principal diagnosis, the systemic infection code should be coded first, followed by the appropriate code from subcategory R65.2-. Codes from subcategory R65.2- can never be assigned as a principal diagnosis. An additional code should be added for any localized infection, if present.
- If sepsis or severe sepsis develops during admission, assign the code for the systemic infection and a code from subcategory R65.2- as a secondary code.
- Septic shock is defined as sepsis with hypotension, which is a failure of the cardiovascular system. Septic shock is used as an additional code when the underlying infection is present.
- For all cases of septic shock, code the systemic infection first (such as A40.-; A41.-; B37.7) followed by code R65.21. Any additional codes for other acute organ dysfunction should also be assigned.

Substance Abuse

- Substance abuse and dependence are classified as mental disorders in ICD-10-CM.
- Alcohol dependence is classified to category F10.2, and nondependent alcohol use is coded to category F10.1.
- The physician documentation must indicate the pattern of use.
- There are codes for alcohol withdrawal and drug withdrawal symptoms. These codes are used in conjunction with the dependence codes.
- When a patient is admitted in withdrawal or when withdrawal develops after admission, the withdrawal code is principal.
- There are procedure codes for rehabilitation, detoxification, and combination rehabilitation and detoxification for both alcohol and drug dependence.

Z-Codes

- Z-codes (Z00–Z99) characterize the purpose for an encounter when a disease or injury is not the reason a patient is seeking healthcare services. Z-codes can be used in any healthcare setting. Certain Z-codes can be assigned as the principal or first listed diagnosis.
- Special main terms for Z-codes in the Alphabetic Index of Diseases include:

Abnormal	Foreign Body
Admission	Healthy
Aftercare Anomaly	History (family)
Attention to	History
(personal) Boarder	Maintenance
Care of	Maladjustment
Carrier	Observation
Checking	Problem with
Complication	Procedure (surgical)
Contraception	Prophylactic
Counseling	Replacement
Delivery	Screening
Dialysis	Status
Donor	Supervision (of)
Examination	Test
Exposure to	Transplant
Fitting of	Unavailability of medical facilities
Follow-up	Vaccination

OUTPATIENT PROCEDURE CODING REVIEW

HCPCS (Healthcare Common Procedure Coding System)
- A coding system describing the physician and nonphysician patient services covered by the government's Medicare and Medicaid programs.
- Designed by CMS and used primarily to report reimbursable services rendered to the patient.
- Consists of two levels of HCPCS codes for ambulatory (outpatient) patients.

LEVEL I—CPT (Current Procedural Terminology) is a coding system developed by the American Medical Association (AMA) to convert descriptions of medical, surgical, and diagnostic services rendered by health care providers into five-digit numerical codes. The codes are updated annually by AMA.

The CPT coding system:
- provides uniform language to accurately designate medical, surgical, and diagnostic services.
- provides effective means of reliable, nationwide communication between physicians, patients, and third-party payers.
- allows for the ability to compare reimbursements for procedures.

Justification for listing of a procedure:
- The procedure is commonly performed by physicians nationally.
- The procedure must be consistent with modern medical practice.

LEVEL II—National Codes
- Updated by CMS
- Five-digit alphanumeric codes
- Codes exist for products, supplies, and services not included in CPT.

CPT and HCPCS are used to code physician and outpatient provider procedures. They are not used in an inpatient or acute care setting.

RULES FOR CODING CPT

1. Determine the service provided by analyzing the statement provided by the physician.
2. Identify the main term(s) in the Alphabetic Index.

   To locate a code in the index, the coder should first look up the procedure or service provided. If the procedure is not listed, look under the anatomic site involved, the condition, the synonym, or the eponym. Follow the guidance of the index in locating the code most accurately describing the service.
3. Write down or note the code number(s) found for the term.
   - If a single code number is given, locate the code in the body of the CPT book. Verify the code and its description against the statement, ensuring they match.
   - If two or more codes separated by a comma are given, locate each code in the body of the CPT book. Read the description of each and select the appropriate code matching the statement.
   - If a range of codes is given, locate the range of codes in the body of the CPT book. Review the description of each entry prior to selecting a code.
4. NEVER code from the Alphabetic Index; look up the codes to verify accuracy.
5. Read all notes that apply to the code selected.
   Notes may appear at the beginning of a section, subsection, before or after a code, or within the code description. Notes are utilized throughout the CPT, requiring special attention and review by the coder. Some of these notes define terms, such as *simple, intermediate,* and *complex wound repair.* Other notes provide specific coding instruction applicable to specific codes.
6. Select the appropriate modifier, if applicable, to complete the code description.
7. Code multiple procedures from highest resource intensive to lowest (most complicated to least complicated).

COMMON ERRORS THAT PREVENT PAYMENT TO PHYSICIANS

1. No documentation or incomplete documentation for services billed
2. Missing signatures
3. Consistently assigning the same level of services
4. Billing of a consult instead of an office visit
5. Using invalid codes in the bill due to use of old coding resources or forms
6. Unbundling procedure codes
7. Not listing the chief complaint
8. Abbreviations that are misinterpreted
9. Billing of services included in global fee as a separate professional fee
10. Not using a modifier or use of an inappropriate modifier for accurate payment of a claim

CPT CODE BOOK FORMAT INFORMATION

Guidelines provide specific instructions about coding for each section. The guidelines contain definitions of terms, explanations of notes, subsection information, unlisted services, and special reports information.

Sections: There are eight major areas into which all CPT codes and descriptions are categorized. The majority of CPT codes are arranged in numerical order in each section. The first six sections are comprised of five-digit numerical codes. The codes in the last two sections, Category II and Category III Codes, are comprised of five-digit codes—four numbers and a letter.

> Evaluation and Management
> Anesthesia
> Surgery
> Radiology
> Pathology/Laboratory
> Medicine
> Category II Codes
> Category III Codes

Category II Codes are optional tracking codes used to measure performance.

Category III Codes are temporary codes for emerging technology, services, and procedures. These codes can be used for data collection purposes or possibly in the FDA approval process. If a Category III code is available, this code must be reported instead of a Category I unlisted code.

Subsections, subcategories, and headings divide the sections into smaller units, based on anatomy, procedure, condition, description, or approach.

Symbols used in CPT coding: The following symbols are special guides that help the coder compare codes and descriptors with the previous year's CPT edition, or that provide additional coding guidance.

- • Bullet is used to indicate a new procedure or service code added since the previous edition of the CPT manual.

- ▲ Triangle indicates that the code has been changed or modified since the last CPT manual edition.

- \+ A plus sign is used to indicate an add-on code.
- ⊘ Null symbol is used to identify a modifier-51 exempt code.

- ►◄ A right and left triangle indicates the beginning and end of the text changes.

- (→) Reference to CPT Assistant, Clinical Examples in Radiology, and CPT Changes
- \# The number sign is used to identify codes that have been resequenced and are not placed numerically.
- ○ Indicates a reinstated/recycled code.
- ★ A star symbol is used to indicate codes that can be used with modifier 95 for synchronous telemedicine services.

Modifiers: Two-character codes added to CPT codes to supply more specific information about the services provided.

Special reports: Detailed reports that include adequate definitions or descriptions of the nature, extent, and need for the procedure, and the time, effort, and equipment necessary to provide the service.

Unlisted procedures: Procedures that are considered unusual, experimental, or new and do not have a specific code number assigned. Unlisted procedure codes are located at the end of the subcategories, or headings, and may be used to identify any procedure that lacks a specific code and requires a "special report" submitted at the time of billing.

CPT Index: Located at the back of the CPT manual and arranged alphabetically. To locate terms in the alphabetic index, look under the

Service/procedure

Anatomic site/body organ

Condition/disease/problem

Synonym

Eponym (procedure named after someone)

Abbreviation or acronym (e.g., CBC)

Notations:

> "see"—sends you to a more appropriate section.

> "see also"—cross-reference to refer to another main term.

CPT Appendices in back section of the CPT manual:

Appendix A:	Lists all modifiers with complete explanations for use
Appendix B:	Contains a complete list of additions to, deletions from, and revisions of the previous year's edition
Appendix C:	Provides clinical examples of Evaluation and Management (E&M) codes
Appendix D:	Contains a listing of the CPT add-on codes
Appendix E:	Contains a list of modifier-51 exempt codes
Appendix F:	Contains a list of modifier-63 exempt codes
Appendix H:	Alphabetical clinical topics listing
Appendix I:	Genetic testing code modifiers
Appendix J:	Electrodiagnostic medicine listing of sensory, motor, and mixed nerves
Appendix K:	Product pending FDA approval
Appendix L:	Vascular families
Appendix M:	Crosswalk to deleted CPT codes
Appendix N:	Summary of resequenced CPT codes
Appendix O:	Multianalyte Assays with Algorithmic Analyses
Appendix P:	CPT Codes that may be used for synchronous telemedicine services

GENERAL E&M CODING GUIDELINES

1. Determine place of service: office, emergency room, or nursing home.
2. Determine type of service: consult, admission, newborn.
3. Determine patient status: new unless seen in last 3 years by the physician or another physician of the same specialty in the same group.
4. Determine the level of each of the three key components:
   A. **History:** problem focused, expanded problem focused, detailed, comprehensive
   B. **Physical examination:** problem focused, expanded problem focused, detailed, comprehensive
   C. **Medical decision making:** straightforward, low, moderate, high
   - New patients, consultations, emergency department services, and initial care: generally require all three key components.
   - Established patients and subsequent care: usually require two of the three key components.
   - Some codes are based on time: critical care, prolonged services.
5. Read Critical Care guidelines carefully. Watch for the procedures that are included in the codes.
6. Read Inpatient Neonatal and Pediatric Critical Care Services and intensive (noncritical) low birth weight services guidelines carefully. Watch for procedures that are inclusive in this area.
7. Be sure to read the coding guidelines for E&M coding carefully.
8. Review definition for "consultations" and determine when consult codes are more appropriate than office visit codes.
9. There are specific codes used for hospital observation services (initial care, subsequent care, and discharge services) and codes for same-day admissions and discharges.
10. When a patient is admitted as an inpatient on the same day that services are provided at another site (office, ER, observation, etc.), only the inpatient services are reported. The E&M services provided in these outpatient settings can be used to determine the level of inpatient services provided.
11. Preventive Care codes are based on the patient's age.

SOME ADDITIONAL AREAS OF INTEREST WHEN CODING WITH CPT

Abortion

- **"Incomplete Abortions" and "Miscarriages"** are alternate terms for missed and spontaneous abortions.
- **Spontaneous abortion** that occurs during any trimester and is completed surgically, assign 59812.
- **Missed abortion** that occurs during the first trimester, assign 59820.
- **Induced abortion**, which combines curettage and evacuation, assign 59851.
- **Induced abortion by dilation and evacuation**, code 59841.
- **Induced abortion by dilation and curettage**, code 59840. Code 58120 is used for a nonobstetrical D&C.

Angioplasty

- **Determination of the site** and whether it is open or percutaneous.
- **Open transluminal angioplasty** of renal or other visceral arteries, aortic, brachiocephalic, or venous sites code from 37246 to 37249.
- **Percutaneous transluminal angioplasty** of renal or other visceral arteries, aortic, brachiocephalic, or venous sites code from 37246 to 37249.
- **Endovascular revascularization (open or percutaneous, transcatheter)** of lower extremities code from 37220 to 37235.
- **PTCA: Percutaneous transluminal coronary angioplasty:** assign code appropriately from 92920 and 92921.
- **Percutaneous transluminal angioplasty** of the peripheral arteries and visceral arteries: includes radiological supervision and interpretation
- **Codes 92928 and 92929** for stent placement include the PTCA and thus the PTCA is not coded separately.

Appendectomy

- There are several codes that are used to describe appendectomies:
  - open surgical appendectomy (including incidental), laparoscopic appendectomy, appendectomy done for a ruptured appendix, and appendectomy done for a specified purpose at the time of other major surgery.

Auditory

- **Simple mastoidectomy** is also called a transmastoid antrotomy (69501).
- **Apicetomy** is the excision of the tip of the petrous bone. This is often performed with a radical mastoidectomy (69530). It would be inappropriate to code 69511 in addition.
- **Tympanostomy** (requiring insertion of ventilating tube). Code 69436, Tympanostomy (requiring insertion of ventilating tube) general anesthesia, and 69433, Tympanostomy (requiring insertion of ventilating tube), local or topic anesthesia, are used for "insertion of tubes."
- **Removal of impacted cerumen** from one or both ears, use code 69210.

Bronchoscopy and Biopsy

- **Surgical bronchoscopy** includes a diagnostic bronchoscopy.
- **Code appropriate endoscopy for each anatomic site examined.**
- **Endobronchial biopsy,** code 31625.
- **Review for types of specimen collection:**
  - **Biopsy** forceps used to remove tissue
  - **Bronchial brush** used to obtain surface cells
  - **Bronchial alveolar lavage (BAL)** used to collect cells from peripheral lung tissue
  - **Cell washings** used to exfoliate cells from crevices

Current Procedural Terminology © 2016 American Medical Association. All Rights Reserved.

Note: Cell washings or brushings are NOT biopsies.
- **Transbronchial biopsy** is performed by positioning the scope in the bronchus nearest to the lesion. A hole is punctured through the bronchus into the lung tissue where the lesion is located. The lesion is then biopsied. Transbronchial lung biopsy is reported with code 31628.
- **Transbronchial needle aspiration biopsy** (31629).
- **Catheter aspiration of tracheobronchial tree at bedside** (31725).

CABG
- To report combined arterial-venous grafts, it is necessary to report two codes:
  - The appropriate combined arterial-venous graft code (33517–33523)
  - The appropriate arterial graft code (33533–33536)
- Procurement of the saphenous vein graft is included in the description of the work for 33517–33523 and is not reported separately.
- Procurement of an upper extremity artery is reported separately.

Casting and Strapping
- Services in the musculoskeletal system include the application or removal of the first cast or traction device only. Subsequent replacement of casts, traction devices, or removals is reported using codes from the 29000–29750 series of codes.
- The codes in the 29000–29750 series of codes have very specific guidelines directing the use of the codes.

Endoscopy
- **Codes specify** the purpose and site of application.
- **Dx endoscopy** is coded only if a surgical procedure was not done. Surgical endoscopy always includes a diagnostic endoscopy.
- **Code as far as the scope is passed.**
- **Stomach endoscopy** is included with UGI endoscopy, not separately.
- **Multiple codes may be necessary** to cover one endoscopic episode.
- **Removal of gastrostomy tube by endoscopy**, code 43247.
- **Colonoscopy:** first determine the route the procedure follows (via colostomy, colotomy, or rectum).
- **Colonoscopy with dilation** of rectum or anorectum, code 45999.
- **Biliary endoscopy** (47550) is only used with 47420 or 47610.
- **EGDs** are coded to 43235–43259.

Eye and Ocular
- **Preliminary iridectomy** is not coded separately if performed as part of a cataract extraction or prior to lens extraction. It is included in the code for the lens extraction.
- Two types of cataract extraction:
  - ICCE: Intracapsular cataract extraction
  - ECCE: Extracapsular cataract extraction
- **Do not code medication injections** used in conjunction with cataract surgery. Injections are considered part of the procedure.
- **Cataract removal includes** the following in codes 66830–66984.
- DO NOT CODE THE FOLLOWING PROCEDURES SEPARATELY: anterior capsulotomy, enzymatic zonulysis, iridectomy, iridotomy, lateral canthotomy, pharmacological agents, posterior capsulotomy, viscoelastic agents, subconjunctival, and subtenon injections.

Female Genital System

- **Codes 57452–57461** are used to report various cervical colposcopic procedures.
- **Code 57455** describes colposcopy with single or multiple biopsies of the cervix.
- **Code 58150** describes total abdominal hysterectomy with or without removal of tube(s) or ovary(s).
- **Code 58611** is an add-on code that describes tubal ligation or transection when done at the time of Cesarean delivery or intra-abdominal surgery.

Fractures/Dislocations

- Treatment of fractures/dislocations can be open or closed.
- Closed treatment means that the fracture or dislocation site is not surgically opened. It is used to describe procedures that treat fractures by three methods: without manipulation, with manipulation, and with or without traction.
- Open treatment implies that the fracture is surgically opened and the fracture is visualized to allow treatment.
- Skeletal fixation is neither open nor closed treatment. Usually pins are placed across the fracture using X-ray guidance.
- Manipulation is used to indicate the attempted reduction or restoration of a fracture or dislocation.

Genitourinary

- Many of the procedures in the urinary system are performed endoscopically—cystoscopy, urethroscopy, cystourethroscopy, ureteroscopy, pyeloscopy, and renal endoscopy.
- Most cystourethroscopy codes are unilateral. When a cysto is performed bilaterally, modifier-50 should be appended.
- Codes in the 52320–52356 series include the insertion and removal of a temporary stent during diagnostic or therapeutic cystourethroscopic intervention(s).
- Cystourethroscopy with removal of a self-retaining/indwelling ureteral stent, planned or staged during the associated normal postoperative follow-up period of the original procedure, is reported by means of code 52310 or 52315 with the modifier-58 appended as appropriate.
- Be careful to differentiate between codes for ureteral and urethral procedures.

GI Biopsy

- **Code only the biopsy** if a single lesion is biopsied but not excised.
- **Code only the biopsy** and list only one time if multiple biopsies are done (from the same or different lesions) and none of the lesions are excised.
- **Code only the excision** if a biopsy of a lesion is taken and the balance of the same lesion is then excised.
- **Code both the biopsy and the excision** if both are performed and if the biopsy is taken from a lesion different from that which is excised, and the code for the excision does not include the phrase "with or without biopsy." If such a phrase is in the code narration, then a separate biopsy code should not be used.
- **Surgical endoscopy** always includes a diagnostic endoscopy.
- **Modifier-59** may be used to explain unusual circumstances when coding both biopsy and removal of a different lesion.

Hernia Repair

- Hernia repair codes are categorized by type (inguinal, femoral, etc.).
- Hernias are further categorized as "initial" or "recurrent" based on whether or not the hernia has required previous repair.
- Age and clinical presentation (reducible versus strangulated).
- Code 49568 is used only with nonlaparscopic incisional or ventral hernia repairs.

Immunizations
- Codes **90460–90474** are used to report the administration of vaccines/toxoids.
- Codes **90476–90749** identify the vaccine PRODUCT alone.
- If a combination vaccine code is provided (MMR) it is not appropriate to report each component of the combination vaccine separately.
- When the physician provides face-to-face counseling of the patient and family during the administration of a vaccine, report codes 90460–90461.
- Do not append modifier-51 to the vaccine/toxoid product codes 90476–90749.

Integumentary
- **Three types of repairs:** Add lengths of repairs together and use one code for repairs of the same location and same type.
  - **Simple:** Superficial wound involving skin and/or subcutaneous tissues and requiring simple suturing.
  - **Intermediate:** Involving skin, subcutaneous tissues, and fascia and requiring layer closure. May also be used when a single closure requires intensive cleaning.
  - **Complex** repairs requiring reconstructive surgery or time-consuming or complicated closures.
- **Debridement is coded separately:** When gross contamination requires cleaning, when appreciable amounts of devitalized or contaminated tissue are removed, and when debridement is carried out separately without primary closure.
- **Lesion size** is best found on the operative report.
- **Benign or malignant lesion(s):** Code each lesion excised separately; simple closure after excision of lesion(s) is included in the code.
- **Adjacent tissue transfers** include excision of tissues, including lesions.
- **Free skin grafts:** Identify by size and location of the defect (recipient area) and the type of graft; includes simple debridement of granulations or recent avulsion.
- There are three code ranges:
  - Use 15002–15005 for initial wound preparation.
  - Use 15040–15261 for autografts and tissue-cultured autografts.
  - Use 15271–15278 for skin substitute grafts (homografts, allografts, and xenografts).
- Repair of donor site requiring skin graft or local flaps is to be added on as an additional procedure.
- Report excision of lesion(s) separately.
- **Excisional biopsy** is used when the entire lesion, whether benign or malignant, is removed.
- **Breast lesion excisions** performed after being identified by pre-op radiological marker (localization wires), use codes 19125 and 19126.
- **Placement of needle localization wires** prior to biopsies, excisions, and other breast procedures, use additional codes 19281–19288.

Laryngoscopy
- Many of the codes used to report laryngoscopies include the use of an operating microscope. Therefore, code 69990, microsurgical techniques, requiring the use of an operating microscope (list separately in addition to code primary procedure), would not be used with any codes that include the use of the microscope.

Lymphatic System: Sentinel Nodes
- **Sentinel node** procedures utilize injection of a radiotracer or blue dye. After absorption of dye, the physician can visualize the node(s). Code 38792 is used for identification of sentinel nodes. For excision of sentinel nodes, see 38500–38542.
- **Use appropriate lymph node excision codes** to report the excision.

- **A second sentinel node** from a different lymphatic chain excised from a separate incision, report the excision and add modifier-59.
- **Lymphoscintigraphy**, code 78195.
- **Injection for gamma probe** node detection with imaging code 38790.

Maternity Care and Delivery

- Antepartum care or services provided above the normally expected care (as defined in the CPT book) should be coded separately.
- Medical problems complicating labor and delivery management may require additional resources and should be identified by using E&M codes in addition to the codes for maternity care.
- For surgical complications of pregnancy, see services in the surgery section.
- If a physician provides all or part of the antepartum and/or postpartum patient care, but does not perform delivery due to termination of pregnancy by abortion or referral to another physician for delivery, see the antepartum and postpartum care codes 59425–59426 and 59430.
- Patients who have had a previous Cesarean delivery and now present with the expectation of a vaginal delivery are coded using codes 59610–59622. If the patient has a successful vaginal delivery after a previous Cesarean delivery (VBAC), use codes 59610–59614. If the attempt is unsuccessful and another Cesarean delivery is carried out, use codes 59618–59622.

Nasal Hemorrhage

- Was it anterior or posterior?
  - If anterior, was the hemorrhage simple or complex?
  - If posterior, was the control of the hemorrhage an initial or subsequent procedure?
- **Anterior nasal hemorrhage** has likely occurred if the physician inserts gauze packing or anterior packing or performs cauterization.
- **Posterior nasal hemorrhage** has likely occurred if the physician inserts nasal stents, tampons, balloon catheters, or posterior packing, or if the patient is taken to the OR for ligation of arteries to control bleeding.
- **Nosebleed subsequent to initial one** (30906).

Neurology/Spine Surgery

- The spinal and spinal cord injection codes reflect the specific spinal anatomy, such as subarachnoid or epidural; the level of the injection (cervical, thoracic, lumbar, or sacral); and the types of substances injected, such as anesthetic steroids, antispasmodics, phenol, etc.
- Injection of contrast material during fluoroscopic guidance is included in codes 62263–62264, 62267, 62270–62273, 62280–62282, and 62320–62326. The fluoroscopic guidance itself is reported by code 77003. Code 62263 describes treatment involving injections of various substances over a multiple-day period. Code 62263 is not reported for each individual injection but is reported once to describe the entire series of injections or infusions.
- Code 62264 describes multiple treatments performed on the same day.
- Other codes in this section refer to laminectomies, excisions, repairs, and shunts. A basic distinction among the codes is the condition, such as herniated disk, as well as the approach used, such as anterior or posterior or costovertebral.
- Lumbar punctures (62270) are also called spinal taps and are used to obtain cerebrospinal fluid by inserting a needle into the subarachnoid space in the lumbar area.
- When coding surgery on the spine, there are many sets of guidelines for the coder to review, including those at the beginning of the subsection, as well as throughout the subsection.
- Co-surgery is common in spinal surgeries. When two surgeons work together, both as primary surgeons, each surgeon should report his or her distinct operative work by adding modifier-62 to the procedure code and any associated add-on codes for that procedure as long as both surgeons continue to work together as primary surgeons.

- Spinal instrumentation is used to stabilize the spinal column during repair procedures. There are two types: segmental and nonsegmental.
  - Segmental instrumentation involves attachment at each end of the spinal area and at least one intermittent fixation.
  - Nonsegmental instrumentation involves attachment at each end and may span several vertebral segments without intermittent fixation.

Pacemakers

1. Is it permanent or temporary?
2. What was the approach (transvenous or epicardial)?
3. What type of device (electrodes and/or pulse generator)?
4. Where were the electrodes placed (atrial, ventricle, or both)?
5. Is this an insertion of a new or replacement permanent pacemaker? Insertion or replacement of a temporary pacemaker? Repair of electrodes? Removal of a pacemaker? Repositioning?
6. Was revision of the skin pocket done?

Thyroid

- **Recall** that **the thyroid has two lobes**, one on each side of the trachea. The procedure may only be unilateral (60220), but it is still considered to be a total lobectomy.
- **Thyroidectomy may be**
  - Total or complete (60240), removing both the lobes and the isthmus. It is not necessary to list the code twice.
  - Partial lobectomy (60210), unilateral, with or without isthmusectomy.
- **Thyroidectomy with neck dissection** (60252 and 60254). Do not assign these codes if an isolated lymph node is excised or biopsied.

Tonsillectomy and Adenoidectomy

- Separate codes describe tonsillectomy and adenoidectomy; tonsillectomy alone, whether primary or secondary; adenoidectomy alone, primary; adenoidectomy alone, secondary.
- Separate codes are reported for procedures performed on patients under age 12, and age 12 or older.
- A primary procedure is one in which no prior tonsillectomy or adenoidectomy has been performed. A secondary procedure is one that is performed to remove residual or regrowth of tonsil or adenoid tissue.

Wound Exploration

- Wound exploration codes (20100–20103) are used when repair of a penetrating wound requires enlargement of the existing defect for exploration, cleaning, and repair.
- If the wound does not need to be enlarged, then only repair codes from the integumentary section are used.

III. Health Data Content and Standards

Patricia J. Schnering, RHIA, CCS
Debra W. Cook, MAEd., RHIA

1. In preparation for an EHR, you are working with a team conducting a total facility inventory of all forms currently used. You must name each form for bar coding and indexing into a document management system. The unnamed document in front of you includes a microscopic description of tissue excised during surgery. The document type you are most likely to give to this form is
    A. recovery room record.
    C. operative report.
    B. pathology report.
    D. discharge summary.

REFERENCE: Abdelhak and Hanken, p 107
                        Bowie and Green, p 181
                        Oachs and Watters, p 18
                        Sayles and Gordon, p 95

2. Patient data collection requirements vary according to health care setting. A data element you would expect to be collected in the MDS but NOT in the UHDDS would be
    A. personal identification.
    C. procedures and dates.
    B. cognitive patterns.
    D. principal diagnosis.

REFERENCE: Abdelhak and Hanken, pp 135–137
                        Sayles and Gordon, p 102

3. In the past, Joint Commission standards have focused on promoting the use of a facility-approved abbreviation list to be used by hospital care providers. With the advent of the Commission's national patient safety goals, the focus has shifted to the
    A. prohibited use of any abbreviations.
    B. flagrant use of specialty-specific abbreviations.
    C. use of prohibited or "dangerous" abbreviations.
    D. use of abbreviations used in the final diagnosis.

REFERENCE: Abdelhak and Hanken, p 111

4. A risk manager needs to locate a full report of a patient's fall from his bed, including witness reports and probable reasons for the fall. She would most likely find this information in the
    A. doctors' progress notes.
    C. incident report.
    B. integrated progress notes.
    D. nurses' notes.

REFERENCE: Abdelhak and Hanken, pp 465–466
                        Bowie and Green, pp 96–97
                        McWay, p 132
                        Oachs and Watters, p 29
                        Sayles and Gordon, p 522

5. For continuity of care, ambulatory care providers are more likely than providers of acute care services to rely on the documentation found in the
    A. interdisciplinary patient care plan.
    B. discharge summary.
    C. transfer record.
    D. problem list.

REFERENCE: Abdelhak and Hanken, p 113
                        Bowie and Green, p 207
                        Sayles and Gordon, p 101

6. Joint Commission does not approve of auto authentication of entries in a health record. The primary objection to this practice is that
   A. it is too easy to delegate use of computer passwords.
   B. evidence cannot be provided that the physician actually reviewed and approved each report.
   C. electronic signatures are not acceptable in every state.
   D. tampering too often occurs with this method of authentication.

REFERENCE: Bowie and Green, p 85
               Oachs and Watters, p 411

7. As part of a quality improvement study you have been asked to provide information on the menstrual history, number of pregnancies, and number of living children on each OB patient from a stack of old obstetrical records. The best place in the record to locate this information is the
   A. prenatal record.   C. postpartum record.
   B. labor and delivery record.   D. discharge summary.

REFERENCE: Abdelhak and Hanken, p 108
               Bowie and Green, p 191

8. As a concurrent record reviewer for an acute care facility, you have asked Dr. Crossman to provide an updated history and physical for one of her recent admissions. Dr. Crossman pages through the medical record to a copy of an H&P performed in her office a week before admission. You tell Dr. Crossman
   A. a new H&P is required for every inpatient admission.
   B. that you apologize for not noticing the H&P she provided.
   C. the H&P copy is acceptable as long as she documents any interval changes.
   D. Joint Commission standards do not allow copies of any kind in the original record.

REFERENCE: Abdelhak and Hanken, p 103
               Bowie and Green, p 145

9. You have been asked to identify every reportable case of cancer from the previous year. A key resource will be the facility's
   A. disease index.   C. physicians' index.
   B. number control index.   D. patient index.

REFERENCE: McWay, p 140
               Oachs and Watters, pp 173–174
               Sayles and Gordon, p 147

10. Discharge summary documentation must include
    A. a detailed history of the patient.
    B. a note from social services or discharge planning.
    C. significant findings during hospitalization.
    D. correct codes for significant procedures.

REFERENCE: Abdelhak and Hanken, p 106
               Bowie and Green, p 158
               Oachs and Watters, pp 114–115
               Sayles and Gordon, p 97

11. The performance of qualitative analysis is an important tool in ensuring data quality. These reviews evaluate
    A. quality of care through the use of preestablished criteria.
    B. adverse effects and contraindications of drugs utilized during hospitalization.
    C. potentially compensable events.
    D. the overall quality of documentation.

REFERENCE: Abdelhak and Hanken, p 126
              Oachs and Watters, p 100

12. Ultimate responsibility for the quality and completion of entries in patient health records belongs to the
    A. chief of staff.   C. HIM director.
    B. attending physician.   D. risk manager.

REFERENCE: Oachs and Watters, p 104

13. The foundation for communicating all patient care goals in long-term care settings is the
    A. legal assessment.   C. interdisciplinary plan of care.
    B. medical history.   D. Uniform Hospital Discharge Data Set.

REFERENCE: Abdelhak and Hanken, p 104
              Oachs and Watters, p 25
              Sayles and Gordon, p 102

14. As part of Joint Commission's National Patient Safety Goal initiative, acute care hospitals are now required to use a preoperative verification process to confirm the patient's true identity and to confirm that necessary documents such as X-rays or medical records are available. They must also develop and use a process for
    A. including the primary caregiver in surgery consults.
    B. including the surgeon in the preanesthesia assessment.
    C. marking the surgical site.
    D. apprising the patient of all complications that might occur.

REFERENCE: Joint Commission
              Sayles and Gordon, p 520

15. Currently, the enforcement of HIPAA Privacy and Security Rules is the responsibility of the
    A. Office for Civil Rights.
    B. FBI.
    C. Office of Inspector General.
    D. Department of Recovery Audit Coordinators.

REFERENCE: Oachs and Watters, pp 59, 283
              Sayles and Gordon, p 450

16. Using the SOAP method of recording progress notes, which entry would most likely include a differential diagnosis?
    A. assessment
    B. plan
    C. subjective
    D. objective

REFERENCE: Bowie and Green, p 99
              Oachs and Watters, p 120
              Sayles and Gordon, p 106

17. You have been asked by a peer review committee to print a list of the medical record numbers of all patients who had CABGs performed in the past year at your acute care hospital. Which secondary data source could be used to quickly gather this information?
    A. disease index
    B. physician index
    C. master patient index
    D. operation index

REFERENCE: Oachs and Watters, p 172
               Sayles and Gordon, pp 147, 174

18. The best example of point-of-care service and documentation is
    A. using an automated tracking system to locate a record.
    B. using occurrence screens to identify adverse events.
    C. doctors using voice recognition systems to dictate radiology reports.
    D. nurses using bedside terminals to record vital signs.

REFERENCE: Abdelhak and Hanken, pp 308–309
               Oachs and Watters, pp 155, 193
               Sayles and Gordon, pp 294, 325

19. Which of the following is a form or view that is typically seen in the health record of a long-term care patient but is rarely seen in records of acute care patients?
    A. pharmacy consultation
    B. medical consultation
    C. physical exam
    D. emergency record

REFERENCE: Abdelhak and Hanken, p 141

20. In determining your acute care facility's degree of compliance with prospective payment requirements for Medicare, the best resource to reference for recent certification standards is the
    A. CARF manual.
    B. hospital bylaws.
    C. Joint Commission accreditation manual.
    D. Federal Register.

REFERENCE: Abdelhak and Hanken, p 448
               Bowie and Green, p 34
               Oachs and Watters, pp 46–47

21. In an acute care hospital, a complete history and physical may not be required for a new admission when
    A. the patient is readmitted for a similar problem within 1 year.
    B. the patient's stay is less than 24 hours.
    C. the patient has an uneventful course in the hospital.
    D. a legible copy of a recent H&P performed in the attending physician's office is available.

REFERENCE: Abdelhak and Hanken, p 103
               Bowie and Green, p 158
               Oachs and Watters, pp 108–109

22. When developing a data collection system, the most effective approach first considers
    A. the end user's needs.
    B. applicable accreditation standards.
    C. hardware requirements.
    D. facility preference.

REFERENCE: Oachs and Watters, p 787

23. A key data item you would expect to find recorded on an ER record but would probably NOT see in an acute care record is the
    A. physical findings.
    B. lab and diagnostic test results.
    C. time and means of arrival.
    D. instructions for follow-up care.

REFERENCE: Abdelhak and Hanken, p 135
                Oachs and Watters, p 116

24. Under which of the following conditions can an original paper-based patient health record be physically removed from the hospital?
    A. when the patient is brought to the hospital emergency department following a motor vehicle accident and, after assessment, is transferred with his health record to a trauma designated emergency department at another hospital
    B. when the director of health records is acting in response to a subpoena duces tecum and takes the health record to court
    C. when the patient is discharged by the physician and at the time of discharge is transported to a long-term care facility with his health record
    D. when the record is taken to a physician's private office for a follow-up patient visit postdischarge

REFERENCE: Abdelhak and Hanken, p 464

25. Using the SOAP style of documenting progress notes, choose the "subjective" statement from the following.
    A. sciatica unimproved with hot pack therapy
    B. patient moving about very cautiously, appears to be in pain
    C. adjust pain medication; begin physical therapy tomorrow
    D. patient states low back pain is as severe as it was on admission

REFERENCE: Abdelhak and Hanken, p 113
                Bowie and Green, p 99
                Oachs and Watters, p 112
                Sayles and Gordon, p 124

26. In 1987, OBRA helped shift the focus in long-term care to patient outcomes. As a result, core assessment data elements are collected on each SNF resident as defined in the
    A. UHDDS.
    B. MDS.
    C. Uniform Clinical Data Set.
    D. Uniform Ambulatory Core Data.

REFERENCE: Abdelhak and Hanken, p 97
                Bowie and Green, p 259
                Oachs and Watters, p 227
                Sayles and Gordon, pp 268–270

27. Before you submit a new form to the Forms Review Committee, you need to track the field name of a particular data field and the security levels applicable to that field. Your best source for this information would be the
    A. facility's data dictionary.
    B. MDS.
    C. Glossary of Health Care Terms.
    D. UHDDS.

REFERENCE: Abdelhak and Hanken, pp 501–505
                Oachs and Watters, p 170
                Sayles and Gordon, p 262

28. You notice on the admission H&P that Mr. McKahan, a Medicare patient, was admitted for disc surgery, but the progress notes indicate that due to some heart irregularities, he may not be at good surgical risk. Because of your knowledge of COP regulations, you expect that a(n) _____ will be added to his health record.
    A. interval summary
    B. consultation report
    C. advance directive
    D. interdisciplinary care plan

REFERENCE: Abdelhak and Hanken, p 106
                      Bowie and Green, p 165
                      Oachs and Watters, p 112

29. An example of objective entry in the health record supplied by a health care practitioner is the
    A. past medical history.
    B. physical assessment.
    C. chief complaint.
    D. review of systems.

REFERENCE: Abdelhak and Hanken, p 106
                      Bowie and Green, p 165
                      Oachs and Watters, p 120
                      Sayles and Gordon, p 124

30. You have been asked to recommend time-limited documentation standards for inclusion in the Medical Staff Bylaws, Rules, and Regulations. The committee documentation standards must meet the standards of both the Joint Commission and the Medicare Conditions of Participation. The standards for the history and physical exam documentation are discussed first. You advise them that the time period for completion of this report should be set at
    A. 12 hours after admission.
    B. 24 hours after admission.
    C. 12 hours after admission or prior to surgery.
    D. 24 hours after admission or prior to surgery.

REFERENCE: Abdelhak and Hanken, p 103
                      Bowie and Green, p 158
                      Oachs and Watters, pp 107–108

31. Based on the following documentation in an acute care record, where would you expect this excerpt to appear?

    "With the patient in the supine position, the right side of the neck was appropriately prepped with betadine solution and draped. I was able to pass the central line which was taped to skin and used for administration of drugs during resuscitation."

    A. physician progress notes
    B. operative record
    C. nursing progress notes
    D. physical examination

REFERENCE: Abdelhak and Hanken, p 107
                      Oachs and Watters, pp 113–114

32. One essential item to be captured on the physical exam is the
    A. general appearance as assessed by the physician.
    B. chief complaint.
    C. family history as related by the patient.
    D. subjective review of systems.

REFERENCE: Abdelhak and Hanken, p 105
               Bowie and Green, p 162
               Oachs and Watters, p 107

33. An example of a primary data source for health care statistics is the
    A. disease index.   C. MPI.
    B. accession register.   D. hospital census.

REFERENCE: Abdelhak and Hanken, p 484

34. During a retrospective review of Rose Hunter's inpatient health record, the health information clerk notes that on day 4 of hospitalization there was one missed dose of insulin. What type of review is this clerk performing?
    A. utilization review   C. legal review
    B. quantitative review   D. qualitative review

REFERENCE: Abdelhak and Hanken, p 125
               Bowie and Green, p 107
               McWay, p 126
               Oachs and Watters, p 125

35. Which of the following is least likely to be identified by a deficiency analysis technician?
    A. missing discharge summary
    B. need for physician authentication of two verbal orders
    C. discrepancy between post-op diagnosis by the surgeon and pathology diagnosis by the pathologist
    D. X-ray report charted on the wrong record

REFERENCE: Abdelhak and Hanken, p 125
               Bowie and Green, p 107
               McWay, p 126
               Oachs and Watters, p 123

36. Which of the following reports would normally be considered a consultation?
    A. tissue examination done by the pathologist
    B. impressions of a cardiologist asked to determine whether patient is at good surgical risk
    C. interpretation of a radiologic study
    D. technical interpretation of electrocardiogram

REFERENCE: Abdelhak and Hanken, p 106
               Bowie and Green, p 161
               Oachs and Watters, p 112

37. The health care providers at your hospital do a very thorough job of periodic open record review to ensure the completeness of record documentation. A qualitative review of surgical records would likely include checking for documentation regarding
    A. the presence or absence of such items as preoperative and postoperative diagnosis, description of findings, and specimens removed.
    B. whether a postoperative infection occurred and how it was treated.
    C. the quality of follow-up care.
    D. whether the severity of illness and/or intensity of service warranted acute level care.

REFERENCE: Abdelhak and Hanken, p 107
               Bowie and Green, p 107
               Oachs and Watters, p 125

38. In your facility, the health care providers from every discipline document progress notes sequentially on the same form. Your facility is utilizing
    A. integrated progress notes.   C. source-oriented records.
    B. interdisciplinary treatment plans.   D. SOAP notes.

REFERENCE: Abdelhak and Hanken, p 113
               Bowie and Green, p 173
               Oachs and Watters, p 111

39. Which of the following services is LEAST likely to be provided by a facility accredited by CARF?
    A. chronic pain management   C. brain injury management
    B. palliative care   D. vocational evaluation

REFERENCE: Abdelhak and Hanken, pp 136–137
               Bowie and Green, p 65
               Oachs and Watters, pp 15, 208

40. Reviewing a medical record to ensure that all diagnoses are justified by documentation throughout the chart is an example of
    A. peer review.   C. qualitative review.
    B. quantitative review.   D. legal analysis.

REFERENCE: Abdelhak and Hanken, p 125
               Bowie and Green, p 107
               McWay, p 126
               Oachs and Watters, p 29

41. Accreditation by Joint Commission is a voluntary activity for a facility and it is
    A. considered unnecessary by most health care facilities.
    B. required for state licensure in all states.
    C. conducted in each facility annually.
    D. required for reimbursement of certain patient groups.

REFERENCE: Abdelhak and Hanken, p 113
               Oachs and Watters, p 32

42. Which of the following indices might be protected from unauthorized access through the use of unique identifier codes assigned to members of the medical staff?
    A. disease index   C. master patient index
    B. procedure index   D. physician index

REFERENCE: Oachs and Watters, p 172

43. Which of the four distinct components of the problem-oriented record serves to help index documentation throughout the record?
    A. database
    B. problem list
    C. initial plan
    D. progress notes

REFERENCE: Abdelhak and Hanken, 112–113
              Bowie and Green, p 97
              Oachs and Watters, p 120

44. You have been asked to report the registry's annual caseload to administration. The most efficient way to retrieve this information would be to use
    A. patient abstracts.
    B. patient index.
    C. accession register.
    D. follow-up files.

REFERENCE: Oachs and Watters, p 174

45. Based on the following documentation in an acute care record, where would you expect this excerpt to appear?

"Initially the patient was admitted to the medical unit to evaluate the x-ray findings and the rub. He was started on Levaquin 500 mg initially and then 250 mg daily. The patient was hydrated with IV fluids and remained afebrile. Serial cardiac enzymes were done. The rub, chest pain, and shortness of breath resolved. EKGs remained unchanged. Patient will be discharged and followed as an outpatient."

    A. discharge summary
    B. physical exam
    C. admission note
    D. clinical laboratory report

REFERENCE: Abdelhak and Hanken, p 107
              Oachs and Watters, p 114

46. The best resource for checking out specific voluntary accreditation standards and guidelines for a rehabilitation facility is the
    A. Conditions of Participation for Rehabilitation Facilities.
    B. Medical Staff Bylaws, Rules, and Regulations.
    C. Joint Commission manual.
    D. CARF manual.

REFERENCE: Oachs and Watters, p 7

47. Stage I of meaningful use focuses on data capture and sharing. Which of the following is included in the menu set of objectives for eligible hospitals in this stage?
    A. use CPOE for medication orders
    B. smoking cessation counseling for MI patients
    C. appropriate use of HL-7 standards
    D. establish critical pathways for complex, high-dollar cases

REFERENCE: CMS

48. Which of the following is a secondary data source that would be used to quickly gather the health records of all juvenile patients treated for diabetes within the past 6 months?
    A. disease index
    B. patient register
    C. pediatric census sheet
    D. procedure index

REFERENCE: Bowie and Green, p 157
              Oachs and Watters, p 172

49. Your job description includes working with agents who have been charged with detecting and correcting overpayments made to your hospital in the Medicare Fee for Service program. You will need to develop a professional relationship with
    A. the OIG.
    B. MEDPAR representatives.
    C. QIO physicians.
    D. recovery audit contractors.

REFERENCE: Bowie and Green, pp 129–130
              Oachs and Watters, p 292

50. A primary focus of screen format design in a health record computer application should be to ensure that
    A. programmers develop standard screen formats for all hospitals.
    B. the user is capturing essential data elements.
    C. paper forms are easily converted to computer forms.
    D. data fields can be randomly accessed.

REFERENCE: Abdelhak and Hanken, pp 114–118
              McWay, pp 131–132
              Oachs and Watters, p 346

51. Before making recommendations to the Executive Committee regarding new physicians who have applied for active membership, the Credentials Committee must query the
    A. peer review organization.
    B. National Practitioner Data Bank.
    C. risk manager.
    D. Health Plan Employer Data and Information Set.

REFERENCE: Abdelhak and Hanken, pp 475–476
              Bowie and Green, p 11
              Oachs and Watters, p 186

52. The lack of a discharge order may indicate that the patient left against medical advice. If this situation occurs, you would expect to see the circumstances of the leave
    A. documented in an incident report and filed in the patient's health record.
    B. reported as a potentially compensable event.
    C. reported to the Executive Committee.
    D. documented in both the progress notes and the discharge summary.

REFERENCE: Oachs and Watters, p 111

53. You recommend that the staff routinely check to verify that a summary on each patient is provided to the attending physician so that he or she can review, update, and recertify the patient as appropriate. The time frame for requiring this summary is at least every
    A. week.
    B. month.
    C. 60 days.
    D. 90 days.

REFERENCE: Abdelhak and Hanken, p 138
              Oachs and Watters, p 115

54. You want to review the one document in your facility that will spell out the documentation requirements for patient records; designate the time frame for completion by the active medical staff; and indicate the penalties for failure to comply with these record standards. Your best resource will be
    A. medical staff bylaws.
    B. quality management plan.
    C. Joint Commission accreditation manual.
    D. medical staff rules and regulations.

REFERENCE: Bowie and Green, p 21
               Oachs and Watters, p 100

55. For inpatients, the first data item collected of a clinical nature is usually
    A. principal diagnosis.   C. admitting diagnosis.
    B. expected payer.   D. review of systems.

REFERENCE: Bowie and Green, p 135
               Oachs and Watters, p 99

56. In addition to diagnostic and therapeutic orders from the attending physician, you would expect every completed inpatient health record to contain
    A. standing orders.   C. stop orders.
    B. telephone orders.   D. discharge order.

REFERENCE: Abdelhak and Hanken, p 105
               Bowie and Green, p 167
               Oachs and Watters, p 111

57. When asked to explain how "review of systems" differs from "physical exam," you explain that the review of systems is used to document
    A. objective symptoms observed by the physician.
    B. past and current activities, such as smoking and drinking habits.
    C. a chronological description of patient's present condition from time of onset to present.
    D. subjective symptoms that the patient may have forgotten to mention or that may have seemed unimportant.

REFERENCE: Bowie and Green, pp 158–159
               Oachs and Watters, p 107

58. Based on the following documentation, where would you expect this excerpt to appear?

"The patient is alert and in no acute distress. Initial vital signs: T98, P 102 and regular, R 20 and BP 120/69..."

    A. physical exam
    B. past medical history
    C. social history
    D. chief complaint

REFERENCE: Abdelhak and Hanken, p 105
               Oachs and Watters, p 107

59. The federally mandated resident assessment instrument used in long-term care facilities consists of three basic components, including the new care area assessment, utilization guidelines, and the
    A. UHDDS.   C. OASIS.
    B. MDS.   D. DEEDS.

REFERENCE: Oachs and Watters, p 119

60. You recommend that the staff at your home health agency routinely check to verify that a summary on each patient is provided to the attending physician so that he or she can review, update, and recertify the patient as appropriate. The time frame for requiring this summary is at least every
    A. week.
    B. month.
    C. 60 days.
    D. 90 days.

REFERENCE: Abdelhak and Hanken, p 138
                Oachs and Watters, p 115

61. To enter the results of a CBC into the computer system, you would use a(n)
    A. laboratory system.
    B. radiology system.
    C. pharmacy system.
    D. order entry/results reporting system.

REFERENCE: Bowie and Green, p 124
                Oachs and Watters, p 98

62. Which of the following would not be an example of a secondary data source?
    A. disease index
    B. accession register
    C. MPI
    D. hospital census

REFERENCE: Abdelhak and Hanken, p 484
                Oachs and Watters, p 481

63. The Recovery Audit Contractor (RAC) program was developed to identify and reduce improper payments for
    A. Medicaid claims.
    B. Medicare claims.
    C. both Medicare claims *and* collection of overpayments.
    D. collection of overpayments.

REFERENCE: McWay, p 71
                Oachs and Watters, p 274

64. You have been asked to give an example of a clinical information system. Which one of the following would you cite?
    A. laboratory information system
    B. financial information system
    C. billing system
    D. admission-discharge-transfer

REFERENCE: McWay, pp 302–303
                Oachs and Watters, p 359

65. The PQRS is a reporting system established by the federal government for physician practices that participate in Medicare for

    A. monetary incentives.
    B. meaningful use incentives.
    C. quality measure reporting.
    D. All answers apply.

REFERENCE: Oachs and Watters, pp 29, 102, 279

66. Surgical case review includes all of the following EXCEPT
    A. determination of surgical justification based on clinical indication(s) in cases where no tissue has been removed.
    B. cases with elements missing in the preoperative anesthesia consultation.
    C. cases where there is a significant discrepancy between preoperative, postoperative, and pathological diagnoses.
    D. cases with serious surgical complications or surgical mortalities.

REFERENCE: Oachs and Watters, p 647

67. While performing routine quantitative analysis of a record, a medical record employee finds an incident report in the record. The employee brings this to the attention of her supervisor. Which best practice should the supervisor follow to deal with this situation?

    A. Remove the incident report and send it to the patient.
    B. Tell the employee to leave the report in the record.
    C. Remove the incident report and have nursing personnel transfer all documentation from the report to the medical record.
    D. Refer this record to the Risk Manager for further review and removal of the incident report.

REFERENCE: Bowie and Green, pp 96–97
               McWay (2008), p 110
               Oachs and Watters, p 72

68. In compiling statistics to report the specific cause of death for all open-heart surgery cases, the quality coordinator assists in documenting

    A. patient care outcomes.
    B. utilization of hospital resources.
    C. delineation of physician privileges.
    D. compliance with OSHA standards.

REFERENCE: McWay, p 153
               Oachs and Watters, pp 558–559

69. Your hospital is required by the Joint Commission and CMS to participate in national benchmarking on specific disease entities for quality of care measurement. This required collection and reporting of disease-specific data is considered

    A. an environment of care.
    B. a group of sentinel events.
    C. a series of core measures.
    D. risk assessment.

REFERENCE: Oachs and Watters, p 639

70. Needlesticks, patient or employee falls, medication errors, or any event not consistent with routine patient care activities would require risk reporting documentation in the form of an

    A. operative report.   C. incident report.
    B. emergency room report.   D. insurance claim.

REFERENCE: Abdelhak and Hanken, p 464
               McWay, p 189
               Oachs and Watters, p 72

71. The Utilization Review Coordinator reviews inpatient records at regular intervals to justify necessity and appropriateness of care to warrant further hospitalization. Which of the following utilization review activities is being performed?

    A. admission review   C. retrospective review
    B. preadmission   D. continued stay review

REFERENCE: Abdelhak and Hanken, pp 471–474
               McWay, p 227
               Oachs and Watters, p 269

72. Which feature is a trademark of an effective PI program?

    A. a one-time cure—all for a facility's problems
    B. an unmanageable project that is too expensive
    C. a cost-containment effort
    D. a continuous cycle of improvement projects over time

REFERENCE: McWay, pp 172, 187–189
               Oachs and Watters, p 632

73. Patient mortality, infection, and complication rates, adherence to living will requirements, adequate pain control, and other documentation that describe end results of care or a measurable change in the patient's health are examples of

    A. outcome measures.   C. sentinel events.
    B. threshold level.   D. incident reports.

REFERENCE: Abdelhak and Hanken, pp 438–439
               McWay, pp 124–128, 183
               Oachs and Watters, p 285

74. Engaging patients and their families in health care decisions is one of the core objectives for

    A. achieving meaningful use of EHRs.
    B. Joint Commission's National Patient Safety goals.
    C. HIPAA 5010 regulations.
    D. establishing flexible clinical pathways.

REFERENCE: Oachs and Watters, p 302

75. Where in the health record would the following statement be located?
    "Microscopic Diagnosis: Liver (needle biopsy), metastatic adenocarcinoma"

    A. operative report   C. anesthesia report
    B. pathology report   D. radiology report

REFERENCE: Abdelhak and Hanken, p 107
               Bowie and Green, p 181
               Oachs and Watters, p 114

Answer Key for Health Data Content and Standards

ANSWER   EXPLANATION

1. B   Although a gross description of tissue removed may be mentioned on the operative note or discharge summary, only the pathology report will contain a microscopic description.

2. B   The other answer choices represent items collected on Medicare inpatients according to UHDDS requirements. Only "cognitive patterns" represents a data item collected more typically in long-term care settings and required in the MDS.

3. C   The Joint Commission requires hospitals to prohibit abbreviations that have caused confusion or problems in their handwritten form, such as "U" for unit, which can be mistaken for "O" or the number "4." Spelling out the unit is preferred.

4. C   Factual summaries investigating unexpected facility events should not be treated as part of the patient's health information and therefore would not be recorded in the health record.

5. D   Patient care plans, pharmacy consultations, and transfer summaries are likely to be found on the records of long-term care patients.

6. B   Auto authentication is a policy adopted by some facilities that allows physicians to state in advance that transcribed reports should automatically be considered approved and signed (or authenticated) when the physician fails to make corrections within a preestablished time frame (e.g., "Consider it signed if I do not make changes within 7 days."). Another version of this practice is when physicians authorize the HIM department to send weekly lists of unsigned documents. The physician then signs the list in lieu of signing each individual report. Neither practice ensures that the physician has reviewed and approved each report individually.

7. A   The antepartum record should include a comprehensive history and physical exam on each OB patient visit with particular attention to menstrual and reproductive history.

8. C   Joint Commission and COP allow a legible copy of a recent H&P done in a doctor's office in lieu of an admission H&P as long as interval changes are documented in the record upon admission. In addition, when the patient is readmitted within 30 days for the same or a related problem, an interval history and physical exam may be completed if the original H&P is readily available.

9. A   The major sources of case findings for cancer registry programs are the pathology department, the disease index, and the logs of patients treated in radiology and other outpatient departments. The number index identifies new health record numbers and the patients to whom they were assigned. The physicians' index identifies all patients treated by each doctor. The patient index links each patient treated in a facility with the health number under which the clinical information can be located.

10. C   "A detailed history of the patient" is incorrect because some reference to the patient's history may be found in the discharge summary but not a detailed history. "A note for social services or discharge planning" is incorrect because the attending physician records the discharge summary. "Correct codes for significant procedures" is incorrect because codes are usually recorded on a different form in the record.

11. D   "Quality of care through the use of preestablished criteria" and "adverse effects and contraindications of drugs utilized during hospitalization" deal with issues directly linked to quality of care reviews. "Potentially compensable events" deals with risk management. Only "the overall quality of documentation" points to a review aimed at evaluating the quality of documentation in the health record.

12. B   Although the nursing staff, hospital administration, and the health information management professional play a role in ensuring an accurate and complete record, the major responsibility lies with the attending physician.

13. C   Unlike the acute care hospital, where most health care practitioners document separately, the patient care plan is the foundation around which patient care is organized in long-term care facilities because it contains the unique perspective of each discipline involved.

ANSWER   EXPLANATION

14. C   The Joint Commission requires hospitals to mark the correct surgical site and to involve the patient in the marking process to help eliminate wrong site surgeries.

15. A   The Office for Civil Rights (OCR) ensures equal access to certain health and human services and protects the privacy and security of health information.

16. A   The assessment statement combines the objective and subjective into a diagnostic conclusion, sometimes in the form of a differential diagnosis, such as "peritonitis versus appendicitis."

17. D   The disease index is a listing in diagnostic code number order. The physician index is a listing of cases in order by physician name or number. The MPI cross-references the patient name and medical record number.

18. D   The other answer choices all refer to a computer application of managing health information, but only "nurses using bedside terminals to record vital signs" deals with the clinical application of data entry into the patient's record at the time and location of service.

19. A   Pharmacy consults are required for elderly patients who typically take multiple medications. These consults review for potential drug interactions and/or discrepancies in medications given and those ordered.

20. D   CMS publishes both proposed and final rules for the Conditions of Participation for hospitals in the daily *Federal Register*.

21. D   "The patient is readmitted for a similar problem within 1 year" is incorrect because an interval H&P can be used when a patient is readmitted for the same or related problem within 30 days. "The patient's stay is less than 24 hours" and "the patient has an uneventful course in the hospital" are incorrect because no matter how long the patient stays or how minor the condition, an H&P is required.

22. A   The needs of the end user are always the primary concern when designing systems.

23. C   The other answer choices are required items in BOTH acute and ER records.

24. B   When the patient is brought to the hospital ED following a motor vehicle accident and, after assessment, is transferred with his health record to a trauma designated ED at another hospital; and when the patient is discharged by the physician and at time of discharge is transported to a long-term care facility with his health record: In these situations a transfer summary or pertinent copies from the inpatient health record may accompany the patient, but the original record stays on the premises.

25. D   "Sciatica unimproved with hot pack therapy" represents the assessment statement, "patient moving about very cautiously, appears to be in pain" the objective, and "adjust pain medications; begin physical therapy tomorrow" the plan.

26. B   OBRA mandates comprehensive functional assessments of long-term care residents using the Minimum Data Set for Long-Term Care.

27. A   "MDS" and "UHDDS" are types of data sets for collecting data in long-term (MDS) and acute care (UHDDS) facilities. A data dictionary should include security levels for each field as well as definitions for all entities.

28. B   COP requires a consultation report on patients who are not a good surgical risk as well as those with obscure diagnoses, patients whose physicians have doubts as to the best therapeutic measure to be taken, and patients for whom there is a question of criminal activity.

29. B   The medical history, including a review of systems and chief complaint, is information supplied by the patient. A physical assessment adds objective data to the subjective data provided by the patient in the history.

30. D   This meets both Joint Commission and COP standards.

31. B   This entry is typical of a surgical procedure.

ANSWER   EXPLANATION

32. A   The medical history (including chief complaint, history of present illness, past medical history, personal history, family history, and a review of systems) is provided by the patient or the most knowledgeable available source. The physical examination adds objective data to the subjective data provided by the patient. This exam begins with the physician's objective assessment of the patient's general condition.

33. D   The other answer choices are examples of secondary data sources.

34. D   Quantitative analysis involves checking for the presence or absence of necessary reports and/or signatures, while qualitative analysis may involve checking documentation consistency, such as comparing a patient's pharmacy drug profile with the medication administration record.

35. C   The other answer choices all represent common checks performed by a quantitative analysis clerk: missing reports, signatures, or patient identification. "Discrepancy between post-op diagnosis by the surgeon and pathology diagnosis by the pathologist" represents a more in-depth review dealing with the quality of the data documented.

36. B   The other answer choices represent routine interpretations that are not normally considered to be consultations.

37. A   "Whether a postoperative infection occurred and how it was treated" represents an appropriate job for the infection control officer. "The quality of follow-up care" represents the clinical care evaluation process, rather than the review of quality documentation. "Whether the severity of illness and/or intensity of service warranted acute level care" is a function of the utilization review program.

38. A   Progress notes may be integrated or they may be separated, with nurses, physicians, and other health care providers writing on designated forms for each discipline.

39. B   The Commission on Accreditation of Rehabilitation Facilities is an independent accrediting agency for rehabilitation facilities. Palliative care is most likely to be provided at a hospice.

40. C   Peer review typically involves quality of care issues rather than quality of documentation issues. Legal analysis ensures that the record entries would be acceptable in a court of law.

41. D   "Considered unnecessary by most health care facilities" is incorrect because advantages of accreditation are numerous and include financial and legal incentives. "Required for state licensure in all states" is incorrect because state licensure is required for accreditation but not the reverse. "Conducted in each facility annually" is incorrect because Joint Commission conducts unannounced on-site surveys approximately every 3 years.

42. D   Because information contained in the physicians' index is considered confidential, identification codes are often used rather than the physicians' names.

43. B   In a POMR, the database contains the history and physical; the problem list includes titles, numbers, and dates of problems, and serves as a table of contents of the record; the initial plan describes diagnostic, therapeutic, and patient education plans; and the progress notes document the progress of the patient throughout the episode of care, summarized in a discharge summary or transfer note at the end of the stay.

44. C   The accession register is a permanent log of all the cases entered into the database. Each number assigned is preceded by the accession year, making it easy to assess annual workloads.

45. A   The excerpt clearly indicates an overall summary of the patient's course in the hospital, which is a common element of the discharge summary.

46. D   The manual published by the Commission on Accreditation of Rehabilitation Facilities will have the most specific and comprehensive standards for a rehabilitation facility.

47. A   See all objectives for Stage I of meaningful use on the HealthIT.hhs.gov website.

ANSWER   EXPLANATION

48. A   The disease index is compiled as a result of abstracting patient code numbers into a computer database, allowing a variety of reports to be generated.

49. D   The RAC program is mandated to find and correct improper Medicare payments paid to health care providers participating in the Medicare reimbursement program. OIG (Office of Inspector General); MEDPAR (Medicare Provider Analysis and Review); QIO (Quality Improvement Organization).

50. B   Both paper-based and computer-based records share similar forms and view design considerations. Among these are the selection and sequencing of essential data items.

51. B   With the passage of the Health Care Quality Improvement Act of 1986, the NPDB was established. Hospitals are required to query the data bank before granting clinical privileges to physicians.

52. D   "Documented in an incident report and filed in the patient's health record" is incorrect because incident reports are written accounts of unusual events that have an adverse effect on a patient, employee, or facility visitor and should never be filed with the patient's record. "Reported as a potentially compensable event" is incorrect because PCEs are occurrences that could result in financial liability at some future time. A patient leaving AMA does not in itself suggest a PCE. "Reported to the Executive Committee" is incorrect because it is not typical to report AMAs to the Executive Committee. The answer is "documented in both the progress notes and the discharge summary" because documenting the event is crucial in protecting the legal interests of the health care team and facility.

53. C   This 60-day time frame is often referred to as the patient's certification period. Recertification can continue every 62 days until the patient is discharged from home health services.

54. D   Although the medical staff bylaws reflect general principles and policies of the medical staff, the rules and regulations outline the details for implementing these principles, including the process and time frames for completing records, and the penalties for failure to comply.

55. C   Clinical data include all health care information collected during a patient's episode of care. During the registration or intake process, the admitting diagnosis, provided by the attending physician, is entered on the face sheet. If the patient is admitted through the ED, the chief complaint listed on the ED record is usually the first clinical data collected. The principal diagnosis is often not known until after diagnostic tests are conducted. Demographic data are not clinical in nature. The review of systems is collected during the history and physical, which is typically done after admission to the hospital.

56. D   Although many patient health records may feasibly contain all of the orders listed, only the discharge order is required to document the formal release of a patient from the facility. Absence of a discharge order would indicate that the patient left against medical advice and this event should be thoroughly documented as well.

57. D   "Objective symptoms observed by the physician" refers to the physical exam. "Past and current activities, such as smoking and drinking habits" refers to the social history. "A chronological description of patient's present condition from time of onset to present" refers to the history of present illness.

58. A   The other answer choices represent components of the medical history as supplied by the patient, while the physical exam is an entry obtained through objective observation and measurement made by the provider.

59. B   The Minimum Data Set is a basic component of the long-term care RAI. UHDDS is used in acute care; OASIS is used in home health; DEEDS is used in emergency departments.

60. C   This 60-day time frame is often referred to as the patient's certification period. Recertification can continue every 62 days until the patient is discharged from home health services.

ANSWER   EXPLANATION

61. A
62. D
63. D
64. A
65. D
66. B
67. D   Incident reports are written accounts of unusual events that have an adverse effect on a patient, employee, or facility visitor and should never be filed with the patient's record.
68. A
69. C
70. C
71. D
72. D
73. A
74. A   There are several core objectives for achieving meaningful use, and engaging patients and their families is one of these objectives.
75. B

REFERENCES

Abdelhak, M. and Hanken, M. A. (2016). *Health information: Management of a strategic resource* (5th ed.). Philadelphia: W. B. Saunders.

Bowie, M. J. and Green, M. A. (2016). *Essentials of health information management: Principles and practices.* (2nd ed.). Clifton Park, NY: Cengage Learning.

CMS. https://www.cms.gov/site-search/search-results.html?q=meaningful%20use%202015 https://www.cms.gov/Medicare/Medicare-Fee-for-Service-Payment/AcuteInpatientPPS/FY2016-IPPS-Final-Rule-Home-Page-Items/FY2016-IPPS-Final-Rule-Tables.html?DLPage=1&DLEntries=10&DLSort=0&DLSortDir=ascending

Joint Commission. National Patient Safety Goals www.jointcommission.org http://www.jointcommission.org/assets/1/6/2015_HAP_NPSG_ER.pdf

McWay, D. C. (2014). *Today's health information management, an integrated approach* (2nd ed.). Clifton Park, NY: Cengage Learning.

Oachs P. and Watters, A. (2016), *Health information management: Concepts, principles and practice* (5th ed.). Chicago: American Health Information Management Association (AHIMA).

Sayles, N. and Gordon, L. (2016). *Health information management technology: An applied approach* (5th ed.). Chicago: American Health Information Management Association (AHIMA).

Competencies for Health Data Content and Standards

Question	CCA Domain					
	1	2	3	4	5	6
1					X	
2	X					
3	X					
4						X
5	X					
6			X			
7			X			
8			X			
9			X			
10			X			
11				X		
12			X			
13			X			
14			X			
15			X			
16	X					
17			X			
18					X	
19			X			
20				X		
21			X			
22					X	
23			X			
24						X
25			X			
26	X					
27			X		X	
28			X			
29			X			
30			X			
31			X			
32			X			
33			X			
34			X			
35			X			
36			X			
37			X			
38			X			
39		X				
40			X			

Question	CCA Domain					
	1	2	3	4	5	6
41			X			
42					X	
43			X			
44			X			
45			X			
46					X	
47			X			
48			X			
49		X				
50					X	
51				X		
52			X			
53			X			
54			X			
55	X					
56			X			
57			X			
58			X			
59				X		
60					X	
61					X	
62					X	
63		X				
64					X	
65		X				
66			X			
67			X			
68			X			
69			X			
70			X			
71			X			
72			X			
73			X			
74			X			
75			X			

IV. Medical Science

Lauralyn Kavanaugh-Burke, DrPH, RHIA, CHES, CHTS-IM

Infectious and Parasitic Diseases

1. The prevention of illness through vaccination occurs due to the formation of
   A. helper B cells.
   B. immunosurveillance.
   C. mast cells.
   D. memory cells.

   REFERENCE: Jones, pp 350–351
                  Scott and Fong, p 307

2. Many bacterial diseases are transmitted directly from person to person. Which of the diseases listed next is a bacterial disease transmitted by way of a tick vector?
   A. Legionnaires' disease
   B. Lyme disease
   C. tetanus
   D. tuberculosis

   REFERENCE: Jones, pp 228–229
                  Moisio, p 434
                  Neighbors and Tannehill-Jones, pp 345, 441
                  Scott and Fong, p 329

3. All of the following are examples of direct transmission of a disease EXCEPT
   A. contaminated foods.
   B. coughing or sneezing.
   C. droplet spread.
   D. physical contact.

   REFERENCE: Scott and Fong, pp 328–329

4. The most common rickettsial disease in the United States is
   A. hantavirus.
   B. Lyme disease.
   C. Rocky Mountain spotted fever.
   D. syphilis.

   REFERENCE: Moisio, pp 434–435
                  Neighbors and Tannehill-Jones, p 64
                  Scott and Fong, p 326

5. The most common bloodborne infection in the United States is
   A. *Helicobacter pylori.*
   B. hepatitis A.
   C. hepatitis C.
   D. hemophilia.

   REFERENCE: Scott and Fong, p 389

6. The causative organism for severe acute respiratory syndrome (SARS) is a
   A. bacterium.
   B. coronavirus.
   C. fungus.
   D. retrovirus.

   REFERENCE: Mayo Clinic (3)
                  Moisio, p 241
                  NLM (5)
                  Scott and Fong, p 360

7. The childhood viral disease that unvaccinated pregnant women should be prevented from contracting because it may be passed to the fetus, thus causing congenital anomalies such as mental retardation, blindness, and deafness, is
   A. rickets.
   B. rubeola.
   C. rubella.
   D. tetanus.

   REFERENCE: Moisio, p 435
                  Neighbors and Tannehill-Jones, p 505

8. United States health care providers are concerned about a possible pandemic of avian flu because
   A. there is no vaccine currently available.
   B. it is caused by a group of viruses that mutate very easily.
   C. the causative virus is being spread around the world by migratory birds.
   D. All answers apply.
   REFERENCE: CDC (2)

9. Ingrid Anderson presents with a skin infection that began as a raised, itchy bump, resembling an insect bite. Within 1 to 2 days, it developed into a vesicle. Now it is a painless ulcer, about 2 cm in diameter, with a black necrotic area in the center. During the history, her doctor learns that she has recently returned from an overseas vacation and becomes concerned that she may have become infected with anthrax. He will prescribe an
   A. antibiotic.   C. antiparasitic.
   B. antineoplastic.   D. antiviral.
   REFERENCE: Scott and Fong, p 360

10. The organism transmitted by a mosquito bite that causes malaria is a
    A. bacteria.   C. protozoa.
    B. prion.   D. virus.
    REFERENCE: Moisio, p 432
                  Neighbors and Tannehill-Jones, p 61
                  Rizzo, p 316
                  Scott and Fong, p 326

11. A pharyngeal culture is taken from a 13-year-old male patient presenting to the ER with fever, painful cervical lymph nodes, purulent tonsillar exudate, and difficulty swallowing. A blood agar culture plate shows complete hemolysis around *Streptococcus pyogenes* bacterial colonies. The patient is given a prescription for erythromycin. The diagnosis in this case is
    A. a group A beta-hemolytic streptococcal throat infection.
    B. a methicillin-resistant *Staphylococcus aureus* skin infection.
    C. tuberculosis with drug-resistant *Mycobacterium tuberculosis*-positive sputum.
    D. meningitis due to *Neisseria meningitidis*-positive cerebrospinal fluid.
    REFERENCE: Estridge and Reynolds, pp 739–742
                  Labtestsonline (7)

12. A 19-year-old college student, who lives on campus in a dormitory, is brought to the ER by his roommates, complaining of a severe headache, nuchal rigidity, fever, and photophobia. The ER physician performs an LP and orders a CSF analysis with a bacterial culture and sensitivity. The young man is admitted to the ICU with a provisional diagnosis of
    A. a group A beta-hemolytic streptococcal throat infection.
    B. a methicillin-resistant *Staphylococcus aureus* skin infection.
    C. tuberculosis with drug-resistant *Mycobacterium tuberculosis*-positive sputum.
    D. meningitis due to *Neisseria meningitidis*-positive cerebrospinal fluid.
    REFERENCE: CDC (12)
                  Labtestsonline (10)

13. There has been a significant increase in the number of cases and deaths from pertussis. Health care professionals attribute this disease trend to which of the following?
    A. A decrease in the number of people immunized with TDaP
    B. An increase in the virulence of the bacteria
    C. Drug-resistant strains of the bacteria
    D. All answers apply.
    REFERENCE: CDC (5)

14. A new strain of influenza, H1N1, is a highly virulent strain that spread all over the world. This type of epidemiological disease pattern is referred to as a(n)
    A. cluster.
    B. outbreak.
    C. epidemic.
    D. pandemic.

REFERENCE: CDC (7)

Neoplasia

15. Dr. Zambrano ordered a CEA test for Mr. Logan, a 67-year-old African American male patient. Dr. Zambrano may be considering a diagnosis of
    A. cancer.   C. cardiomyopathy.
    B. carpal tunnel syndrome.   D. congestive heart failure.

REFERENCE: NLM (4)

16. Which disease is a malignancy of the lymphatic system?
    A. cystic fibrosis   C. neutropenia
    B. Hodgkin's disease   D. Von Willebrand's disease

REFERENCE: Jones, p 355
              Moisio, p 216
              Neighbors and Tannehill-Jones, p 142
              Rizzo, p 363
              Scott and Fong, p 305

17. _____ is the most common type of skin cancer and _____ is the most deadly type of skin cancer.
    A. Malignant melanoma, basal cell carcinoma
    B. Basal cell carcinoma, malignant melanoma
    C. Oat cell carcinoma, squamous cell carcinoma
    D. Squamous cell carcinoma, oat cell carcinoma

REFERENCE: Jones, pp 117, 122–123, 934–935, 939–940
              Neighbors and Tannehill-Jones, pp 455–456
              Rizzo, p 125
              Scott and Fong, p 75
              Sormunen, pp 114, 115

18. Cancer derived from epithelial tissue is classified as a(n)
    A. adenoma.   C. lipoma.
    B. carcinoma.   D. sarcoma.

REFERENCE: Jones, p 931
              Neighbors and Tannehill-Jones, pp 30–31
              Rizzo, p 83
              Sormunen, p 302

19. The most fatal type of lung cancer is
    A. adenocarcinoma.   C. small cell cancer.
    B. large cell cancer.   D. squamous cell cancer.

REFERENCE: Scott and Fong, p 362

20. A pathological diagnosis of transitional cell carcinoma is made. The examined tissue was removed from the
    A. bladder.
    B. esophagus.
    C. oral cavity.
    D. pleura.

REFERENCE: Neighbors and Tannehill-Jones, p 294

21. The patient's pathology report revealed the presence of Reed–Sternberg cells. This is indicative of
    A. Hodgkin's disease.
    B. leukemia.
    C. non-Hodgkin's lymphoma.
    D. sarcoma.

REFERENCE: Neighbors and Tannehill-Jones, p 142

22. Which of the following BEST summarizes the current treatment of cervical cancer?
    A. A new three-shot vaccination series protects against the types of HPV that cause most cervical cancer cases.
    B. All stages have extremely high cure rates.
    C. Early detection and treatment of cervical cancer does not improve patient survival rates.
    D. Over 99% of cases are linked to long-term HPV infections.

REFERENCE: CDC (1)

23. A 63-year-old patient with terminal pancreatic cancer has started palliative chemotherapy. Palliative means
    A. alleviating or eliminating distressing symptoms of the disease.
    B. increasing the immune response to fight infections.
    C. quick destruction of cancerous cells.
    D. the combining of several medications to cure the cancer.

REFERENCE: ACS (3)
                Woodrow, p 229

24. Mary Smith, a 48-year-old patient, is receiving an IV mixture of four different medications to treat stage 2 invasive ductal breast carcinoma. Each of the medications acts upon a different aspect of the cancer cells. This mixture is typically termed a(n)
    A. amalgamation.
    B. cocktail.
    C. blend.
    D. mash-up.

REFERENCE: CDC (8)

Endocrine, Nutritional, and Metabolic Disorders

25. Mary Mulholland has diabetes. Her physician has told her about some factors that put her more at risk for infections. Which of the following factors would probably NOT be applicable?
    A. hypoxia
    B. increased glucose in body fluids
    C. increased blood supply
    D. both hypoxia and increased blood supply

REFERENCE: Neighbors and Tannehill-Jones, pp 253–257

26. Which of the organs listed below has endocrine and exocrine functions?
    A. kidney
    B. liver
    C. lung
    D. pancreas

REFERENCE: Moisio, p 266
                Neighbors and Tannehill-Jones, p 259
                Rizzo, pp 97, 290–291
                Scott and Fong, p 212

27. Which of the following is an effect of insulin?
    A. decreases glycogen concentration in liver
    B. increases blood glucose
    C. increases the breakdown of fats
    D. increases glucose metabolism

REFERENCE: Moisio, pp 301–302, 304
                Neighbors and Tannehill-Jones, pp 315–318
                Rizzo, pp 290–291
                Scott and Fong, pp 222–223
                Sormunen, p 554

28. Diabetic microvascular disease occurs
    A. as a direct result of elevated serum glucose.
    B. as a result of elevated fat in blood.
    C. due to damage to nerve cells.
    D. only in patients with type 1 diabetes.

REFERENCE: Neighbors and Tannehill-Jones, p 371
                Rizzo, p 292
                Scott and Fong, pp 227–229

29. Old age, obesity, and a family history of diabetes are all characteristics of
    A. type 1 diabetes.   C. juvenile diabetes.
    B. type 2 diabetes.   D. IDDM.

REFERENCE: Rizzo, p 292
                Scott and Fong, p 228

30. Clinical manifestations of this disease include polydipsia, polyuria, polyphagia, weight loss, and hyperglycemia. Which of the following tests would be ordered to confirm the disease?
    A. fasting blood sugar   C. glucose tolerance test
    B. glucagon   D. postprandial blood sugar

REFERENCE: Neighbors and Tannehill-Jones, pp 315–318
                Rizzo, p 292
                Scott and Fong, pp 229–230

31. Which of the following is characteristic of Graves' disease?
    A. It is an autoimmune disease.   C. It usually cannot be treated.
    B. It most commonly affects males.   D. It usually affects the elderly.

REFERENCE: Jones, p 560
                Neighbors and Tannehill-Jones, p 309
                Rizzo, pp 287, 294
                Scott and Fong, p 310

32. A toxic goiter has what distinguishing characteristic?
    A. iodine deficiency   C. presence of muscle spasm
    B. parathyroid involvement   D. thyroid hyperfunction

REFERENCE: Moisio, p 304
                Neighbors and Tannehill-Jones, pp 308–310
                Rizzo, p 294
                Sormunen, p 567

33. How can Graves' disease be treated?
    A. antithyroid drugs
    B. radioactive iodine therapy
    C. surgery
    D. All answers apply.

REFERENCE: Jones, pp 560–561
              Neighbors and Tannehill-Jones, p 309
              Rizzo, p 294
              Sormunen, p 567

Blood and Blood-Forming Conditions

34. The etiology of aplastic anemia is
    A. acute blood loss.
    B. bone marrow failure.
    C. chronic blood loss.
    D. inadequate iron intake.

REFERENCE: Jones, pp 331, 337, 340
              Moisio, p 213
              Neighbors and Tannehill-Jones, pp 139–140
              Scott and Fong, p 246

35. A 75-year-old patient has a sore tongue with tingling and numbness of the hands and feet. She has headaches and is fatigued. Following diagnostic workup, the doctor orders monthly injections of vitamin B_{12}. This patient most likely has which of the following conditions?
    A. aplastic anemia
    B. autoimmune hemolytic anemia
    C. pernicious anemia
    D. sickle cell anemia

REFERENCE: Jones, p 332
              Moisio, p 213
              Neighbors and Tannehill-Jones, pp 137–138
              Scott and Fong, p 245

36. Which one of the following is NOT a pathophysiological factor in anemia?
    A. excessive RBC breakdown
    B. lack of RBC maturation
    C. loss of bone marrow function
    D. loss of spleen function

REFERENCE: Jones, pp 331–333, 338–341
              Neighbors and Tannehill-Jones, pp 136–137
              Rizzo, p 315
              Scott and Fong, pp 245–246

37. In systemic circulation, which of the following vessels carries oxygenated blood?
    A. right vena cava
    B. renal arteries
    C. pulmonary veins
    D. left ventricle

REFERENCE: Jones, pp 380–382
              Moisio, pp 176–178
              Rizzo, pp 322, 335
              Scott and Fong, pp 328–330
              Sormunen, p 206

38. O_2 is carried in the blood
   A. bound to hemoglobin.   C. plasma.
   B. in the form of carbonic acid.   D. serum.

REFERENCE: Moisio, p 208
                   Neighbors and Tannehill-Jones, pp 133–134
                   Rizzo, pp 219, 224
                   Sormunen, p 247

39. In general, excessive RBC breakdown could result in
   A. Crohn's disease.   C. high bilirubin levels.
   B. elevated BUN.   D. peptic ulcers.

REFERENCE: Labtestsonline (1)
                   Neighbors and Tannehill-Jones, p 259
                   NLM (1)

40. In _____ anemia, the red blood cells become shaped like elongated crescents in the presence of low oxygen concentration.
   A. aplastic   C. sickle cell
   B. folic acid   D. vitamin B_{12}

REFERENCE: Jones, p 333
                   Moisio, p 213
                   Rizzo, p 315
                   Scott and Fong, p 246

41. A 72-year-old white male patient is on Coumadin therapy. Which of the following tests is commonly ordered to monitor the patient's Coumadin levels?
   A. bleeding time   C. partial thromboplastin time
   B. blood smear   D. prothrombin time

REFERENCE: Jones, p 339
                   Labtestsonline (3)
                   Moisio, p 219
                   NLM (2)

42. An African American couple are undergoing genetic counseling to determine the likelihood of producing children with a recessively genetic blood condition. The genetic tests reveal that the father carries the trait to produce abnormal hemoglobin, HbS, which causes crystallization in RBCs and deforms their shape when O_2 is low. This condition causes painful crises and multiple infarcts and is termed
   A. hemophilia.   C. sickle cell anemia.
   B. thalassemia.   D. iron-deficiency anemia.

REFERENCE: Estridge and Reynolds, pp 328–330
                   Labtestsonline (4)

Mental Disorders

43. The most common etiology of dementia in the United States is
   A. autism.   C. alcohol abuse.
   B. Alzheimer's disease.   D. anxiety disorder.

REFERENCE: Jones, p 1084
                   Neighbors and Tannehill-Jones, pp 343–344

44. Contributing factors of mental disorders include
    A. heredity.
    C. trauma.
    B. stress.
    D. heredity, stress, and trauma.

REFERENCE: Jones, pp 1008, 1010
               Neighbors and Tannehill-Jones, p 532

45. Why are there "black box warnings" on antidepressant medications regarding children and adolescents?
    A. Antidepressants increase the risk of suicidal thinking and behavior in some children and adolescents.
    B. Dosage requirements must be significantly higher in children and adolescents compared to adults.
    C. There is no established medical need for treatment of depression in children and adolescents.
    D. Antidepressants interfere with physiological growth patterns in children and adolescents.

REFERENCE: FDA (2)
               Woodrow, p 379

Nervous System/Sense Organ Disorders

46. The leading cause of blindness in the United States is a vision-related pathology caused by diabetes. It is called
    A. retinal detachment.
    C. retinopathy.
    B. retinoblastoma.
    D. rhabdomyosarcoma.

REFERENCE: Jones, pp 569, 606–607, 1075–1077
               Moisio, p 403
               Neighbors and Tannehill-Jones, pp 318, 371–372
               Scott and Fong, p 192

47. Which of the following is a hereditary disease of the cerebral cortex that includes progressive muscle spasticity and mental impairment leading to dementia?
    A. Huntington's disease
    C. Bell's palsy
    B. Lou Gehrig's disease
    D. Guillain–Barré syndrome

REFERENCE: Jones, pp 277–278
               Moisio, p 294
               Neighbors and Tannehill-Jones, pp 484–485
               Scott and Fong, p 473

48. A disease of the inner ear with fluid disruption in the semicircular canal that causes vertigo is
    A. labyrinthitis.
    C. Meniere's disease.
    B. mastoiditis.
    D. both labyrinthitis and Meniere's disease.

REFERENCE: Moisio, pp 411–412
               Neighbors and Tannehill-Jones, p 381
               Scott and Fong, pp 198–199

49. A treatment for sensorineural hearing loss is
    A. cochlear implants.
    C. removal of impacted cerumen.
    B. myringotomy.
    D. stapedectomy.

REFERENCE: Jones, p 628
               Scott and Fong, p 199

50. A condition that involves the fifth cranial nerve, also known as "tic douloureux," causes intense pain in the eye and forehead; lower lip, the section of the cheek closest to the ear and the outer segment of the tongue; or the upper lip, nose, and cheek.
    A. Bell's palsy
    B. thrush
    C. trigeminal neuralgia
    D. Tourette's disorder

REFERENCE: Jones, pp 283, 288
               Moisio, p 396
               Scott and Fong, p 178

51. The hypothalamus and the thalamus are part of the
    A. brainstem.
    B. cerebellum.
    C. exocrine system.
    D. limbic system.

REFERENCE: NCBI

52. Photophobia or visual aura preceding a severe headache is characteristic of
    A. malnutrition.
    B. mastitis.
    C. migraines.
    D. myasthenia gravis.

REFERENCE: Jones, pp 275–276
               Neighbors and Tannehill-Jones, p 340
               Scott and Fong, p 160

53. A "pill-rolling" tremor of the hand is a characteristic symptom of
    A. epilepsy.
    B. Guillain–Barré syndrome.
    C. myasthenia gravis.
    D. Parkinson's disease.

REFERENCE: Jones, pp 282–283, 1066–1067
               Neighbors and Tannehill-Jones, pp 342–343
               Scott and Fong, p 159

54. Etiologies of dementia include
    A. brain tumors.
    B. ischemia.
    C. trauma.
    D. All answers apply.

REFERENCE: Neighbors and Tannehill-Jones, pp 343–345
               Sormunen, p 597

55. Which of the following pieces of equipment records the electrical activity of the brain?
    A. EEG
    B. EMG
    C. ECG
    D. EKG

REFERENCE: Jones, p 290
               Moisio, p 397
               NLM (5)

Cardiac Disorders

56. Which of the following conditions is NOT a predisposing risk associated with essential hypertension?
    A. age
    B. cigarette smoking
    C. low dietary sodium intake
    D. obesity

REFERENCE: Jones, p 404
               Neighbors and Tannehill-Jones, p 160
               Scott and Fong, pp 289–290

57. Which of the following is a lethal arrhythmia?
    A. atrial fibrillation
    B. atrial tachycardia
    C. bradycardia
    D. ventricular fibrillation

REFERENCE: Jones, p 411
               Neighbors and Tannehill-Jones, p 174

58. Diastole occurs when
    A. cardiac insufficiency is present.
    B. the atria contracts.
    C. the ventricles contract.
    D. the ventricles fill.

REFERENCE: Jones, pp 384, 387
               Neighbors and Tannehill-Jones, p 154
               Scott and Fong, pp 285–286
               Sormunen, p 207

59. Henry experienced sudden sharp chest pain that he described as heavy and crushing. His pain and past medical history caused Dr. James to suspect that Henry was having an acute myocardial infarction (AMI). Which of the following tests is a more specific marker for an AMI?
    A. AST
    B. CK-MB
    C. LDH1
    D. Troponin I

REFERENCE: Labtestsonline (2)

60. Margaret Vargas needs to have her mitral valve replaced. Her surgeon will discuss which of the following issues with her before the surgery?
    A. A mechanical valve will require that she take a "blood thinner" for the rest of her life.
    B. A biological valve (usually porcine) will last 10 to 15 years.
    C. A mechanical valve increases the risk of blood clots that can cause stroke.
    D. All answers apply.

REFERENCE: NHLBI

61. A common cardiac glycoside medication that increases the force of the cardiac contraction without increasing the oxygen consumption, thereby increasing the cardiac output is typically given to patients with heart failure. However, there is a very narrow therapeutic window between effectiveness and toxicity, and the patient must be monitored closely. This common cardiac medication is
    A. COX-2 inhibitor.
    B. nitroglycerin.
    C. digoxin.
    D. acetylsalicylic acid.

REFERENCE: NLM (9)
               Woodrow, pp 31, 503–504

Respiratory Disorders

62. Each of the following conditions fall under the category of COPD EXCEPT
    A. chronic bronchitis.
    B. emphysema.
    C. pneumonia.
    D. smoking.

REFERENCE: Moisio, pp 238, 240
               Neighbors and Tannehill-Jones, pp 194–196
               Scott and Fong, pp 361–362

63. Which of the following sequences correctly depicts the flow of blood through the heart to the lungs in order for gas exchange to occur?
    A. right atrium, right ventricle, lungs, pulmonary artery
    B. right atrium, right ventricle, pulmonary artery, lungs
    C. right ventricle, right atrium, lungs, pulmonary artery
    D. right ventricle, right atrium, pulmonary artery, lungs

REFERENCE: Jones, pp 380–382
               Moisio, pp 176–177
               Scott and Fong, pp 277–279
               Sormunen, p 206

64. Gas exchange in the lungs takes place at the
    A. alveoli.   C. bronchioles.
    B. bronchi.   D. trachea.

REFERENCE: Neighbors and Tannehill-Jones, p 187
               Scott and Fong, p 277
               Sormunen, p 345

65. Most carbon dioxide is carried in the
    A. blood as CO_2 gas.   C. blood plasma in the form of carbonic acid.
    B. blood bound to hemoglobin.   D. red blood cells.

REFERENCE: Scott and Fong, p 239
               Sormunen, p 247

66. The presence of fluid in the alveoli of the lungs is characteristic of
    A. COPD.   C. pneumonia.
    B. Crohn's disease.   D. tuberculosis.

REFERENCE: Neighbors and Tannehill-Jones, pp 197–198

67. Which of the following BEST describes tuberculosis?
    A. a chronic, systemic disease whose initial infection is in the lungs
    B. an acute bacterial infection of the lung
    C. an ordinary lung infection
    D. a viral infection of the lungs

REFERENCE: Neighbors and Tannehill-Jones, pp 199–201
               Scott and Fong, pp 359–360
               Sormunen, p 272

68. A sweat test was done on a patient with the following symptoms: frequent respiratory infections, chronic cough, and foul-smelling bloody stools. Which of the following diseases is probably suspected?
    A. cystic breast disease   C. cystic lung disease
    B. cystic fibrosis   D. cystic pancreas

REFERENCE: Neighbors and Tannehill-Jones, p 494

69. *Mycobacterium tuberculosis* is the organism that causes tuberculosis (TB), typically a respiratory disorder. It is currently experiencing resurgence in the United States and many other countries. What is the average time frame in which all patients with new, previously untreated TB must have daily antibiotic therapy?
    A. 4–7 days
    B. 6–9 months
    C. 6–9 weeks
    D. 4–7 years

REFERENCE: CDC (4)
                Labtestsonline (13)

70. Which of the following is a severe, chronic, two-phased, bacterial respiratory infection that has become increasingly difficult to treat because many antibiotics are no longer effective against it?
    A. SARS
    B. MDR-TB
    C. MRSA
    D. H1N1

REFERENCE: CDC (6)

Digestive System Disorders

71. Which of the following anatomical parts is involved in both the respiratory and digestive systems?
    A. larynx
    B. nasal cavity
    C. pharynx
    D. trachea

REFERENCE: Moisio, p 233
                Scott and Fong, pp 348–349
                Sormunen, pp 344, 383

72. Most of the digestion of food and absorption of nutrients occur in the
    A. ascending colon.
    B. esophagus.
    C. small intestine.
    D. stomach.

REFERENCE: Neighbors and Tannehill-Jones, p 185
                Scott and Fong, pp 383–384
                Sormunen, p 374

73. A chronic inflammatory bowel disease where affected segments of the bowel may be separated by normal bowel tissue is characteristic of
    A. appendicitis.
    B. Crohn's disease.
    C. diverticulitis.
    D. Graves' disease.

REFERENCE: Moisio, p 270
                Neighbors and Tannehill-Jones, pp 239–240
                Sormunen, p 392

74. Early detection programs apply screening guidelines to detect cancers at an early stage, which provides the likelihood of increased survival and decreased morbidity. Which of the following would NOT be a diagnostic or screening test for colorectal cancer?
    A. double contrast barium enema
    B. sigmoidoscopy
    C. fecal occult blood test
    D. upper GI X-ray

REFERENCE: ACS (1)
                Scott and Fong, p 392

75. Prevention programs identify risk factors and use strategies to modify attitudes and behaviors to reduce the chance of developing cancers. Which of the following would NOT be an identified risk factor for colorectal cancer?
    A. alcohol use
    B. physical inactivity
    C. a high-fiber diet
    D. obesity

REFERENCE: ACS (2)

76. The first stage of alcoholic liver disease is
    A. alcoholic hepatitis.
    B. cirrhosis.
    C. fatty liver.
    D. jaundice.

REFERENCE: Neighbors and Tannehill-Jones, p 262

77. Portal hypertension can contribute to all of the following EXCEPT
    A. ascites.
    B. dilation of the blood vessels lining the intestinal tract.
    C. esophageal varices.
    D. kidney failure.

REFERENCE: Mayo Clinic (1)
                Neighbors and Tannehill-Jones, pp 263–264

78. Which of the following is a risk factor involved in the etiology of gallstones?
    A. being overweight
    B. being an adolescent
    C. low-fat diets
    D. the presence of a peptic ulcer

REFERENCE: Mayo Clinic (4)

79. Increasing peristalsis of the intestines, increasing salivation, and a slowing heart rate are examples of
    A. automatic nervous system responses.
    B. higher brain functions.
    C. parasympathetic nervous system responses.
    D. sympathetic nervous system responses.

REFERENCE: Jones, p 263
                Scott and Fong, pp 176–177
                Sormunen, p 585

80. One of the most common causes of peptic ulcer disease is the consumption of aspirin and NSAIDs. Another common cause is infection by *Helicobacter pylori,* and the usual treatment for this condition is use of
    A. antivirals.
    B. antibiotics.
    C. antifungals.
    D. antiemetics.

REFERENCE: NLM (10)
                Woodrow, p 300

Genitourinary Conditions

81. Genital warts are caused by
    A. HAV.
    B. HIV.
    C. HPV.
    D. VZV.

REFERENCE: Jones, p 716
                  Moisio, p 436
                  Scott and Fong, p 460

82. A physician prescribes a diuretic for his patient. He could be treating any of the following disorders EXCEPT
    A. congestive heart failure.   C. pneumonia.
    B. mitral stenosis.   D. pulmonary edema.

REFERENCE: Neighbors and Tannehill-Jones, p 172

83. Common kidney stone treatments that allow small particles to be flushed out of the body through the urinary system include all of the following EXCEPT
    A. extracorporeal shock wave lithotripsy.
    B. fluid hydration.
    C. ureteroscopy and stone basketing.
    D. using medication to dissolve the stone(s).

REFERENCE: Neighbors and Tannehill-Jones, pp 286–287

84. Which of the following tubes conveys sperm from the seminal vesicle to the urethra?
    A. ejaculatory duct   C. oviduct
    B. epididymis   D. vas deferens

REFERENCE: Moisio, p 332

85. The most common type of vaginitis is
    A. yeast.   C. viral.
    B. protozoan.   D. both yeast and protozoan.

REFERENCE: Neighbors and Tannehill-Jones, pp 397–398

86. _____ is usually the first symptom of benign prostate hyperplasia.
    A. Abdominal pain   C. Difficulty in urinating
    B. Burning pain during urination   D. Pelvic pain

REFERENCE: Neighbors and Tannehill-Jones, pp 142, 397–398
                  Scott and Fong, pp 457–458

87. A 37-year-old female goes to her family physician complaining of dysuria, urgency, fever, and malaise. A UA is performed, and upon gross examination is found to be turbid and has an unusual odor. Microscopic examination reveals a rod-shaped microorganism. A 24-hour culture produces a colony count greater than 100,000/mL of *Escherichia coli.* This would indicate a diagnosis of
    A. UTI.   C. PID.
    B. FUO.   D. KUB.

REFERENCE: Estridge and Reynolds, pp 751–753
                  Labtestsonline (5)

88. Microbiological lab culture and sensitivity tests were performed on the skin scrapings of a groin lesion on a 27-year-old male patient who presented to a local health department clinic. The results confirm infection with *Treponema pallidum*. He was given a prescription for penicillin and told to return for a follow-up visit in 2 weeks. His diagnosis is
   A. syphilis.
   B. HIV.
   C. herpes.
   D. HPV.

REFERENCE: CDC (13)
                  Labtestsonline (11)

89. A common contraceptive that is implanted in the uterus induces slight endometrial inflammation, which attracts neutrophils to the uterus. These neutrophils are toxic to sperm and prevent the fertilization of the ovum. This contraception is termed
   A. oral contraceptives.
   B. progestin injections.
   C. spermicides.
   D. an IUD.

REFERENCE: Jones, pp 755–756

Pregnancy, Childbirth, Perperium Conditions

90. Cervical cerclage is a procedure used to help prevent
   A. breathing restrictions.
   B. miscarriage.
   C. torsion.
   D. torticollis.

REFERENCE: Jones, pp 802, 817

91. A 28-year-old female presents to her general practitioner with morning nausea and vomiting, weight gain, and two missed menstrual cycles. The physician orders a pregnancy test. What chemical in the urine does this lab test detect?
   A. alpha-fetoprotein
   B. creatine phosphokinase
   C. carcinoembryonic antigen
   D. human chorionic gonadotropin

REFERENCE: Estridge and Reynolds, pp 471–472
                  Labtestsonline (9)

92. What common vitamin should be taken by pregnant women to substantially reduce the occurrence of neural tube defects, such as spina bifida, in a developing fetus?
   A. folic acid
   B. calcium
   C. B_{12}
   D. E

REFERENCE: CDC (10)

Skin/Subcutaneous Tissue Disorders

93. Impetigo can be
   A. spread through autoinoculation.
   B. caused by *Streptococcus pyogenes.*
   C. caused by *Staphylococcus aureus.*
   D. either spread through autoinoculation or caused by *Streptococcus pyogenes.*

REFERENCE: Jones, pp 121, 855
                  Neighbors and Tannehill-Jones, pp 438, 510
                  Scott and Fong, pp 72

94. Pain is a symptom of which of the following conditions?
    A. first-degree burn (superficial)
    B. second-degree burn (partial thickness)
    C. third-degree burn (full thickness)
    D. both first-degree burn (superficial) and second-degree burn (partial thickness)

REFERENCE: Jones, pp 116–117
                Neighbors and Tannehill-Jones, p 356
                Scott and Fong, pp 76–77

95. Necrosis extending down to the underlying fascia is characteristic of a decubitus ulcer in stage
    A. one.   C. three.
    B. two.   D. four.

REFERENCE: Scott and Fong, pp 77, 79

96. Scabies, a highly contagious condition that produces intense pruritus and a rash, is caused by
    A. pediculosis capitis.   C. candidiasis.
    B. itch mites.   D. ringworm.

REFERENCE: Jones, pp 124–125
                Moisio, p 108
                Neighbors and Tannehill-Jones, p 446

97. When a decubitus ulcer has progressed to a stage in which osteomyelitis is present, the ulcer has extended to the
    A. bone.   C. muscle.
    B. fascia.   D. subcutaneous tissue.

REFERENCE: Neighbors and Tannehill-Jones, p 764
                Scott and Fong, p 79

Musculoskeletal and Connective Tissue Disorders

98. Softening of the bone in children is termed _____.
    A. Raynaud's disease   C. rickets
    B. Reye's syndrome   D. rubella

REFERENCE: Rizzo, p 144
                Scott and Fong, p 110

99. The Phalen's wrist flexor test is a noninvasive method for diagnosing
    A. carpal tunnel syndrome.   C. severe acute respiratory syndrome.
    B. Down syndrome.   D. Tourette's syndrome.

REFERENCE: NINDS

100. Rheumatoid arthritis typically affects the
    A. intervertebral disks.
    B. hips and shoulders.
    C. knees and small joints of the hands and feet.
    D. large, weight-bearing joints.

REFERENCE: Jones, p 230
                Moisio, p 149
                Neighbors and Tannehill-Jones, pp 82–83, 109–111
                Scott and Fong, pp 106–107

101. Fractures occur in patients with osteoporosis due to
    A. falling from loss of balance.
    B. fibrous joint adhesions tearing apart small bones.
    C. loss of bone mass.
    D. a tendency to fall from a lack of joint mobility.

REFERENCE: Jones, pp 174–175
               Moisio, p 149
               Neighbors and Tannehill-Jones, pp 105–107
               Scott and Fong, p 109

102. Henrietta Dawson presents with a chief complaint of pain and weakness in her arms and neck. After an H and P and a review of diagnostic tests that include a myelogram, her doctor diagnoses a herniated nucleus pulposus at the _____ level of her spine.
    A. cervical   C. sacral
    B. lumbar   D. thoracic

REFERENCE: Jones, pp 160, 228, 277
               Moisio, p 147
               Sormunen, pp 158, 161

103. Carpal tunnel syndrome is caused by entrapment of the
    A. medial nerve.   C. tibial nerve.
    B. radial nerve.   D. ulnar nerve.

REFERENCE: Jones, p 270
               Moisio, p 142
               Neighbors and Tannehill-Jones, pp 122–123
               NINDS
               Sormunen, p 158

Congenital Disorders

104. Sex-linked genetic diseases
    A. are transmitted during sexual activity.
    B. involve a defect on a chromosome.
    C. occur equally between males and females.
    D. occur only in males.

REFERENCE: Neighbors and Tannehill-Jones, pp 478–479
               Scott and Fong, pp 470–471

105. Before leaving the hospital, all newborns are screened for an autosomal recessive genetic disorder of defective enzymatic conversion in protein metabolism. With early detection and a protein-restricted diet, brain damage is prevented. This disease is
    A. cystic fibrosis.   C. phenylketonuria.
    B. hereditary hemochromatosis.   D. Tay–Sachs disease.

REFERENCE: Neighbors and Tannehill-Jones, p 491
               Scott and Fong, p 472

106. Which of the following is a congenital condition that is the most severe neural tube defect?
    A. meningocele   C. severe combined immunodeficiency
    B. myelomeningocele   D. spina bifida occulta

REFERENCE: Neighbors and Tannehill-Jones, p 484

Perinatal Conditions

107. Children at higher risk for sudden infant death syndrome (SIDS) include those
    A. with sleep apnea.
    B. with respiratory problems.
    C. who are premature infants.
    D. All answers apply.

REFERENCE: Jones, pp 455, 867–868
                        Neighbors and Tannehill-Jones, p 515
                        Scott and Fong, p 362

Injuries and Poisonings

108. Sam Spade has been severely injured in an MVA because he was not wearing a seat belt. The organ in his body, situated at the upper left of his abdominal cavity, under the ribs, that is part of his lymphatic system has been ruptured, and he is bleeding internally. Sam needs a surgical procedure known as
    A. sequestrectomy.
    B. sialoadenectomy.
    C. sigmoidoscopy.
    D. splenectomy.

REFERENCE: Jones, p 345
                        Moisio, p 219
                        Sormunen, pp 275, 399

109. John Palmer was in a car accident and sustained severe chest trauma resulting in a tension pneumothorax. Manifestations of this disorder include all of the following EXCEPT
    A. severe chest pain.
    B. dyspnea.
    C. shock.
    D. clubbing.

REFERENCE: Jones, p 454
                        Neighbors and Tannehill-Jones, pp 204–207

Immune System Conditions

110. A bee stung little Bobby. He experiences itching, erythema, and respiratory distress caused by laryngeal edema and vascular collapse. In the emergency room where he is given an epinephrine injection, Bobby is diagnosed with
    A. allergic rhinitis.
    B. allergic sinusitis.
    C. anaphylactic shock.
    D. asthma.

REFERENCE: Jones, pp 965, 974
                        Neighbors and Tannehill-Jones, p 178

111. Which of the following cells produce histamine in a type I hypersensitivity reaction?
    A. lymphocyte
    B. macrophages
    C. mast cells
    D. neutrophils

REFERENCE: Jones, p 106
                        Neighbors and Tannehill-Jones, p 76

112. Which one of the following cells produces antibodies?
    A. A cells
    B. cytotoxic T cells
    C. helper T cells
    D. plasma cells

REFERENCE: Neighbors and Tannehill-Jones, pp 21, 52, 74

113. A patient, who is HIV positive, has raised red or purple lesions that appear on his skin, in his mouth, and most anywhere on his body. What is the stage of his disease process in today's medical terminology?
    A. ARC
    B. AIDS
    C. AZT
    D. HIV positive

REFERENCE: Jones, pp 714–715
               Neighbors and Tannehill-Jones, pp 91–93

114. Which of the following autoimmune diseases affects tissues of the nervous system?
    A. Goodpasture's syndrome
    B. Hashimoto's disease
    C. myasthenia gravis
    D. rheumatoid arthritis

REFERENCE: Jones, pp 281–282, 356
               Neighbors and Tannehill-Jones, pp 83–85
               Scott and Fong, pp 136, 310

115. Full-blown AIDS sets in as
    A. CD4 receptors increase.
    B. helper T-cell concentrations decrease.
    C. HIV virus concentrations decrease.
    D. immunity to HIV increases.

REFERENCE: Scott and Fong, pp 316–319
               Sormunen, p 271

116. The HPV vaccine, Gardasil, is recommended for all children/young adults between the ages of 9 and 26 years. It is a quadrivalent vaccine. What is the definition of quadrivalent?
    A. It must be administered every 4 years to be effective.
    B. It is administered in a series of four shots over a 6-month period.
    C. It prevents infection from the four most prevalent types of HPV that cause cervical cancer.
    D. It reduces the risk of infection by four times.

REFERENCE: CDC (3)
               FDA (1)
               Labtestsonline (12)

117. Some immunizations, such as tetanus, require a second application, to strengthen or "remind" the immune system in response to antigens. The subsequent injections are termed
    A. alerting shots.
    B. warning shots.
    C. booster shots.
    D. unnecessary shots.

REFERENCE: CDC (9)

118. Why must influenza immunizations be developed and administered on an annual basis?
    A. The virus mutates significantly each year.
    B. People develop resistance to the vaccine.
    C. The immunization is only strong enough for one year.
    D. The pharmaceutical companies produce the lowest dosage possible.

REFERENCE: CDC (11)

Pharmacology

119. The drug commonly used to treat bipolar mood swings is
   A. Lanoxin.
   B. Lasix.
   C. lithium carbonate.
   D. lorazepam.

REFERENCE: Woodrow, p 385

120. Penicillin is effective in the treatment of all of the following diseases EXCEPT
   A. influenza.
   B. Lyme disease.
   C. strep throat.
   D. syphilis.

REFERENCE: Jones, pp 453, 1070
               Neighbors and Tannehill-Jones, p 62

121. The positive belief in a drug and its ability to cure a patient's illness, even if this drug is an inactive or inert substance, typically positively influences a patient's perception of their outcome. This effect is termed a
   A. synergistic effect.
   B. potentiation effect.
   C. placebo effect.
   D. antagonistic effect.

REFERENCE: Sormunen, pp 79, 92
               Woodrow, pp 32, 352

122. The interaction of two drugs working together to where each simultaneously helps the other achieve an effect that neither could produce alone is termed a
   A. placebo effect.
   B. synergistic effect.
   C. potentiation effect.
   D. antagonistic effect.

REFERENCE: Woodrow, p 33

123. The opposing interaction of two drugs in which one decreases or cancels out the effects of the other is termed a
   A. placebo effect.
   B. potentiation effect.
   C. synergistic effect.
   D. antagonistic effect.

REFERENCE: Woodrow, p 33

Surgical and Medical Procedures

124. A stapedectomy is a common treatment for
   A. atherosclerosis.
   B. multiple sclerosis.
   C. otosclerosis.
   D. scoliosis.

REFERENCE: Jones, p 630
               Moisio, pp 412–413
               Neighbors and Tannehill-Jones, pp 377–378
               Scott and Fong, p 198

125. A procedure performed with an instrument that freezes and destroys abnormal tissues (including seborrheic keratoses, basal cell carcinomas, and squamous cell carcinomas) is
   A. cryosurgery.
   B. electrodesiccation.
   C. phacoemulsification.
   D. photocautery.

REFERENCE: Moisio, p 110

126. Maria Giovanni is in the hospital recovering from colon resection surgery. Based on her symptoms, her doctors are concerned about the possibility that she has developed a pulmonary embolism. Which of the following procedures will provide the definitive diagnosis?
    A. chest X-ray
    B. lung scan
    C. pulmonary angiography
    D. none of the above

REFERENCE: Neighbors and Tannehill-Jones, p 206
                Scott and Fong, p 362

127. A surgical procedure that cuts into the skull to drain blood from a subdural hematoma in order to decrease the intracranial pressure is termed a(n)
    A. craniectomy.
    B. craniotomy.
    C. angioplasty.
    D. hemispherectomy.

REFERENCE: NLM (6)

128. A surgical procedure that is performed to realign and stabilize a fractured femur with a rod and screws is referred to as a(n)
    A. closed reduction with external fixation.
    B. closed reduction with internal fixation.
    C. osteotomy.
    D. open reduction with internal fixation.

REFERENCE: Jones, pp 180–181
                Moisio, p 152

129. Which of the following procedures is typically performed on children to facilitate the drainage of serous exudate behind the tympanic membrane in chronic otitis media?
    A. cochlear implants
    B. stapedectomy
    C. myringotomy with tympanostomy tubes
    D. cerumen evacuation

REFERENCE: Jones, p 624
                Moisio, p 413

130. Coronary arteries may become blocked, either partially or totally, due to atherosclerosis and lead to an AMI. Which of the following procedures would be used to improve the coronary blood flow by building an alternate route for the blood to bypass the blockage by inserting a portion of another blood vessel, typically the saphenous vein?
    A. PTCA
    B. CABG
    C. carotid endarterectomy
    D. cardiac catheterization

REFERENCE: Jones, p 1086
                Moisio, pp 185–186

131. A standard surgical procedure used for the treatment of early-stage breast cancer involves the removal of the cancerous tumor, skin, breast tissue, areola, nipple, and most of the axillary lymph nodes, but leaves the underlying chest muscles intact. This procedure is termed a(n)
    A. modified radical mastectomy.
    B. partial mastectomy.
    C. lumpectomy.
    D. incisional breast biopsy.

REFERENCE: Jones, pp 760, 936
                Moisio, p 361
                WebMD.com (1)

132. The least invasive restrictive gastric surgery used to reduce the size of the stomach to facilitate weight loss in obese patients is
    A. a gastric bypass.
    B. Roux-en-Y gastric surgery.
    C. laparoscopic gastric banding.
    D. a biliopancreatic diversion.

REFERENCE: WebMD.com (2)

133. Which of the following procedures would be performed for the removal of the gall bladder due to excessive gallstone formation?
    A. ERCP
    B. cholangiography
    C. hemicolectomy
    D. cholecystectomy

REFERENCE: WebMD.com (3)
              NLM (7)

Laboratory Tests

134. A patient's history includes the following documentation:
    • Small ulcers (chancres) appeared on the genitalia and resolved after 4 to 6 weeks
    • Elevated temperature, skin rash, and enlarged lymph nodes

    Which procedure will be used to initially diagnose the patient?
    A. bone marrow test   C. serology test
    B. chest X-ray   D. thyroid scan

REFERENCE: Jones, p 328
              Moisio, p 437
              Neighbors and Tannehill-Jones, pp 417–420

135. Diagnostic testing for meningitis usually involves
    A. blood cultures.   C. stool C and S.
    B. cerebrospinal fluid analysis. D. testing urine.

REFERENCE: Jones, p 292
              Neighbors and Tannehill-Jones, p 333

136. Which of the following is a liver function test?
    A. AST (SGOT)   C. ECG
    B. BUN   D. TSH

REFERENCE: Neighbors and Tannehill-Jones, p 259
              Sormunen, p 389

137. A serum potassium level of 2.8 would indicate
    A. Addison's disease.   C. diabetic ketoacidosis.
    B. anemia.   D. hypokalemia.

REFERENCE: Mayo Clinic (2)
              NLM (3)

138. An elevated serum amylase would be characteristic of
    A. acute pancreatitis.
    B. gallbladder disease.
    C. postrenal failure.
    D. prerenal failure.

REFERENCE: Neighbors and Tannehill-Jones, pp 269–270

139. A 68-year-old female patient has no visible bleeding, but remains anemic. Her physician is concerned about possible gastrointestinal bleeding. Which of the following tests might be ordered?
    A. DEXA scan
    B. guaiac smear test
    C. Pap smear test
    D. prostatic-specific antigen test

REFERENCE: Estridge and Reynolds, pp 680–681
              Sormunen, p 388

140. When a physician orders a liver panel, which of the following tests are NOT included?
    A. albumin
    B. alkaline phosphatase
    C. bilirubin
    D. creatinine

REFERENCE: Estridge and Reynolds, pp 608–609

141. A 13-year-old patient is brought to her pediatrician with a 2-week history of fatigue, an occasional low-grade fever, and malaise. The pediatrician indicates it is a possible infection but needs to know what type of infection. She orders a hematology laboratory test to determine the relative number and percentage of each type of leukocytes. This test is referred to as a
    A. hematocrit.
    B. CBC.
    C. WBC diff.
    D. hemoglobin determination.

REFERENCE: Estridge and Reynolds, p 198

142. A 62-year-old female presents to her family doctor complaining of fatigue; constantly feeling cold, especially in her hands and feet; weakness; and pallor. O_2 must be transported to the cells and exchanged with CO_2, which is then transported back to the lungs to be expelled. A hematology laboratory test that evaluates the oxygen-carrying capacity of blood is referred to as a
    A. hematocrit.
    B. CBC.
    C. WBC diff.
    D. hemoglobin determination.

REFERENCE: Estridge and Reynolds, pp 206–207
              Labtestsonline (15)

143. A 57-year-old male patient is having his annual physical. Due to a family history of coronary artery disease and his sedentary lifestyle, his doctor orders a total blood cholesterol panel. What is the optimal level of total cholesterol in the blood for adults?
    A. <200 mg/dL
    B. 200–239 mg/dL
    C. 300–339 mg/dL
    D. >500 mg/dL

REFERENCE: Estridge and Reynolds, pp 662–667
              Labtestsonline (6)

144. An 81-year-old male with arteriosclerosis and a long-standing history of taking Coumadin presents to his physician's office for his biweekly prothrombin time (PT) test. The PT test is one of the most common hemostasis tests used as a presurgery screening and monitoring Coumadin (warfarin) therapy. This test evaluates
    A. coagulation of the blood.
    B. the iron-binding capacity of RBCs.
    C. the oxygen-carrying capacity of RBCs.
    D. the type and cross-match of blood.

REFERENCE: Estridge and Reynolds, p 394
                 Labtestsonline (8)

Radiological Tests and Procedures

145. The key diagnostic finding for typical pneumonia is
    A. abnormal chemical electrolytes.   C. lung consolidation on CXR.
    B. elevated WBC.   D. a positive sputum culture.

REFERENCE: Neighbors and Tannehill-Jones, pp 197–198

146. A radiological test for bone mineral density (BMD) is a useful diagnostic tool for diagnosing
    A. osteoarthritis.   C. osteoporosis.
    B. osteomyelitis.   D. rheumatoid arthritis.

REFERENCE: Jones, p 184
                 Neighbors and Tannehill-Jones, pp 105–107

Anatomy and Physiology

147. The state of balance or normality that the human body continuously tries to attain is referred to as
    A. pathogenesis.   C. etiology.
    B. iatrogenic.   D. homeostasis.

REFERENCE: Neighbors and Tannehill-Jones, p 4

148. The progress of a disease, including initiating factors, signs and symptoms, physical manifestations, residual sequela, prognosis, and finally, the end result, is termed
    A. pathogenesis.   C. etiology.
    B. iatrogenic.   D. homeostasis.

REFERENCE: Neighbors and Tannehill-Jones, p 4

149. When the body's immune system reverses itself and attacks the organs and tissues, this process is called
    A. allergy.   C. immunodeficiency.
    B. autoimmunity.   D. immunosuppression.

REFERENCE: Neighbors and Tannehill-Jones, p 21

150. The process of cancer development, from exposure through the cellular changes of hyperplasia to neoplasia, is termed
    A. pathogenesis.   C. carcinogenesis.
    B. metastasis.   D. staging.

REFERENCE: Neighbors and Tannehill-Jones, p 36

151. Which type of joint, such as the sutures of the skull, has no movement?
   A. synarthrosis
   B. amphiarthrosis
   C. diarthrosis
   D. arthritis

REFERENCE: Neighbors and Tannehill-Jones, p 100

152. Which type of diagnostic test involves the use of electromagnetic waves to produce very detailed images of soft tissue structures of the body?
   A. MRI
   B. CAT or CT scan
   C. X-ray
   D. electrophoresis

REFERENCE: Neighbors and Tannehill-Jones, p 102

153. Which valve is between the left atrium and left ventricle?
   A. tricuspid
   B. mitral
   C. pulmonary
   D. aortic

REFERENCE: Neighbors and Tannehill-Jones, p 152

154. On an EKG, what signifies the electronic stimulation of the ventricles?
   A. the spacing of the waves
   B. the QRS wave
   C. the P wave
   D. the height of the waves

REFERENCE: Neighbors and Tannehill-Jones, p 153

155. The nose, mouth, sinuses, pharynx, and larynx make up the
   A. upper gastrointestinal tract.
   B. lower gastrointestinal tract.
   C. the upper respiratory tract.
   D. lower respiratory tract.

REFERENCE: Neighbors and Tannehill-Jones, p 186

156. What is the large serous membrane that covers the abdominal organs and lines the abdominal wall?
   A. perineum
   B. pleural membrane
   C. pericardial membrane
   D. peritoneum

REFERENCE: Neighbors and Tannehill-Jones, p 226

157. The muscular contractions that move food through the alimentary canal from the mouth to the anus is referred to as
   A. paralysis.
   B. peritonitis.
   C. pleural effusion.
   D. peristalsis.

REFERENCE: Neighbors and Tannehill-Jones, p 227

158. The _____ is the largest solid organ of the body, but the _____ is the largest organ overall.
   A. skin, brain
   B. intestine, liver
   C. brain, latissimus dorsi
   D. liver, skin

REFERENCE: Neighbors and Tannehill-Jones, p 258

159. Which structure transports urine from the kidneys to the bladder?
   A. urethra
   B. meatus
   C. ureter
   D. vas deferens

REFERENCE: Neighbors and Tannehill-Jones, p 278

160. In which gender is the urethra significantly longer?
   A. males
   B. females
   C. It is the same length regardless of gender.
   D. It depends on the height of the individual.

REFERENCE: Neighbors and Tannehill-Jones, p 278

161. Which endocrine gland secretes melatonin, which controls the circadian rhythm of an individual?
  A. pineal
  B. adrenal medulla
  C. beta cells of the pancreas
  D. alpha cells of the pancreas

REFERENCE: Neighbors and Tannehill-Jones, p 303

162. Which endocrine gland secretes epinephrine, which activates the "fight or flight" response and increases blood pressure and metabolism?
  A. pineal
  B. adrenal medulla
  C. beta cells of the pancreas
  D. alpha cells of the pancreas

REFERENCE: Neighbors and Tannehill-Jones, p 303

163. In which brain lobe is the processing of smell and hearing stimuli performed?
  A. occipital
  B. frontal
  C. parietal
  D. temporal

REFERENCE: Neighbors and Tannehill-Jones, p 328

164. In which brain lobe is the processing of emotions, intellect, and personality performed?
  A. occipital
  B. frontal
  C. parietal
  D. temporal

REFERENCE: Neighbors and Tannehill-Jones, p 328

165. Which set of muscles controls the movement of the eye up and down?
  A. superior and inferior rectus
  B. medial and lateral rectus
  C. superior and inferior oblique
  D. medial and lateral oblique

REFERENCE: Neighbors and Tannehill-Jones, p 360

166. Which of the following is not one of the five layers of the epidermis?
  A. stratum corneum
  B. stratum spinosum
  C. stratum fascia
  D. stratum lucidum

REFERENCE: Neighbors and Tannehill-Jones, p 432

Additional Questions

167. Which step of the "chain of infection" is disrupted by eliminating the standing water in old tires, birdbaths, and empty buckets when combatting the Zika virus epidemic?
  A. identifying the susceptible host
  B. eliminating the reservoir
  C. stopping the direct transmission
  D. killing the virus particle

REFERENCE: CDC (12)

168. Which of the following issues seems to be the main contributing factor to the rise of antibiotic-resistant bacterial organisms such as methicillin-resistant *Staphylococcus aureus*?
  A. the over-prescribing of antibiotics to treat bacterial and viral infections
  B. patient non-compliance in the use of antibiotics when the patient does not take all of the medicine for the allotted time
  C. the use of antibacterial soaps and other products that contain triclosan and/or triclocarban
  D. All answers apply.

REFERENCE: WebMD (2)

169. One of the common manifestations of the Zika virus exposure in utero is severe fetal brain malformation due to the virus attacking and destroying the neurons. This condition is called
    A. encephalitis.   C. microcephaly.
    B. meningitis.   D. myelomeningocele.

REFERENCE: CDC (13)

170. Which of the following conditions is typically treated with the insertion of a pacemaker?
    A. Sick-sinus syndrome   C. third-degree heart block
    B. bradyarrhythmias   D. All answers apply.

REFERENCE: WebMD (4)

171. A cardiac condition where there is an abnormality in the way the electricity passes through the sinoatrial (SA) node and the atrioventricular (AV) node to generate a pulse or heartbeat is called
    A. heart block.   C. acute myocardial infarction.
    B. hypertrophic cardiomyopathy.   D. tachycardia.

REFERENCE: WebMD (5)

172. A mild, atypical lung infection with inflammation and fluid buildup, usually caused by *Mycoplasma pneumoniae* or other bacteria, in which the patient is mildly ill but does not require hospitalization and is treated with antibiotics is termed
    A. walking pneumonia.   C. emphysema.
    B. pneumoconiosis.   D. intrinsic asthma.

REFERENCE: CDC (14)

173. Which of the following is the most effective method for the prevention of influenza?
    A. intramuscular injection vaccine
    B. coughing into the crook of the elbow
    C. Flu-Mist nasal spray vaccine
    D. handwashing

REFERENCE: CDC (15)

174. What is the name of the protein that gives breads, cereals, baked goods, and pasta their structure, but can cause serious gastrointestinal complications when ingested by individuals with celiac disease?
    A. carbohydrate   C. glucose
    B. gluten   D. antioxidant

REFERENCE: WebMD (1)

175. Several recent studies suggest that this issue/condition is now the third leading cause of death in the United States, is responsible for at least 10% of all deaths in the United States, and is an under-recognized and therefore under-reported cause of death in the United States. This issue/condition is
    A. medical errors.   C. handguns.
    B. epidemics.   D. car accidents.

REFERENCE: Johns Hopkins Medicine

176. A severe allergic reaction which can be life-threatening, due to a swollen throat, difficulty breathing, rash, and dizziness that must be treated with injectable epinephrine is termed
    A. asthma.   C. arrhythmia.
    B. amyloidosis   D. anaphylaxis.

REFERENCE: WebMD (3)

Answer Key for Medical Science

1.	D	50.	C	99.	A	147.	D
2.	B	51.	D	100.	C	148.	A
3.	A	52.	C	101.	C	149.	B
4.	C	53.	D	102.	A	150.	C
5.	C	54.	D	103.	A	151.	A
6.	B	55.	A	104.	B	152.	A
7.	C	56.	C	105.	C	153.	B
8.	D	57.	D	106.	B	154.	B
9.	A	58.	D	107.	D	155.	C
10.	C	59.	B	108.	D	156.	D
11.	A	60.	D	109.	D	157.	D
12.	D	61.	C	110.	C	158.	D
13.	D	62.	C	111.	C	159.	C
14.	D	63.	B	112.	D	160.	A
15.	A	64.	A	113.	B	161.	A
16.	B	65.	D	114.	C	162.	B
17.	B	66.	C	115.	B	163.	D
18.	B	67.	A	116.	C	164.	B
19.	C	68.	B	117.	C	165.	A
20.	A	69.	B	118.	A	166.	C
21.	A	70.	B	119.	C	167.	B
22.	A	71.	C	120.	A	168.	D
23.	A	72.	C	121.	C	169.	C
24.	B	73.	B	122.	B	170.	D
25.	C	74.	D	123.	D	171.	A
26.	D	75.	C	124.	C	172.	A
27.	D	76.	C	125.	A	173.	A
28.	A	77.	D	126.	C	174.	B
29.	B	78.	A	127.	B	175.	A
30.	C	79.	C	128.	D	176.	D
31.	A	80.	B	129.	C		
32.	D	81.	C	130.	B		
33.	D	82.	C	131.	A		
34.	B	83.	C	132.	C		
35.	C	84.	A	133.	D		
36.	D	85.	D	134.	C		
37.	D	86.	C	135.	B		
38.	A	87.	A	136.	A		
39.	C	88.	A	137.	C		
40.	C	89.	D	138.	A		
41.	D	90.	B	139.	B		
42.	C	91.	D	140.	D		
43.	B	92.	A	141.	C		
44.	D	93.	D	142.	D		
45.	A	94.	D	143.	A		
46.	C	95.	C	144.	A		
47.	A	96.	B	145.	C		
48.	D	97.	A	146.	C		
49.	A	98.	C				

REFERENCES

American Cancer Society (ACS). http://www.cancer.org

    ACS (1)

        http://www.cancer.org/healthy/findcancerearly/index

        http://www.cancer.org/healthy/findcancerearly

    ACS (2)

        http://www.cancer.org/acs/groups/cid/documents/webcontent/003096-pdf.pdf

        http://www.cancer.org/acs/groups/cid/documents/webcontent/003096-pdf.pdf

    ACS (3)

        http://www.cancer.org/acs/groups/cid/documents/webcontent/003092-pdf.pdf

Centers for Disease Control and Prevention (CDC). http://www.cdc.gov/index.htm

    CDC (1)

        http://www.cdc.gov/std/Hpv/STDFact-HPV-vaccine-young-women.htm#why

    CDC (2)

        http://www.cdc.gov/flu/avian/gen-info/pdf/avian_facts.pdf

    CDC (3)

        http://www.cdc.gov/Features/HPVvaccine/

    CDC (4)

        http://www.cdc.gov/tb/topic/treatment/default.htm

    CDC (5)

        http://www.cdc.gov/pertussis/outbreaks-faqs.html

    CDC (6)

        http://www.cdc.gov/tb/topic/treatment/default.htm

    CDC (7)

        http://www.cdc.gov/flu/spotlights/pandemic-global-estimates.htm

    CDC (8)

        http://www.cdc.gov/cancer/breast/basic_info/

    CDC (9)

        http://www.cdc.gov/vaccines/vac-gen/default.htm

    CDC (10)

        http://www.cdc.gov/NCBDDD/folicacid/about.html

    CDC (11)

        http://www.cdc.gov/vaccines/vac-gen/default.htm

Estridge, B. H. and Reynolds, A. P. (2012). *Basic clinical laboratory techniques* (6th ed.). Clifton Park, NY: Cengage Learning.

Food and Drug Administration (FDA). http://www.fda.gov/default.htm

        http://www.fda.gov/BiologicsBloodVaccines/Vaccines/ApprovedProducts/ucm094042.htm

Jones, B. D. (2016). *Comprehensive medical terminology* (5th ed.). Clifton Park, NY: Cengage Learning.

Labtestsonline. http://www.labtestsonline.org

    Labtestsonline (1)

        http://www.labtestsonline.org/understanding/analytes/bilirubin/glance.html

    Labtestsonline (2)

        http://www.labtestsonline.org/understanding/analytes/troponin/related.html

    Labtestsonline (3)

        http://www.labtestsonline.org/understanding/analytes/pt/test.html

    Labtestsonline (4)

        http://labtestsonline.org/understanding/conditions/sickle

    Labtestsonline (5)

        http://labtestsonline.org/understanding/analytes/urinalysis/tab/test

Labtestsonline (6)
http://labtestsonline.org/understanding/analytes/cholesterol/tab/test
Labtestsonline (7)
http://labtestsonline.org/understanding/analytes/strep/tab/sample
Labtestsonline (8)
http://labtestsonline.org/understanding/analytes/pt/tab/sample
Labtestsonline (9)
https://labtestsonline.org/understanding/wellness/pregnancy/first-trimester/hcg
Labtestsonline (10)
http://labtestsonline.org/understanding/conditions/meningitis?start=3
Labtestsonline (11)
http://labtestsonline.org/understanding/analytes/syphilis/tab/glance
Labtestsonline (12)
http://www.cdc.gov/vaccines/vpd-vac/hpv/default.htm
Labtestsonline (13)
http://labtestsonline.org/understanding/conditions/tuberculosis/?start=4

Mayo Clinic. http://www.mayoclinic.com
Mayo Clinic (1)
http://www.mayoclinic.com/print/esophageal-varices/DS00820/
Mayo Clinic (2)
http://www.mayoclinic.com/health/diabetic-ketoacidosis/DS00674
Mayo Clinic (3)
http://www.mayoclinic.org/diseases-conditions/sars/basics/causes/con-20024278
Mayo Clinic (4)
http://www.mayoclinic.org/diseases-conditions/gallstones/basics/risk-factors/con-20020461

Moisio, M. A. (2010). *Medical terminology for insurance and coding*. Clifton Park, NY: Cengage Learning.

National Center for Biotechnology Information (NCBI)
https://www.ncbi.nlm.nih.gov/pmc/articles/PMC2917081/

National Library of Medicine. http://www.nlm.nih.gov/medlineplus/
NLM (1)
http://www.nhlbi.nih.gov/health/dci/Diseases/ha/ha_diagnosis.html
http://www.nlm.nih.gov/medlineplus/ency/article/003479.htm
NLM (2)
http://www.nlm.nih.gov/medlineplus/ency/article/003652.htm
NLM (3)
http://www.nlm.nih.gov/medlineplus/ency/article/003498.htm
NLM (4)
http://www.nlm.nih.gov/medlineplus/ency/article/003574.htm
NLM (5)
http://www.nlm.nih.gov/medlineplus/ency/article/007192.htm

Neighbors, M. and Tannehill-Jones, R. (2015). *Human diseases* (4th ed.). Clifton Park, NY: Cengage Learning.

NHLBI—National Heart Lung and Blood Institute. http://www.nhlbi.nih.gov
http://www.nhlbi.nih.gov/health/dci/Diseases/hvd/hvd_treatments.html

NINDS—National Institute of Neurological Disorders and Stroke.
http://www.ninds.nih.gov/disorders/carpal_tunnel/detail_carpal_tunnel.htm

Rizzo, D. C. (2016). *Fundamentals of anatomy and physiology*. (4th ed.). Clifton Park, NY: Cengage Learning.

Scott, A. S. and Fong, P. E. (2014). *Body structures and functions* (12th ed.). Clifton Park, NY: Cengage Learning.

Sormunen, C. (2010). *Terminology for allied health professionals* (6th ed.). Clifton Park, NY: Cengage Learning.

Woodrow, R. (2015). *Essentials of pharmacology for health occupations* (7th ed.). Clifton Park, NY: Cengage Learning.

Medical Sciences Competencies

Questions	CCA Competencies
1–176	Domain 1

V. Classification Systems and Secondary Data Sources

Marissa Lajaunie, MBA, RHIA

1. Which system is a classification of health and health-related domains that describe body functions and structures, domains of activities and participation, and environmental factors that interact with all of these components?
   A. International Classification of Primary Care (ICPC-2)
   B. International Classification on Functioning, Disability, and Health (ICF)
   C. National Drug Codes
   D. Clinical Care Classification (CCC)

REFERENCE:　　　Oachs and Watters, p 148
　　　　　　　　　Sayles and Gordon, pp 125–126

2. A physician performed an outpatient surgical procedure on the eye orbit of a patient with Medicare. Upon searching the CPT codes and consulting with the physician, the coder is unable to find a code for the procedure. The coder should assign
   A. an unlisted Evaluation and Management code from the E/M section.
   B. an unlisted procedure code located in the eye and ocular adnexa section.
   C. a HCPCS Level Two (alphanumeric) code.
   D. an ophthalmologic treatment service code.

REFERENCE:　　　AMA (2016), pp 67–68
　　　　　　　　　Green, p 515
　　　　　　　　　Smith, pp 24–26

3. A system of preferred terminology for naming disease processes is known as a
   A. set of categories.　　　　　　　C. medical nomenclature.
   B. classification system.　　　　　　D. diagnosis listing.

REFERENCE:　　　Abdelhak and Hanken, p 256
　　　　　　　　　Bowie and Green, p 318
　　　　　　　　　Green, p 9
　　　　　　　　　McWay, pp 149–150
　　　　　　　　　Oachs and Watters, p 143
　　　　　　　　　Sayles and Gordon, p 114

4. Which of the following is NOT included as a part of the minimum data maintained in the MPI?
   A. principal diagnosis　　　　　　　C. full name (last, first, and middle)
   B. patient medical record number　　D. date of birth

REFERENCE:　　　Abdelhak and Hanken, p 130
　　　　　　　　　Bowie and Green, pp 252–255
　　　　　　　　　McWay, pp 139–140
　　　　　　　　　Oachs and Watters, pp 129–131
　　　　　　　　　Sayles and Gordon, pp 56–58

5. The Health Information Department receives research requests from various committees in the hospital. The Medicine Committee wishes to review all patients having a diagnosis of anterolateral myocardial infarction within the past 6 months. Which of the following would be the best source to identify the necessary charts?
   A. operation index　　　　　　　　C. disease index
   B. consultation index　　　　　　　D. physician's index

REFERENCE:　　　Bowie and Green, p 257
　　　　　　　　　McWay, p 140
　　　　　　　　　Oachs and Watters, p 172
　　　　　　　　　Sayles and Gordon, pp 147, 174

6. One of the major functions of the cancer registry is to ensure that patients receive regular and continued observation and management. How long should patient follow-up be continued?
   A. until remission occurs
   B. 10 years
   C. for the life of the patient
   D. 1 year

REFERENCE: Abdelhak and Hanken, pp 490–491
                McWay, pp 142–143
                Oachs and Watters, pp 173–175
                Sayles and Gordon, pp 175–178

7. In reviewing the medical record of a patient admitted for a left herniorrhaphy, the coder discovers an extremely low potassium level on the laboratory report. In examining the physician's orders, the coder notices that intravenous potassium was ordered. The physician has not listed any indication of an abnormal potassium level or any related condition on the discharge summary. The best course of action for the coder to take is to
   A. confer with the physician and ask him or her to list the condition as a final diagnosis if he or she considers the abnormal potassium level to be clinically significant.
   B. code the record as is.
   C. code the condition as abnormal blood chemistry.
   D. code the abnormal potassium level as a complication following surgery.

REFERENCE: Green, pp 15–16
                Oachs and Watters, pp 232–234

8. DSM-5 is used most frequently in what type of healthcare setting?
   A. behavioral health centers
   B. ambulatory surgery centers
   C. home health agencies
   D. nursing homes

REFERENCE: Bowie (2017b), p 569
                Green, pp 950–952
                McWay, p 152
                Oachs and Watters, p 150
                Sayles and Gordon, pp 127–128

9. A coder notes that a patient is taking prescription Pilocarpine. The final diagnoses on the discharge summary are congestive heart failure and diabetes mellitus. The coder should query the physician about adding a diagnosis of
   A. arthritis.
   B. glaucoma.
   C. bronchitis.
   D. laryngitis.

REFERENCE: Green, pp 15–16, 176–178
                Woodrow, p 345

10. The patient is diagnosed with congestive heart failure. A drug of choice is
    A. ibuprofen.
    B. oxytocin.
    C. haloperidol.
    D. digoxin.

REFERENCE: Woodrow, p 503

11. ICD-10-CM utilizes a placeholder character. This is used as a 5th character placeholder at certain 6 character codes to allow for future expansion. The placeholder character is
    A. "Z."
    B. "O."
    C. "1."
    D. "x."

REFERENCE: Bowie (2017b), p 51
                Green, p 74

12. The local safety council requests statistics on the number of head injuries occurring as a result of skateboarding accidents during the last year. To retrieve this data, you will need to have the correct
    A. CPT code.
    B. Standard Nomenclature of Injuries codes.
    C. ICD-10-CM codes.
    D. HCPCS Level II codes.

REFERENCE: Bowie (2017b), p 421
                Green, pp 207–208, 211–212
                McWay, pp 154–155
                Schraffenberger, p 566

13. All children will be entered into which of the following registries at birth, and thus will continue to be monitored by the registry in their geographic area?
    A. Birth defects registry   C. Cancer registry
    B. Trauma registry   D. Immunization registry

REFERENCE: McWay, p 141
                Oachs and Watters, p 180
                Sayles and Gordon, p 182

14. In general, all three key components (history, physical examination, and medical decision making) for the E/M codes in CPT should be met or exceeded when
    A. the patient is established.
    B. a new patient is seen in the office.
    C. the patient is given subsequent care in the hospital.
    D. the patient is seen for a follow-up inpatient consultation.

REFERENCE: AMA (2016), pp 11–12
                Bowie (2017a), p 45
                Green, pp 541–542, 546

15. This registry collects data on recipients of heart valves and pacemakers.
    A. Transplant registry   C. Cancer registry
    B. Implant registry   D. Hypertension registry

REFERENCE: McWay, p 141
                Oachs and Watters, pp 178–179
                Sayles and Gordon, pp 180–181

16. Which classification system was developed to standardize terminology and codes for use in clinical laboratories?
    A. Systematized Nomenclature of Human and Veterinary Medicine International (SNOMED)
    B. Systematized Nomenclature of Pathology (SNOP)
    C. Read Codes
    D. Logical Observation Identifiers, Names and Codes (LOINC)

REFERENCE: Abdelhak and Hanken, p 200
                McWay, p 151
                Oachs and Watters, pp 155–156

17. Which classification system is used to classify neoplasms according to site, morphology, and behavior?
    A. International Classification of Diseases for Oncology (ICD-O)
    B. Systematized Nomenclature of Human and Veterinary Medicine International (SNOMED)
    C. Diagnostic and Statistical Manual of Mental Disorders (DSM)
    D. Current Procedural Terminology (CPT)

REFERENCE: Abdelhak and Hanken, p 282
                Oachs and Watters, pp 147–148

18. According to the UHDDS, a procedure that is surgical in nature, carries a procedural or anesthetic risk, or requires special training is defined as a
    A. principal procedure.   C. operating room procedure.
    B. significant procedure.   D. therapeutic procedure.

REFERENCE: Green, pp 356, 383
                Schraffenberger, p 83

19. You need to analyze data on the types of care provided to Medicare patients in your geographic area by DRG. Which of the following would be most helpful?
    A. National Practitioner Data Bank
    B. MEDPAR
    C. Vital Statistics
    D. RxNorm

REFERENCE: McWay, p 187
                Oachs and Watters, pp 185–186
                Sayles and Gordon, p 185

20. An encoder that prompts the coder to answer a series of questions and choices based on the documentation in the medical record is called a(n)
    A. logic-based encoder.   C. grouper.
    B. automated codebook.   D. automatic code assignment.

REFERENCE: Sayles and Gordon, p 75

21. Which of the following classification systems was designed with electronic systems in mind and is currently being used for problem lists, ICU unit monitoring, patient care assessments, data collection, medical research studies, clinical trials, disease surveillance, and images?
    A. SNOMED CT   C. ICDPC-2
    B. SNDO   D. GEM

REFERENCE: Abdelhak and Hanken, pp 266–268
                McWay, pp 150–151
                Oachs and Watters, pp 153–155

22. The Unified Medical Language System (UMLS) is a project sponsored by the
    A. National Library of Medicine.   C. World Health Organization.
    B. CMS.   D. Office of Inspector General.

REFERENCE: McWay, p 151
                Oachs and Watters, pp 162–164
                Sayles and Gordon, pp 187–188

23. You have recently been hired as the Medical Staff Coordinator at your local hospital. Which database/registry will you utilize most often?
   A. Trauma Registry
   B. MEDPAR
   C. LOINC
   D. National Practitioner Data Bank (NPDB)

REFERENCE: McWay, p 270
               Oachs and Watters, p 186
               Sayles and Gordon, p 185

24. You need to retrieve information on a particular physician in your facility. Specifically, you need to know how many cases he saw during the month of May. What would be your best source of information?
   A. Healthcare Integrity and Protection Data Banks (HIPDB)
   B. Physician Index
   C. MEDLINE database
   D. National Practitioner Data Bank (NPDB)

REFERENCE: McWay, p 140
               Oachs and Watters, p 172
               Sayles and Gordon, pp 174–175

25. You just completed a process through which you reviewed a patient record and entered the required elements into a database. What is this process called?
   A. Case finding
   B. Staging
   C. Abstracting
   D. Nomenclature

REFERENCE: McWay, p 140
               Oachs and Watters, p 191
               Sayles and Gordon, p 74

26. Which system is used primarily to report services and supplies for reimbursement purposes?
   A. LOINC
   B. HCPCS
   C. NLM
   D. ASTM

REFERENCE: Green, pp 471–473
               McWay, p 164
               Oachs and Watters, pp 148–149
               Sayles and Gordon, p 130

27. You are looking at statistics for your facility that include average length of stay (ALOS) and discharge data by DRG. What type of data are you reviewing?
   A. Aggregate data
   B. Patient-identifiable data
   C. MPI data
   D. Protocol data

REFERENCE: McWay, p 208
               Oachs and Watters, p 170
               Sayles and Gordon, p 53

28. In which registry would you expect to find an Injury Severity Score (ISS)?
   A. Cancer Registry
   B. Birth Defects Registry
   C. Trauma Registry
   D. Transplant Registry

REFERENCE: Oachs and Watters, pp 175–176
               Sayles, pp 178–179

29. At the request of one physician, a second physician provides advice regarding the evaluation and management of a specific problem. This is called
    A. a referral.
    C. risk factor intervention.
    B. a consultation.
    D. concurrent care.

REFERENCE: AMA (2016), pp 19–20
              Bowie (2017a), pp 66–67
              Green, pp 568–570
              Smith, pp 207–208

30. Which of the following systems facilitates capturing standardized data with the electronic documentation of patient at the point of care?
    A. Continuity of Care Record (CCR)
    B. Clinical Care Classification (CCC)
    C. Clinical Documentation Architecture (CDA)
    D. Continuity of Care Document (CCD)

REFERENCE: Oachs and Watters, p 156

31. The most widely discussed and debated unique patient identifier is the
    A. patient's date of birth.
    B. patient's first and last names.
    C. patient's social security number.
    D. Unique Physician Identification Number (UPIN).

REFERENCE: Oachs and Watters, p 105

32. A nomenclature of codes and medical terms that provides standard terminology for reporting physicians' services for third-party reimbursement is
    A. Current Medical Information and Terminology (CMIT).
    B. Current Procedural Terminology (CPT).
    C. Systematized Nomenclature of Pathology (SNOP).
    D. Diagnostic and Statistical Manual of Mental Disorders (DSM).

REFERENCE: Bowie (2017a), p 2
              Green, p 10
              Oachs and Watters, pp 149–150
              Schraffenberger and Kuehn, p 10

33. A cancer program is surveyed for approval by the
    A. American Cancer Society.
    B. Commission on Cancer of the American College of Surgeons.
    C. State Department of Health.
    D. Joint Commission on Accreditation of Healthcare Organizations.

REFERENCE: Abdelhak and Hanken, p 491
              Oachs and Watters, p 175
              Sayles and Gordon, p 177

34. The nursing staff would most likely use which of the following to facilitate aggregation of data for comparison at local, regional, national, and international levels?
    A. READ codes
    C. SPECIALIST Lexicon
    B. ABC codes
    D. LOINC

REFERENCE: Bowie and Green, p 323
              McWay, p 164

35. The Level II (national) codes of the HCPCS coding system are maintained by the
    A. American Medical Association.
    B. CPT Editorial Panel.
    C. local fiscal intermediary.
    D. Centers for Medicare and Medicaid Services.

REFERENCE: Bowie (2017a), pp 9–10
               Bowie and Green, p 30

36. A patient is admitted with pneumonia. Cultures are requested to determine the infecting organism. Which of the following, if present, would alert the coder to ask the physician whether or not this should be coded as gram-negative pneumonia?
    A. pseudomonas   C. staphylococcus
    B. clostridium   D. listeria

REFERENCE: Green, pp 15–17

37. The Level I (CPT) codes of the HCPCS coding system are maintained by the
    A. American Medical Association.
    B. American Hospital Association.
    C. local fiscal intermediary.
    D. Centers for Medicare and Medicaid Services.

REFERENCE: Bowie (2017a), p 9–10
               Bowie and Green, p 30
               Green, p 471
               McWay, p 416

38. A physician excises a 3.1 cm malignant lesion of the scalp that requires full-thickness graft from the thigh to the scalp. In CPT, which of the following procedures should be coded?
    A. full-thickness skin graft to scalp only
    B. excision of lesion; full-thickness skin graft to scalp
    C. excision of lesion; full-thickness skin graft to scalp; excision of skin from thigh
    D. code 15004 for surgical preparation of recipient site; full-thickness skin graft to scalp

REFERENCE: Green, pp 651–654, 661–663
               Smith, pp 62–64, 73–76

39. A patient is seen by a surgeon who determines that an emergency procedure is necessary. Identify the modifier that may be reported to indicate that the decision to do surgery was made on this office visit.
    A. -25   B. -55   C. -57   D. -58

REFERENCE: AMA (2016), p 710
               Bowie (2017a), p 21
               Green, pp 519, 521, 571
               Smith, p 204

40. A patient develops difficulty during surgery and the physician discontinues the procedure. Identify the modifier that may be reported by the physician to indicate that the procedure was discontinued.
    A. -52   B. -53   C. -73   D. -74

REFERENCE: AMA (2016), p 710
               Bowie (2017a), pp 21–22
               Green, pp 519, 521
               Smith, p 47

41. A barrier to widespread use of automated code assignment is
    A. inadequate technology.
    C. resistance by physicians.
    B. poor quality of documentation.
    D. resistance by HIM professionals.

REFERENCE: Oachs and Watters, pp 281, 348

42. In assigning E/M codes, three key components are used. These are
    A. history, examination, counseling.
    B. history, examination, time.
    C. history, nature of presenting problem, time.
    D. history, examination, medical decision making.

REFERENCE: AMA (2016), pp 9–10
               Bowie (2017a), pp 45–46
               Green, p 546
               Smith, p 189

43. Mrs. Jones had an appendectomy on November 1. She was taken back to surgery on November 2 for evacuation of a hematoma of the wound site. Identify the modifier that may be reported for the November 2 visit.
    A. -58   B. -76   C. -78   D. -79

REFERENCE: AMA (2016), p 711
               Bowie (2017a), p 26
               Green, pp 520, 524
               Smith, p 49

44. The primary goal of a hospital-based cancer registry is to
    A. improve patient care.
    B. allocate hospital resources appropriately.
    C. determine the need for professional and public education programs.
    D. monitor cancer incidence.

REFERENCE: Abdelhak and Hanken, p 491
               McWay, pp 142–143

45. A secondary data source that houses and aggregates extensive data about patients with a certain diagnosis is a(n)
    A. disease index.
    C. disease registry.
    B. master patient index.
    D. admissions register.

REFERENCE: Bowie and Green, p 257
               Oachs and Watters, p 172

46. After reviewing the following excerpt from CPT, code 27646 would be interpreted as

27645	Radical resection of tumor; tibia
27646	Fibula
27647	Talus or calcaneus

    A. 27646   radical resection of tumor; tibia and fibula.
    B. 27646   radical resection of tumor; fibula.
    C. 27646   radical resection of tumor; fibula or tibia.
    D. 27646   radical resection of tumor; fibula, talus, or calcaneus.

REFERENCE: Bowie (2017a), pp 5–6
               Green, p 701
               Smith, p 20

47. A population-based cancer registry that is designed to determine rates and trends in a defined population is a(n)
    A. incidence-only population-based registry.
    B. cancer control population-based registry.
    C. research-oriented population-based registry.
    D. patient care population-based registry.

REFERENCE: Abdelhak and Hanken, p 491
               Oachs and Watters, p 173
               Sayles and Gordon, p 175

48. Given the diagnosis "carcinoma of axillary lymph nodes and lungs, metastatic from breast," what is the primary cancer site(s)?
    A. axillary lymph nodes   C. breast
    B. lungs   D. A and B

REFERENCE: Bowie (2017b), p 107
               Green, pp 168–172
               Schraffenberger, pp 139, 152–155

49. According to CPT, in which of the following cases would an established E/M code be used?
    A. A home visit with a 45-year-old male with a long history of drug abuse and alcoholism. The man is seen at the request of Adult Protective Services for an assessment of his mental capabilities.
    B. John and his family have just moved to town. John has asthma and requires medication to control the problem. He has an appointment with Dr. You and will bring his records from his previous physician.
    C. Tom is seen by Dr. X for a sore throat. Dr. X is on call for Tom's regular physician, Dr. Y. The last time that Tom saw Dr. Y was a couple of years ago.
    D. A 78-year-old female with weight loss and progressive agitation over the past 2 months is seen by her primary care physician for drug therapy. She has not seen her primary care physician in 4 years.

REFERENCE: AMA (2016), pp 4–5
               Bowie (2017a), pp 41–42
               Green, pp 542–543
               Smith, pp 186–187

50. In order to use the inpatient CPT consultation codes, the consulting physician must
    A. order diagnostic tests.
    B. document his findings in the patient's medical record.
    C. communicate orally his opinion to the attending physician.
    D. use the term "referral" in his report.

REFERENCE: AMA (2016), pp 19–22
               Bowie (2017a), pp 65–67
               Smith, pp 207–208

51. The attending physician requests a consultation from a cardiologist. The cardiologist takes a detailed history, performs a detailed examination, and utilizes moderate medical decision making. The cardiologist orders diagnostic tests and prescribes medication. He documents his findings in the patient's medical record and communicates in writing with the attending physician. The following day the consultant visits the patient to evaluate the patient's response to the medication, to review results from the diagnostic tests, and to discuss treatment options. What codes should the consultant report for the two visits?
    A. an initial inpatient consult and a follow-up consult
    B. an initial inpatient consult for both visits
    C. an initial inpatient consult and a subsequent hospital visit
    D. an initial inpatient consult and initial hospital care

REFERENCE: AMA (2016), pp 19–22
               Bowie (2017a), pp 65–67
               Green, pp 569–572
               Smith, pp 207–208

52. According to the American Medical Association, medical decision making is measured by all of the following except the
    A. number of diagnoses or management options.
    B. amount and complexity of data reviewed.
    C. risk of complications.
    D. specialty of the treating physician.

REFERENCE: AMA (2016), p 10
               Bowie (2017a), pp 56-59
               Green, p 548
               Smith, p 197

53. CPT provides Level I modifiers to explain all of the following situations EXCEPT
    A. when a service or procedure is partially reduced or eliminated at the physician's discretion.
    B. when one surgeon provides only postoperative services.
    C. when a patient sees a surgeon for follow-up care after surgery.
    D. when the same laboratory test is repeated multiple times on the same day.

REFERENCE: AMA (2016), pp 709–714
               Bowie (2017a), pp 13–15, 41–43
               Green, pp 519–527

54. The best place to ascertain the size of an excised lesion for accurate CPT coding is the
    A. discharge summary.   C. operative report.
    B. pathology report.   D. anesthesia record.

REFERENCE: Green, pp 651–654
               Smith, pp 61–63

55. Which of the following is expected to enable hospitals to collect more specific information for use in patient care, benchmarking, quality assessment, research, public health reporting, strategic planning, and reimbursement?
    A. LOINC   C. NDC
    B. ICD-10-CM   D. NANDA

REFERENCE: Abdelhak and Hanken, p 255
               Bowie (2017b), pp 2–3

56. Case definition is important for all types of registries. Age will certainly be an important criterion for accessing a case in a(n) _____ registry.
    A. implant
    B. trauma
    C. HIV/AIDS
    D. birth defects

REFERENCE: Oachs and Watters, p 177

57. To gather statistics for surgical services provided on an outpatient basis, which of the following codes are needed?
    A. ICD-10-CM codes
    B. evaluation and management codes
    C. HCPCS Level II codes
    D. CPT codes

REFERENCE: Bowie and Green, p 257
                McWay, p 164
                Schraffenberger and Kuehn, p 10

58. The Cancer Committee at your hospital requests a list of all patients entered into your cancer registry in the last year. This information would be obtained by checking the
    A. disease index.
    B. tickler file.
    C. suspense file.
    D. accession register.

REFERENCE: Oachs and Watters, p 174
                Sayles and Gordon, p 175

59. The reference date for a cancer registry is
    A. January 1 of the year in which the registry was established.
    B. the date when data collection began.
    C. the date that the Cancer Committee is established.
    D. the date that the cancer program applies for approval by the American College of Surgeons.

REFERENCE: Abdelhak and Hanken, p 491

60. The abstract completed on the patients in your hospital contains the following items: patient demographics; prehospital interventions; vital signs on admission; procedures and treatment prior to hospitalization; transport modality; and injury severity score. The hospital uses these data for its
    A. AIDS registry.
    B. diabetes registry.
    C. implant registry.
    D. trauma registry.

REFERENCE: Abdelhak and Hanken, p 497
                Oachs and Watters, pp 175–176
                Sayles and Gordon, pp 178–179

61. In relation to birth defects registries, active surveillance systems
    A. use trained staff to identify cases in all hospitals, clinics, and other facilities through review of patient records, indexes, vital records, and hospital logs.
    B. are commonly used in all 50 states.
    C. miss 10% to 30% of all cases.
    D. rely on reports submitted by hospitals, clinics, or other sources.

REFERENCE: Abdelhak and Hanken, p 492

62. In regard to quality of coding, the degree to which the same results (same codes) are obtained by different coders or on multiple attempts by the same coder refers to
    A. reliability.
    B. validity.
    C. completeness.
    D. timeliness.

REFERENCE: Oachs and Watters, pp 254–255

63. The Healthcare Cost and Utilization Project (HCUP) consists of a set of databases that include data on inpatients whose care is paid for by third-party payers. HCUP is an initiative of the
    A. Agency for Healthcare Research and Quality.
    B. Centers for Medicare and Medicaid Services.
    C. National Library of Medicine.
    D. World Health Organization.

REFERENCE: McWay, p 175
               Oachs and Watters, p 190

64. The coding supervisor notices that the coders are routinely failing to code all possible diagnoses and procedures for a patient encounter. This indicates to the supervisor that there is a problem with
    A. completeness.   C. reliability.
    B. validity.   D. timeliness.

REFERENCE: Oachs and Watters, pp 254–255

65. When coding free skin grafts, which of the following is NOT an essential item of data needed for accurate coding?
    A. recipient site   C. size of defect
    B. donor site   D. type of repair

REFERENCE: Bowie (2017a), p 127
               Green, pp 661–663
               Smith, pp 73–77

66. In CPT, Category III codes include codes
    A. to describe emerging technologies.
    B. to measure performance.
    C. for use by nonphysician practitioners.
    D. for supplies, drugs, and durable medical equipment.

REFERENCE: AMA (2016), p 687
               Bowie (2017a), pp 9–10
               Smith, p 4

67. The information collected for your registry includes patient demographic information, diagnosis codes, functional status, and histocompatibility information. This type of registry is a
    A. birth defects registry. C. transplant registry.
    B. diabetes registry.   D. trauma registry.

REFERENCE: Oachs and Watters, pp 179–180

68. Patient Jamey Smith has been seen at Oceanside Hospital three times prior to this current encounter. Unfortunately, because of clerical errors, Jamey's information was entered into the MPI incorrectly on the three previous admissions and consequently has three different medical record numbers. The unit numbering system is used at Oceanside Hospital. Jamey's previous entries into the MPI are as follows:

09/03/14	Jamey Smith	MR# 10361
03/10/15	Jamey Smith Doe	MR# 33998
07/23/16	Jamie Smith Doe	MR# 36723

The next available number to be assigned at Oceanside Hospital is 41369. Duplicate entries in the MPI should be scrubbed and all of Jamey's medical records should be filed under medical record number
  A. 10361.
  B. 33998.
  C. 36723.
  D. 41369.

REFERENCE: Bowie and Green, pp 252–256
                McWay, pp 139–140

69. The method of calculating errors in a coding audit that allows for benchmarking with other hospitals, and permits the reviewer to track errors by case type, is the
  A. record-over-record method.
  B. benchmarking method.
  C. code method.
  D. focused review method.

REFERENCE: Schraffenberger and Kuehn, p 319

70. The most common type of registry located in hospitals of all sizes and in every region of the country is the
  A. trauma registry.
  B. cancer registry.
  C. AIDS registry.
  D. birth defects registry.

REFERENCE: Bowie and Green, p 262
                McWay, p 142

71. A radiologist is asked to review a patient's CT scan that was taken at another facility. The modifier – 26 attached to the code indicates that the physician is billing for what component of the procedure?
  A. professional
  B. technical
  C. global
  D. confirmatory

REFERENCE: Bowie (2017a), 19–20
                Green, p 519

72. The committee that is responsible for establishing the quality improvement priorities of the cancer program and for monitoring the effectiveness of quality improvement activities is the
  A. Medical Staff Committee.
  B. Cancer Committee.
  C. Governing Board Committee.
  D. Quality Improvement Committee.

REFERENCE: Abdelhak and Hanken, p 492

73. According to CPT, antepartum care includes all of the following EXCEPT
  A. initial and subsequent history.
  B. physical examination.
  C. monthly visits up to 36 weeks.
  D. routine chemical urinalysis.

REFERENCE: Bowie (2017a), p 338
                Green, pp 831–832
                Smith, p 142

74. The Cancer Committee at Wharton General Hospital wants to compare long-term survival rates for pancreatic cancer by evaluating medical versus surgical treatment of the cancer. The best source of these data is the
    A. disease index.
    B. operation index.
    C. master patient index.
    D. cancer registry abstracts.

REFERENCE: Abdelhak and Hanken, pp 490–492
               McWay, pp 142–143
               Oachs and Watters, pp 173–175

75. A list or collection of clinical words or phrases with their meanings is a
    A. data dictionary.
    B. language.
    C. medical nomenclature.
    D. clinical vocabulary.

REFERENCE: Oachs and Watters, p 144

76. The main difference between concurrent and retrospective coding is
    A. when the coding is done.
    B. what classification system is used.
    C. the credentials of the coder.
    D. the involvement of the physician.

REFERENCE: Sayles and Gordon, p 64
               Schraffenberger and Kuehn, p 30

77. A PEG procedure would most likely be done to facilitate
    A. breathing.
    B. eating.
    C. urination.
    D. None of these answers apply.

REFERENCE: Schraffenberger, p 389

78. CMS published a final rule indicating a compliance date to implement ICD-10-CM and ICD-10-PCS. The use of these two code sets became effective on
    A. January 1, 2014.
    B. October 1, 2014.
    C. January 1, 2015.
    D. October 1, 2015.

REFERENCE: Bowie (2017b), p 4
               Schraffenberger, pp xi–xii

79. Mappings between ICD-9-CM and ICD-10-CM were developed and released by the National Center for Health Statistics (NCHS) to facilitate the transition from one code set to another. They are called
    A. GEMS (General Equivalency Mappings).
    B. Medical Mappings.
    C. Code Maps.
    D. ICD Code Maps.

REFERENCE: Green, pp 86–87
               Oachs and Watters, pp 145–146

80. The code structure for ICD-10-CM differs from the code structure of ICD-9-CM. An ICD-10-CM code consists of
    A. five alphanumeric characters.
    B. 10 characters.
    C. three to seven characters.
    D. seven digits.

REFERENCE: Bowie (2017b), p 51
               Green, pp 72–74

81. The first character for all of the codes assigned in ICD-10-CM is
    A. an alphabet.   C. an alphabet or a number.
    B. a number.   D. a digit.

REFERENCE: Bowie (2017b), pp 12–20
                 Green, pp 72–74

82. ICD-10-PCS was implemented in the United States to code
    A. hospital inpatient procedures.   C. hospital inpatient diagnoses.
    B. physician office procedures.   D. hospital outpatient diagnoses.

REFERENCE: Bowie (2017b), pp 3–4, 465
                 Green, p 79

83. ICD-10-PCS codes have a unique structure. An example of a valid code in the ICD-10-PCS system is
    A. L03.311.   C. B2151.
    B. 013.2.   D. 2W3FX1Z.

REFERENCE: Bowie (2017b), pp 465–468
                 Green, pp 80–81
                 Schraffenberger, pp 65–71

84. ICD-10-PCS utilizes the third character in the Medical and Surgical section to identify the "root operation." The name of the root operation that describes "cutting out or off, without replacing a portion of a body part" is
    A. destruction.   C. excision.
    B. extirpation.   D. removal.

REFERENCE: Bowie (2017b), p 479
                 Green, p 392
                 Schraffenberger, p 50

85. In ICD-10-PCS, to code "removal of a thumbnail," the root operation would be
    A. removal.   C. fragmentation.
    B. extraction.   D. extirpation.

REFERENCE: Bowie (2017b), p 479
                 Green, p 392
                 Schraffenberger, p 51

86. In ICD-10-CM, the final character of the code indicates laterality. An unspecified side code is also provided should the site not be identified in the medical record. If no bilateral code is provided and the condition is bilateral, the ICD-10-CM Official Coding Guidelines direct the coder to
    A. assign the unspecified side code.
    B. assign separate codes for both the left and right side.
    C. not assign a code.
    D. query the physician.

REFERENCE: Bowie (2017b), p 39
                 Green, p 250

87. An example of a valid code in ICD-10-CM is
    A. 576.212D.   C. 329.6677.
    B. Z3A.34   D. BJRT23x.

REFERENCE: Bowie (2017b), pp 12–20
                 Green, p 73

Answer Key for Classification Systems and Secondary Data Sources

NOTE: Explanations are provided for those questions that require mathematical calculations and questions that are not clearly explained in the references that are cited.

ANSWER		EXPLANATION
1.	B	
2.	B	
3.	C	
4.	A	
5.	C	
6.	C	
7.	A	A coder should never assign a code on the basis of laboratory results alone. If findings are clearly outside the normal range and the physician has ordered additional testing or treatment, it is appropriate to consult with the physician as to whether a diagnosis should be added or whether the abnormal finding should be listed.
8.	A	
9.	B	Pilocarpine is used to treat open-angle and angle-closure glaucoma to reduce intraocular pressure.
10.	D	Digoxin is used for maintenance therapy in congestive heart failure, atrial fibrillation, atrial flutter, and paroxysmal atrial tachycardia. Ibuprofen is an anti-inflammatory drug. Oxytocin is used to initiate or improve uterine contractions at term, and haloperidol is used to manage psychotic disorders.
11.	D	
12.	C	HCPCS codes (Levels I and II) would only give the code for any procedures that were performed and would not identify the diagnosis code or cause of the accident. The correct name of the nomenclature for athletic injuries is the Standard Nomenclature of Athletic Injuries and is used to identify sports injuries. It has not been revised since 1976.
13.	D	
14.	B	All three key components (history, physical examination, and medical decision making) are required for new patients and initial visits. At least two of the three key components are required for established patients and subsequent visits.
15.	B	
16.	D	
17.	A	
18.	B	
19.	B	
20.	A	
21.	A	
22.	A	
23.	D	
24.	B	
25.	C	
26.	B	
27.	A	
28.	C	
29.	B	
30.	B	
31.	C	
32.	B	
33.	B	

Current Procedural Terminology © 2016 American Medical Association. All Rights Reserved.

ANSWER   EXPLANATION

34.   B
35.   D
36.   A
37.   A
38.   B
39.   C
40.   B
41.   B
42.   D
43.   C
44.   A
45.   C
46.   B
47.   A
48.   C
49.   C
50.   B
51.   C
52.   D
53.   C
54.   C
55.   B
56.   D
57.   D
58.   D
59.   B
60.   D
61.   A
62.   A
63.   A
64.   A
65.   B
66.   A
67.   C
68.   A
69.   A
70.   B
71.   A   With CPT radiology codes, there are three components that have to be considered. These are the professional, technical, and global components. The professional component describes the services of a physician who supervises the taking of an X-ray film and the interpretation with report of the results. The technical component describes the services of the person who uses the equipment, the film, and other supplies. The global component describes the combination of both professional and technical components. If the billing radiologist's services include only the supervision and interpretation component, the radiologist bills the procedure code and adds the modifier –26 to indicate that he or she did only the professional component of the procedure.

	ANSWER	EXPLANATION

72. B
73. C
74. D
75. D
76. A
77. B
78. D
79. A
80. C
81. A
82. A
83. D   Immobilization of Left Hand Using Splint
        2W3FX1Z is a billable ICD-10-PCS procedure code that can be used to specify a medical procedure.
84. C
85. B
86. B
87. B   ICD-10-CM codes begin with an alphabetical letter. There is a decimal after the third character. Codes can consist of three to seven characters.

ICD-10-CM Official Guidelines for Coding and Reporting FY 2017
Chapter 15: Pregnancy, Childbirth, and the Puerperium
(15.b.1) Selection of OB Principal or First-listed Diagnosis
Routine outpatient prenatal visits
For routine outpatient prenatal visits when no complications are present, a code from category Z34, Encounter for supervision of normal pregnancy, should be used as the first-listed diagnosis. These codes should not be used in conjunction with chapter 15 codes.
Chapter 21: Factors influencing health status and contact with health services (Z00-Z99)
(21.c.11) Encounters for Obstetrical and Reproductive Services
See Section I.C.15. Pregnancy, Childbirth, and the Puerperium, for further instruction on the use of these codes.
Codes in category Z3A, Weeks of gestation, may be assigned to provide additional information about the pregnancy. The date of the admission should be used to determine weeks of gestation for inpatient admissions that encompass more than one gestational week.

REFERENCES

Abdelhak, M. and Hanken, M.A. (2016). *Health information: Management of a strategic resource* (5th ed.). St. Louis, MO: Saunders Elsevier.

American Medical Association (AMA). (2016). *Current procedural terminology (CPT) 2017 professional edition*. Chicago: Author.

Bowie, M. J. (2017a). *Understanding current procedural terminology and HCPCS coding systems* (4th ed.). Clifton Park, NY: Cengage Learning.

Bowie, M. J. (2017b). *Understanding ICD-10-CM and ICD-10-PCS: A worktext* (3rd ed.). Clifton Park, NY: Cengage Learning.

Bowie, M. J. and Green, M. A. (2016). *Essentials of health information management: Principles and practices* (3rd ed.). Clifton Park, NY: Cengage Learning.

Green, M. (2016). *3-2-1 Code it* (5th ed.). Clifton Park, NY: Cengage Learning.

McWay, D. C. (2014). *Today's health information management: An integrated approach* (2nd ed.). Clifton Park, NY: Cengage Learning.

Oachs, P. and Watters, A. (2016). *Health information management: Concepts, principles and practice* (5th ed.). Chicago: American Health Information Management Association (AHIMA).

Sayles, N. and Gordon, L. (2016). *Health information management technology: An applied approach* (5th ed.). Chicago: American Health Information Management Association (AHIMA).

Schraffenberger, L. A. (2016). *Basic ICD-10-CM/and ICD-10-PCS Coding 2016*. Chicago: American Health Information Management Association (AHIMA).

Schraffenberger, L. A. and Kuehn, L. (2010). *Effective management of coding services* (4th ed.). Chicago: American Health Information Management Association (AHIMA).

Smith, G. (2016). *Basic current procedural terminology and HCPCS coding 2016*. Chicago: American Health Information Management Association (AHIMA).

Woodrow, R., Colbert, B. J., and Smith, D. M. (2015). *Essentials of pharmacology for health professions* (7th ed.). Clifton Park, NY: Cengage Learning.

Classification Systems and Secondary Data Sources

Question	CCA Domain					
	1	2	3	4	5	6
1	X					
2	X					
3	X					
4					X	
5			X			
6	X					
7	X					
8	X					
9	X					
10	X					
11	X					
12			X			
13	X					
14	X					
15	X					
16	X					
17	X					
18	X					
19			X			
20					X	
21	X					
22					X	
23				X		
24					X	
25					X	
26		X				
27					X	
28	X					
29	X					
30					X	
31					X	
32	X					
33				X		
34					X	
35	X					
36	X					
37	X					
38	X					
39	X					
40	X					
41					X	
42	X					
43	X					
44	X					
45					X	

Question	CCA Domain					
	1	2	3	4	5	6
46	X					
47	X					
48	X					
49	X					
50	X					
51	X					
52	X					
53	X					
54	X					
55					X	
56	X					
57	X					
58			X			
59	X					
60	X					
61			X			
62				X		
63				X		
64				X		
65	X					
66	X					
67	X					
68			X			
69				X		
70	X					
71	X					
72	X					
73	X					
74	X					
75	X					
76	X					
77	X					
78				X		
79	X					
80	X					
81	X					
82	X					
83	X					
84	X					
85	X					
86	X					
87	X					

VI. ICD-10-CM/PCS Coding

Shelley C. Safian, PhD, RHIA, CCS-P, COC, CPC-I,
AHIMA-Approved ICD-10-CM/PCS Trainer

ICD-10-CM CODING SECTION

Infectious and Parasitic Diseases

1.   The patient was admitted with AIDS-related Kaposi's sarcoma of the skin.
     A.   B20, C46.1   C.   B20, C46.7
     B.   C46.0, B20   D.   B20, C46.0

REFERENCE: Bowie (2017b), pp 83–84
                Schraffenberger, pp 113–119, 125

2.   A patient was admitted with severe sepsis due to MRSA with septic shock and acute respiratory failure with hypoxia.
     A.   R65.21, A41.02, J96.02
     B.   A41.02, R65.21, J96.01
     C.   A49.01, R65.21, J96.01
     D.   J96.01, R65.21, A41.02

REFERENCE: Bowie (2017b), pp 77–79, 255–256
                Schraffenberger, pp 121–122, 353–354

3.   Patient was initially admitted and treated for an amebic abscess of the liver. During the stay, the patient developed a "hospital acquired bacterial pneumonia."
     A.   A06.4, J15.9, Y95   C.   A06.4, J18.9, Y95
     B.   A06.4, J15.8, Y95   D.   A06.4, J95.89, Y95

REFERENCE: Bowie (2017b), pp 75–76, 251–252, 433

4.   A patient is admitted with fever and severe headache. The physician's diagnostic statement at discharge is: Fever and severe headache possibly due to viral meningitis.
     A.   A87.9, R50.9, R51   C.   A87.9
     B.   A87.8, R50.9, R51   D.   A87.8

REFERENCE: Bowie (2017b), p 81
                Schraffenberger, pp 112, 341, 554–555

5.   Positive HIV test in a patient who is asymptomatic and has a high-risk lifestyle for HIV infection.
     A.   B20, Z20.6, Z72.89   C.   B20, Z20.6, Z72.89
     B.   B20, Z21, Z72.89   D.   Z21, Z72.89

REFERENCE: Bowie (2017b), p 83
                Schraffenberger, pp 123–124

6.   A 32-year-old female patient presents with right arm (dominant) paralysis due to childhood poliomyelitis.
     A.   A80.39   C.   B91, G83.21
     B.   A80.39, G83.21   D.   A80.39, G83.3

REFERENCE: Bowie (2017b), pp 50, 81
                Schraffenberger, pp 17, 240

Neoplasms

7. A patient is admitted for chemotherapy for treatment of liver metastasis from previous breast cancer. She had a mastectomy 4 months ago. Chemotherapy is given today.
   A. C78.7, C85.3, Z51.11
   B. C85.3, C78.7, Z51.11
   C. C78.7, C85.3
   D. Z51.11, C78.7, Z85.3

REFERENCE: Bowie (2017b), p 450
               Schraffenberger, pp 17, 141–143, 240

8. A patient with a history of malignant neoplasm of the lung status post lobectomy was admitted after experiencing a violent seizure lasting more than several minutes. During the course of the hospitalization the patient has continued to have seizures. Workup revealed metastatic lesions to the brain. The patient's seizures were treated with IV Dilantin.
   A. C79.3, Z85.118, R56.9
   B. C79.31, R56.9
   C. C79.31, R56.9, Z85.118
   D. R56.9, C79.32, Z85.118

REFERENCE: Bowie (2017b), p 106
               Schraffenberger, pp 17, 240

9. A patient is admitted to the hospital for treatment of dehydration following chemotherapy as treatment for right ovarian cancer.
   A. E86.0, C56.1
   B. E86.9, C56.1
   C. C56.1, E86.9
   D. C56.1, E86.0

REFERENCE: Bowie (2017b), p 113
               Schraffenberger, pp 17, 142–145, 240

10. A patient has malignant melanoma of the skin of the back, nose, and scalp. The patient will be scheduled to undergo a radical excision of the melanoma.
   A. C43.9
   B. C43.59, C43.31, C43.4
   C. C4A.59, C4A.4
   D. C44.300, C44.509

REFERENCE: Bowie (2017b), p 101
               Schraffenberger, pp 17, 240, pp 346–350

11. A patient is admitted with abdominal pain. A CT and MRI of the abdomen reveal a malignant neoplasm to the head of the pancreas with metastatic disease to the peritoneal cavity.
   A. C25.1, C78.6
   B. C78.89, C78.89
   C. C25.0, C78.6
   D. D01.7, C78.6

REFERENCE: Bowie (2017b), p 111
               Kuehn, pp 346–350

12. A patient presents to an outpatient clinic with a large growth on the left side of the neck. Examination reveals primary malignant neoplasm of lymph nodes. Confirmed diagnosis of nodular lymphocyte predominant Hodgkin lymphoma, lymph nodes of head, face, and neck.
   A. C77.0
   B. C81.01
   C. C76.0
   D. C77.9

REFERENCE: Bowie (2017b), p 111
               Schraffenberger, pp 17, 240, 346–350

Endocrine, Nutritional, and Metabolic Diseases and Immunity Disorders

13. A female, 68 years old, was admitted with type 2 diabetes mellitus with a diabetic ulcer of the left heel involving the subcutaneous layer of the skin. The patient will be scheduled for wound care with whirlpool treatments.

   A. E11.621, L97.421
   B. E11.620, L97.421
   C. E11.621
   D. L97.421, E11.621

REFERENCE: Bowie (2017b), p 152
               Kuehn, pp 187–189, 403–404

14. A 67-year-old man is admitted with acute dehydration secondary to lymphocytic colitis that is due to acute gastroenteritis. He is treated with IV fluids for the dehydration.

   A. K52.9, E86.0
   B. E11.2, K52.9, E86.0
   C. E86.0, E12.9, K59.2
   D. E86.0, K52.9

REFERENCE: Bowie (2017b), p 157
               Schraffenberger, pp 17, 240 193–194, 375

15. A patient was found at home in a hypoglycemic coma. This patient had never been diagnosed as being diabetic.

   A. E16.2
   B. E15
   C. E16.1
   D. E16.9

REFERENCE: Bowie (2017b), p 155
               Kuehn, pp 189–190

16. A patient is admitted with aplastic anemia secondary to chemotherapy administered for multiple myeloma initial encounter.

   A. D61.1, T45.1x5A, C90.00
   B. T45.1x5A, C90.00, D61.3
   C. C90.00, T45.1x5A, D61.1
   D. D61.1, T45.1x5A, D61.3

REFERENCE: Bowie (2017b), p 131
               Schraffenberger, pp 17, 148–150, 174, 240, 604–606

17. A male patient is admitted with gastrointestinal hemorrhage resulting in acute blood-loss anemia. A bleeding scan fails to reveal the source of the bleed.

   A. K92, D63.8
   B. K92.1, D62
   C. K92.2, D62
   D. K92.2, D63.8

REFERENCE: Bowie (2017b), p 272
               Kuehn, pp 171, 378–379

18. A patient is admitted with severe protein calorie malnutrition.

   A. E42
   B. E43
   C. E46
   D. E40

REFERENCE: Bowie (2017b), p 157
               Schraffenberger, p 17, 191–192, 240

Diseases of the Blood and Blood-Forming Organs

19. A patient is admitted with idiopathic thrombocytopenia and purpura.
    A. D61
    B. D69.3, D61
    C. D69.49
    D. D69.3

REFERENCE: Bowie (2017b), p 132
                    Kuehn, pp 172–173

20. A patient is admitted with sickle cell anemia with crisis.
    A. D57.00, D57.3
    B. D57.00
    C. D57.1
    D. D57.819

REFERENCE: Bowie (2017b), p 129
                    Schraffenberger, p 17, 240, p 168

21. A patient is admitted with sickle cell vasoocclusive pain crisis.
    A. D57.00
    B. D57.00, D57.3
    C. D57.819
    D. D57.1

REFERENCE: Bowie (2017b), p 129
                    Schraffenberger, pp 17, 168, 240

22. A patient is readmitted for post-op anemia due to acute blood loss. Patient is 5 days status post-cholecystectomy.
    A. D62, R58
    B. K91.840, D62
    C. K91.89, D62
    D. D62, K91.840

REFERENCE: Bowie (2017b), p 131
                    Kuehn, p 171

23. A patient is admitted with anemia due to end-stage renal disease. The patient is treated for anemia.
    A. N18.6, D63.8
    B. D63.1, N18.6
    C. D63.1, N18.5
    D. D63.1

REFERENCE: Bowie (2017b), p 131
                    Schraffenberger, pp 17, 171, 240, 447

24. A patient is admitted for treatment of anemia, neutropenia, and thrombocytopenia.
    A. D70.8, D69.59, D59.2
    B. D61.810
    C. D70.8, D69.59, D59.2, D61.810
    D. D64.9, D70.9, D69.6

REFERENCE: Bowie (2017b), pp 131–135
                    Schraffenberger, pp 17, 171–173, 240

Mental Disorders

25. A patient is admitted with severe recurrent major depression without psychotic features.
    A. F33.0
    B. F33.3
    C. F32.2
    D. F33.2

REFERENCE: Bowie (2017b), p 172
                    Schraffenberger, pp 17, 215–216, 240

26. A patient is admitted with acute alcohol intoxication with a blood alcohol level of 113 mg/100 ml.
    A. Y90.5, F10.129
    B. F10.129, Y90.5
    C. F10.129, Y90.6
    D. F10.129, Y90.4

REFERENCE: Bowie (2017b), p 168
                      Kuehn, pp 209–211

27. A patient is admitted with withdrawal delirium tremens with alcohol dependence.
    A. F10.221
    B. F10.222
    C. F10.121
    D. F10.231

REFERENCE: Bowie (2017b), p 168
                      Schraffenberger, pp 17, 209–211, 240

28. A patient is admitted with catatonic schizophrenia.
    A. F20
    B. F14.221
    C. F20.2
    D. F14.29

REFERENCE: Bowie (2017b), p 171
                      Keuhn, pp 215–216

29. A patient is diagnosed with chronic paranoia due to cocaine dependence with intoxication and drug delirium.
    A. F14.129
    B. F14.280, F14.221
    C. F14.159
    D. F14.19, F22

REFERENCE: Bowie (2017b), p 168
                      Schraffenberger, pp 212–213

30. A patient is diagnosed with psychogenic paroxysmal tachycardia.
    A. I47.9
    B. F54
    C. I47.8, F54
    D. I47.9, F54

REFERENCE: Bowie (2017b), pp 173, 235
                      Schraffenberger, pp 215–216, 315–316

Diseases of the Nervous System and Sense Organs

31. A patient is admitted with sensorineural deafness of the left ear. The patient was fitted for a hearing aid.
    A. H90.71
    B. H90.72
    C. H90.42
    D. H90.41

REFERENCE: Bowie (2017b), p 216
                      Schraffenberger, p 292

32. A patient is a type 2 diabetic with chronic kidney disease dependent on dialysis.
    A. E09.29, N18.6, Z99.2
    B. E11.22, N18.6, Z99.2
    C. E11.21, N18.6, Z99.2
    D. E13.21, N18.6, Z99.2

REFERENCE: Bowie (2017b), p 152
                      Schraffenberger, pp 451–453

33. A patient has intractable status epilepticus.
    A. G40.311   C. G40.31
    B. G40.301   D. G40.201

REFERENCE: Bowie (2017b), p 189
                Schraffenberger, p 241

34. A patient is diagnosed with early onset Alzheimer's disease and early onset dementia, and
    frequently wanders away from home.
    A. G30.8, F02.81, Z91.83   C. G30.0, F02.81, Z91.83
    B. F02.81, G30.0, Z91.73   D. G30.0, Z91.73

REFERENCE: Bowie (2017b), p 188
                Schraffenberger, pp 236, 688

35. A patient is admitted with poliovirus meningitis.
    A. G02, A80.9   C. A80.3, G02
    B. A80.9, G02   D. A80.0, G02

REFERENCE: Bowie (2017b), p 81
                Schraffenberger, pp 112–113, 228

36. A patient is admitted for pain control secondary to metastatic carcinoma of the spinal cord.
    A. G89.3, C79.49
    B. C79.51, C80.1, G89.3
    C. C79.49, C80.1 , G89.3
    D. G89.3, C79.49, C80.1

REFERENCE: Bowie (2017b), pp 114, 191
                Schraffenberger, pp 128–130, 146–150

Diseases of the Circulatory System

37. A patient is admitted with a thrombosis of the right middle cerebral artery, with hemiplegia
    affecting the right dominant side.
    A. I66.01, I69.351   C. I63.311
    B. I63.311, I69.353   D. I66.01, I69.851

REFERENCE: Bowie (2017b), p 237
                Schraffenberger, pp 317–319

38. A patient is admitted with multiple problems. He has hypertensive kidney disease, CKD stage
    III, and acute systolic congestive heart failure.
    A. N18.3, I12.9, I50.21   C. I12.9, N18.3, I50.21
    B. I50.21, I12.9, N18.3   D. I12.9

REFERENCE: Bowie (2017b), p 237
                Schraffenberger, pp 301–303, 312–315, 481–483

39. A patient is admitted with acute ST inferolateral wall myocardial infarction. Several days later
    during the same episode of care, the patient sustained a subsequent non-ST subendocardial
    myocardial infarction.
    A. I21.09, I22.8   C. I22.2, I21.02
    B. I21.02, I22.8   D. I21.19, I22.2

REFERENCE: Bowie (2017b), p 230
                Schraffenberger, pp 307–308

40. A patient with a diagnosis of coronary artery disease with ischemic chest pain. No history of CABG.
   A. I25.119
   B. I25.119, I20.9
   C. I25.9
   D. I25.10, I20.9

REFERENCE: Bowie (2017b), p 230
               Schraffenberger, pp 309–310

41. A patient with atherosclerotic peripheral vascular disease of the left lower leg with intermittent claudication. Past surgical history is negative.
   A. I70.219
   B. I70.212
   C. I70.298
   D. I70.208

REFERENCE: Bowie (2017b), p 238

Diseases of the Respiratory System

42. A patient presents to the outpatient department for a chest X-ray. The physician's order lists the following reasons for the chest X-ray: fever and cough, rule out pneumonia. The radiologist reports that the chest X-ray is positive for double pneumonia.
   A. J18.9
   B. J18.8
   C. J18.1
   D. J12.9

REFERENCE: Bowie (2017b), p 251

43. A patient has aspiration pneumonia with pneumonia due to *Staphylococcus aureus*.
   A. J15.211
   B. J69.0
   C. J69.0, J15
   D. J69.0, J15.211

REFERENCE: Bowie (2017b), pp 251–254
               Schraffenberger, pp 343, 350–351

44. A patient is admitted with acute respiratory failure with hypercapnia due to acute asthmatic bronchitis with status asthmaticus. Treatment consisted of IV steroids.
   A. J45.902, J96.02
   B. J96.02, J45.902
   C. J45.901, J96.02
   D. J45.52, J96.02

REFERENCE: Bowie (2017b), pp 253–255
               Schraffenberger, pp 348–349, 353–356

45. A patient is admitted for treatment of influenza and pneumonia.
   A. J11.1, J18.9
   B. J11.00
   C. J11.08, J11.1
   D. J11.1

REFERENCE: Bowie (2017b), p 251
               Schraffenberger, p 341

46. A patient is admitted with acute exacerbation chronic obstructive pulmonary disease with a history of tobacco dependence.
   A. J44.1, Z87.891
   B. J44.9, Z72.0
   C. J44.0, Z87.891
   D. J44.1, Z72.0

REFERENCE: Bowie (2017b), p 253
               Schraffenberger, pp 335, 347–348

47. A patient is admitted with extrinsic asthma with status asthmaticus with bronchospasm.
    A. J45.901
    B. J45.32
    C. J45.902
    D. J45.90

REFERENCE: Bowie (2017b), p 253
              Schraffenberger, pp 348–349

48. A patient is admitted for infection of the tracheostomy stoma secondary to cellulitis of the neck.
    A. L03.221, J95.02
    B. J95.02, L03.221
    C. J95.03, L03.221
    D. J95.09, L03.221

REFERENCE: Bowie (2017b), p 255
              Schraffenberger, pp 352–353, 397–398

Diseases of the Digestive System

49. A patient is admitted to the hospital for repair of a recurrent incarcerated ventral hernia. The surgery is canceled after the chest X-ray revealed lower lobe pneumonia. The patient is placed on antibiotics for treatment of the pneumonia.
    A. K43.0, J18.9, Z53.09
    B. J18.9, K43.0, Z53.09
    C. K43.6, J18.9
    D. J18.9, J43.6

REFERENCE: Bowie (2017b), p 251
              Schraffenberger, pp 341, 373–374, 683

50. A patient is admitted with acute gastric ulcer with hemorrhage and perforation.
    A. K25.0, K25.1
    B. K25.6
    C. K25.4, K25.6
    D. K25.2

REFERENCE: Bowie (2017b), p 265
              Schraffenberger, pp 371–372

51. A patient has diverticulitis of the large bowel with abscess. Patient was treated with IV antibiotics.
    A. K57.92
    B. K57.12
    C. K57.20
    D. K57.52

REFERENCE: Bowie (2017b), p 269
              Schraffenberger, pp 368–369

52. A patient is admitted with acute gangrenous cholecystitis with cholelithiasis.
    A. K80.00
    B. K80.12
    C. K81.0, K80.80
    D. K80.32

REFERENCE: Bowie (2017b), p 270
              Schraffenberger, pp 376–378

53. A patient is admitted with bleeding esophageal varices with alcoholic liver cirrhosis and portal hypertension. The patient is alcohol dependent.
    A. K76.6, I85.11, K70.30
    B. I85.11, K76.6, K70.30
    C. I85.01, K70.30, F10.288, K76.6
    D. K70.0. I85.11, K76.6

REFERENCE: Bowie (2017b), p 238
              Schraffenberger, pp 209–211, 292–293, 368–369

54. A patient is admitted for rectal bleeding. The laboratory results reveal chronic blood-loss anemia. The CT and the bleeding scan results of the abdomen revealed that the rectal bleeding is due to Crohn's disease of the descending colon.
   A. K50.118, D50.0
   B. K50.111, D50.0
   C. K50.011, D50.0
   D. K50.911, D50.0

REFERENCE: Bowie (2017b), p 269
              Schraffenberger, pp 166, 374–375

Diseases of the Genitourinary System

55. A patient is admitted with acute urinary tract infection due to *E. coli*.
   A. N39.0, B96.20
   B. N11.9, B96.20
   C. N30.90, B96.20
   D. N10, B96.20

REFERENCE: Bowie (2017b), pp 316–320
              Schraffenberger, pp 127–128, 454–455

56. A patient admitted with gross hematuria and benign prostatic hypertrophy.
   A. R31.0, N40.0
   B. R31.0, N40.1
   C. N40.0, R31.0
   D. N40.1, R31.0

REFERENCE: Bowie (2017b), p 322
              Schraffenberger, pp 454–455, 550–551

57. A male patient presents to the ED with acute renal failure. He is also being treated for hypertension.
   A. I12.9, N17.9
   B. N17.9, I15.9
   C. N17.9, I12.9
   D. N17.9, I10

REFERENCE: Bowie (2017b), p 318
              Schraffenberger, pp 302, 452–453

58. A patient is admitted with acute hemorrhagic cystitis. The patient was treated with IV antibiotics.
   A. N30.00
   B. N30.91
   C. N30.01
   D. N30.81

REFERENCE: Bowie (2017b), p 320
              Schraffenberger, pp 353–354

59. A patient is admitted with chronic kidney disease stage III due to hypertension and type 1 diabetes mellitus.
   A. E11.22, I12.0, N18.3
   B. E10.22, I12.0, N18.3
   C. I12.9, N18.3, E10.22
   D. E08.22, I12.0, N18.3

REFERENCE: Bowie (2017b), pp 152, 228
              Schraffenberger, pp 188, 302–303, 451–453

60. A patient has end-stage kidney disease, which resulted from malignant hypertension.
   A. I12.0, N18.6
   B. I10, N18.6
   C. I13.11, N18.6
   D. I15.1, N18.6

REFERENCE: Bowie (2017b), p 228
              Schraffenberger, pp 302–303, 452–453

Complications of Pregnancy, Childbirth, and the Puerperium

61. A woman has a vaginal delivery of a full-term liveborn infant after 38 weeks gestation.
    A. O80, Z37.0, Z3A.38
    B. O80, Z37.0
    C. Z3A.38, O80, Z37.0
    D. Z37.0, Z3A.38, O80

    REFERENCE: Bowie (2017b), p 342
    Schraffenberger, pp 486–487, 497–498

62. A patient is admitted with pregnancy-induced hypertension with severe edema and 24 weeks gestation.
    A. O14.12
    B. I10, Z33.1
    C. O13.2, Z3A.24
    D. O14.00, Z3A.24

    REFERENCE: Bowie (2017b), p 337
    Schraffenberger, pp 488–489, 501

63. A patient is admitted with obstructed labor due to breech presentation. A single liveborn infant was delivered via Cesarean section. Do not assign the code for the procedure.
    A. O32.1xx0
    B. O32.1xx1, Z37.0
    C. O32.8xx0, Z37.0
    D. O32.6xx0, Z37.0

    REFERENCE: Bowie (2017b), p 338
    Schraffenberger, pp 489, 500

64. A patient is admitted for gestational diabetes, insulin controlled, 28 weeks gestation.
    A. O24.414
    B. E11.69, O09.892
    C. O24.419, Z3A.28
    D. O24.414, Z3A.28

    REFERENCE: Bowie (2017b), p 337
    Schraffenberger, pp 482–484, 488–489

65. A patient is seen in the ED at 22 weeks gestation who is HIV positive.
    A. B20, O98.712, Z3A.22
    B. O98.712, Z21, Z3A.22
    C. Z21, O98.712
    D. P98.712, B20

    REFERENCE: Bowie (2017b), p 344
    Schraffenberger, pp 482–484, 488–490

66. A patient is admitted who is 39 weeks gestation and has a normal delivery of a single full-term newborn. During the same episode of care, patient experiences a 36-hour delayed hemorrhage following the delivery.
    A. O80, O72.2, Z37.0
    B. O72.2, Z37.0
    C. Z3A.39, O72.2, Z37.0
    D. O80, Z37.0, O72.2

    REFERENCE: Bowie (2017b), p 342
    Schraffenberger, pp 499–500

Diseases of the Skin and Subcutaneous Tissue

67. A patient had a cholecystectomy 3 days ago and is now readmitted with cellulitis at the site of the operative incision.
    A. T81.4, K68.11, 95.61
    B. T81.4xxA, L03.311
    C. K68.11, B95.61
    D. L03.31, T81.4xxA

    REFERENCE: Bowie (2017b), p 281
    Schraffenberger, pp 397–398, 612–613

68. A patient is admitted with an open wound to the left finger with cellulitis due to a dog bite, initial encounter. The patient is given IV antibiotics for treatment of the infection.
    A. L03.012
    B. L03.011
    C. S61.201A
    D. L03.012, S61.201A, W54.0xxA

REFERENCE: Bowie (2017b), p 281
                Schraffenberger, pp 397–398, 584, 629–632

69. A patient is admitted with diabetes mellitus type II; diabetic heel ulcer with necrosis of the muscle.
    A. E11.621, L97.403
    B. E10.622, L97.403
    C. E11.622, L97.403
    D. E10.628, L97.403

REFERENCE: Bowie (2017b), p 152
                Schraffenberger, pp 188, 397

70. A patient is admitted with dermatitis due to prescription topical antibiotic cream used as directed by a physician, initial encounter.
    A. L08.89, T49.0x5
    B. L25.1, T49.0x5A
    C. L02.91, T49.0x5
    D. T49.0x5, L25.1

REFERENCE: Bowie (2017b), pp 281–284
                Schraffenberger, pp 398–399, 607

71. A patient is admitted with a pressure ulcer of the left buttock stage 2.
    A. L89.322
    B. L98.411
    C. L89.152
    D. L03.317

REFERENCE: Bowie (2017b), p 286
                Schraffenberger, pp 402–403

72. A patient is admitted with a stage 1 pressure ulcer of the sacrum. During the hospitalization, the ulcer progressed to a stage 2.
    A. L89.125
    B. L89.151, L89.152
    C. L89.152
    D. L89.153

REFERENCE: Bowie (2017b), p 286
                Schraffenberger, pp 402–403

Diseases of the Musculoskeletal System and Connective Tissue

73. A patient has a pathological fracture of the left femur due to metastatic bone cancer. The past medical history is significant for surgical removal of cancer of the lung.
    A. C79.51, S72.92xG, Z85.118
    B. M84.552A, C79.51, Z85.118
    C. C79.51, S72.92xS, Z85.118
    D. C79.51, M84.552, Z85.118

REFERENCE: Bowie (2017b), pp 101–105
                Schraffenberger, pp 150–151, 432–433, 663

74. A patient is admitted with a back pain. A myelogram demonstrated the reason for the back pain is a herniated lumbar intervertebral disc with radiculopathy.
    A. M51.26, M54.16
    B. M84.552, C79.51, Z85.118
    C. M51.26
    D. M51.16

REFERENCE: Bowie (2017b), pp 302–303
                Schraffenberger, pp 416, 418–422

75. A patient is admitted with pyogenic arthritis of the right hip due to group A *streptococcus*. Treatment consisted of IV antibiotics.
    A. M16.11, A49.1
    B. M16.7, A49.1
    C. M00.251, B95.0
    D. M00.851

REFERENCE: Bowie (2017b) pp 229-300
              Schraffenberger, pp 127–128, 420–423

76. A patient is admitted with a fracture to the L1 vertebrae secondary to postmenopausal senile osteoporosis, initial encounter.
    A. M80.08
    B. M80.88
    C. M80.88xA
    D. M80.08xA

REFERENCE: Bowie (2017b), p 303
              Schraffenberger, pp 431–432

77. A patient developed a malunion of the left medial condyle humeral fracture. The original injury occurred 4 months ago.
    A. S42.462K
    B. S42.462G
    C. S42.462P
    D. S42.462D

REFERENCE: Bowie (2017b), p 404
              Schraffenberger, pp 577–578

78. A patient was admitted for removal of internal pins from the left ankle. One month ago the patient sustained a traumatic displaced bimalleolar fracture to the left ankle.
    A. S82.842K
    B. S82.842D
    C. S82.842S
    D. S84.842G

REFERENCE: Bowie (2017b), p 404
              Schraffenberger, pp 567–568, 574–578

Congenital Anomalies

79. A newborn infant is born in the hospital, vaginal delivery, with a unilateral hard cleft palate and cleft lip.
    A. Q37.1, Z38.00
    B. Q37.2, Z38.00
    C. Z38.00, Q37.1
    D. Z38.00, Q37.2

REFERENCE: Bowie (2017b), p 449
              Schraffenberger, pp 529, 537–536

80. A newborn infant is born in the hospital, vaginal delivery. Physical examination demonstrates molding of the baby's scalp, which resolved prior to discharge without treatment.
    A. Z38.00, Q82.9
    B. Z38.00, Q82.8
    C. Z38.00, L98.8
    D. Z38.00

REFERENCE: Bowie (2017b), p 449
              Schraffenberger, p 662

81. A newborn infant is transferred to Community General Hospital for treatment of an esophageal atresia. What codes should be reported for Community General Hospital?
    A. Z38.00, Q39.0
    B. Q39.0
    C. Z38.00, Q39.1
    D. Q39.1

REFERENCE: Bowie (2017b), p 369
              Schraffenberger, pp 531–532

82. A patient is admitted with cervical spina bifida with hydrocephalus.
    A. Q76.0
    B. Q05
    C. Q05.0
    D. Q05.5

REFERENCE: Bowie (2017b), p 366
               Schraffenberger, pp 528–529

83. A newborn infant is born in the hospital, delivered vaginally, and sustained a fracture of the clavicle due to birth trauma.
    A. Z38.00, P13.4
    B. Z38.00, S42.009A
    C. P13.4
    D. Z38.00, P13.4, S42.009A

REFERENCE: Bowie (2017b), p 449
               Schraffenberger, pp 512, 623

84. A full-term infant born in the hospital, vaginal delivery, was diagnosed with polycystic kidneys.
    A. Z38.00, Q61.11
    B. Z38.00, Q61.19
    C. Z38.00, Q61.3
    D. Z38.00, Q61.8

REFERENCE: Bowie (2017b), p 449
               Schraffenberger, pp 512–513, 523

Certain Conditions Originating in the Perinatal Period

85. A full-term newborn, vaginal delivery, was born in the hospital to a mother who is addicted to cocaine; however, the infant tested negative.
    A. Z38.00, F14.10
    B. Z38.00, F14.129
    C. Z38.00, F14.20
    D. Z38.00, Z03.79

REFERENCE: Bowie (2017b), p 449

86. A preterm infant, 34 weeks gestation, is born via Cesarean section and has severe birth asphyxia.
    A. Z38.01, P84, P07.37
    B. Z38.01, P84, R09.01
    C. Z38.01, P84, R09.02
    D. Z38.01, P84, R09.2, P07.37

REFERENCE: Bowie (2017b), pp 358, 449
               Schraffenberger, pp 512–513, 518–519, 523–524

87. A preterm infant born in the hospital, vaginal delivery, 36 weeks gestation, is treated for neonatal jaundice.
    A. Z38.00, P59.9, P07.39
    B. Z38.00, P59.8, P07.39
    C. Z38.00, P59.29, P07.39
    D. Z38.00, P59.3, P07.39

REFERENCE: Bowie (2017b), pp 357, 449
               Schraffenberger, pp 512–513. 518, 523–524

88. A 1-week-old infant is admitted to the hospital with a diagnosis of urinary tract infection contracted prior to birth. The urine culture is positive for *E. coli*.
    A. P39.3
    B. P39.3, N39.0, A49.8
    C. P39.3, N30.90, A49.8
    D. P39.3, B96.20

REFERENCE: Bowie (2017b), p 356
               Schraffenberger, pp 522–523

89. An infant has hypoglycemia and a mother with diabetes.
    A. P70.0   C. P70.1
    B. P70.2   D. P70.4

REFERENCE: Bowie (2017b), p 357
                  Schraffenberger, pp 512–513

90. A full-term newborn, vaginal delivery, born in the hospital. The birth is complicated by cord compression, which affected the newborn.
    A. Z38.00, P02.5   C. Z38.00, P02.4
    B. P02.5   D. Z38.00, P02.69

REFERENCE: Bowie (2017b), pp 354, 449
                  Schraffenberger, pp 517–518, 523–524

Symptoms, Signs, and Ill-Defined Conditions

91. A patient is admitted with right lower quadrant abdominal pain. The discharge diagnosis is listed as abdominal pain due to gastroenteritis or diverticulosis.
    A. K52.9, K57.90   C. R10.31, K52.9, K57.90
    B. K57.90, K52.9   D. K52.9, K57.90, R10.31

REFERENCE: Bowie (2017b), p 269
                  Schraffenberger, pp 367–368, 375, 550–551

92. A patient was admitted with hemoptysis; a CT of the chest revealed a lung mass.
    A. R91.8   C. R04.2
    B. R91.8, R04.2   D. R91.8, F04.1

REFERENCE: Bowie (2017b), pp 384–389
                  Schraffenberger, pp 550–551, 555–556

93. A woman has a Pap smear that detected cervical high-risk human papillomavirus (HPV). The DNA test was positive.
    A. R87.810   C. R87.820
    B. R87.9   D. R87.811

REFERENCE: Bowie (2017b), p 389
                  Schraffenberger, pp 556–557

94. A patient is admitted with malignant ascites with widespread metastatic peritoneal lesions, primary site sigmoid colon; sigmoid colon resection 6 months ago.
    A. R18.8, C78.6, Z85.038   C. C78.6, R18.0, Z85.038
    B. R18.8, C78.6, C18.9   D. R18.0, C78.6, C18.9

REFERENCE: Bowie (2017b), p 384
                  Schraffenberger, pp 154–155, 550–551, 690–691

95. A patient is admitted with fever due to bacteremia.
    A. R78.81   C. R78.81, F50.81
    B. R50.9   D. R78.81, R50.9

REFERENCE: Bowie (2017b), pp 387–388
                  Schraffenberger, pp 546–547, 554–555

96. A patient is admitted that has urinary retention secondary to benign prostatic hypertrophy.
    A. N40.0, R33.8   C. N40.1, R33.8
    B. N40.1, R39.11, R33.9   D. N40.3, R33.8

REFERENCE: Bowie (2017b), p 322
                Schraffenberger, pp 454–455, 550–551

Injury and Poisoning

97. A patient is admitted with a nondisplaced fracture of the left medial malleolus, initial encounter. The fracture was treated with a cast.
    A. S82.52xB   C. S82.62xA
    B. S82.55xA   D. S82.63xA

REFERENCE: Bowie (2017b), p 405
                Schraffenberger, pp 574–575

98. A patient is admitted with an anaphylactic reaction due to eating strawberries, initial encounter.
    A. T78.04xA   C. T78.2
    B. T78.49   D. T78.04

REFERENCE: Bowie (2017b), p 411
                Schraffenberger, p 610

99. A patient is admitted with a through and through gunshot wound to the right upper quadrant of the abdomen, which involves a moderate laceration to the liver, initial encounter.
    A. S36.118A, W34.00xA   C. S36.115A
    B. S36.115A, S31.101A   D. S31.130A, S36.115A, W34.00xA

REFERENCE: Bowie (2017b), p 404
                Schraffenberger, pp 583, 630–632

100. A woman experienced third-degree burns to her left thigh and second-degree burns to her right and left foot, initial encounter. She stated that the burns were from an accidental spill of hot coffee at a nearby café.
    A. T24.319A, T25.229A, Y92.511   C. T24.312A, T25.221A, T25.222A, X10.0xxA, Y92.511
    B. T24.31xA, T24.331A, T24.332A   D. T24.719A, T25.222A, T25.221A

REFERENCE: Bowie (2017b), p 406
                Schraffenberger, pp 586, 587, 629–633, 640

101. A patient is seen for a cast removal. Six weeks ago, the patient underwent open reduction internal fixation for a displaced fracture of the left radial styloid process.
    A. S52.512D   C. S52.515A
    B. Z47.89   D. Z47.2

REFERENCE: Bowie (2017b), p 404
                Schraffenberger, pp 576–578

102. A patient is admitted with a left wrist laceration, with embedded glass that involved the radical nerve, initial encounter.
    A. S64.22xA   C. S61.512, S64.22xA
    B. S62.522A   D. S61.522A, S64.22xA

REFERENCE: Bowie (2017b), p 404
                Schraffenberger, pp 584–585

103. A patient is admitted with a left nondisplaced comminuted patella fracture, a displaced left spiral fracture of the shaft of the fibula, and a displaced comminuted fracture of the shaft of the left tibia, initial encounter.
    A. S82.045A, S82.442A
    B. S82.045, S82.252A
    C. S82.252A, S82.442A, S82.045A
    D. S82.045A, S82.442A, S82.255A

REFERENCE: Bowie (2017b), p 405
              Schraffenberger, pp 574–576

104. A patient is admitted with dizziness as a result of taking phenobarbital as prescribed, initial encounter.
    A. R42, T42.4x1A   C. T42.4x2A, R42
    B. R42, T42.3x5A   D. T42.4x1A, R42

REFERENCE: Bowie (2017b), p 385
              Schraffenberger, pp 550–551, 598–599

105. A patient is admitted for control of exacerbation of chronic obstructive lung disease. The patient had stopped taking the prednisone as prescribed due to gaining weight, a known side effect for this drug.
    A. J44.1, T38.0x6A, Z91.14   C. J44.0, T38.0x6A, Z91.14
    B. T38.0x6A, J44.1, Z91.14   D. T38.0x6A, Z91.14, J44.0

REFERENCE: Bowie (2017b), p 253
              Schraffenberger, pp 347–348, 609

106. A patient is admitted for intentional overdose of valium and acute respiratory failure with hypoxia.
    A. J96.01, T42.4x2A   C. T42.4x2A, J96.01
    B. J96.01, T42.4x2A, R09.02   D. T42.4x2A, J96.00, R09.02

REFERENCE: Bowie (2017b), pp 255, 409
              Schraffenberger, pp 354, 607–608

Z-Codes

107. A patient is being admitted for chemotherapy for primary lung cancer, left lower lobe.
    A. Z51.11   C. C34.32, Z51.11
    B. Z51.11, Z85.118   D. Z51.11, C34.32

REFERENCE: Bowie (2017b), p 450
              Schraffenberger, pp 146–151, 662

108. The patient presents for a screening examination for lung cancer.
    A. Z03.89   C. Z12.2
    B. C78.00   D. C34.90

REFERENCE: Bowie (2017b), p 444
              Schraffenberger, p 662

109. A patient is admitted for observation for a head injury. The patient was struck while playing football. The patient also suffered a minor laceration to the forehead. Head injury was ruled out.
    A. Z71.4
    B. S01.81xA, Z71.4
    C. S01.81xA
    D. Z04.3, S01.81xA

REFERENCE: Bowie (2017b), pp 402, 454
                 Schraffenberger, pp 584–585, 662

ICD-10-PCS CODING SECTION

Identify the correct root operation for the following:

110. Excision gallbladder
    A. Resection
    B. Excision
    C. Incision
    D. Removal

    REFERENCE: Bowie (2017b), pp 477–482
                     Schraffenberger, pp 384–385

111. Excision descending colon
    A. Resection
    B. Excision
    C. Incision
    D. Bypass

    REFERENCE: Bowie (2017b), pp 477–482
                     Kuehn, pp 9, 41–45, 71–76, 135
                     Schraffenberger, pp 389–390

112. Removal of a foreign body right external auditory canal
    A. Removal
    B. Extirpation
    C. Inspection
    D. Excision

    REFERENCE: Bowie (2017b), pp 477–482
                     Kuehn, p 84
                     Schraffenberger, p 288

113. Amputation first left toe
    A. Excision
    B. Amputation
    C. Resection
    D. Detachment

    REFERENCE: Bowie (2017b), pp 477–482

114. Reduction fracture right femoral shaft
    A. Transfer
    B. Reduction
    C. Reposition
    D. Reattachment

    REFERENCE: Bowie (2017b), pp 477–483
                     Schraffenberger, p 435

115. Colon polyp fulguration
    A. Excision
    B. Destruction
    C. Extraction
    D. Detachment

    REFERENCE: Bowie (2017b), pp 477–482
                      Schraffenberger, p 380

116. Reattachment fourth finger
    A. Reattachment
    B. Reposition
    C. Transfer
    D. Repair

    REFERENCE: Bowie (2017b), pp 477–482
                      Schraffenberger, p 435

117. Cystoscopy
    A. Inspection
    B. Endoscopy
    C. Insertion
    D. Drainage

    REFERENCE: Bowie (2017b), pp 477–482
                      Schraffenberger, pp 460–467

118. Removal deep left vein thrombosis
    A. Excision
    B. Removal
    C. Resection
    D. Extirpation

    REFERENCE: Bowie (2017b), pp 477–482

119. Total left knee replacement
    A. Insertion
    B. Resection
    C. Excision
    D. Replacement

    REFERENCE: Bowie (2017b), pp 477–482
                      Schraffenberger, pp 434–440

120. Lysis of abdominal adhesions
    A. Excision
    B. Division
    C. Incision
    D. Release

    REFERENCE: Bowie (2017b), pp 477–482
                      Schraffenberger, pp 462–467

121. Percutaneous angioplasty right coronary artery
    A. Dilation
    B. Restriction
    C. Insertion
    D. Excision

    REFERENCE: Bowie (2017b), pp 477–482
                   Schraffenberger, pp 323–326

122. Ligation right fallopian tube
    A. Restriction
    B. Occlusion
    C. Dilation
    D. Bypass

    REFERENCE: Bowie (2017b), pp 477–482
                   Schraffenberger, pp 462–463

123. Removal cardiac pacemaker
    A. Change
    B. Excision
    C. Revision
    D. Removal

    REFERENCE: Bowie (2017b), pp 477–482

124. Creation of arteriovenous graft brachial artery left arm for hemodialysis
    A. Bypass
    B. Creation
    C. Alteration
    D. Insertion

    REFERENCE: Bowie (2017b), pp 477–482
                   Schraffenberger, pp 195–198

125. Lithotripsy left ureter with removal of fragment
    A. Drainage
    B. Fragmentation
    C. Removal
    D. Extirpation

    REFERENCE: Bowie (2017b), pp 477–482

126. Endometrial ablation of cervical polyps
    A. Destruction
    B. Excision
    C. Removal
    D. Extraction

    REFERENCE: Bowie (2017b), pp 477–483
                   Schraffenberger, pp 462–463

127. Angioplasty abdominal iliac artery
    A. Dilation
    B. Repair
    C. Angioplasty
    D. Insertion

    REFERENCE: Bowie (2017b), pp 477–482

128. Radiofrequency ablation right kidney
    A. Excision
    B. Removal
    C. Destruction
    D. Ablation

    REFERENCE: Bowie (2017b), pp 477–482
                      Schraffenberger, pp 462–465

129. Cryoablation external genital warts
    A. Destruction
    B. Cryoablation
    C. Excision
    D. Resection

    REFERENCE: Bowie (2017b), pp 477–482
                      Schraffenberger, pp 407–412

130. Gastric lap band for treatment of morbid obesity
    A. Dilation
    B. Occlusion
    C. Restriction
    D. Bypass

    REFERENCE: Bowie (2017b), pp 477–482

131. Excisional debridement of a chronic skin ulcer
    A. Debridement
    B. Extraction
    C. Incision
    D. Resection

    REFERENCE: Bowie (2017b), pp 477–482

132. Application of free skin graft to the nose status post excision malignant neoplasm
    A. Transfer
    B. Creation
    C. Replacement
    D. Alteration

    REFERENCE: Bowie (2017b), pp 477–482

133. Spinal fusion cervical C1–C2
    A. Arthrodesis
    B. Repair
    C. Creation
    D. Fusion

    REFERENCE: Bowie (2017b), pp 477–482

134. Tracheostomy
    A. Bypass
    B. Creation
    C. Reposition
    D. Insertion

    REFERENCE: Bowie (2017b), pp 477–482

135. Percutaneous needle biopsy left lung
    A. Incision
    B. Excision
    C. Drainage
    D. Resection

    REFERENCE: Bowie (2017b), pp 477–482

136. Extraction left intraocular lens, open
    A. Extirpation
    B. Fragmentation
    C. Extraction
    D. Excision

    REFERENCE: Bowie (2017b), pp 477–482

137. Uterine dilation and curettage
    A. Extraction
    B. Dilation
    C. Excision
    D. Destruction

    REFERENCE: Bowie (2017b), pp 477–482

138. Excision right popliteal artery with graft replacement, open
    A. Excision
    B. Resection
    C. Replacement
    D. Repair

    REFERENCE: Bowie (2017b), pp 477–482

139. Mitral valve ring annuloplasty, open
    A. Supplement
    B. Replacement
    C. Resection
    D. Repair

    REFERENCE: Bowie (2017b), pp 477–482

140. Left common carotid endarterectomy, open
    A. Excision
    B. Resection
    C. Extraction
    D. Release

    REFERENCE: Bowie (2017b), pp 477–482

141. Excision malignant lesion skin of left ear
    A. 0HB3XZZ
    B. 0HC3XZZ
    C. 0H53XZZ
    D. 0HD3XZZ

    REFERENCE: Bowie (2017b), pp 474–495

142. Left below the knee amputation, proximal tibia/fibula
    A. 0YBJ0ZZ
    B. 0Y6H0ZZ
    C. 0Y6J0Z1
    D. 0Y6J0Z3

    REFERENCE: Bowie (2017b), pp 474–495

143. Thoracoscopic pleurodesis right side
    A. 0BVN4ZZ
    B. 0BPQ40Z
    C. 0B5N4ZZ
    D. 0BCN4ZZ

    REFERENCE: Bowie (2017b), pp 474–495

144. Extraction left intraocular lens without replacement, percutaneous
    A. 08DK3ZZ
    B. 08PK3JZ
    C. 08QK3ZZ
    D. 08BK3ZZ

    REFERENCE: Bowie (2017b), pp 474–495

145. Routine insertion of indwelling Foley catheter
    A. 0T9B7ZZ
    B. 0T9B70Z
    C. 0T9C80Z
    D. 0T9C8ZZ

    REFERENCE: Bowie (2017b), pp 474–495

146. EGD with removal FB from duodenum
    A. 0DC98ZZ
    B. 0DF98ZZ
    C. 0D898ZZ
    D. 0D798ZZ

    REFERENCE: Bowie (2017b), pp 474–495

147. Facelift, open
    A. 0WQ20ZZ
    B. 0WU20KZ
    C. 0WB20ZZ
    D. 0W020ZZ

    REFERENCE: Bowie (2017b), pp 474–495

148. Normal delivery with episiotomy
    A. 10E0XZZ, 0W8NXZZ
    B. 0WQNXZZ
    C. 10E0XZZ, 0WBNXZZ
    D. 0WMN0ZZ

    REFERENCE: Bowie (2017b), pp 474–495

149. Percutaneous endoscopic clipping cerebral aneurysm
    A. 03VG4CZ
    B. 03LG0DZ
    C. 03BG0ZZ
    D. 03CG0ZZ

    REFERENCE: Bowie (2017b), pp 474–495

150. Left knee arthroscopy with reposition of the anterior horn medial meniscus
    A. 0MQP4ZZ
    B. 0MQP3ZZ
    C. 0MSP0ZZ
    D. 0MSP4ZZ

    REFERENCE: Bowie (2017b), pp 474–495

151. Heart transplant using porcine heart, open
    A. 02YA0Z2
    B. 02QA0ZZ
    C. 02YA0Z0
    D. 02Y0Z1

    REFERENCE: Bowie (2017b), pp 474–495

152. ESWL left ureter
    A. 0TF7XZZ
    B. 0TP930Z
    C. 0TB63ZZ
    D. 0TC63ZZ

    REFERENCE: Bowie (2017b), pp 474–495

153. Reattachment severed left ear
    A. 09WJXZZ
    B. 09Q1XZZ
    C. 09M1XZZ
    D. 09S1XZZ

    REFERENCE: Bowie (2017b), pp 474–495

154. Transuretheral cystoscopy with removal of right ureteral calculus
    A. 0TB68ZZ
    B. 0TJ98ZZ
    C. 0TF68ZZ
    D. 0TC68ZZ

    REFERENCE: Bowie (2017b), pp 474–495

155. Open reduction fracture left tibia
    A. 0QSH0ZZ
    B. 0QSH04Z
    C. 0QWH04Z
    D. 0QQH0ZZ

    REFERENCE: Bowie (2017b), pp 474–495

156. Percutaneous insertion Greenfield IVC filter
    A. 06H03DZ
    B. 06L03DZ
    C. 06Q03ZZ
    D. 06V03DZ

    REFERENCE: Bowie (2017b), pp 474–495

157. Incision and drainage external perianal abscess
    A. 0D9Q30Z
    B. 0D9RX0Z
    C. 0D9QXZZ
    D. 0D9QX0Z

    REFERENCE: Bowie (2017b), pp 474–495

158. Removal FB left cornea
    A. 08B8XZZ
    B. 0858XZZ
    C. 08D8XZZ
    D. 08C9XZZ

    REFERENCE: Bowie (2017b), pp 474–495

159. Percutaneous transposition left radial nerve
    A. 01X40ZZ
    B. 01S63ZZ
    C. 01Q63ZZ
    D. 01860ZZ

    REFERENCE: Bowie (2017b), pp 474–495

160. Right TRAM pedicle flap reconstruction status post mastectomy, muscle only open
    A. 0KXK0Z4
    B. 0KXF0ZZ
    C. 0KXK0Z6
    D. 0KXK0ZZ

    REFERENCE: Bowie (2017b), pp 474–495

161. Laparotomy with exploration and adhesiolysis of the left ureter
    A. 0TN74ZZ
    B. 0TN70ZZ
    C. 0TN73ZZ
    D. 0T8N0ZZ

    REFERENCE: Bowie (2017b), pp 474–495

162. Thoracentesis right pleural effusion
    A. 0W930ZZ
    B. 0W9C3ZZ
    C. 0W993ZZ
    D. 0W9C30Z

    REFERENCE: Bowie (2017b), pp 474–495

163. Percutaneous radiofrequency ablation of the left vocal cord
    A. 0CBV3ZZ
    B. 0CPS30Z
    C. 0C5V3ZZ
    D. 0CYV0ZZ

    REFERENCE: Bowie (2017b), pp 474–495

164. Excision malignant lesion upper lip
    A. 0CC00ZZ
    B. 0CQ00ZZ
    C. 0CT00ZZ
    D. 0CB0XZZ

    REFERENCE: Bowie (2017b), pp 474–495

165. Laparoscopic appendectomy
    A. 0DBJ4ZZ
    B. 0DTJ4ZZ
    C. 0DNJ4ZZ
    D. 0DTJ8ZZ

    REFERENCE: Bowie (2017b), pp 474–495

166. Nonexcisional debridement left heel ulcer
    A. 0HDNXZZ
    B. 0HBNXZZ
    C. 0HQNXZZ
    D. 0H5LXZZ

    REFERENCE: Bowie (2017b), pp 474–495

167. Transurethral cystoscopy with fragmentation of bladder neck stones
    A. 0TBC8ZZ
    B. 0TPC8ZZ
    C. 0TFC8ZZ
    D. 0TPB8ZZ

    REFERENCE: Bowie (2017b), pp 474–495

168. Laparoscopy with bilateral occlusion fallopian tubes using external clips
    A. 0UH843Z
    B. 0U774DZ
    C. 0UL74CZ
    D. 0UW84DZ

    REFERENCE: Bowie (2017b), pp 474–495

169. Incision scar contracture right knee
    A. 0H8KXZZ
    B. 0HBKXZZ
    C. 0HNKXZZ
    D. 0HQKXZZ

    REFERENCE: Bowie (2017b), pp 474–495

170. Colonoscopy with sigmoid colon polypectomy
    A. 0DFN8ZZ
    B. 0DBN8ZZ
    C. 0DCM8ZZ
    D. 0D5N8ZZ

    REFERENCE: Bowie (2017b), pp 474–495

171. A percutaneous fascia transfer to cover defect of the anterior neck
    A. 0JX53ZZ
    B. 0JX43ZZ
    C. 0JR43ZZ
    D. 0JQ43ZZ

    REFERENCE: Bowie (2017b), pp 474–495

172. Percutaneous embolization left uterine artery using coils
    A. 04VF3DZ
    B. 04QF3ZZ
    C. 04LF3DU
    D. 04LF3CZ

    REFERENCE: Bowie (2017b), pp 474–495

173. Endoscopic retrograde cholangiopancreatography with lithotripsy of the pancreatic duct
    A. 0FCD8ZZ
    B. 0FJD8ZZ
    C. 0FFD8ZZ
    D. 0FJD8ZZ

    REFERENCE: Bowie (2017b), pp 474–495

174. Open left neck total lymphadenectomy
    A. 07T20ZZ
    B. 07B20ZZ
    C. 07520ZZ
    D. 07C20ZZ

    REFERENCE: Bowie (2017b), pp 474–495

175. Percutaneous chest tube placement left pneumothorax
    A. 0W9B30Z
    B. 0W9D30Z
    C. 0W9B3ZZ
    D. 0W9D3ZZ

    REFERENCE: Bowie (2017b), pp 474–495

176. Laparoscopy with excision old sutures from the peritoneum
    A. 0DBW4ZZ
    B. 0DNW4ZZ
    C. 0DPW4JZ
    D. 0DPW4ZZ

    REFERENCE: Bowie (2017b), pp 474–495

177. Closed reduction with percutaneous internal fixation left femoral neck fracture
    A. 0QSC34Z
    B. 0QS734Z
    C. 0QS934Z
    D. 0QS7X4Z

    REFERENCE: Bowie (2017b), pp 474–495

178. Laparotomy and drain placement left lobe liver abscess
    A. 0F900ZZ
    B. 0F900ZZ
    C. 0F9030Z
    D. 0F9200Z

    REFERENCE: Bowie (2017b), pp 474–495

179. Hysteroscopy with D&C, diagnostic
    A. 0UDB8ZX
    B. 0UDN82X
    C. 0U898ZZ
    D. 0U798ZZ

    REFERENCE: Bowie (2017b), pp 474–495

180. Laparoscopy with destruction of endometriosis left ovary
    A. 0UB14ZZ
    B. 0UT14ZZ
    C. 0UP340Z
    D. 0U514ZZ

    REFERENCE: Bowie (2017b), pp 474–495

181. Distal interphalangeal (DIP) amputation left thumb
    A. 0X6M0Z3
    B. 0XGM022
    C. 0XGM021
    D. 0XGM020

    REFERENCE: Bowie (2017b), pp 474–495

182. Removal right index fingernail
    A. 0HDQXZZ
    B. 0HPRXZZ
    C. 0HNQXZZ
    D. 0HTQXZZ

    REFERENCE: Bowie (2017b), pp 474–495

183. Percutaneous drainage abdominal ascites
    A. 0W9G3ZZ
    B. 0W9F3ZZ
    C. 0W930ZZ
    D. 0W9H3ZZ

    REFERENCE: Bowie (2017b), pp 474–495

184. Transurethral endoscopic ablation right hepatic duct
    A. 0F558ZZ
    B. 0FB58ZZ
    C. 0FT04ZZ
    D. 0FP040Z

    REFERENCE: Bowie (2017b), pp 474–495

185. ERCP with balloon dilation cystic duct
    A. 0F784DZ
    B. 0F788ZZ
    C. 0F783DZ
    D. 0FT83ZZ

    REFERENCE: Bowie (2017b), pp 474–495

186. Stopping of postoperative tonsillectomy hemorrhaging is coded to which root operation?
    A. Revision   C. Control
    B. Repair   D. Change

    REFERENCE: Bowie (2017b), pp 474–481

187. In the Medical Surgical Section, the third character position represents?
    A. Body System   C. Root Operation
    B. Approach   D. Qualifier

    REFERENCE: Bowie (2017b), pp 474–481

188. In the Medical Surgical Section, the second character position represents?
    A. Body System   C. Qualifier
    B. Body Part   D. Approach

    REFERENCE: Bowie (2017b), pp 475–476

189. In the Medical Surgical Section, the seventh character position represents?
    A. Qualifier   C. Body System
    B. Device   D. Approach

    REFERENCE: Bowie (2017b), p 492

190 In the Medical Surgical Section, the fourth character position represents?
A. Section   C. Body System
B. Body Part   D. Approach

REFERENCE: Bowie (2017b), p 486

191. A complete redo of a knee replacement requiring a new prosthesis is coded to which root operation(s)?
A. Removal, Replacement   C. Change
B. Replacement   D. Insertion

REFERENCE: Bowie (2017b), pp 477–481

192. Reposition of a malfunctioning pacemaker lead is coded to which root operation?
A. Change   C. Replacement
B. Revision   D. Reposition

REFERENCE: Bowie (2017b), pp 477–481

193. Dilation of the ureter with insertion of a stent is coded to which root operation?
A. Insertion   C. Supplemental
B. Dilation   D. Inspection

REFERENCE: Bowie (2017b), pp 477–481

194. ERCP. Identify the approach.
A. External   C. Percutaneous
B. Endoscopic   D. Open

REFERENCE: Bowie (2017b), p 489

195. Percutaneous insertion nephrostomy tube. Identify the approach.
A. External   C. Percutaneous
B. Open   D. Percutaneous Endoscopic

REFERENCE: Bowie (2017b), p 489

196. Fulguration of anal warts. Identify the approach.
A. Percutaneous   C. Destruction
B. External   D. Open

REFERENCE: Bowie (2017b), p 489

197. Percutaneous placement of pacemaker lead. Identify the approach.
A. External
B. Via Natural or Artificial Opening
C. Percutaneous Endoscopic
D. Percutaneous

REFERENCE: Bowie (2017b), p 489

198. ESWL left ureter. Identify the approach.
A. Percutaneous
B. Via Natural or Artificial Opening
C. External
D. Open

REFERENCE: Bowie (2017b), p 489

199. Laparoscopy with destruction of endometriosis. Identify the approach.
    A. Percutaneous
    B. Via Natural or Artificial Opening
    C. Percutaneous Endoscopic
    D. External

    REFERENCE: Bowie (2017b), p 489
                   Kuehn, pp 43–44

200. Colonoscopy. Identify the approach.
    A. Percutaneous
    B. Via Natural or Artificial Opening Endoscopic
    C. Percutaneous Endoscopic
    D. External

    REFERENCE: Bowie (2017b), p 489
                   Kuehn, pp 42–44

Use this information to answer questions 201–203.
Present on admission (POA) guidelines were established to identify and report diagnoses that are present at the time of a patient's admission. The reporting options for each ICD-10-CM code are
    A. Y = Yes
    B. N = No
    C. U = Unknown
    D. W = Clinically Undetermined
    E. Unreported/Not Used (Exempt from POA) Reporting

201. The physician explicitly documents that a condition is not present at the time of admission.
    A. Y = Yes
    B. N = No
    C. U = Unknown
    D. W = Clinically Undetermined
    E. Unreported/Not Used (Exempt from POA) Reporting

    REFERENCE: Kuehn, p 85

202. The physician documents that the patient has diabetes that was diagnosed prior to admission.
    A. Y = Yes
    B. N = No
    C. U = Unknown
    D. W = Clinically Undetermined
    E. Unreported/Not Used (Exempt from POA) Reporting

    REFERENCE: Kuehn, p 85

203. The medical record documentation is unclear as to whether the condition was present on admission.
    A. Y = Yes
    B. N = No
    C. U = Unknown
    D. W = Clinically Undetermined
    E. Unreported/Not Used (Exempt from POA) Reporting
    REFERENCE: Kuehn, p 85

Answer Key for ICD-10-CM/PCS Coding

1.	D	52.	A	103.	C	154.	D
2.	B	53.	C	104.	B	155.	A
3.	A	54.	B	105.	A	156.	A
4.	C	55.	A	106.	C	157.	C
5.	D	56.	A	107.	D	158.	D
6.	C	57.	D	108.	C	159.	B
7.	D	58.	C	109.	D	160.	C
8.	C	59.	C	110.	A	161.	B
9.	A	60.	A	111.	B	162.	C
10.	B	61.	A	112.	B	163.	C
11.	C	62.	C	113.	D	164.	D
12.	B	63.	B	114.	C	165	B
13.	A	64.	D	115.	B	166.	A
14.	D	65.	B	116.	A	167.	C
15.	B	66.	D	117.	A	168.	C
16.	A	67.	B	118.	D	169.	C
17.	C	68.	D	119.	D	170.	B
18.	B	69.	A	120.	D	171.	B
19.	D	70.	B	121.	A	172.	C
20.	B	71.	A	122.	B	173.	C
21.	A	72.	C	123.	D	174.	A
22.	D	73.	B	124.	B	175.	A
23.	B	74.	D	125.	D	176.	C
24.	D	75.	C	126.	A	177.	B
25.	D	76.	D	127.	A	178.	D
26.	B	77.	C	128.	C	179.	A
27.	D	78.	B	129.	A	180.	D
28.	C	79.	C	130.	C	181.	A
29.	B	80.	D	131.	B	182.	A
30.	D	81.	B	132.	C	183.	A
31.	C	82.	C	133.	D	184.	A
32.	B	83.	A	134.	A	185.	B
33.	A	84.	B	135.	B	186.	C
34.	C	85.	D	136.	C	187.	C
35.	B	86.	A	137.	A	188.	A
36.	A	87.	A	138.	C	189.	A
37.	D	88.	D	139.	A	190.	B
38.	C	89.	C	140.	C	191.	A
39.	D	90.	A	141.	A	192.	B
40.	A	91.	C	142.	C	193.	A
41.	B	92.	B	143.	C	194.	B
42.	A	93.	A	144.	A	195.	C
43.	D	94.	C	145.	B	196.	B
44.	A	95.	D	146.	A	197.	D
45.	B	96.	C	147.	D	198.	C
46.	A	97.	B	148.	A	199.	C
47.	C	98.	A	149.	A	200.	B
48.	B	99.	D	150.	D	201.	B
49.	A	100.	C	151.	A	202.	A
50.	D	101.	A	152.	A	203.	C
51.	C	102.	D	153.	C		

REFERENCES

Bowie, M. J. (2017b). *Understanding ICD-10-CM and ICD-10-PCS: A worktext* (3rd ed.). Clifton Park, NY: Cengage Learning.

Kuehn, L. M. and Jorwic, T. M. (2017). *ICD-10-PCS: An applied approach* (2017 ed.). Chicago: American Health Information Management Association (AHIMA).

Schraffenberger, L. A. (2016). *Basic ICD-10-CM and ICD-10-PCS coding, 2016.* American Health Information Management Association (AHIMA). Chicago, IL.

ICD-10-CM/PCS Chapter Competencies

Question	CCA Domain
1–203	1

VII. CPT Coding

Marissa Lajaunie, MBA, RHIA

Evaluation and Management

1. Patient is admitted to the hospital with acute abdominal pain. The attending medical physician requests a surgical consult. The consultant agrees to see the patient and conducts a comprehensive history and physical examination. To rule out pancreatitis, the physician orders lab work, along with an ultrasound of the gallbladder and an abdominal x-ray. Due to the various diagnosis possibilities and the tests reviewed, a moderate medical decision was made.

   A. 99244
   B. 99222
   C. 99254
   D. 99204

   REFERENCE: AMA, 2017
   Bowie (2017a), pp 66–67
   Green, pp 548–554
   Johnson and Linker, pp 136–137
   Kuehn, pp 60–61
   Smith (2016), p 208

2. An established patient returns to the physician's office for follow-up on his hypertension and diabetes. The physician takes the blood pressure and references the patient's last three glucose tests. The patient is still running above-normal glucose levels, so the physician decides to adjust the patient's insulin. An expanded history was taken and a physical examination was performed.

   A. 99213
   B. 99232
   C. 99202
   D. 99214

   REFERENCE: AMA, 2017
   Bowie (2017a), p 45
   Green, pp 541–543
   Johnson and Linker, p 133
   Kuehn, pp 54–56
   Smith (2016), p 206

3. Patient arrives in the emergency room via a medical helicopter. The patient has sustained multiple life-threatening injuries due to a multiple car accident. The patient goes into cardiac arrest 10 minutes after arrival. An hour and 30 minutes of critical care time is spent trying to stabilize the patient. Code only critical care.

   A. 99285, 99288, 99291
   B. 99291, 99292
   C. 99291, 99292, 99285
   D. 99282

   REFERENCE: AMA, 2017
   Bowie (2017a), pp 68–69
   Green, pp 573–576
   Johnson and Linker, pp 138–140
   Kuehn, p 63
   Smith (2016), p 209

4. The physician provided services to a new patient who was in a rest home for an ulcerative sore on the hip. A problem-focused history and physical examination were performed and a straightforward medical decision was made.
    A. 99304   C. 99324
    B. 99325   D. 99334
REFERENCE: AMA, 2017
               Bowie (2017a), p 74
               Green, pp 577–578
               Johnson and Linker, p 142
               Kuehn, pp 65–66
               Smith (2016), p 210

5. A doctor provides critical care services in the emergency department for a patient in respiratory failure. He initiates ventilator management and spends an hour and 10 minutes providing critical care for this patient. Code only critical care.
    A. 99281, 99291, 99292, 94002   C. 99291, 94002
    B. 99291, 99292, 94002   D. 99291
REFERENCE: AMA, 2017
               Bowie (2017a), pp 68–69
               Green, pp 573–576
               Johnson and Linker, pp 138–140
               Kuehn, p 63
               Smith (2016), p 209

6. Services were provided to a patient in the emergency room after the patient twisted her ankle stepping down from a curb. The emergency room physician ordered x-rays of the ankle, which came back negative for a fracture. A problem-focused history and physical examination were performed and ankle strapping was applied. A prescription for pain was given to the patient. Code the emergency room visit only.
    A. 99201   C. 99281
    B. 99282   D. 99211
REFERENCE: AMA, 2017
               Bowie (2017a), pp 67–68
               Green, pp 572–573
               Johnson and Linker, p 138
               Kuehn, p 62
               Smith (2016), pp 208–209

7. An established patient was seen in her primary physician's office. The patient fell at home and came to the physician's office for an examination. Due to a possible concussion, the patient was sent to the hospital to be admitted as an observation patient. A detailed history and physical examination were performed and the medical decision was low complexity. The patient stayed overnight and was discharged the next afternoon.
    A. 99214, 99234   C. 99218
    B. 99214, 99218, 99217   D. 99218, 99217
REFERENCE: AMA, 2017
               Bowie (2017a), pp 63–64
               Green, pp 563–564
               Johnson and Linker, pp 133–134
               Kuehn, pp 56–57
               Smith (2016), p 207

8. An out-of-town patient presents to a walk-in clinic to have a prescription refilled for a nonsteroidal anti-inflammatory drug. The physician performs a problem-focused history and physical examination with a straightforward decision.
   A. 99211
   B. 99201
   C. 99212
   D. 99202

REFERENCE: AMA, 2017
   Bowie (2017a), pp 41–42
   Green, pp 541–551
   Johnson and Linker, p 133
   Keuhn, pp 54–56
   Smith (2016), p 206

9. An office consultation is performed for a postmenopausal woman who is complaining of spotting in the past 6 months with right lower-quadrant tenderness. A detailed history and physical examination were performed with a low-complexity medical decision.
   A. 99242
   B. 99243
   C. 99253
   D. 99254

REFERENCE: AMA, 2017
   Bowie (2017a), 65–67
   Green, pp 541–551
   Johnson and Linker, pp 136–137
   Kuehn, pp 60–61
   Smith (2016), pp 207–208

Anesthesia

10. Code anesthesia for upper abdominal ventral hernia repair.
    A. 00832
    B. 00750
    C. 00752
    D. 00830

REFERENCE: AMA, 2017
   Bowie (2017a), pp 93–96
   Green, pp 596–604, 619
   Johnson and Linker, pp 157–159
   Kuehn, pp 86–87
   Smith (2016), pp 245–250

11. Code anesthesia for total hip replacement.
    A. 01210
    B. 01402
    C. 01230
    D. 01214

REFERENCE: AMA, 2017
   Bowie (2017a), pp 93–96
   Green, pp 596–604, 619
   Kuehn, pp 86–87
   Smith (2016), pp 245–250

12. Code anesthesia for vaginal hysterectomy.
    A. 00846
    B. 00944
    C. 00840
    D. 01963

REFERENCE: AMA, 2017
             Green, pp 596–604, 619
             Kuehn, pp 86–87
             Smith (2016), pp 245–250

13. Code anesthesia for placement of vascular shunt in forearm.
    A. 01844
    B. 01850
    C. 00532
    D. 01840

REFERENCE: AMA, 2017
             Bowie (2017a), pp 93–96
             Green, pp 596–604, 621
             Smith (2016), pp 245–250

14. Code anesthesia for decortication of left lung.
    A. 01638
    B. 00542
    C. 00546
    D. 00500

REFERENCE: AMA, 2017
             Bowie (2017a), p 96
             Green, pp 596–604, 617
             Kuehn, pp 86–87
             Smith (2016), pp 245–250

15. Code anesthesia for total shoulder replacement.
    A. 01760
    B. 01630
    C. 01402
    D. 01638

REFERENCE: AMA, 2017
             Bowie (2017a), pp 93–96
             Green, pp 596–604, 621
             Kuehn, pp 86–87
             Smith (2016), pp 245–250

16. Code anesthesia for cesarean section.
    A. 00840
    B. 01961
    C. 00940
    D. 01960

REFERENCE: AMA, 2017
             Bowie (2017a), pp 93–96
             Green, pp 596–604, 623
             Kuehn, pp 86–87
             Smith (2016), pp 245–250

17. Code anesthesia for procedures on bony pelvis.
    A. 00400   C. 01120
    B. 01170   D. 01190

REFERENCE: AMA, 2017
                Bowie (2017a), pp 93–96
                Green, pp 596–604, 620
                Kuehn, pp 86–87
                Smith (2016), pp 245–250

18. Code anesthesia for corneal transplant.
    A. 00144   C. 00147
    B. 00140   D. 00190

REFERENCE: AMA, 2017
                Bowie (2017a), pp 93–96
                Green, pp 596–604, 620
                Kuehn, pp 86–87
                Smith (2016), pp 245–250

Surgery—Integumentary System

19. Patient presents to the hospital for skin grafts due to previous third-degree burns. The burn eschar of the back was removed. Once the eschar was removed, the defect size measured 10 cm x 10 cm. A skin graft from a donor bank was placed onto the defect and sewn into place as a temporary wound closure.
    A. 15002, 15130   C. 15002, 15200
    B. 15002, 15271, 15272, 15272, 15272   D. 15002, 15273

REFERENCE: AMA, 2017
                Bowie (2017a), 127–128
                Green, pp 662–663
                Smith (2016), pp 73–76
                Keuhn, pp 114–116
                Smith (2016), pp 73–76

20. Patient presents to the operating room for excision of a 4.5-cm malignant melanoma of the left forearm. A 6 cm x 6 cm rotation flap was created for closure.
    A. 14021   C. 14301
    B. 11606, 14020   D. 11606, 15100

REFERENCE: AMA, 2017
                Bowie (2017a), p 126
                Green, pp 651–654, 661
                Kuehn, pp 110–111, 116
                Smith (2011), pp 26–27
                Smith (2016), pp 61–63, 76–77

21. Female patient has a percutaneous needle biopsy of the left breast lesion in the lower outer quadrant. Following the biopsy frozen section results, the physician followed this with an excisional removal of the same lesion.
    A. 19100, 19125
    B. 19100, 19120-LT
    C. 19120-LT
    D. 19100, 19120, 19120

REFERENCE: AMA, 2017
               Bowie (2017a), p 127
               Green, pp 651–654, 669–672
               Smith (2011), p 30
               Smith (2016), pp 79–80

22. Patient presents to the emergency room with lacerations of right lower leg that involved the fascia. Lacerations measured 5 cm and 2.7 cm.
    A. 11406, 11403
    B. 12034
    C. 12032, 12031
    D. 12032

REFERENCE: AMA, 2017
               Bowie (2017a), p 123
               Green, pp 658–660
               Smith (2011), p 21
               Smith (2016), pp 67–69

23. A 10-square-centimeter epidermal autograft to the face from the back.
    A. 15110
    B. 15115
    C. 15110, 15115
    D. 15120

REFERENCE: AMA, 2017
               Bowie (2017a), p 127
               Green, p 661
               Smith (2011), p 27
               Smith (2016), pp 74–76

24. Nonhuman graft for temporary wound closure. Patient has a 5-cm defect on the scalp.
    A. 15275, 15276
    B. 15271
    C. 15275
    D. 15271, 15272

REFERENCE: AMA, 2017
               Green, p 661

25. Patient is admitted for a blepharoplasty of the left lower eyelid and a repair for a tarsal strip of the left upper lid.
    A. 67917-E1, 15822-E2
    B. 67917-E1, 15820-E2
    C. 67917-E1
    D. 67917-E1, 15823-E2

REFERENCE: AMA, 2017
               Bowie (2017a), pp 133, 384–385
               Green, p 665
               Smith (2011), p 165

26. Patient presents to the emergency room with lacerations sustained in an automobile accident. Repairs of the 3.3-cm skin laceration of the left leg that involved the fascia, 2.5-cm and 3-cm lacerations of the left arm involving the fascia, and 2.7 cm of the left foot, which required simple sutures, were performed. Sterile dressings were applied.
   A. 12032, 12032-59, 12031-59, 12002-59   C. 12034, 12002-59
   B. 12002, 12002-59   D. 13151, 12032-59, 12032-59, 12001-59

REFERENCE: AMA, 2017
              Bowie (2017a), pp 123–125
              Green, pp 658–660
              Smith (2011), p 24
              Smith (2016), pp 67–69

27. Patient presents to the operating room for excision of three lesions. The 1.5-cm and 2-cm lesions of the back were excised with one excision. The 0.5-cm lesion of the hand was excised. The pathology report identified both back lesions as squamous cell carcinoma. The hand lesion was identified as seborrheic keratosis.
   A. 11604, 11420   C. 11403, 11642, 11642
   B. 11402, 11420, 11403   D. 11602, 11402

REFERENCE: AMA, 2017
              Bowie (2017a), p 120
              Green, pp 651–654
              Smith (2011), pp 21–22
              Smith (2016), pp 62–64

28. Patient presents to the radiology department where a fine-needle aspiration of the breast is performed utilizing computed tomography.
   A. 19085, 77012   C. 19125
   B. 19100   D. 10022, 77012

REFERENCE: AMA, 2017
              Bowie (2017a), pp 115–116, 412
              Green, pp 669, 887–888
              Smith (2011), p 29

29. Patient presents to the operating room where a 3.2-cm malignant lesion of the shoulder was excised and repaired with simple sutures. A 2-cm benign lesion of the cheek was excised and was repaired with a rotation skin graft.
   A. 11604, 11442, 14040, 12001   C. 15002, 15120
   B. 14040, 11604   D. 17264, 17000, 12001

REFERENCE: AMA, 2017
              Bowie (2017a), pp 120–121, 126
              Green, pp 651–654, 660–661
              Smith (2011), pp 26–27
              Smith (2016), pp 61–63, 73–77

30. Patient was admitted to the hospital for removal of excessive tissue due to massive weight loss. Liposuction of the abdomen and bilateral thighs was performed.
    A. 15830
    B. 15830, 15833, 15833
    C. 15877, 15879-50
    D. 15839

REFERENCE: AMA, 2017
                   Bowie (2017a), p 133

Surgery—Musculoskeletal

31. Patient presents to the hospital with ulcer of the right foot. Patient is taken to the operating room where a revision of the right metatarsal head is performed.
    A. 28104-RT
    B. 28111-RT
    C. 28288-RT
    D. 28899-RT

REFERENCE: AMA, 2017
                   Green, pp 680–690, 701

32. Patient presents to the emergency room following a fall. X-rays were ordered for the lower leg and results showed a fracture of the proximal left tibia. The emergency room physician performed a closed manipulation of the fracture with skeletal traction.
    A. 27532-LT
    B. 27536-LT
    C. 27530-LT
    D. 27524-LT

REFERENCE: AMA, 2017
                   Green, pp 680–689, 701
                   Smith (2011), pp 42–44
                   Smith (2016), pp 85–86

33. Trauma patient was rushed to the operating room with multiple injuries. Open reduction with internal fixation of intertrochanteric femoral fracture, and open reduction of the tibial and fibula shaft with internal fixation was performed.
    A. 27245, 27759
    B. 20690
    C. 27248, 27756
    D. 27244, 27758

REFERENCE: AMA, 2017
                   Green, pp 680–689, 699–701
                   Smith (2011), pp 42–44
                   Smith (2016), pp 85–86

34. Open I&D of a deep abscess of the cervical spine.
    A. 22010
    B. 22015
    C. 10060
    D. 10140

REFERENCE: AMA, 2017
                   Green, pp 692–694

35. Patient presents to the emergency room following an assault. Examination of the patient reveals blunt trauma to the face. Radiology reports that the patient suffers from a fracture to the frontal skull and a blow-out fracture of the orbital floor. Patient is admitted and taken to the operating room where a periorbital approach to the orbital fracture is employed and an implant is inserted.

A. 21407, 21275   C. 21390

B. 21387, 61330   D. 61340, 21401

REFERENCE: AMA, 2017
               Green, pp 689–690
               Smith (2011), pp 42–44
               Smith (2016), pp 85–86

36. Patient presents with a traumatic partial amputation of the second, third, and fourth fingers on the right hand. Patient was taken to the operating room where completion of the amputation of three fingers was performed with direct closure.

A. 26910-F6, 26910-F7, 26910-F8   C. 26951-F6, 26951-F7, 26951-F8

B. 26843-RT   D. 26550-RT

REFERENCE: AMA, 2017
               Green, p 698

37. Patient is brought to the emergency room following a shark attack. The paramedics have the patient's amputated foot. The patient is taken directly to the operating room to reattach the patient's foot.

A. 28800   C. 28110

B. 28200, 28208   D. 20838

REFERENCE: AMA, 2017
               Green, p 701

38. Patient presents to the hospital with a right index trigger finger. Release of the trigger finger was performed.

A. 26060-F7   C. 26170-F6

B. 26055-F6   D. 26110

REFERENCE: AMA, 2017
               Green, p 698

39. Patient had been diagnosed with a bunion. Patient was taken to the operating room where a simple resection of the base of the proximal phalanx along with the medial eminence was performed. Kirschner wire was placed to hold the joint in place.

A. 28292   C. 28293

B. 28290   D. 28294

REFERENCE: AMA, 2017
               Green, p 701
               Smith (2011), pp 47–49

Surgery—Respiratory

40. Patient has a bronchoscopy with endobronchial biopsies of three sites.
    A. 31625, 31625, 31625
    B. 31625
    C. 31622, 31625
    D. 31622, 31625, 31625, 31625

REFERENCE: AMA, 2017
              Bowie (2017a), pp 188–189
              Green, pp 713–714
              Smith (2011), p 61
              Smith (2016), pp 97–98

41. Patient presents to the surgical unit and undergoes unilateral nasal endoscopy, partial ethmoidectomy, and maxillary antrostomy.
    A. 31254, 31256-51
    B. 31201, 31225-51
    C. 31290, 31267-51
    D. 31233, 31231-51

REFERENCE: AMA, 2017
              Bowie (2017a), pp 83–84
              Green, pp 706–710
              Smith (2011), p 59
              Smith (2016), pp 92–93

42. Patient has been diagnosed with metastatic laryngeal carcinoma. Patient underwent subtotal supraglottic laryngectomy with radical neck dissection.
    A. 31540
    B. 31367
    C. 31365
    D. 31368

REFERENCE: AMA, 2017
              Green, pp 711–712

43. Patient was involved in an accident and has been sent to the hospital. During transport the patient develops breathing problems and, upon arrival at the hospital, an emergency transtracheal tracheostomy was performed. Following various x-rays, the patient was diagnosed with traumatic pneumothorax. A thoracentesis with insertion of tube was performed.
    A. 31603, 31612
    B. 31610, 32555
    C. 31603, 32554
    D. 31603, 32555

REFERENCE: AMA, 2017
              Green, pp 713–714

44. Patient with laryngeal cancer has a tracheoesophageal fistula created and has a voicebox inserted.
    A. 31611
    B. 31580
    C. 31395
    D. 31502

REFERENCE: AMA, 2017
              Green, pp 713–714

45. Upper lobectomy of the right lung with repair of the bronchus.
   A. 32480
   B. 32486
   C. 32320
   D. 32480, 32501

REFERENCE: AMA, 2017
              Bowie (2017a), pp 191–192
              Green, pp 715–718
              Smith (2011), pp 61–62

46. Patient with a deviated nasal septum that was repaired by septoplasty.
   A. 30400
   B. 30620
   C. 30520
   D. 30630

REFERENCE: AMA, 2017
              Green, pp 706–708

47. Lye burn of the larynx repaired by laryngoplasty.
   A. 31599
   B. 16020
   C. 31360
   D. 31540

REFERENCE: AMA, 2017
              Green, pp 711–712

48. Bronchoscopy with multiple transbronchial right upper and right lower lobe lung biopsy with fluoroscopic guidance.
   A. 31628-RT, 76000-RT
   B. 31717-RT, 31632-RT
   C. 32405-RT
   D. 31628-RT, 31632-RT

REFERENCE: AMA, 2017
              Bowie (2017a), pp 188–189
              Green, pp 713–716
              Smith (2011), p 61
              Smith (2016), pp 97–98

49. Patient has recurrent spontaneous pneumothorax, which has resulted in a chemical pleurodesis by thoracoscopy.
   A. 32650
   B. 32310, 32601
   C. 32601
   D. 32960

REFERENCE: AMA, 2017
              Green, pp 716–717

50. Laryngoscopic stripping of vocal cords for leukoplakia of the vocal cords.
   A. 31535
   B. 31540
   C. 31541
   D. 31570

REFERENCE: AMA, 2017
              Bowie (2017a), pp 186–187
              Green, pp 711–712
              Smith (2016), pp 95–96

Surgery—Cardiovascular System

51. Patient returns to the operating room following open-heart bypass for exploration of blood vessel to control postoperative bleeding in the chest.
    A. 35820
    B. 20101
    C. 35761
    D. 35905

REFERENCE: AMA, 2017
               Green, p 752

52. Patient undergoes construction of apical aortic conduit with an insertion of a single-ventricle ventricular assist device.
    A. 33404
    B. 33975
    C. 33977
    D. 33975, 33404

REFERENCE: AMA, 2017
               Green, p 744

53. Patient presents to the operating room where a CABG x 3 is performed using the mammary artery and two sections of the saphenous vein.
    A. 33534, 33511
    B. 33534, 33518, 33511
    C. 33535
    D. 33533, 33518

REFERENCE: AMA, 2017
               Bowie (2017a), pp 212–213
               Green, p 739
               Smith (2011), pp 74–75
               Smith (2016), pp 105–106

54. Patient complains of recurrent syncope following carotid thromboendarterectomy. Patient returns 2 weeks after initial surgery and undergoes repeat carotid thromboendarterectomy.
    A. 33510
    B. 35301
    C. 35201
    D. 35301, 35390

REFERENCE: AMA, 2017
               Green, p 749
               Smith (2011), pp 78–79

55. Patient is admitted with alcohol cirrhosis and has a TIPS procedure performed.
    A. 35476, 36011, 36481
    B. 37183
    C. 37182
    D. 37140

REFERENCE: AMA, 2017
               Green, pp 757–758

56. Eighty-year-old patient has carcinoma and presents to the operating room for placement of a tunneled implantable centrally inserted venous access port.
    A. 36558
    B. 36571
    C. 36561
    D. 36481

REFERENCE: AMA, 2017
               Green, pp 755–757
               Smith (2011), pp 79–80
               Smith (2016), pp 110–112

57. Patient presents to the operating room and undergoes an endovascular repair of an infrarenal abdominal aortic aneurysm utilizing a unibody bifurcated prosthesis.
   A. 34800, 34813
   B. 34802
   C. 34804
   D. 35081

REFERENCE: AMA, 2017
            Bowie (2017a), pp 217–218
            Green, p 738
            Smith (2011), pp 76–77

58. The physician punctures the left common femoral to examine the right common iliac.
   A. 36245
   B. 36246
   C. 36247
   D. 36140

REFERENCE: AMA, 2017
            Bowie (2017a), pp 223–224
            Green, p 754

59. Patient has a history of PVD for many years and experiences chest pains. The patient underwent Doppler evaluation, which showed a common femoral DVT. Patient is now admitted for thromboendarterectomy.
   A. 35371
   B. 35372
   C. 37224
   D. 35256

REFERENCE: AMA, 2017
            Smith (2011), pp 78–79

60. Patient undergoes percutaneous transluminal iliac artery balloon angioplasty.
   A. 37228
   B. 37220
   C. 37222
   D. 37224

REFERENCE: AMA, 2017
            Green, p 750
            Smith (2016), pp 112–113

Surgery—Hemic and Lymphatic Systems, Mediastinum, and Diaphragm

61. Patient has breast carcinoma and is now undergoing sentinel node biopsy. Patient was injected for sentinel node identification and two deep axillary lymph nodes showed up intensely. These two lymph nodes were completely excised. Path report was positive for metastatic carcinoma.
   A. 38525, 38790
   B. 38589
   C. 38308, 38790
   D. 38525, 38792

REFERENCE: AMA, 2017
            Green, pp 761–764

62. Patient has a history of hiatal hernia for many years, which has progressively gotten worse. The decision to repair the hernia was made and the patient was sent to the operating room where the repair took place via the thorax and abdomen.
   A. 39545
   B. 43336
   C. 43332
   D. 39503

REFERENCE: AMA, 2017
            Green, pp 772–773

63. Patient has a bone marrow aspiration of the iliac crest and of the tibia.
    A. 38220, 38220-59
    B. 38221
    C. 38230
    D. 38220

REFERENCE: AMA, 2017
            Bowie (2017a), pp 235, 237
            Green, p 763

64. Trauma patient is rushed to the operating room with multiple injuries. The patient had his spleen removed due to a massive rupture, with repair of the lacerated diaphragm.
    A. 38115, 39501
    B. 38120, 39599
    C. 38102, 39540
    D. 38100, 39501

REFERENCE: AMA, 2017
            Green, pp 762, 772–773

65. Laparoscopic retroperitoneal lymph node biopsy.
    A. 38570
    B. 38780
    C. 49323
    D. 38589

REFERENCE: AMA, 2017
            Green, pp 761–764

66. Excision of mediastinal cyst.
    A. 11400
    B. 39200
    C. 17000
    D. 39400

REFERENCE: AMA, 2017
            Bowie (2017a), p 246

67. Patient diagnosed with cystic hygroma of the axilla, which was excised.
    A. 38555
    B. 11400
    C. 38550
    D. 38300

REFERENCE: AMA, 2017
            Bowie (2017a), p 237

68. Laparoscopy with multiple biopsies of retroperitoneal lymph nodes.
    A. 38570
    B. 38571
    C. 38570-22
    D. 38572

REFERENCE: AMA, 2017
            Green, pp 761–764

69. Cannulation of the thoracic duct.
    A. 38794
    B. 36810
    C. 36260
    D. 38999

REFERENCE: AMA, 2017
            Bowie (2017a), p 239

70. Patient has been on the bone marrow transplant recipient list for 3 months. A perfect match was made and the patient came in and received a peripheral stem cell transplant.
    A. 38242
    B. 38230
    C. 38241
    D. 38240

REFERENCE: AMA, 2017
              Green, p 763

Surgery—Digestive System

71. Laparoscopic gastric banding.
    A. 43842
    B. 43843
    C. 43770
    D. 43771

REFERENCE: AMA, 2017
              Green, pp 785–786

72. Patient presents with a history of upper abdominal pain. Cholangiogram was negative and patient was sent to the hospital for ERCP. During the procedure the sphincter was incised and a stent was placed for drainage.
    A. 43260, 43262, 43264
    B. 43262
    C. 43275
    D. 43274

REFERENCE: AMA, 2017
              Smith (2011), pp 92–93

73. Patient presents to the emergency room with right lower abdominal pains. Emergency room physician suspects possible appendicitis. Patient was taken to the operating room where a laparoscopic appendectomy was performed. Pathology report was negative for appendicitis.
    A. 44950
    B. 44950, 49320
    C. 44970
    D. 44979

REFERENCE: AMA, 2017
              Bowie (2017a), p 271
              Green, p 790
              Smith (2011), p 97

74. Morbidly obese patient comes in for vertical banding of the stomach.
    A. 43848
    B. 43659
    C. 43842
    D. 43999

REFERENCE: AMA, 2017
              Green, pp 785–786

75. Patient underwent anoscopy followed by colonoscopy. The physician examined the colon to 60 cm.
    A. 46600, 45378
    B. 46600, 45378-59
    C. 45378
    D. 45999

REFERENCE: AMA, 2017
              Green, pp 791–792
              Smith (2011), p 93
              Smith (2016), pp 119–120

76. Injection snoreplasty for treatment of palatal snoring.
    A. 42299
    B. 42145
    C. 42999
    D. 40899

REFERENCE: AMA, 2017
               Green, pp 778–779

77. Patient arrives to the hospital and has a Nissen fundoplasty done laparoscopically.
    A. 43410
    B. 43415
    C. 43502
    D. 43280

REFERENCE: AMA, 2017
               Green, pp 785–786
               Smith (2011), p 97

78. Young child presents with cleft lip and cleft palate. This is the first attempt of repair, which includes major revision of the cleft palate and unilateral cleft lip repair.
    A. 42200, 40701
    B. 42225, 40700
    C. 42220, 40720
    D. 42215, 40700

REFERENCE: AMA, 2017
               Green, pp 779–778

79. Patient has a history of chronic alcohol abuse with portal hypertension. Patient has been vomiting blood for the past 3 days and presented to his physician's office. Patient was sent to the hospital for evaluation and an EGD was performed. Biopsy findings showed gastritis, esophagitis, and bleeding esophageal varices, which were injected with sclerosing solution.
    A. 43235, 43244, 43204
    B. 43239, 43244
    C. 43239, 43243
    D. 43239, 43243, 43204

REFERENCE: AMA, 2017
               Bowie (2017a), pp 260–261
               Green, pp 782–784
               Smith (2011), p 92
               Smith (2016), pp 116–118

Surgery—Urinary System

80. Patient is admitted for contact laser vaporization of the prostate. The physician performed a TURP and transurethral resection of the bladder neck at the same time.
    A. 52648
    B. 52648, 52450, 52500
    C. 52450, 53500
    D. 52648, 52450

REFERENCE: AMA, 2017
               Bowie (2017a), p 299
               Green, pp 807–808
               Smith (2011), p 122

81. Patient comes to the hospital with a history of right flank pain. Urine tests are negative. Radiology examination reveals that the patient has renal cysts. Patient is now admitted for laparoscopic ablation of the cysts.
    A. 50541   C. 50280
    B. 50390   D. 50920

REFERENCE: AMA, 2017
              Bowie (2017a), pp 292–293
              Green, pp 800–802

82. Patient has extensive bladder cancer. She underwent a complete cystectomy with bilateral pelvic lymphadenectomy and creation of ureteroileal conduit.
    A. 51575, 50820   C. 51595
    B. 50825, 51570, 38770   D. 51550, 38770

REFERENCE: AMA, 2017
              Bowie (2017a), p 296

83. Patient presents to the hospital with right ureteral calculus. Patient is taken to the operating room where a cystoscopy with ureteroscopy is performed to remove the calculus.
    A. 52353   C. 51065
    B. 52310   D. 52352

REFERENCE: AMA, 2017
              Green, pp 803–806
              Smith (2011), pp 111–112
              Smith (2016), p 132

84. Female with 6 months of stress incontinence. Outpatient therapies are not working and the patient decides to have the problem fixed. Laparoscopic urethral suspension was completed.
    A. 51992   C. 51840
    B. 51990   D. 51845

REFERENCE: AMA, 2017
              Green, p 803

85. Patient has ovarian vein syndrome and has ureterolysis performed.
    A. 58679   C. 52351
    B. 58660   D. 50722

REFERENCE: AMA, 2017
              Green, p 803

86. Male patient has been diagnosed with benign prostatic hypertrophy and undergoes a transurethral destruction of the prostate by radiofrequency thermotherapy.
    A. 52648   C. 52601
    B. 53852   D. 53850

REFERENCE: AMA, 2017
              Bowie (2017a), p 300

87. Nephrectomy with resection of half of the ureter.
    A. 50220   C. 50230, 50650
    B. 50234   D. 50546

REFERENCE: AMA, 2017
                Green, pp 801–803

88. Male with urinary incontinence. Sling procedure was performed 6 months ago and now the patient has returned for a revision of the sling procedure.
    A. 53449   C. 53440
    B. 53442   D. 53431

REFERENCE: AMA, 2017
                Bowie (2017a), p 300

89. Excision of 2.5-cm bladder tumor with cystoscopy.
    A. 51550   C. 52235
    B. 51530   D. 51060

REFERENCE: AMA, 2017
                Bowie (2017a), p 299
                Green, pp 804–806
                Smith (2016), p 132

90. Closure of ureterocutaneous fistula.
    A. 50930   C. 57310
    B. 50920   D. 50520

REFERENCE: AMA, 2017
                Green, p 803

Surgery—Male Genital System

91. Removal of nephrostomy tube with fluoroscopic guidance.
    A. 50387   C. 99212
    B. 50389   D. 99213

REFERENCE: AMA, 2017
                Bowie (2017a), p 291

92. Patient has been diagnosed with prostate cancer. Patient arrived in the operating room where a therapeutic orchiectomy is performed.
    A. 54560   C. 55899
    B. 54530   D. 54520

REFERENCE: AMA, 2017
                Green, pp 819–820
                Smith (2011), p 122

93. Patient undergoes laparoscopic orchiopexy for intra-abdominal testes.
    A. 54650   C. 54692
    B. 54699   D. 55899

REFERENCE: AMA, 2017
              Green, pp 819–820
              Smith (2011), p 122

94. Scrotal wall abscess drainage.
    A. 55100   C. 54700
    B. 55150   D. 55110

REFERENCE: AMA, 2017
              Bowie (2017a), p 310

95. Hydrocelectomy of spermatic cord.
    A. 55500   C. 55041
    B. 55000   D. 55520

REFERENCE: AMA, 2017
              Bowie (2017a), pp 311–312

96. Patient has been followed by his primary care physician for elevated PSA. Patient underwent prostate needle biopsy in the physician's office 2 weeks ago and the final pathology was positive for carcinoma. Patient is admitted for prostatectomy. The frozen section of the prostate and one lymph node is positive for prostate cancer with metastatic disease to the lymph node. Prostatectomy became a radical perineal with bilateral pelvic lymphadenectomy.
    A. 55845   C. 55815, 38562
    B. 55815   D. 38770

REFERENCE: AMA, 2017
              Green, pp 821–822
              Smith (2011), p 122

97. Male presented to operating room for sterilization by bilateral vasectomy.
    A. 55200   C. 55250
    B. 55400   D. 55450

REFERENCE: AMA, 2017
              Green, pp 820–821

98. Laser destruction of penile condylomas.
    A. 54057   C. 17270
    B. 17106   D. 54055

REFERENCE: AMA, 2017
              Smith (2016), p 136

99. First-stage repair for hypospadias with skin flaps.
    A. 54300   C. 54322
    B. 54308, 14040   D. 54304

REFERENCE: AMA, 2017
              Bowie (2017a), pp 309–310

100. Priapism operation with spongiosum shunt.
    A. 54450   C. 54430
    B. 54352   D. 55899

REFERENCE: AMA, 2017
                        Bowie (2017a),pp 309–310

Surgery—Female Genital System

101. Patient was admitted to the hospital with sharp pelvic pains. A pelvic ultrasound was ordered and the results showed a possible ovarian cyst. The patient was taken to the operating room where a laparoscopic destruction of two corpus luteum cysts was performed.
    A. 49321   C. 58561
    B. 58925   D. 58662

REFERENCE: AMA, 2017
                        Smith (2011), p 534

102. Patient was admitted with a cystocele and rectocele. An anterior colporrhaphy was performed.
    A. 57250   C. 57240
    B. 57260   D. 57110

REFERENCE: AMA, 2017
                        Bowie (2017a), p 325

103. Patient has a Bartholin's gland cyst that was marsupialized.
    A. 54640   C. 58999
    B. 10060   D. 56440

REFERENCE: AMA, 2017
                        Bowie (2017a), pp 321–333

104. Patient is at a fertility clinic and undergoes intrauterine embryo transplant.
    A. 58679   C. 58323
    B. 58322   D. 58974

REFERENCE: AMA, 2017
                        Bowie (2017a), p 330

105. Patient has been diagnosed with carcinoma of the vagina, and she has a radical vaginectomy with complete removal of the vaginal wall.
    A. 57107   C. 58150
    B. 57110   D. 57111

REFERENCE: AMA, 2017
                        Smith (2011), p 133

106. Patient has been diagnosed with uterine fibroids and undergoes a total abdominal hysterectomy with bilateral salpingo-oophorectomy.
    A. 58200
    B. 58150
    C. 58262
    D. 58150, 58720

REFERENCE: AMA, 2017
               Bowie (2017a), p 327
               Green, p 829
               Johnson and Linker, pp 360–362
               Smith (2011), p 133
               Smith (2016), pp 140–142

107. Hysteroscopy with D&C and polypectomy.
    A. 58563
    B. 58558
    C. 58120, 58100, 58555
    D. 58558, 58120

REFERENCE: AMA, 2017
               Bowie (2017a), p 328
               Green, pp 827–829
               Smith (2011), p 132
               Smith (2016), p 141

108. Laparoscopic tubal ligation utilizing Endoloop.
    A. 58670
    B. 58615
    C. 58671
    D. 58611

REFERENCE: AMA, 2017
               Bowie (2017a), pp 328–329
               Green, pp 828–829

109. Laser destruction of extensive herpetic lesions of the vulva.
    A. 17106
    B. 17004
    C. 56515
    D. 56501

REFERENCE: AMA, 2017
               Smith (2011), p 131

110. Patient undergoes hysteroscopy with excision uterine fibroids.
    A. 58545
    B. 58140
    C. 58561
    D. 58140, 49320

REFERENCE: AMA, 2017
               Bowie (2017a), p 328
               Green, pp 827–829
               Smith (2011), p 132
               Smith (2016), p 141

Surgery—Maternity Care and Delivery

111. Attempted vaginal delivery in a previous cesarean section patient, which resulted in a repeat cesarean section.
    A. 59409   C. 59620
    B. 59612   D. 59514

REFERENCE: AMA, 2017
              Bowie (2017a), p 342
              Green, pp 830–834
              Smith (2016), p 142

112. Patient is admitted to the hospital following an ultrasound at 25 weeks, which revealed fetal pleural effusion. A fetal thoracentesis was performed.
    A. 59074   C. 32555
    B. 32554   D. 76815

REFERENCE: AMA, 2017
              Bowie (2017a), p 338

113. Patient in late stages of labor arrives at the hospital. Her OB physician is not able to make the delivery and the house physician delivers the baby vaginally. Primary care physician resumes care after delivery. Code the delivery.
    A. 59409   C. 59620
    B. 59612   D. 59400

REFERENCE: AMA, 2017
              Bowie (2017a), pp 340–341
              Green, pp 830–834
              Smith (2016), p 142

114. Patient is 24 weeks pregnant and arrives in the emergency room following an automobile accident. No fetal movement or heartbeat noted. Patient is taken to the OB ward where prostaglandin is given to induce abortion.
    A. 59200   C. 59821
    B. 59855   D. 59410

REFERENCE: AMA, 2017
              Green, pp 830–834

115. Patient is 6 weeks pregnant and complains of left-sided abdominal pains. Patient is suspected of having an ectopic pregnancy. Patient has a laparoscopic salpingectomy with removal of the ectopic tubal pregnancy.
    A. 59120   C. 59121
    B. 59200   D. 59151

REFERENCE: AMA, 2017
              Bowie (2017a), pp 348–349
              Green, pp 830–834

116. Cesarean delivery with antepartum and postpartum care.
    A. 59610
    B. 59514
    C. 59400
    D. 59510

REFERENCE: AMA, 2017
                Bowie (2017a), pp 340–342
                Green, pp 830–834
                Smith (2016), p 142

117. A pregnant patient has an incompetent cervix, which was repaired using a vaginal cerclage.
    A. 57700
    B. 57531
    C. 59320
    D. 59325

REFERENCE: AMA, 2017
                Bowie (2017a), p 339

118. A D&C is performed for postpartum hemorrhage.
    A. 59160
    B. 58120
    C. 58558
    D. 58578

REFERENCE: AMA, 2017
                Bowie (2017a), pp 338–339

119. Hysterotomy for hydatidifom mole and tubal ligation.
    A. 58285, 58600
    B. 58150, 58605
    C. 51900, 58605
    D. 59100, 58611

REFERENCE: AMA, 2017
                Bowie (2017a), pp 328–329, 338–339

120. D&C performed for patient with a diagnosis of incomplete abortion at 8 weeks.
    A. 59812
    B. 59820
    C. 58120
    D. 59160

REFERENCE: AMA, 2017
                Green, pp 830–834

Surgery—Endocrine System

121. Patient comes in for a percutaneous needle biopsy of the thyroid gland.
    A. 60000
    B. 60270
    C. 60699
    D. 60100

REFERENCE: AMA, 2017
                Green, p 835

122. Laparoscopic adrenalectomy, complete.
    A. 60650
    B. 60650-50
    C. 60659
    D. 60540

REFERENCE: AMA, 2017
                Green, p 836

123. Left carotid artery excision for tumor of carotid body.
    A. 60650
    B. 60600
    C. 60605
    D. 60699

REFERENCE: AMA, 2017
              Green, p 836

124. Patient undergoes total thyroidectomy with parathyroid autotransplantation.
    A. 60240, 60512
    B. 60520, 60500
    C. 60260, 60512
    D. 60650, 60500

REFERENCE: AMA, 2017
              Green, p 835

125. Unilateral partial thyroidectomy.
    A. 60252
    B. 60210
    C. 60220
    D. 60520

REFERENCE: AMA, 2017
              Green, p 835

Surgery—Nervous System

126. Patient comes in through the emergency room with a wound that was caused by an electric saw. Patient is taken to the operating room where two ulna nerves are sutured.
    A. 64837
    B. 64892, 69990
    C. 64836, 64837
    D. 64856, 64859

REFERENCE: AMA, 2017
              Smith (2011), p 153

127. Laminectomy and excision of intradural lumbar lesion.
    A. 63272
    B. 63267
    C. 63282
    D. 63252

REFERENCE: AMA, 2017
              Green, pp 843, 845–846
              Smith (2011), p 149

128. Patient comes in for steroid injection for lumbar herniated disk. Marcaine and Aristocort were injected into the L2-L3 space.
    A. 64520
    B. 64483
    C. 62322
    D. 64714

REFERENCE: AMA, 2017
              Smith (2011), p 148
              Smith (2016), p 148

129. Patient with Parkinson's disease is admitted for insertion of a brain neurostimulator pulse generator with one electrode array.
   A. 61885
   B. 61850, 61863
   C. 61888
   D. 61867, 61870

REFERENCE: AMA, 2017
             Bowie (2017a), p 367
             Green, p 841
             Smith (2011), p 145

130. Patient has rhinorrhea, which requires repair of the CSF leak with craniotomy.
   A. 63707
   B. 63709
   C. 62100
   D. 62010

REFERENCE: AMA, 2017
             Green, pp 838–840
             Smith (2011), pp 143–144

131. Patient has metastatic brain lesions. Patient undergoes stereotactic radiosurgery gamma knife of two lesions.
   A. 61533
   B. 61500
   C. 61796, 61797
   D. 61796

REFERENCE: AMA, 2017
             Bowie (2017a), p 367

132. Patient has right sacroiliac joint dysfunction and requires a right S2-S3 paravertebral facet joint anesthetic nerve block with image guidance.
   A. 62311
   B. 64493
   C. 64490
   D. 64520

REFERENCE: AMA, 2017
             Green, p 847
             Smith (2011), pp 152–153

133. Patient requires repair of a 6-cm meningocele.
   A. 63700
   B. 63709
   C. 63180
   D. 63702

REFERENCE: AMA, 2017
             Smith (2011), pp 151–152

134. Patient comes in through the emergency room with a laceration of the posterior tibial nerve. Patient is taken to the operating room where the nerve requires transposition and suture.
   A. 64856
   B. 64831, 64832, 64876
   C. 64840, 64874
   D. 64834, 64859, 64872

REFERENCE: AMA, 2017
             Green, p 849
             Smith (2011), p 153

Surgery—Eye and Ocular Adnexa

135. Patient returns to the physician's office complaining of obscured vision. Patient has had cataract surgery 6 months prior. Patient requires laser discission of secondary cataract.
    A. 66821   C. 67835
    B. 66940   D. 66830

REFERENCE: AMA, 2017
               Bowie (2017a), pp 379–380
               Green, pp 852–853
               Smith (2011), pp 162–163
               Smith (2016), pp 151–152

136. Patient undergoes enucleation of left eye, and muscles were reattached to an implant.
    A. 65135-LT   C. 65730-LT
    B. 65105-LT   D. 65103-LT

REFERENCE: AMA, 2017
               Smith (2011), p 161

137. Patient suffers from strabismus and requires surgery. Recession of the lateral rectus (horizontal) muscle with adjustable sutures was performed.
    A. 67340, 67500   C. 67332, 67334
    B. 67314, 67320   D. 67311, 67335

REFERENCE: AMA, 2017
               Bowie (2017a), pp 384–385
               Green, pp 853–854
               Smith (2011), p 165
               Smith (2016), p 154

138. Radial keratotomy.
    A. 92071   C. 65767
    B. 65855   D. 65771

REFERENCE: AMA, 2017
               Green, pp 852–853
               Smith (2011), pp 162–163

139. Correction of trichiasis by incision of lid margin.
    A. 67840   C. 67835
    B. 67830   D. 67850

REFERENCE: AMA, 2017
               Smith (2011), p 165

140. Patient undergoes ocular resurfacing construction utilizing stem cell allograft from a cadaver.
    A. 67320   C. 68371
    B. 66999   D. 65781

REFERENCE: AMA, 2017
               Green, pp 853–854
               Smith (2011), pp 162–163

141. Patient presents for procedure for aphakia penetrating corneal transplant.
    A. 65755   C. 65750
    B. 65730   D. 65765

REFERENCE: AMA, 2017
               Bowie (2017a), pp 379–380
               Green, p 852
               Smith (2011), pp 162–163

142. Lagophthalmos correction with implantation using gold weight.
    A. 67912   C. 67901
    B. 67911   D. 67121

REFERENCE: AMA, 2017
               Smith (2011), p 165

143. Lacrimal fistula closure.
    A. 68760   C. 68700
    B. 68761   D. 68770

REFERENCE: AMA, 2017
               Bowie (2017a), pp 379–380
               Green, pp 854–855
               Smith (2011), pp 165–166

Surgery—Auditory

144. Patient comes into the office for removal of impacted earwax.
    A. 69210   C. 69222
    B. 69200   D. 69000

REFERENCE: AMA, 2017
               Bowie (2017a), pp 394–395
               Green, pp 856–857
               Smith (2011), p 120

145. Patient with a traumatic rupture of the eardrum. Repaired with tympanoplasty with incision of
     the mastoid. Repair of ossicular chain not required.
    A. 69641   C. 69642
    B. 69646   D. 69635

REFERENCE: AMA, 2017
               Bowie (2017a), pp 396–397
               Green, pp 857–858
               Smith (2011), p 173

146. Patient came in for excision of a middle ear lesion.
    A. 11440   C. 69552
    B. 69540   D. 69535

REFERENCE: AMA, 2017
               Green, pp 857–858
               Smith (2011), p 173

147. Patient with chronic otitis media requiring transtympanic eustachian tube catheterization.
     A. 69420
     B. 69424
     C. 69421
     D. 69401

REFERENCE: AMA, 2017
              Bowie (2017a), p 397
              Green, pp 857–858
              Smith (2011), p 173

148. Modified radical mastoidectomy.
     A. 69511
     B. 69505
     C. 69635
     D. 69641

REFERENCE: AMA, 2017
              Green, pp 857–858
              Smith (2011), p 173

149. Decompression internal auditory canal.
     A. 69979
     B. 69915
     C. 69970
     D. 69960

REFERENCE: AMA, 2017
              Green, p 858
              Smith (2011), pp 172–173

150. Myringoplasty.
     A. 69620
     B. 69635
     C. 69610
     D. 69420

REFERENCE: AMA, 2017
              Bowie (2017a), pp 369–397
              Green, pp 857–858

151. Insertion of cochlear device inner ear.
     A. 69711
     B. 69949
     C. 69930
     D. 69960, 69990

REFERENCE: AMA, 2017
              Bowie (2017a), p 398
              Green, p 858
              Smith (2011), p 173

152. Patient with Bell's palsy requiring a total facial nerve decompression.
     A. 64742
     B. 64771
     C. 69955
     D. 64864

REFERENCE: AMA, 2017
              Green, p 858
              Smith (2011), p 173

153. Drainage of simple external ear abscess.
    A. 69000
    B. 69100
    C. 10060
    D. 69020

REFERENCE: AMA, 2017
            Green, pp 856–857
            Smith (2011), p 173

Radiology

154. Administration of initial oral radionuclide therapy for hyperthyroidism.
    A. 78015
    B. 77402
    C. 78099
    D. 79005

REFERENCE: AMA, 2017
            Green, p 908

155. Patient comes into the outpatient department at the local hospital for an MRI of the cervical spine with contrast. Patient status post automobile accident.
    A. 72156
    B. 72142
    C. 72149
    D. 72126

REFERENCE: AMA, 2017
            Green, pp 881, 889
            Smith (2016), pp 167–168

156. Obstetric patient comes in for a pelvimetry with placental placement.
    A. 74710
    B. 76946
    C. 76805
    D. 76825

REFERENCE: AMA, 2017
            Bowie (2017), p 408

157. Patient comes into his physician's office complaining of wrist pain. Physician gives the patient an injection and sends the patient to the hospital for an arthrography. Code the complete procedure.
    A. 73115
    B. 73100
    C. 73110
    D. 25246, 73115

REFERENCE: AMA, 2017
            Bowie (2017a), pp 154–155, 407–408

158. Patient has carcinoma of the breast and undergoes proton beam delivery of radiation to the breast with a single port.
    A. 77523
    B. 77432
    C. 77520
    D. 77402

REFERENCE: AMA, 2017
            Bowie (2017a), pp 413–415
            Green, p 903
            Smith (2016), pp 171–173

159. CT scan of the head with contrast.
    A. 70460
    B. 70542
    C. 70551
    D. 70470

REFERENCE: AMA, 2017
              Bowie (2017a), pp 407–408
              Green, pp 887–888
              Smith (2016), pp 167–168

160. Patient undergoes x-ray of the foot with three views.
    A. 73620
    B. 3610
    C. 73630
    D. 27648, 73615

REFERENCE: AMA, 2017
              Green, pp 884–885
              Smith (2016), pp 167–168

161. Unilateral mammogram with computer-aided detection with further physician review and interpretation.
    A. 77065, 77067
    B. 77065-22
    C. 77066-52, 77065
    D. 77065

REFERENCE: AMA, 2017
              Bowie (2017a), p 412
              Green, pp 895–896

162. Pregnant female comes in for a complete fetal and maternal evaluation via ultrasound.
    A. 76856
    B. 76805
    C. 76811
    D. 76810

REFERENCE: AMA, 2017
              Bowie (2017), pp 411–412
              Green, p 894

163. Ultrasonic guidance for the needle biopsy of the liver. Code the complete procedure.
    A. 47000, 76942
    B. 47000, 76937
    C. 47000, 76999
    D. 47000, 77002

REFERENCE: AMA, 2017
              Bowie (2017a), pp 274–275, 411–412
              Green, p 894

Pathology and Laboratory

164. What code is used for a culture of embryos less than 4 days old?
    A. 89251
    B. 89272
    C. 89268
    D. 89250

REFERENCE: AMA, 2017
              Bowie (2017a), p 429
              Green, pp 936–937

165. Basic metabolic panel (calcium, total) and total bilirubin.
   A. 80048, 82247
   B. 80053
   C. 80053
   D. 82239, 80400, 80051

REFERENCE: AMA, 2017
              Bowie (2017a), 425–426, 428
              Green, pp 923–924, 927–928
              Smith (2016), pp 178–180

166. Huhner test and semen analysis.
   A. 89325
   B. 89258
   C. 89310
   D. 89300

REFERENCE: AMA, 2017
              Green, pp 931–932

167. Chlamydia culture.
   A. 87110
   B. 87106
   C. 87118
   D. 87109, 87168

REFERENCE: AMA, 2017
              Green, pp 785–786

168. Partial thromboplastin time utilizing whole blood.
   A. 85732
   B. 85730
   C. 85245
   D. 85246

REFERENCE: AMA, 2017
              Smith (2016), p 182

169. Pathologist bills for gross and microscopic examination of medial meniscus.
   A. 88300
   B. 88302, 88311
   C. 88325
   D. 88304

REFERENCE: AMA, 2017
              Bowie (2017a), p 429
              Green, pp 934–936
              Smith (2016), p 182

170. Cytopathology of cervical Pap smear with automated thin-layer preparation utilizing computer screening and manual rescreening under physician supervision.
   A. 88175
   B. 88148
   C. 88160, 88141
   D. 88161

REFERENCE: AMA, 2017
              Bowie (2017a), p 429
              Green, pp 932–933

171. Pathologist performs a postmortem examination, including the brain, of an adult. Tissue is sent to the lab for microscopic examination.
   A. 88309
   B. 88025
   C. 88099
   D. 88028

REFERENCE: AMA, 2017
              Green, p 932
              Smith (2016), p 182

172. Clotting factor VII.
    A. 85220
    B. 85240
    C. 85362
    D. 85230

REFERENCE: AMA, 2017
              Green, pp 928–929
              Smith (2016), p 182

Medicine Section

173. IV push of one antineoplastic drug.
    A. 96401
    B. 96409
    C. 96411
    D. 96413

REFERENCE: AMA, 2017
              Bowie (2017a), p 445
              Green, pp 972–973
              Smith (2016), p 237

174. One-half hour of IV chemotherapy by infusion followed by IV push of a different drug.
    A. 96413
    B. 96413, 96411
    C. 96413, 96409
    D. 96409, 96411

REFERENCE: AMA, 2017
              Bowie (2017a), p 445
              Green, pp 972–973
              Smith (2016), p 237

175. Caloric vestibular test using air, monothermal.
    A. 92543, 92700
    B. 92543, 92543
    C. 92538
    D. 92543

REFERENCE: AMA, 2017
              Bowie (2017a), p 441

176. Patient presents to the emergency room with chest pains. The patient is admitted as a 23-hour observation. The cardiologist orders cardiac workup and the patient undergoes left heart catheterization via the left femoral artery with visualization of the coronary arteries and left ventriculography. The physician interprets the report. Code the heart catheterization.
    A. 93452, 93455
    B. 93452, 93458
    C. 93458
    D. 93459

REFERENCE: AMA, 2017
              Johnson and Linker, pp 286–289

177. Patient with hematochromatosis had a therapeutic phlebotomy performed on an outpatient basis.
    A. 99195
    B. 36522
    C. 36514
    D. 99199

REFERENCE: AMA, 2017
              Bowie (2017a), p 446

178. A physician performs a PTCA with drug-eluting stent placement in the left anterior descending artery and angioplasty only in the right coronary artery.
    A. 92928-LD, 92929-RC
    B. 92928-LD, 92920-RC
    C. 92928-LD, 92920-RC
    D. 92920-RC, 92929-LD

REFERENCE: AMA, 2017
              Bowie (2017a), pp 441–442
              Smith (2016), pp 225–228

179. Transesophageal echocardiography (TEE) with probe placement, image, and interpretation and report.
    A. 93307
    B. 93303, 93325
    C. 93312, 93313, 93314
    D. 93312

REFERENCE: AMA, 2017
              Bowie (2017a), pp 441–442

180. Which code listed below would be used to report an esophageal electrogram during an EPS?
    A. 93600
    B. 93615
    C. 93612
    D. 93616

REFERENCE: AMA, 2017
              Smith (2016), p 227

181. Cardioversion of cardiac arrhythmia by external forces.
    A. 92961
    B. 92950
    C. 92960
    D. 92970

REFERENCE: AMA, 2017
              Bowie (2017a), p 441

182. Osteopathic manipulative treatment to three body regions.
    A. 98926
    B. 98941
    C. 97110
    D. 97012

REFERENCE: AMA, 2017
              Green, p 975

183. Patient presents to the Respiratory Therapy Department and undergoes a pulmonary stress test. CO_2 production with O_2 uptake with recordings was also performed.
    A. 94450
    B. 94620
    C. 94002
    D. 94621

REFERENCE: AMA, 2017
              Bowie (2017a), p 443

For the following questions, you will be utilizing the codes provided for the scenarios. You will need to code appropriate CPT codes only.

184. Patient presents to the hospital for debridement of a diabetic ulcer of the left ankle. The patient has a history of recurrent ulcers. Medication taken by the patient includes Diabeta and the patient was covered in the hospital with insulin sliding scales. The decubitus ulcer was debrided down to the bone.

11043	Debridement, muscle and/or fascia (includes epidermis, dermis, and subcutaneous tissue, if performed); first 20 cm^2 or less
11044	Debridement, bone (includes epidermis, dermis, subcutaneous tissue, muscle and/or fascia, if performed); first 20 cm^2 or less
+11046	Each additional 20 cm^2 thereof (List separately in addition to code for primary procedure.) (Use 11046 in conjunction with 11043.)
+11047	Each additional 20 cm^2, or part thereof (List separately in addition to code for primary procedure.) (Use 11047 in conjunction with 11047.)

A. 11043, +11047

B. 11043, +11046

C. 11044

D. 11044, +11047

REFERENCE: AMA, 2017

Bowie (2017a), pp 116–117

185. Patient presents to the emergency room following a fall from a tree. X-rays were ordered for the left upper arm, which showed a fracture of the humerus shaft. The emergency room physician performed a closed reduction of the fracture and placed the patient in a long arm spica cast. Code the diagnoses and procedures, excluding the x-ray.

Code	Description
24500	Closed treatment of humeral shaft fracture; without manipulation
24505	Closed treatment of humeral shaft fracture; with manipulation, with or without skeletal traction
24515	Open treatment of humeral shaft fracture with plate/screws, with or without cerclage
29065	Application, cast; shoulder to hand (long arm) LT Left side

A. 24505-LT

B. 24515-LT

C. 24505-LT, 29065

D. 24500-LT

REFERENCE: AMA, 2017

Bowie (2017a), p 155

Green, pp 697–698

Smith (2016), pp 84–86

186. Patient was admitted with hemoptysis and underwent a bronchoscopy with transbronchial lung biopsy. Following the bronchoscopy, the patient was taken to the operating room where a left lower lobe lobectomy was performed without complications. Pathology reported large cell carcinoma of the left lower lobe.

31625	Bronchoscopy with bronchial or endobronchial biopsy, with or without fluoroscopic guidance
31628	Bronchoscopy with transbronchial lung biopsy, with or without fluoroscopic guidance
32405	Biopsy, lung or mediastinum, percutaneous needle
32440	Removal of lung, total pneumonectomy
32480	Removal of lung, other than total pneumonectomy, single lobe (lobectomy)
32484	Removal of lung, other than total pneumonectomy, single segment (segmentectomy)

A. 31625

B. 31628, 32480

C. 32405, 32484

D. 32440

REFERENCE:　AMA, 2017
　　　　　　　Bowie (2017a), pp 188, 191
　　　　　　　Green, pp 713–716
　　　　　　　Smith (2016), pp 97–99

187. Patient was admitted for right upper quadrant pain. Workup included various x-rays that showed cholelithiasis. Patient was taken to the operating room where a laparoscopic cholecystectomy was performed. During the procedure, the physician was unable to visualize through the ports and an open cholecystectomy was elected to be performed. An intraoperative cholangiogram was performed. Pathology report states acute and chronic cholecystitis with cholelithiasis.

| 47605 | Cholecystectomy with cholangiography |
| 47563 | Laparoscopy, surgical; cholecystectomy with cholangiography |

A. 47563

B. 47563, 47605

C. 47605

REFERENCE:　AMA, 2017
　　　　　　　Bowie (2017a), pp 274–276
　　　　　　　Green, p 796

188. Patient presents to the emergency room complaining of right forearm/elbow pain after racquetball last night. Patient states that he did not fall, but overworked his arm. Past medical history is negative and the physical examination reveals the patient is unable to supinate. A four-view x-ray of the right elbow is performed and is negative. The physician signs the patient out with right elbow sprain. Prescription of Motrin is given to the patient.

73040	X-ray of shoulder, arthrography radiological supervision and interpretation
73070	X-ray of elbow, two views
73080	X-ray of elbow, complete, minimum of three views
99281	E/M visit to emergency room—problem-focused history, problem-focused exam, straightforward medical decision
99282	E/M visit to emergency room—expanded problem-focused history, expanded problem-focused exam, and medical decision of low complexity
-25	Significant, separately identifiable evaluation and management service by the same physician on the same day of the procedure or other service

  A. 73080   C. 73080, 99282, 73040

  B. 99281, 73070   D. 99281-25, 73080

REFERENCE: AMA, 2017
                      Bowie (2017a), pp 67–68, 407–408
                      Smith (2016), pp 167, 208–209

189. A physician orders a lipid panel on a 54-year-old male with hypercholesterolemia, hypertension, and a family history of heart disease. The lab employee in his office performs and reports the total cholesterol and HDL cholesterol only.

80061	Lipid panel; this panel must include the following: Cholesterol, serum, total (82465); Lipoprotein, direct measurement, high density cholesterol (HDL cholesterol) (83718); Triglycerides (84478)
82465	Cholesterol, serum or whole blood, total
83718	Lipoprotein, direct measurement; high density cholesterol (HDL cholesterol)
84478	Triglycerides
-52	Reduced services

  A. 80061   C. 82465, 83718

  B. 80061-52   D. 82465, 84478

REFERENCE: AMA, 2017
                      Bowie (2017a), p 428
                      Green, pp 927–928
                      Smith (2016), pp 178–182

190. Chronic nontraumatic rotator cuff tear. Arthroscopic subacromial decompression with coracoacromial ligament release, and open rotator cuff repair.

23410	Repair of ruptured musculotendinous cuff (e.g., rotator cuff); open, acute
23412	Repair of ruptured musculotendinous cuff (e.g., rotator cuff) open; chronic
29821	Arthroscopy, shoulder, surgical; synovectomy, complete
29823	Arthroscopy, shoulder, surgical; debridement, extensive
+29826	Arthroscopy, shoulder, surgical; decompression of subacromial space with partial acromioplasty, with coracoacromial ligament release (List separately in addition to code from primary procedure.)
29827	Arthroscopy, shoulder, surgical; with rotator cuff repair
-59	Distinct procedural service

A. 29823

C. 29826, 29821

B. 23412, 29826-59

D. 23410

REFERENCE: AMA, 2017
Bowie (2017a), pp 154–155, 165–166
Smith (2016), pp 85–86, 89

191. The patient is on vacation and presents to a physician's office with a lacerated finger. The physician repairs the laceration and gives a prescription for pain control and has the patient follow up with his primary physician when he returns home. The physician fills out the superbill as a problem-focused history and physical examination with straightforward medical decision making. Also checked is a laceration repair for a 1.5-cm finger wound.

99201	New patient office visit with a problem-focused history, problem-focused examination and straightforward medical decision making
99212	Established patient office visit with a problem-focused history, problem-focused examination and straightforward medical decision making
12001	Simple repair of superficial wounds of scalp, neck, axillae, external genitalia, trunk, and/or extremities (including hands and feet); 2.5 cm or less
13131	Repair, complex, forehead, cheeks, chin, mouth, neck, axillae, genitalia, hands, and/or feet; 1.1 cm to 2.5 cm
-25	Significant separately identifiable evaluation and management service by the same physician or other qualified health care professional on the same day of the procedure or other service

A. 99212, 13131

C. 99212, 12001

B. 12001

D. 99201-25

REFERENCE: AMA, 2017
Green, 542–543, 658–660
Smith (2016), pp 67–68, 206

192. A 69-year-old established female patient presents to the office with chronic obstructive lung disease, congestive heart failure, and hypertension. The physician conducts a comprehensive history and physical examination and makes a medical decision of moderate complexity. Physician admits the patient from the office to the hospital for acute exacerbation of CHF.

99212	Established office visit for problem-focused history and exam, straightforward medical decision making
99214	Established office visit for a detailed history and physical exam, moderate medical decision making
99222	Initial hospital care for comprehensive history and physical exam, moderate medical decision making
99223	Initial hospital care for comprehensive history and physical exam, high medical decision making

A. 99214
B. 99223
C. 99222
D. 99212

REFERENCE: AMA, 2017
Bowie (2017a), pp 61–62
Green, pp 566–567
Smith (2016), p 207

193. Established 42-year-old patient comes into your office to obtain vaccines required for his trip to Sri Lanka. The nurse injects intramuscularly the following vaccines: hepatitis A and B vaccines, cholera vaccine, and yellow fever vaccine. As the coding specialist, what would you report on the CMS 1500 form?
   A. office visit, hepatitis A and B vaccine, cholera vaccine, and yellow fever vaccine
   B. office visit, intramuscular injection; HCPCS Level II codes
   C. office visit; administration of two or more single vaccines; vaccine products for hepatitis A and B, cholera, and yellow fever
   D. administration of two or more single vaccines; vaccine products for hepatitis A and B, cholera, and yellow fever

REFERENCE: AMA, 2017
Green, pp 948–949
Smith (2016), p 220

194. Patient presents to the operating room where the physician performed, using imaging guidance, a percutaneous breast biopsy utilizing a rotating biopsy device.

19000	Puncture aspiration of cyst of breast
19081	Biopsy, breast, with imaging of the biopsy specimen, percutaneous; first lesion, including stereotactic guidance
19120	Excision of cyst, fibroadenoma, or other benign or malignant tumor, aberrant breast tissue, duct lesion, nipple or areolar lesion (except 19300), open, male or female, one or more lesions
19125	Excision of breast lesion identified by preoperative placement of radiological marker, open; single lesion
19283	Placement of breast localization device(s) (ed clip, metallic pellet, wire/needle, radioactive seeds), percutaneous; first lesion, including stereotactic guidance

A. 19081
B. 19125, 19283
C. 19120
D. 19000

REFERENCE: AMA, 2017
Bowie (2017a), p 137
Green, pp 669–670
Smith (2016), pp 79–80

195. Facelift utilizing the superficial musculoaponeurotic system (SMAS) flap technique.

15788	Chemical peel, facial; epidermal
15825	Rhytidectomy; neck with platysmal tightening (platysmal flap, P-flap)
15828	Rhytidectomy; cheek, chin, and neck
15829	Rhytidectomy; SMAS flap

A. 15825   C. 15829
B. 15788   D. 15828

REFERENCE: AMA, 2017
                    Green, pp 661–665

196. Tracheostoma revision with flap rotation.

31613	Tracheostoma revision; simple, without flap rotation
31614	Tracheostoma revision; complex, with flap rotation
31750	Tracheoplasty; cervical
31830	Revision of tracheostomy scar

A. 31830   C. 31614
B. 31750   D. 31613

REFERENCE: AMA, 2017
                    Bowie (2017a), pp 187–188

197. Blood transfusion of three units of packed red blood cells.

36430	Transfusion, blood or blood components
36455	Exchange transfusion; blood, other than newborn
36460	Transfusion, intrauterine, fetal

A. 36430   C. 36460
B. 36430, 36430, 36430   D. 36455

REFERENCE: AMA, 2017
                    Bowie (2017), p 223

198. Two-year-old patient returns to the hospital for cleft palate repair where a secondary lengthening procedure takes place.

40720	Plastic repair of cleft lip/nasal deformity; secondary, by re-creation of defect and reclosure
42145	Palatopharyngoplasty
42220	Palatoplasty for cleft palate; secondary lengthening procedure
42226	Lengthening of palate and pharyngeal flap

A. 40720   C. 42226
B. 42220   D. 42145

REFERENCE: AMA, 2017

199. Tonsillectomy on a 14-year-old.

42820	Tonsillectomy and adenoidectomy; under age 12
42821	Tonsillectomy and adenoidectomy; age 12 or over
42825	Tonsillectomy, primary or secondary; under age 12
42826	Tonsillectomy, primary or secondary; age 12 or over

A. 42820   C. 42825
B. 42821   D. 42826

REFERENCE: AMA, 2017
              Green, p 780

200. Laparoscopic repair of umbilical hernia.

49580	Repair umbilical hernia, under age 5 years, reducible
49585	Repair umbilical hernia, age 5 years or over, reducible
49652	Laparoscopy, surgical, repair, ventral, umbilical, spigelian, or epigastric hernia (includes mesh insertion when performed); reducible
49654	Laparoscopy, surgical, repair, incisional hernia (includes mesh insertion when performed); reducible

A. 49580   C. 49585
B. 49654   D. 49652

REFERENCE: AMA, 2017
              Bowie (2017a), pp 277–278

201. Ureterolithotomy completed laparoscopically.

50600	Ureterotomy with exploration or drainage (separate procedure)
50945	Laparoscopy, surgical ureterolithotomy
52325	Cystourethroscopy; with fragmentation of ureteral calculus
52352	Cystourethroscopy, with urethroscopy and/or pyeloscopy; with removal or manipulation of calculus (ureteral catheterization is included)

A. 52352   C. 50600
B. 52325   D. 50945

REFERENCE: AMA, 2017
              Bowie (2017a), p 295

202. Patient undergoes partial nephrectomy for carcinoma of the kidney.

50220	Nephrectomy, including partial ureterectomy, any open approach including rib resection
50234	Nephrectomy with total ureterectomy and bladder cuff; through same incision
50240	Nephrectomy, partial
50340	Recipient nephrectomy (separate procedure)

A. 50234   C. 50340
B. 50220   D. 50240

REFERENCE: AMA, 2017
              Bowie (2017a), pp 289–290
              Green, pp 800–802

203. Patient presents to the operating room for fulguration of bladder tumors. The cystoscope was inserted and entered the urethra, which was normal. Bladder tumors measuring approximately 1.5 cm were removed.

50957	Ureteral endoscopy through established ureterostomy, with or without irrigation, instillation, or ureteropyelography, exclusive of radiologic service; with fulguration and/or incision, with or without biopsy
51530	Cystotomy; for excision of bladder tumor
52214	Cystourethroscopy, with fulguration of trigone, bladder neck, prostatic fossa, urethra, or periurethral glands
52234	Cystourethroscopy, with fulguration (including cryosurgery or laser surgery) and/or resection of small bladder tumor(s) (0.5 up to 2.0 cm)

A. 52234
B. 50957

C. 52214
D. 51530

REFERENCE: AMA, 2017
Bowie (2017a), p 299
Green, pp 806–807
Smith (2016), pp 131–132

204. Excision of Cowper's gland.

53220	Excision or fulguration of carcinoma of urethra
53250	Excision of bulbourethral gland (Cowper's gland)
53260	Excision or fulguration; urethral polyp(s), distal urethra
53450	Urethromeatoplasty, with mucosal advancement

A. 53250
B. 53450

C. 53260
D. 53220

REFERENCE: AMA, 2017
Bowie (2017a), p 300

205. Placement of double-J stent.

52320	Cystourethroscopy (including ureteral catheterization); with removal of ureteral calculus
52330	Cystourethroscopy; with manipulation, without removal of ureteral calculus
52332	Cystourethroscopy with insertion of indwelling ureteral stent (e.g., Gibbons or double-J type)
52341	Cystourethroscopy, with treatment of ureteral stricture (e.g., balloon dilation, laser electrocautery, and incision)

A. 52341
B. 52320

C. 52330, 52332
D. 52332

REFERENCE: AMA, 2017
Bowie (2017a), p 299
Green, pp 806–807
Smith (2016), pp 131–132

206. Litholapaxy, 3 cm calculus.

50590	Lithotripsy, extracorporeal shock wave
52317	Litholapaxy, simple or small (< 2.5 cm)
52318	Litholapaxy, complicated or large (over 2.5 cm)
52353	Cystourethroscopy, with ureteroscopy and/or pyeloscopy; with lithotripsy

A. 52353
B. 50590

C. 52318
D. 52317

REFERENCE: AMA, 2017
              Bowie (2017a), p 299

207. Patient presented to the operating room where an incision was made in the epigastric region for a repair of ureterovisceral fistula.

50520	Closure of nephrocutaneous or pyelocutaneous fistula
50525	Closure of nephrovisceral fistula, including visceral repair; abdominal approach
50526	Closure of nephrovisceral fistula, including visceral repair; thoracic approach
50930	Closure of ureterovisceral fistula (including visceral repair)

A. 50526
B. 50930

C. 50520
D. 50525

REFERENCE: AMA, 2017
              Bowie (2017a), p 295

208. Amniocentesis.

57530	Trachelectomy, amputation of cervix (separate procedure)
57550	Excision of cervical stump, vaginal approach
59000	Amniocentesis, diagnostic
59200	Insertion of cervical dilator (separate procedure)

A. 59000
B. 59200

C. 57550
D. 57530

REFERENCE: AMA, 2017
              Bowie (2017a), p 338

209. Patient is admitted to the hospital with facial droop and left-sided paralysis. CT scan of the brain shows subdural hematoma. Burr holes were performed to evacuate the hematoma.

61150	Burr hole(s) or trephine; with drainage of brain abscess or cyst
61154	Burr hole(s) with evacuation and/or drainage of hematoma, extradural or subdural
61156	Burr hole(s); with aspiration of hematoma or cyst, intracerebral
61314	Craniectomy or craniotomy for evacuation of hematoma, infratentorial; extradural or subdural

A. 61156
B. 61314

C. 61154
D. 61150

REFERENCE: AMA, 2017
              Green, pp 838–840

210. Spinal tap.

62268	Percutaneous aspiration, spinal cord cyst or syrinx
62270	Spinal puncture, lumbar diagnostic
62272	Spinal puncture, therapeutic, for drainage of cerebrospinal fluid (by needle or catheter)
64999	Unlisted procedure, nervous system

A. 62272   C. 62268
B. 64999   D. 62270

REFERENCE: AMA, 2017
               Bowie (2017a), pp 368–369

211. Injection of anesthesia for nerve block of the brachial plexus.

64413	Injection, anesthetic agent; cervical plexus
64415	Injection, anesthetic agent; brachial plexus, single
64510	Injection, anesthetic agent; stellate ganglion (cervical sympathetic)
64530	Injection, anesthetic agent; celiac plexus, with or without radiologic monitoring

A. 64415   C. 64530
B. 64413   D. 64510

REFERENCE: AMA, 2017
               Bowie (2017a), p 370
               Green, pp 596–598

212. SPECT bone imaging.

77080	Dual energy x-ray absorptiometry (DXA), bone density study, one or more sites; axial skeleton (e.g., hips, pelvis, spine)
76977	Ultrasound bone density measurement and interpretation, peripheral site(s), any method
78300	Bone and/or joint imaging; limited area
78320	Bone and/or joint imaging; tomographic (SPECT)

A. 76977   C. 77080
B. 78320   D. 76977

REFERENCE: AMA, 2017
               Bowie (2017), pp 415–416

213. Vitamin B_{12}

82180	Ascorbic acid (vitamin C), blood
82607	Cyanocobalamin (vitamin B_{12})
84590	Vitamin A
84591	Vitamin, not otherwise specified

A. 84590   C. 84591
B. 82180   D. 82607

REFERENCE: AMA, 2017
               Green, pp 927–928
               Smith (2016), p 182

214. Hepatitis C antibody.

86803	Hepatitis C antibody
86804	Hepatitis C antibody; confirmatory test (e.g., immunoblot)
87520	Infectious agent detection by nucleic acid (DNA or RNA); hepatitis C, direct probe technique
87522	Infectious agent detection by nucleic acid (DNA or RNA); hepatitis C, quantification

A. 86804   C. 87522
B. 86803   D. 87520

REFERENCE: AMA, 2017
             Green, p 930

215. Creatinine clearance.

82550	Creatine kinase (CK), (CPK); total
82565	Creatinine; blood
82575	Creatinine; clearance
82585	Cryofibrinogen

A. 82550   C. 82575
B. 82565   D. 82585

REFERENCE: AMA, 2017
             Green, pp 927–928
             Smith (2016), p 182

216. Comprehensive electrophysiologic evaluation (EPS) with induction of arrhythmia.

93618	Induction of arrhythmia by electrical pacing
93619	Comprehensive electrophysiologic evaluation with right atrial pacing and recording, right ventricular pacing and recording, His bundle recording, including insertion and repositioning of multiple electrode catheters, without induction or attempted induction of arrhythmia
93620	Comprehensive electrophysiologic evaluation including insertion and repositioning of multiple electrode catheters with induction or attempted induction of arrhythmia; with right atrial pacing and recording, right ventricular pacing and recording, His bundle recording
+93623	Programmed stimulation and pacing after intravenous drug infusion (list separately in addition to code for primary procedure)
93640	Electrophysiologic evaluation of single- or dual-chamber pacing cardioverter-defibrillator leads including defibrillation threshold evaluation (induction of arrhythmia, evaluation of sensing and pacing for arrhythmia termination) at time of initial implantation or replacement

A. 93618, 93620   C. 93640, 93623
B. 93620   D. 93619, 93620

REFERENCE: AMA, 2017
             Bowie (2017a), pp 441–442

217. Patient presents to the hospital for a two-view chest x-ray for a cough. The radiology report comes back negative. What would be the correct code to report to the insurance company?

71010 Radiologic examination, chest, single view, frontal
71020 Radiologic examination, chest, two views, frontal and lateral
71035 Radiologic examination, chest, special views

    A. 71010
    B. 71020
    C. 71035

REFERENCE: AMA, 2017
               Bowie (2017a), pp 407–408

Answer Key for CPT Coding

1. C
2. A
3. B
4. C
5. D
6. C
7. D
8. B
9. B
10. C
11. D
12. B
13. A
14. B
15. D
16. B
17. C
18. A
19. D   The supply of skin substitutes graft(s) should be reported separately.
20. C
21. C
22. B
23. B
24. C   The supply of skin substitutes graft(s) should be reported separately.
25. B
26. C
27. A   If two lesions are removed with one excision, only one excision code would be reported.

28. D
29. B
30. C
31. D
32. A
33. D
34. A   Codes 10060 and 10140 are used for I&Ds of superficial abscesses.
35. C
36. C
37. D
38. B
39. A
40. B
41. A
42. D

43. C
44. A
45. D
46. C
47. A
48. D
49. A
50. B
51. A
52. B   Creation of conduit is included in code 33975.
53. D
54. B
55. C
56. C
57. C
58. A
59. A
60. B
61. D
62. B
63. A
64. D
65. A
66. B
67. C
68. A
69. A
70. D
71. C
72. D   Radiology codes would be used for the supervision and interpretation.
73. C
74. C
75. C
76. A
77. D
78. D
79. C
80. A
81. A
82. C
83. D
84. B
85. D
86. B
87. A
88. B
89. C
90. B
91. B

92.	D
93.	C
94.	A
95.	A
96.	B
97.	C
98.	A
99.	D
100.	C
101.	D
102.	C
103.	D
104.	D
105.	D
106.	B
107.	B
108.	C
109.	C
110.	C
111.	C
112.	A
113.	A
114.	B
115.	D
116.	D
117.	C
118.	A
119.	D	When tubal ligation is performed at the same time as hysterotomy, use 58611 in addition to 59100.
120.	A
121.	D
122.	A
123.	C
124.	A
125.	B
126.	C
127.	A
128.	C
129.	A
130.	C
131.	C
132.	B
133.	D
134.	C
135.	A

136.	B
137.	D
138.	D
139.	B
140.	D
141.	C
142.	A
143.	D
144.	A
145.	D
146.	B
147.	D
148.	B
149.	D
150.	A
151.	C
152.	C
153.	A
154.	D
155.	B
156.	A
157.	D
158.	C
159.	A
160.	C
161.	D
162.	C
163.	A
164.	D
165.	A
166.	D
167.	A
168.	B
169.	D
170.	A
171.	B
172.	D
173.	B
174.	B
175.	C
176.	C
177.	A
178.	B
179.	D
180.	B
181.	C
182.	A

(Continues)

183. D
184. C
185. A   Casting is included in the surgical procedure.
186. B
187. C
188. D
189. C   In order to use the code for the panel, every test must have been performed.
190. B   Code both the arthroscopic procedure and the open procedure. Both need to be reported because there were two separate procedures. Modifier-59 must be added to code 29826 because it is a component of the comprehensive procedure 23412. That is allowed if an appropriate modifier is used per NCCI edits.
191. D
192. C   According to CPT guidelines, when a patient is admitted to the hospital on the same day as an office visit, the office visit is not billable.

193. D   According to the CPT coding and guidelines for vaccines, only a separate identifiable Evaluation Management code may be billed in addition to the vaccine. In this scenario, the patient was seen only for his vaccines. This guideline immediately eliminates all the other answers.
194. A
195. C
196. C
197. A   Report this code only once no matter how many units were given.
198. B
199. D
200. D
201. D
202. D
203. A
204. A
205. D
206. C
207. B
208. A
209. C
210. D
211. A
212. B
213. D
214. B
215. C
216. B
217. B

REFERENCES

American Medical Association (AMA). (2016). *Physician's current procedural terminology (CPT) 2017 professional edition.* Chicago: Author.

Bowie, M. J. (2017a). *Understanding current procedural terminology and HCPCS coding systems* (5th ed.). Clifton Park, NY: Cengage Learning.

Green, M. (2016). *3-2-1 Code It!* (5th ed.). Clifton Park, NY: Cengage Learning.

Johnson, S. L. and Linker, R. (2017). *Understanding medical coding: A comprehensive guide* (4th ed.). Clifton Park, NY: Cengage Learning.

Keuhn, L. (2016). *Procedural Coding and Reimbursement for Physician Services: Applying Current Procedural Terminology and HCPCS.* Chicago: American Health Information Management Association (AHIMA).

Smith, G. (2011). *Coding surgical procedures: Beyond the basics.* Clifton Park, NY: Cengage Learning.

Smith, G. (2016). *Basic current procedural terminology and HCPCS coding, 2016.* Chicago: American Health Information Management Association (AHIMA).

CPT Coding Competencies

Questions	CCA Domain
1–217	1

VIII. Medical Billing and Reimbursement Systems

Shelley C. Safian, PhD, RHIA, CCS-P, COC, CPC-I,

AHIMA-Approved ICD-10-CM/PCS Trainer

1. The case-mix management system that utilizes information from the Minimum Data Set (MDS) in long-term care settings is called
   A. Medicare Severity Diagnosis Related Groups (MS-DRGs).
   B. Resource Based Relative Value System (RBRVS).
   C. Resource Utilization Groups (RUGs).
   D. Ambulatory Patient Classifications (APCs).

REFERENCE: Green, p 344
               Green and Rowell, p 30

2. The prospective payment system used to reimburse home health agencies for patients with Medicare utilizes data from the
   A. MDS (Minimum Data Set).
   B. OASIS (Outcome and Assessment Information Set).
   C. UHDDS (Uniform Hospital Discharge Data Set).
   D. UACDS (Uniform Ambulatory Core Data Set).

REFERENCE: Green, p 423
               Green and Rowell, p 30
               Oachs and Watters, p 230

3. Under APCs, the payment status indicator "N" means that the payment
   A. is for ancillary services.
   B. is for a clinic or an emergency visit.
   C. is discounted at 50%.
   D. is packaged into the payment for other services.

REFERENCE: Green and Rowell, p 334
               Oachs and Watters, p 229

4. All of the following items are "packaged" under the Medicare ASC payments, EXCEPT for
   A. implanted prosthetic devices.   C. splints and casts.
   B. medical supplies.   D. brachytherapy.

REFERENCE: Green, pp 640–644
               Oachs and Watters, p 230

5. Under the RBRVS, each HCPCS/CPT code contains three components, each having assigned relative value units. These three components are
   A. geographic index, wage index, and cost of living index.
   B. fee-for-service, per diem payment, and capitation.
   C. conversion factor, CMS weight, and hospital-specific rate.
   D. physician work, practice expense, and malpractice insurance expense.

REFERENCE: Green, p 1011
               Green and Rowell, pp 340–343

6. The prospective payment system used to reimburse hospitals for Medicare hospital outpatients is called
   A. APGs.   C. APCs.
   B. RBRVS.   D. MS-DRGs.

REFERENCE: Bowie and Green, p 328
               Green, pp 1002, 1007–1008
               Green and Rowell, pp 333–334

7. A Medicare patient was seen by Dr. Zachary, who is a nonparticipating physician. The charge for the office visit was $125. The Medicare beneficiary had already met his deductible. The Medicare Fee Schedule amount is $100. Dr. Zachary does not accept assignment. The office manager will apply a practice termed as "balance billing," which means that the patient is
   A. financially liable for the Medicare Fee Schedule amount.
   B. financially liable for charges in excess of the Medicare Fee Schedule, up to a limit.
   C. not financially liable for any amount.
   D. financially liable for only the deductible.

REFERENCE: Green and Rowell, pp 340–342
               Kuehn, p 324

8. The prospective payment system based on resource utilization groups (RUGs) is used for reimbursement to _____ for patients with Medicare.
   A. freestanding ambulatory surgery centers
   B. hospital-based outpatients
   C. intermediate care facilities
   D. skilled nursing facilities

REFERENCE: Green, pp 1006–1007
               Green and Rowell, p 30
               Oachs and Watters, p 227
               Schraffenberger, p 544

9. The _____ is a statement sent to the provider to explain payments made by third-party payers.
   A. remittance advice   C. attestation statement
   B. advance beneficiary notice   D. acknowledgment notice

REFERENCE: Green, p 1030
               Green and Rowell, p 89

10. HIPAA administrative simplification provisions require all of the following code sets to be used EXCEPT
   A. ICD-10-CM.   C. DSM.
   B. CDT.   D. CPT.

REFERENCE: Green, p 1034

11. The computer-to-computer transfer of data between providers and third-party payers in a data format agreed upon by both parties is called
   A. HIPAA (Health Insurance Portability and Accountability Act).
   B. electronic data interchange (EDI).
   C. health information exchange (HIE).
   D. health data exchange (HDE).

REFERENCE: Green, p 1030
               Green and Rowell, pp 81–83

12. A computer software program that assigns appropriate MS-DRGs according to the information provided for each episode of care is called a(n)
   A. encoder.   C. grouper.
   B. case-mix analyzer.   D. scrubber.

REFERENCE: Oachs and Watters, p 432

13. The standard claim form used by hospitals to request reimbursement for inpatient and outpatient procedures performed or services provided is called the
    A. UB-04.
    B. CMS-1500.
    C. CMS-1491.
    D. CMS-1600.

REFERENCE: Green and Rowell, pp 353–354
               Oachs and Watters, p 235

14. Under ASC PPS, when multiple procedures are performed during the same surgical session, a payment reduction is applied. The procedure in the highest level group is reimbursed at _____ and all remaining procedures are reimbursed at _____.
    A. 50%, 25%
    B. 100%, 50%
    C. 100%, 25%
    D. 100%, 75%

REFERENCE: Oachs and Watters, p 229

15. The _____ refers to a statement sent to the patient to show how much the provider billed, how much Medicare reimbursed the provider, and what the patient must pay the provider.
    A. Medicare summary notice
    B. remittance advice
    C. advance beneficiary notice
    D. coordination of benefits

REFERENCE: Green and Rowell, p 342–343, 520
               Oachs and Watters, p 235

16. Currently, which prospective payment system is used to determine the payment to the "physician" for physician services covered under Medicare Part B, such as outpatient surgery performed on a Medicare patient?
    A. MS-DRGs
    B. APCs
    C. RBRVS
    D. ASC PPS

REFERENCE: Oachs and Watters, p 229

17. Which of the following best describes the situation of a provider who agrees to accept assignment for Medicare Part B services?
    A. The provider is reimbursed at 15% above the allowed charge.
    B. The provider is paid according to the Medicare Physician Fee Schedule (MPFS) plus 10%.
    C. The provider cannot bill the patients for the balance between the MPFS amount and the total charges.
    D. The provider is a nonparticipating provider.

REFERENCE: Green, p 1011
               Green and Rowell, pp 510–511

18. When the MS-DRG payment received by the hospital is lower than the actual charges for providing the inpatient services for a patient with Medicare, then the hospital
    A. makes a profit.
    B. can bill the patient for the difference.
    C. absorbs the loss.
    D. can bill Medicare for the difference.

REFERENCE: Oachs and Watters, p 224

19. Under ASC PPS, bilateral procedures are reimbursed at _____ of the payment rate for their group.
   A. 50%   C. 200%
   B. 100%   D. 150%

REFERENCE: Oachs and Watters, p 229

Use the following table to answer questions 20 through 23.

Plantation Hospital's TOP 10 MS-DRGs

MS-DRG	Description	Number of Patients	CMS Relative Weight
470	Major joint replacement or reattachment of lower extremity w/o MCC	2,750	1.9871
392	Esophagitis, gastroent & misc. digestive disorders w/o MCC	2,200	0.7121
194	Simple pneumonia & pleurisy w CC	1,150	1.0235
247	Perc cardiovasc proc 2 drug-eluting stent w/o MCC	900	2.1255
293	Heart failure & shock w/o CC/MCC	850	0.8765
313	Chest pain	650	0.5489
292	Heart failure & shock w CC	550	1.0134
690	Kidney & urinary tract infections w/o MCC	400	0.8000
192	Chronic obstructive pulmonary disease w/o CC/MCC	300	0.8145
871	Septicemia w/o MV 96+ hours w MCC	250	1.7484

20. The case-mix index (CMI) for the top 10 MS-DRGs above is
   A. 1.164.   C. 0.782.
   B. 1.278.   D. 1.097.

REFERENCE: Abdelhak and Hanken, p 671
               Oachs and Watters, pp 223–224
               Sayles and Gordon, p 401

21. Which individual MS-DRG has the highest reimbursement?
   A. 247   C. 871
   B. 470   D. 293

REFERENCE: Oachs and Watters, pp 223–224

22. Based on this patient volume, during this time period, the MS-DRG that brings in the highest "total" reimbursement to the hospital is
   A. 470.   C. 392.
   B. 247.   D. 871.

REFERENCE: Oachs and Watters, pp 223–224
               Sayles and Gordon, pp 401–402

23. Based on this patient volume, the MS-DRG that brings in the highest total profit to the hospital is
   A. 470.
   B. 247.
   C. 392.
   D. It cannot be determined from this information.

REFERENCE: Casto and Forrestal, p 127
               Oachs and Watters, pp 223–224
               Sayles and Gordon, p 269

24. The Health Insurance Portability and Accountability Act (HIPAA) requires the retention of health insurance claims and accounting records for a minimum of ____ years, unless state law specifies a longer period.
   A. six
   B. five
   C. seven
   D. ten

REFERENCE: Green and Rowell, p 151
               Oachs and Watters, p 311

25. ____ is knowingly making false statements or representation of material facts to obtain a benefit or payment for which no entitlement would otherwise exist.
   A. Fraud
   B. Whistle-blowing
   C. Abuse
   D. Assault

REFERENCE: Abdelhak and Hanken, p 672
               Oachs and Watters, p 282

26. These are assigned to every HCPCS/CPT code under the Medicare hospital outpatient prospective payment system to identify how the service or procedure described by the code would be paid.
   A. geographic practice cost indices
   B. major diagnostic categories
   C. minimum data set
   D. payment status indicator

REFERENCE: Green, p 1011
               Green and Rowell, p 334

27. The term used to indicate that the service or procedure is reasonable and necessary for the diagnosis or treatment of illness or injury consistent with generally accepted standards of care is
   A. appropriateness.
   B. evidence-based medicine.
   C. benchmarking.
   D. medical necessity.

REFERENCE: Green, pp 22–23
               Green and Rowell, pp 377–378

28. This law prohibits a physician from referring Medicare patients to clinical laboratory services where the doctor or a member of his family has a financial interest.
   A. the False Claims Act
   B. the Civil Monetary Penalties Act
   C. the Federal Antikickback Statute
   D. the Stark I Law

REFERENCE: Bowie and Green, p 325
               Green, p 1028
               Green and Rowell, p 114

29. ____ are errors in medical care that are clearly identifiable, preventable, and serious in their consequences for patients.
    A. Misadventures
    B. Adverse preventable events
    C. Never events or sentinel events
    D. Potential compensable events

REFERENCE: Bowie and Green, p 326
               Sayles and Gordon, p 503

30. When a provider, knowingly or unknowingly, uses practices that are inconsistent with accepted medical practice and that directly or indirectly result in unnecessary costs to the Medicare program, this is called
    A. fraud.
    B. abuse.
    C. unbundling.
    D. hypercoding.

REFERENCE: Abdelhak and Hanken, p 672
               Green, pp 12, 529–530
               Oachs and Watters, p 282
               Sayles and Gordon, p 123

31. What prospective payment system reimburses the provider according to prospectively determined rates for a 60-day episode of care?
    A. home health resource groups
    B. inpatient rehabilitation facility
    C. long-term care Medicare severity diagnosis-related groups
    D. the skilled nursing facility prospective payment system

REFERENCE: Bowie and Green, p 313
               Green and Rowell, p 326
               Oachs and Watters, p 230
               Sayles and Gordon, p 442

32. If the Medicare non-PAR approved payment amount is $128.00 for a proctoscopy, what is the total Medicare approved payment amount for a doctor who does not accept assignment, applying the limiting charge for this procedure?
    A. $140.80   C. $192.00
    B. $143.00   D. $147.20

REFERENCE: Green and Rowell, pp 340–342, 468–469

33. Under the inpatient prospective payment system (IPPS), there is a 3-day payment window (formerly referred to as the 72-hour rule). This rule requires that outpatient preadmission services that are provided by a hospital up to three calendar days prior to a patient's inpatient admission be covered by the IPPS MS-DRG payment for
    A. diagnostic services.
    B. therapeutic (or nondiagnostic) services whereby the inpatient principal diagnosis code (ICD-10-CM) exactly matches the code used for preadmission services.
    C. therapeutic (or nondiagnostic) services whereby the inpatient principal diagnosis code (ICD-10-CM) does not match the code used for preadmission services.
    D. diganostic services *and* therapeutic (or nondiagnostic) services whereby the inpatient principal diagnosis code (ICD-10-CM) exactly matches the code used for preadmission services.

REFERENCE: Bowie and Green, p 313
               Green, p 1002
               Green and Rowell, p 331

34. This initiative was instituted by the government to eliminate fraud and abuse and recover overpayments, and involves the use of _____. Charts are audited to identify Medicare overpayments and underpayments. These entities are paid based on a percentage of money they identify and collect on behalf of the government.
    A. Clinical Data Abstraction Centers (CDAC)
    B. Quality Improvement Organizations (QIO)
    C. Medicare Code Editors (MCE)
    D. Recovery Audit Contractors (RAC)

REFERENCE: Green and Rowell, pp 126–127
                Oachs and Watters, p 258
                Sayles and Gordon, 453

35. When a patient is discharged from the inpatient rehabilitation facility and returns within three calendar days (prior to midnight on the third day) this is called a(n)
    A. interrupted stay.   C. per diem.
    B. transfer.   D. qualified discharge.

REFERENCE: Oachs and Watters, pp 231–233

36. In a global payment methodology, which is sometimes applied to radiological and similar types of procedures that involve professional and technical components, all of the following are part of the "technical" components EXCEPT
    A. radiological equipment.   C. radiological supplies.
    B. physician services.   D. radiologic technicians.

REFERENCE: Green and Rowell, pp 373–374
                Oachs and Watters, p 222
                Sayles and Gordon, pp 263–264, 675

37. Changes in case-mix index (CMI) may be attributed to all of the following factors EXCEPT
    A. changes in medical staff composition.
    B. changes in coding rules.
    C. changes in services offered.
    D. changes in coding productivity.

REFERENCE: Oachs and Watters, p 255
                Sayles and Gordon, pp 401–402

38. This prospective payment system replaced the Medicare physician payment system of "customary, prevailing, and reasonable (CPR)" charges whereby physicians were reimbursed according to their historical record of the charge for the provision of each service.
    A. Medicare Physician Fee Schedule (MPFS)
    B. Medicare Severity-Diagnosis Related Groups (MS-DRGs)
    C. Global payment
    D. Capitation

REFERENCE: Green, p 1011
                Green and Rowell, pp 340–343

39. CMS-identified "Hospital-Acquired Conditions" mean that when a particular diagnosis is not "present on admission," CMS determines it to be
    A. medically necessary.
    B. reasonably preventable.
    C. a valid comorbidity.
    D. the principal diagnosis.

REFERENCE: Oachs and Watters, p 226
                Sayles and Gordon, p 653

40. This process involves the gathering of charge documents from all departments within the facility that have provided services to patients. The purpose is to make certain that all charges are coded and entered into the billing system.
    A. precertification
    B. insurance verification
    C. charge capturing
    D. revenue cycle

REFERENCE: Diamond, p 10
               Oachs and Watters, p 247
               Sayles and Gordon, p 424

41. The Correct Coding Initiative (CCI) edits contain a listing of codes under two columns titled "comprehensive codes" and "component codes." According to the CCI edits, when a provider bills Medicare for a procedure that appears in both columns for the same beneficiary on the same date of service,
    A. code only the component code.
    B. do not code either one.
    C. code only the comprehensive code.
    D. code both the comprehensive code and the component code.

REFERENCE: Green, p 1024
               Green and Rowell, pp 267–268
               Oachs and Watters, p 236

42. The following type of hospital is considered excluded when it applies for and receives a waiver from CMS. This means that the hospital does not participate in the inpatient prospective payment system (IPPS)
    A. rehabilitation hospital
    B. long-term care hospital
    C. psychiatric hospital
    D. cancer hospital

REFERENCE: Green, p 1001
               Sayles and Gordon, p 440

43. These are financial protections to ensure that certain types of facilities (e.g., children's hospitals) recoup all of their losses due to the differences in their APC payments and the pre-APC payments.
    A. limiting charge   C. hold harmless
    B. indemnity insurance   D. pass through

REFERENCE: Green, p 989

44. LCDs and NCDs are review policies that describe the circumstances of coverage for various types of medical treatment. They advise physicians which services Medicare considers reasonable and necessary and may indicate the need for an advance beneficiary notice. They are developed by the Centers for Medicare and Medicaid Services (CMS) and Medicare Administrative Contractors. LCD and NCD are acronyms that stand for
    A. local covered determinations and noncovered determinations.
    B. local coverage determinations and national coverage determinations.
    C. list of covered decisions and noncovered decisions.
    D. local contractor's decisions and national contractor's decisions.

REFERENCE: Green, pp 488, 920
               Green and Rowell, p 309
               Oachs and Watters, p 243

Use the following table to answer questions 45 through 50.

EXAMPLE OF A CHARGE DESCRIPTION MASTER (CDM) FILE LAYOUT

Charge Service Code	Item Service Description	General Ledger Key	HCPCS Code		Charge	Revenue Code	Activity Date
			Medicare	Medicaid			
49683105	CT scan; head; w/out contrast	3	70450	70450	500.00	0351	1/1/2017
49683106	CT scan; head; with contrast	3	70460	70460	675.00	0351	1/1/2017

45. This information is printed on the UB-04 claim form to represent the cost center (e.g., lab, radiology, cardiology, respiratory, etc.) for the department in which the item is provided. It is used for Medicare billing.
   A. HCPCS
   B. revenue code
   C. charge/service code
   D. general ledger key

REFERENCE: Green, pp 1014–1015
              Green and Rowell, pp 346–349
              Oachs and Watters, p 251

46. This information is used because it provides a uniform system of identifying procedures, services, or supplies. Multiple columns can be available for various financial classes.
   A. HCPCS code
   B. revenue code
   C. general ledger key
   D. charge/service code

REFERENCE: Green, p 471
              Green and Rowell, pp 300–301
              Oachs and Watters, p 148
              Sayles and Gordon, p 130

47. This information provides a narrative name of the services provided. This information should be presented in a clear and concise manner. When possible, the narratives from the HCPCS/CPT book should be utilized.
   A. general ledger key
   B. HCPCS
   C. item/service description
   D. revenue code

REFERENCE: Green, p 474
              Green and Rowell, 320–321

48. This information is the numerical identification of the service or supply. Each item has a unique number with a prefix that indicates the department number (the number assigned to a specific ancillary department) and an item number (the number assigned by the accounting department or the business office) for a specific procedure or service represented on the chargemaster.
   A. charge/service code
   B. HCPCS code
   C. revenue code
   D. general ledger key

REFERENCE: Green, p 471
              Green and Rowell, pp 346–348

49. This information is used to assign each item to a particular section of the general ledger in a particular facility's accounting section. Reports can be generated from this information to include statistics related to volume in terms of numbers, dollars, and payer types.
    A. general ledger key
    B. charge/service code
    C. revenue code
    D. HCPCS code

REFERENCE: Oachs and Watters, p 848

50. Under ASC-PPS the patient is responsible for paying the coinsurance amount based on ____ of the national median charge for the services rendered.
    A. 50%
    B. 15%
    C. 20%
    D. 80%

REFERENCE: Bowie and Green, p 314
                Green, p 1009
                Oachs and Watters, p 229

51. ____ is a joint federal and state program that provides health care coverage to low-income populations and certain aged and disabled individuals.
    A. TRICARE
    B. Medicare Part A
    C. Medicaid
    D. Medicare Part B

REFERENCE: Green, p 995
                Oachs and Watters, p 35
                Sayles and Gordon, p 26

52. The DNFB report includes all patients who have been discharged from the facility but for whom, for one reason or another, the billing process is not complete. DNFB is an acronym for _____.
    A. diagnosis not finally balanced
    B. days not fiscally balanced
    C. dollars not fully billed
    D. discharged no final bill

REFERENCE: Oachs and Watters, p 255
                Sayles and Gordon, p 801

53. The limiting charge is a percentage limit on fees specified by legislation that the nonparticipating physician may bill Medicare beneficiaries above the non-PAR fee schedule amount. The limiting charge is
    A. 10%.
    B. 15%.
    C. 20%.
    D. 50%.

REFERENCE: Green and Rowell, pp 340–342

Use the following case scenario to answer questions 54 through 58.

A patient with Medicare is seen in the physician's office.
The total charge for this office visit is $250.00.
The patient has previously paid his deductible under Medicare Part B.
The PAR Medicare Fee Schedule amount for this service is $200.00.
The non-PAR Medicare Fee Schedule amount for this service is $190.00.

54. The patient is financially liable for the coinsurance amount, which is
A. 80%.
B. 100%.
C. 20%.
D. 15%.

REFERENCE: Green and Rowell, pp 340–342

55. If this physician is a participating physician who accepts assignment for this claim, the total amount the physician will receive is
A. $200.00.
B. $250.00.
C. $218.50.
D. $190.00.

REFERENCE: Green and Rowell, pp 340–342

56. If this physician is a nonparticipating physician who does NOT accept assignment for this claim, the total amount the physician will receive is
A. $250.00.
B. $200.00.
C. $218.50.
D. $190.00.

REFERENCE: Green and Rowell, pp 340–342

57. If this physician is a participating physician who accepts assignment for this claim, the total amount of the patient's financial liability (out-of-pocket expense) is
A. $200.00.
B. $40.00.
C. $160.00.
D. $30.00.

REFERENCE: Green and Rowell, pp 340–342

58. If this physician is a nonparticipating physician who does NOT accept assignment for this claim, the total amount of the patient's financial liability (out-of-pocket expense) is
A. $66.50.
B. $38.00.
C. $190.00.
D. $152.00.

REFERENCE: Green and Rowell, pp 340–342

59. A Medicare Summary Notice (MSN) is sent to _____ as their EOB.
A. physicians
B. patients (beneficiaries)
C. hospitals
D. skilled nursing facilities

REFERENCE: Clack Renfoe, and Rimmer, p 98
Green, p 1031
Oachs and Watters, p 235

60. There are times when documentation is incomplete or insufficient to support the diagnoses found in the chart. The most common way of communicating with the physician for answers is by
A. e-mailing physicians.
B. using physician query forms.
C. calling the physician's office.
D. leaving notes in the chart.

REFERENCE: Green, pp 15–18
Oachs and Watters, p 254
Sayles and Gordon, p 464

61. Under APCs, payment status indicator "X" means
A. ancillary services.
B. clinic or emergency department visit (medical visits).
C. significant procedure, multiple procedure reduction applies.
D. significant procedure, not discounted when multiple.

REFERENCE: Diamond, pp 278–279
Green and Rowell, p 334
Oachs and Watters, p 228

62. Under APCs, payment status indicator "V" means
   A. ancillary services.
   B. clinic or emergency department visit (medical visits).
   C. inpatient procedure.
   D. significant procedure, not discounted when multiple.

REFERENCE: Diamond, p 279
               Green and Rowell p 334
               Oachs and Watters, pp 228–229

63. Under APCs, payment status indicator "S" means
   A. ancillary services.
   B. clinic or emergency department visit (medical visits).
   C. significant procedure, multiple procedure reduction applies.
   D. significant procedure, multiple procedure reduction does not apply.

REFERENCE: Diamond, p 279
               Green, p 1007
               Green and Rowell, p 334
               Oachs and Watters, pp 228–229

64. Under APCs, payment status indicator "T" means
   A. ancillary services.
   B. clinic or emergency department visit (medical visits).
   C. significant procedure, multiple procedure reduction applies.
   D. significant procedure, not discounted when multiple.

REFERENCE: Diamond, p 279
               Green, p 1007
               Green and Rowell, p 334
               Oachs and Watters, p 229

65. Under APCs, payment status indicator "C" means
   A. ancillary services.
   B. inpatient procedures/services.
   C. significant procedure, multiple procedure reduction applies.
   D. significant procedure, not discounted when multiple.

REFERENCE: Diamond, p 278
               Green and Rowell, p 334
               Oachs and Watters, p 229

66. This is a 10-digit, intelligence-free, numeric identifier designed to replace all previous provider legacy numbers. This number identifies the physician universally to all payers. This number is issued to all HIPAA-covered entities. It is mandatory on the CMS-1500 and UB-04 claim forms.
   A. National Practitioner Databank (NPD)
   B. Universal Physician Number (UPN)
   C. Master Patient Index (MPI)
   D. National Provider Identifier (NPI)

REFERENCE: Green and Rowell, p 134
               Oachs and Watters, p 181
               Sayles and Gordon, p 183

67. In the managed care industry, there are specific reimbursement concepts, such as "capitation." All of the following statements are true in regard to the concept of "capitation," EXCEPT
    A. each service is paid based on the actual charges.
    B. the volume of services and their expense do not affect reimbursement.
    C. capitation means paying a fixed amount per member per month.
    D. capitation involves a group of physicians or an individual physician.

REFERENCE: Green, p 996
                  Green and Rowell, pp 48–51

68. Which of the following statements is FALSE regarding the use of modifiers with the CPT codes?
    A. All modifiers will alter (increase or decrease) the reimbursement of the procedure.
    B. Some procedures may require more than one modifier.
    C. Modifiers are appended to the end of the CPT code.
    D. Not all procedures need a modifier.

REFERENCE: Clack, Renfroe, and Rimmer, pp 25–26
                  Green, p 517
                  Green and Rowell, pp 48–49
                  Oachs and Watters, p 221
                  Sayles and Gordon, p 440

69. This document is published by the Office of Inspector General (OIG) every year. It details the OIG's focus for Medicare fraud and abuse for that year. It gives health care providers an indication of general and specific areas that are targeted for review. It can be found on the Internet on CMS' website.
    A. the OIG's Evaluation and Management Documentation Guidelines
    B. the OIG's Model Compliance Plan
    C. the Federal Register
    D. the OIG's Workplan

REFERENCE: Oachs and Watters, p 292
                  Sayles and Gordon, p 457

70. Accounts Receivable (A/R) refers to
    A. claims for which money has not yet come in.
    B. the amount the hospital was paid.
    C. claims for which money has been received.
    D. denials that have been returned to the hospital.

REFERENCE: Green and Rowell, p 97
                  Oachs and Watters, p 256
                  Sayles and Gordon, p 427

71. The following coding system(s) is/are utilized in the MS-DRG prospective payment methodology for assignment and proper reimbursement.
    A. HCPCS/CPT codes
    B. ICD-10-CM/ICD-10-PCS codes
    C. both HCPCS/CPT codes and ICD-10-CM/ICD-10-PCS codes
    D. NPI codes

REFERENCE: Green, pp 1002–1004
                  Oachs and Watters, p 224
                  Sayles and Gordon, pp 440–441

72. The following coding system(s) is/are utilized in the Inpatient Psychiatric Facilities (IPFs) prospective payment methodology for assignment and proper reimbursement.
    A. HCPCS/CPT codes
    B. ICD-10-CM/ICD-10-PCS codes
    C. both HCPCS/CPT codes and ICD-10-CM/ICD-10-PCS codes
    D. Revenue codes

REFERENCE: Green, p 1009
              Green and Rowell pp 335–337
              Oachs and Watters, p 233
              Sayles and Gordon, p 440

73. An Advance Beneficiary Notice (ABN) is a document signed by the
    A. utilization review coordinator indicating that the patient stay is not medically necessary.
    B. physician advisor indicating that the patient's stay is denied.
    C. patient indicating whether he/she wants to receive services that Medicare probably will not pay for.
    D. provider indicating that Medicare will not pay for certain services.

REFERENCE: Green, p 488
              Green and Rowell, pp 383–384

74. CMS identified Hospital-Acquired Conditions (HACs). Some of these HACs include foreign objects retained after surgery, blood incompatibility, and catheter-associated urinary tract infection. The importance of the HAC payment provision is that the hospital
    A. will receive additional payment for these conditions when they are not present on admission.
    B. will not receive additional payment for these conditions when they are not present on admission.
    C. will receive additional payment for these conditions whether they are present on admission or not.
    D. will not receive additional payment for these conditions when they are present on admission.

REFERENCE: Green and Rowell, pp 331–333
              Oachs and Watters, p 225
              Sayles and Gordon, p 437

75. Under Medicare Part B, all of the following statements are true and are applicable to nonparticipating physician providers, EXCEPT
    A. providers must file all Medicare claims.
    B. nonparticipating providers have a higher fee schedule than that for participating providers.
    C. fees are restricted to charging no more than the "limiting charge" on nonassigned claims.
    D. collections are restricted to only the deductible and coinsurance due at the time of service on an assigned claim.

REFERENCE: Green and Rowell, pp 510–512

76. Under Medicare, a beneficiary has lifetime reserve days. All of the following statements are true, EXCEPT
    A. the patient has a total of 60 lifetime reserve days.
    B. lifetime reserve days are usually reserved for use during the patient's final (terminal) hospital stay.
    C. lifetime reserve days are paid under Medicare Part B.
    D. lifetime reserve days are not renewable, meaning once a patient uses all of his or her lifetime reserve days, the patient is responsible for the total charges.

REFERENCE: Green and Rowell, pp 498–499
              Oachs and Watters, p 207

77. When a provider bills separately for procedures that are a part of the major procedure, this is called
   A. fraud.
   B. packaging.
   C. unbundling.
   D. discounting.

REFERENCE: Green and Rowell, p 293
                Oachs and Watters, p 286
                Sayles and Gordon, p 450

78. Health care claims transactions use one of three electronic formats, **including** which one of those listed below?
   A. CMS-1500 flat-file format.
   B. National Claim Format.
   C. ANSI ASC X12N 837 format.
   D. Medicare Summary Notice format.

REFERENCE: Green, pp 1032–1033
                Green and Rowell, p 135

79. The process by which health care facilities and providers ensure their financial viability by increasing revenue, improving cash flow and enhancing the patient's experience is called
   A. patient orientation.
   B. revenue cycle management.
   C. accounts receivable.
   D. auditing.

REFERENCE: Green, pp 1017–1018

80. Under the APC methodology, discounted payments occur when
   A. there are two or more (multiple) procedures that are assigned to status indicator "T."
   B. there are two or more (multiple) procedures that are assigned to status indicator "S."
   C. modifier-78 is used to indicate a procedure is terminated after the patient is prepared but before anesthesia is started.
   D. pass-through drugs are assigned to status indicator "K."

REFERENCE: Green, pp 1007–1008
                Green and Rowell, pp 349–353
                Oachs and Watters, p 229
                Sayles and Gordon, pp 289–291

81. This prospective payment system is for _____ and utilizes a Patient Assessment Instrument (PAI) to classify patients into case-mix groups (CMGs).
   A. skilled nursing facilities
   B. inpatient rehabilitation facilities
   C. home health agencies
   D. long-term acute care hospitals

REFERENCE: Green and Rowell, p 337
                Oachs and Watters, p 231
                Sayles and Gordon, p 103

82. Home Health Agencies (HHAs) utilize a data entry software system developed by the Centers for Medicare and Medicaid Services (CMS). This software is available to HHAs at no cost through the CMS website or on a CD-ROM.
   A. PACE (Patient Assessment and Comprehensive Evaluation)
   B. HAVEN (Home Assessment Validation and Entry)
   C. HHASS (Home Health Agency Software System)
   D. PEPP (Payment Error Prevention Program)

REFERENCE: Green and Rowell, p 326
                Oachs and Watters, p 230

83. This information is published by the Medicare Administrative Contractors (MACs) to describe when and under what circumstances Medicare will cover a service. The ICD-10-CM, ICD-10-PCS, and CPT/HCPCS codes are listed in the memoranda.
    A. LCD (Local Coverage Determinations)
    B. SI/IS (Severity of Ilness/Intensity of Service Criteria)
    C. OSHA (Occupational Safety and Health Administration)
    D. PEPP (Payment Error Prevention Program)

REFERENCE: Green and Rowell, p 309
               Oachs and Watters, p 243

84. The term "hard coding" refers to
    A. HCPCS/CPT codes that are coded by the coders.
    B. HCPCS/CPT codes that appear in the hospital's chargemaster and will be included automatically on the patient's bill.
    C. ICD-10-CM/ICD-10-PCS codes that are coded by the coders.
    D. ICD-10-CM/ICD-10-PCS codes that appear in the hospital's chargemaster and that are automatically included on the patient's bill.

REFERENCE: Oachs and Watters, p 252

85. This is the amount collected by the facility for the services it bills.
    A. costs
    B. charges
    C. reimbursement
    D. contractual allowance

REFERENCE: Oachs and Watters, p 102
               Sayles and Gordon, p 54

86. Assume the patient has already met his or her deductible and that the physician is a Medicare participating (PAR) provider. The physician's standard fee for the services provided is $120.00. Medicare's PAR fee is $60.00. How much reimbursement will the physician receive from Medicare?
    A. $120.00   C. $ 48.00
    B. $ 60.00   D. $ 96.00

REFERENCE: Green and Rowell, pp 340–342

87. This accounting method attributes a dollar figure to every input required to provide a service.
    A. cost accounting   C. reimbursement
    B. charge accounting   D. contractual allowance

REFERENCE: Kuehn, p 320
               Oachs and Watters, p 838
               Sayles and Gordon, p 547

88. This is the amount the facility actually bills for the services it provides.
    A. costs   C. reimbursement
    B. charges   D. contractual allowance

REFERENCE: Green and Rowell, p 319
               Oachs and Watters, pp 185, 220, 838

89. This is the difference between what is charged and what is paid.
    A. costs   C. reimbursement
    B. customary   D. contractual allowance

REFERENCE: Green and Rowell, pp 319, 342
               Kuehn, pp 320–326

90. When appropriate, under the outpatient PPS, a hospital can use this CPT code in place of, but not in addition to, a code for a medical visit or emergency department service.
    A. CPT Code 99291 (critical care)
    B. CPT Code 99358 (prolonged evaluation and management service)
    C. CPT Code 35001 (direct repair of aneurysm)
    D. CPT Code 50300 (donor nephrectomy)
REFERENCE: Green, pp 575, 580
              Kuehn, p 63

91. To monitor timely claims processing in a hospital, a summary report of "patient receivables" is generated frequently. Aged receivables can negatively affect a facility's cash flow; therefore, to maintain the facility's fiscal integrity, the HIM manager must routinely analyze this report. Though this report has no standard title, it is often called the
    A. remittance advice.
    B. periodic interim payments.
    C. DNFB (discharged, no final bill).
    D. chargemaster.
REFERENCE: Oachs and Watters, pp 254–255
              Sayles and Gordon, p 501

92. Assume the patient has already met his or her deductible and that the physician is a nonparticipating Medicare provider but does accept assignment. The standard fee for the services provided is $120.00. Medicare's PAR fee is $60.00 and Medicare's non-PAR fee is $57.00. What is the amount Medicare will pay the beneficiary on this claim?
    A. $120.00   C. $57.00
    B. $60.00   D. $45.60
REFERENCE: Green and Rowell, pp 340–342

93. CMS assigns one _____ to each APC and each _____ code.
    A. payment status indicator, HCPCS
    B. CPT code, HCPCS
    C. MS-DRG, CPT
    D. payment status indicator, ICD-10-CM and ICD-10-PCS
REFERENCE: Green, pp 1007–1008
              Green and Rowell, p 334

94. All of the following statements are true of MS-DRGs, EXCEPT
    A. a patient claim may have multiple MS-DRGs.
    B. the MS-DRG payment received by the hospital may be lower than the actual cost of providing the services.
    C. special circumstances can result in a cost outlier payment to the hospital.
    D. there are several types of hospitals that are excluded from the Medicare inpatient PPS.
REFERENCE: Green and Rowell, pp 329–330
              Oachs and Watters, p 223

95. This program, formerly called CHAMPUS (Civilian Health and Medical Program—Uniformed Services), is a health care program for active members of the military and other qualified family members.
    A. TRICARE   C. Indian Health Service
    B. CHAMPVA   D. workers' compensation
REFERENCE: Clack, Renfroe, and Rimmer, pp 15–16
              Green and Rowell, p 585
              Oachs and Watters, p 213
              Sayles and Gordon, pp 433–434

96. When health care providers are found guilty under any of the civil false claims statutes, the Office of Inspector General is responsible for negotiating these settlements and the provider is placed under a
   A. Fraud Prevention Memorandum of Understanding.
   B. Noncompliance Agreement.
   C. Corporate Integrity Agreement.
   D. Recovery Audit Contract.

REFERENCE: Oachs and Watters, p 297

97. Regarding hospital emergency department and hospital outpatient evaluation and management CPT code assignment, which statement is true?
   A. Each facility is accountable for developing and implementing its own methodology.
   B. The level of service codes reported by the facility must match those reported by the physician.
   C. Each facility must use the same methodology used by physician coders based on the history, examination, and medical decision-making components.
   D. Each facility must use acuity sheets with acuity levels and assign points for each service performed.

REFERENCE: Green, p 538

98. CMS adjusts the Medicare Severity DRGs and the reimbursement rates every
   A. calendar year beginning January 1.
   B. quarter.
   C. month.
   D. fiscal year beginning October 1.

REFERENCE: Oachs and Watters, p 223

99. In calculating the fee for a physician's reimbursement, the three relative value units are each multiplied by the
   A. geographic practice cost indices.
   B. national conversion factor.
   C. usual and customary fees for the service.
   D. cost of living index for the particular region.

REFERENCE: Green, p 1011
                Green and Rowell, pp 340–342

100. If a participating provider's usual fee for a service is $700.00 and Medicare's allowed amount is $450.00, what amount is written off by the physician?
   A. none of it is written off   C. $340.00
   B. $250.00   D. $391.00

REFERENCE: Green and Rowell, pp 340–342

101. Health plans that use _____ reimbursement methods issue lump-sum payments to providers to compensate them for all the health care services delivered to a patient over a specific period of time.
   A. episode-of-care (EOC)   C. fee-for-service
   B. capitation   D. bundled

REFERENCE: Abdelhak and Hanken, p 33
                Green and Rowell, pp 48–49
                Kuehn, p 321
                Oachs and Watters, p 221
                Sayles and Gordon, p 440

102. _____ offers voluntary, supplemental medical insurance to help pay for physician's services, outpatient hospital services, medical services, and medical-surgical supplies not covered by the hospitalization plan.
   A. Medicare Part A
   B. Medicare Part B
   C. Medicare Part C
   D. Medicare Part D

REFERENCE: Abdelhak and Hanken, p 34
               Oachs and Watters, p 208
               Sayles and Gordon, p 431

103. Commercial insurance plans usually reimburse health care providers under some type of _____ payment system, whereas the federal Medicare program uses some type of _____ payment system.
   A. prospective, retrospective
   B. retrospective, concurrent
   C. retrospective, prospective
   D. prospective, concurrent

REFERENCE: Green and Rowell, pp 318–320
               Oachs and Watters, pp 28, 30, 205
               Sayles and Gordon, p 441

104. When the third-party payer refuses to grant payment to the provider, this is called a
   A. denied claim.
   B. clean claim.
   C. rejected claim.
   D. unprocessed claim.

REFERENCE: Green, p 29
               Oachs and Watters, p 257

105. Some services are performed by a nonphysician practitioner (such as a Physician Assistant). These services are an integral yet incidental component of a physician's treatment. A physician must have personally performed an initial visit and must remain actively involved in the continuing care. Medicare requires direct supervision for these services to be billed. This is called
   A. "Technical component" billing.
   B. "Assignment" billing.
   C. "Incident to" billing.
   D. "Assistant" billing.

REFERENCE: Green and Rowell, pp 341–346

106. When payments can be made to the provider by EFT, this means that the reimbursement is
   A. sent to the provider by check.
   B. sent to the patient, who then pays the provider.
   C. combined with all other payments from the third party payer.
   D. directly deposited into the provider's bank account.

REFERENCE: Clack, Renfroe, and Rimmer, p 98
               Green and Rowell, p 89

107. The following services are excluded under the Hospital Outpatient Prospective Payment System (OPPS) Ambulatory Payment Classification (APC) methodology.
   A. surgical procedures
   B. durable medical equipment
   C. clinic/emergency visits
   D. radiology/radiation therapy

REFERENCE: Green, pp 1007–1008, 1010
               Green and Rowell, p 111

Current Procedural Terminology © 2016 American Medical Association. All Rights Reserved.

108. A HIPPS (Health Insurance Prospective Payment System) code is a five-character alphanumeric code. A HIPPS code is used by home health agencies (HHA) and _____
    A. ambulatory surgery centers (ASCs) and skilled nursing facilities (SNFs).
    B. physical therapy (PT) centers and inpatient rehabilitation facilities (IRFs).
    C. ambulatory surgery centers (ASCs) and physical therapy (PT) centers.
    D. skilled nursing facilities (SNFs) and inpatient rehabilitation facilities (IRFs).

REFERENCE: cms.gov

109. The Centers for Medicare and Medicaid Services (CMS) will make an adjustment to the MS-DRG payment for certain conditions that the patient was not admitted with, but were acquired during the hospital stay. Therefore, hospitals are required to report an indicator for each diagnosis. This indicator is referred to as
    A. a sentinel event.
    B. a payment status indicator.
    C. a hospital acquired condition.
    D. present on admission.

REFERENCE: Abdelhak and Hanken, p 284
               Green, p 1005
               Green and Rowell, pp 331–332
               Oachs and Watters, p 225
               Sayles and Gordon, p 437

110. A patient is admitted for a diagnostic workup for cachexia. The final diagnosis is malignant neoplasm of lung with metastasis. The present on admission (POA) indicator is
    A. Y = Present at the time of inpatient admission.
    B. N = Not present at the time of inpatient admission.
    C. U = Documentation is insufficient to determine if condition was present at the time of admission.
    D. W = Provider is unable to clinically determine if condition was present at the time of admission.

REFERENCE: Green, p 1005
               Oachs and Watters, p 225
               Sayles and Gordon, p 437

111. A patient undergoes outpatient surgery. During the recovery period, the patient develops atrial fibrillation and is subsequently admitted to the hospital as an inpatient. The present on admission (POA) indicator is
    A. Y = Present at the time of inpatient admission.
    B. N = Not present at the time of inpatient admission.
    C. U = Documentation is insufficient to determine if condition was present at the time of admission.
    D. W = Provider is unable to clinically determine if condition was present at the time of admission.

REFERENCE: Green, p 1005
               Oachs and Watters, p 225
               Sayles and Gordon, p 437

112. A patient is admitted to the hospital for a coronary artery bypass surgery. Postoperatively, he develops a pulmonary embolism. The present on admission (POA) indicator is
    A. Y = Present at the time of inpatient admission.
    B. N = Not present at the time of inpatient admission.
    C. U = Documentation is insufficient to determine if condition was present at the time of admission.
    D. W = Provider is unable to clinically determine if condition was present at the time of admission.

REFERENCE: Green, p 1005
              Oachs and Watters, p 225
              Sayles and Gordon, p 437

113. The nursing initial assessment upon admission documents the presence of a decubitus ulcer. There is no mention of the decubitus ulcer in the physician documentation until several days after admission. The present on admission (POA) indicator is
    A. Y = Present at the time of inpatient admission.
    B. N = Not present at the time of inpatient admission.
    C. U = Documentation is insufficient to determine if condition was present at the time of admission.
    D. W = Provider is unable to clinically determine if condition was present at the time of admission.

REFERENCE: Green, p 1005
              Oachs and Watters, p 225
              Sayles and Gordon, p 437

114. The present on admission (POA) indicator is required to be assigned to the _____ diagnosis(es) for _____claims on _____admissions.
    A. principal and secondary, Medicare, inpatient
    B. principal, all, inpatient
    C. principal and secondary, all, inpatient and outpatient
    D. principal, Medicare, inpatient and outpatient

REFERENCE: Green, p 1005
              Oachs and Watters, p 225
              Sayles and Gordon, p 437

115. The prospective payment system (PPS) requiring the use of DRGs for inpatient care was implemented in 1983. This PPS is used to manage the costs for
    A. home health care.
    B. medical homes.
    C. inpatient hospital stays.
    D. assisted living facilities.

REFERENCE: Oachs and Watters, p 233
              Sayles and Gordon, p 28

116. Coinsurance payments are paid by the _____ and determined by a specified ratio.
    A. physician
    B. third-party payer
    C. facility
    D. patient (insured)

REFERENCE: Green and Rowell, p 28
              Oachs and Watters, p 205
              Sayles and Gordon, p 426

117. Terminally ill patients with life expectancies of _____ may opt to receive hospice services.
    A. 6 months or less
    B. 6 months to a year
    C. one year or more
    D. one year or less
REFERENCE: Oachs and Watters, p 208
                      Sayles and Gordon, p 40

118. State Medicaid programs are required to offer medical assistance for
    A. all individuals age 65 and over.
    B. individuals with qualified financial need.
    C. patients with end stage renal disease.
    D. patients receiving dialysis for permanent kidney failure.
REFERENCE: Oachs and Watters, p 210
                      Sayles and Gordon, p 27

119. A lump-sum payment distributed among the physicians who performed the procedure or interpreted its results and the health care facility that provided equipment, supplies, and technical support is known as
    A. capitation.
    B. fee-for-service.
    C. a prospective payment system.
    D. a global payment.
REFERENCE: Green and Rowell, pp 273–275
                      Oachs and Watters, p 222
                      Sayles and Gordon, p 440

120. Of the following, which is a hospital-acquired condition (HAC)?
    A. air embolism
    B. Stage I pressure ulcer
    C. traumatic wound infection
    D. breach birth
REFERENCE: Green, p 1005
                      Green and Rowell, pp 331–333
                      Oachs and Watters, p 225
                      Sayles and Gordon, p 437

121. APCs are groups of services that the OPPS will reimburse. Which one of the following services is not included in APCs?
    A. radiation therapy
    B. preventive services
    C. screening exams
    D. organ transplantation
REFERENCE: Oachs and Watters, p 228

122. A patient is being cared for in her home by a qualified agency participating in Medicare. The data-entry software used to conduct all patient assessments is known as
    A. HHRG.
    B. RBRVS.
    C. HAVEN.
    D. IRVEN.
REFERENCE: Green, pp 442, 1007
                      Green and Rowell, p 326
                      Oachs and Watters, p 230

123. There are seven criteria for high-quality clinical documentation. All of these elements are included EXCEPT
   A. precise.
   B. complete.
   C. consistent.
   D. covered (by third-party payer).

REFERENCE: Oachs and Watters, p 267

124. A three-digit code that describes a classification of a product or service provided to a patient is a
   A. ICD-10-CM code.
   B. CPT code.
   C. HCPCS Level II code.
   D. Revenue code.

REFERENCE: Oachs and Watters, p 251
             Sayles and Gordon, p 130

125. The category "Commercial payers" includes private health information and
   A. Medicare/Medicaid.
   B. employer-based group health insurers.
   C. TriCare.
   D. Blue Cross Blue Shield.

REFERENCE: Green, p 993
             Green and Rowell, pp 442–443

126. ICD-10-PCS procedure codes are used on which of the following forms to report services provided to a patient?
   A. UB-04
   B. CMS-1500
   C. CMS-1491
   D. MDC 02

REFERENCE: Green, p 993

127. _____ classifies inpatient hospital cases into groups that are expected to consume similar hospital resources.
   A. IPPS
   B. CMS
   C. DRG
   D. MAC

REFERENCE: Green, p 1002
             Green and Rowell, pp 326–327

128. Based on CMS's DRG system, other systems have been developed for payment purposes. The one that classifies the non-Medicare population, such as HIV patients, neonates, and pediatric patients, is known as
   A. AP-DRGs.
   B. RDRGs.
   C. IR-DRGs.
   D. APR-DRGs.

REFERENCE: Green, p 1004

129. For those qualified, the _____ rule states that hospitals are paid a graduated per diem rate for each day of the patient's stay, not to exceed the prospective payment DRG rate.
    A. POA Indicator
    B. MS-DRG
    C. IPPS Transfer
    D. OASIS

REFERENCE: Green, p 1005
                    Green and Rowell, p 331

130. In a hospital, a document that contains a computer-generated list of procedures, services, and supplies, along with their revenue codes and charges for each item, is known as a(n)
    A. encounter form.
    B. superbill.
    C. revenue master.
    D. chargemaster.

REFERENCE: Green, p 1014

Answer Key for Medical Billing and Reimbursement Systems

ANSWER   EXPLANATION

1.   C
2.   B
3.   D
4.   D
5.   D
6.   C
7.   B
8.   D
9.   A
10. C
11. B
12. C
13. A   The UB-04 is used by hospitals. The CMS-1500 is used by physicians and other noninstitutional providers and suppliers. The CMS-1491 is used by ambulance services.
14. B
15. A
16. D
17. C   Since the provider accepts assignment, he will accept the Medicare Physician Fee Schedule (MPFS) payment as payment in full.
18. C
19. D
20. B   12781.730/10,000 = 1.278

MS-DRG	Description	Number of Patients	CMS Relative Weight	Total CMS Relative Weight
470	Major joint replacement or reattachment of lower extremity w/o MCC	2,750	1.9871	5464.525
392	Esophagitis, gastroent & misc. digestive disorders w/o MCC	2,200	0.7121	1566.620
194	Simple pneumonia & pleurisy w CC	1,150	1.0235	1177.025
247	Perc cardiovasc proc 2 drug-eluting stent w/o MCC	900	2.1255	1912.950
293	Heart failure & shock w/o CC/MCC	850	0.8765	745.025
313	Chest pain	650	0.5489	356.785
292	Heart failure & shock w CC	550	1.0134	557.350
690	Kidney & urinary tract infections w/o MCC	400	0.8000	320.000
192	Chronic obstructive pulmonary disease w/o CC/MCC	300	0.8145	244.350
871	Septicemia w/o MV 96+ hours w MCC	250	1.7484	437.100
	Total	10,000		12781.730
	Case-Mix Index Total CMS Relative Weights (12781.730) divided by (10,000) patients			1.278

ANSWER   EXPLANATION

21.   A   (See table on answer key under question 20.)

22.   A   (See table on answer key under question 20.)

23.   D   Total profit cannot be determined from this information alone. A comparison of the total charges on the bills and the PPS amount (reimbursement amount) that the hospital would receive for each MS-DRG could identify the total profit.

24.   A

25.   A

26.   D

27.   D

28.   D

29.   C

30.   B

31.   A

32.   D   The limiting charge is 15% above Medicare's approved payment amount for doctors who do NOT accept assignment ($128.00 × 1.15 = $147.20).

33.   D

34.   D

35.   A

36.   B

37.   D   Coding productivity will not directly affect CMI. Inaccuracy or poor coding quality can affect CMI.

38.   A   The Medicare Physician Fee Schedule (MPFS) reimburses providers according to predetermined rates assigned to services.

39.   B

40.   C

41.   C

42.   D   Cancer hospitals can apply for and receive waivers from the Centers for Medicare and Medicaid Services (CMS) and are therefore excluded from the inpatient prospective payment system (MS-DRGs). Rehabilitation hospitals are reimbursed under the Inpatient Rehabilitation Prospective Payment System (IRF PPS). Long-term care hospitals are reimbursed under the Long-Term Care Hospital Prospective Payment System (LTCH PPS). Skilled nursing facilities are reimbursed under the Skilled Nursing Facility Prospective Payment System (SNF PPS).

43.   C

44.   B

45.   B

46.   A

47.   C

48.   A

49.   A

50.   C

51.   C

52.   D

53.   B

54.   C

ANSWER   EXPLANATION

55.   A   If a physician is a participating physician who accepts assignment, he will receive the lesser of "the total charges" or "the PAR Medicare Fee Schedule amount." In this case, the Medicare Fee Schedule amount is less; therefore, the total received by the physician is $200.00.

56.   C   If a physician is a nonparticipating physician who does not accept assignment, he can collect a maximum of 15% (the limiting charge) over the non-PAR Medicare Fee Schedule amount. In this case, the non-PAR Medicare Fee Schedule amount is $190.00 and 15% over this amount is $28.50; therefore, the total that he can collect is $218.50.

57.   B   The PAR Medicare Fee Schedule amount is $200.00. The patient has already met the deductible. Of the $200.00, the patient is responsible for 20% ($40.00). Medicare will pay 80% ($160.00). Therefore, the total financial liability for the patient is $40.00.

58.   A   If a physician is a nonparticipating physician who does not accept assignment, he may collect a maximum of 15% (the limiting charge) over the non-PAR Medicare Fee Schedule amount.

$190.00 = non-PAR Medicare Fee Schedule amount

$190.00 × 0.20 = $38.00 = patient liable for 20% coinsurance (patient previously met the deductible)

$190.00 × 0.80 = $152.00 = Medicare pays 80%

$190.00 × 0.15 = $28.50 = 15% (limiting charge) over non-PAR Medicare Fee Schedule amount Physician can balance bill and collect from the patient the difference between the non-PAR Medicare Fee Schedule amount and the total charge amount. Therefore, the patient's financial liability is $38.00 (coinsurance) + 28.50 (limiting charge) = $66.50.

59.   B

60.   B

61.   A   Under the APC system, there exists a list of status indicators (also called service indicators, payment status indicators, or payment indicators). This indicator is provided for every HCPCS/CPT code and identifies how the service or procedure would be paid (if covered) by Medicare for hospital outpatient visits.

62.   B   Under the APC system, there exists a list of status indicators (also called service indicators, payment status indicators, or payment indicators). This indicator is provided for every HCPCS/CPT code and identifies how the service or procedure would be paid (if covered) by Medicare for hospital outpatient visits.

63.   D   Under the APC system, there exists a list of status indicators (also called service indicators, payment status indicators, or payment indicators). This indicator is provided for every HCPCS/CPT code and identifies how the service or procedure would be paid (if covered) by Medicare for hospital outpatient visits. Payment Status Indicator (PSI) "S" means that if a patient has more than one CPT code with this PSI, none of the procedures will be discounted or reduced. They will all be paid at 100%.

64.   C   Under the APC system, there exists a list of status indicators (also called service indicators, payment status indicators, or payment indicators). This indicator is provided for every HCPCS/CPT code and identifies how the service or procedure would be paid (if covered) by Medicare for hospital outpatient visits. Payment Status Indicator (PSI) "T" means that if a patient has more than one CPT code with this PSI, the procedure with the highest weight will be paid at 100% and all others will be reduced or discounted and paid at 50%.

ANSWER   EXPLANATION

65.   B   Under the APC system, there exists a list of status indicators (also called service indicators, payment status indicators, or payment indicators). This indicator is provided for every HCPCS/CPT code and identifies how the service or procedure would be paid (if covered) by Medicare for hospital outpatient visits.

66.   D

67.   A

68.   A

69.   D

70.   A

71.   B

72.   B

73.   C

74.   B   When these conditions are not present on admission, it is assumed that it was hospital acquired and therefore, the hospital may not receive additional payment.

75.   B   Under Medicare Part B, Congress has mandated special incentives to increase the number of health care providers signing PAR (participating) agreements with Medicare. One of those incentives includes a 5% higher fee schedule for PAR providers than for non-PAR (nonparticipating) providers.

76.   C   Lifetime reserve days are applicable for hospital inpatient stays that are payable under Medicare Part A, not Medicare Part B.

77.   C

78.   C

79.   B

80.   A   Discounts are applied to those multiple procedures identified by CPT codes with status indicator "T."

81.   B

82.   B

83.   A   Local Coverage Determinations (LCDs) were formerly called local medical review policies (LMRPs).

84.   B

85.   C

86   C   If the physician is a participating physician (PAR) who accepts the assignment, he will receive the lesser of the "total charges" or the "PAR amount" (on the Medicare Physician Fee Schedule). Since the PAR amount is lower, the physician collects 80% of the PAR amount ($60.00) × .80 = $48.00, from Medicare. The remaining 20% ($60.00 × .20 = $12.00) of the PAR amount is paid by the patient to the physician. Therefore, the physician will receive $48.00 directly from Medicare.

87   A

88.   B

89   D

90.   A   When a patient meets the definition of critical care, the hospital must use CPT Code 99291 to bill for outpatient encounters in which critical care services are furnished. This code is used instead of another E&M code.

ANSWER   EXPLANATION

91.   C   DNFB stands for "Discharged, No Final Bill"

92.   D   Since the physician is a nonparticipating physician, he will receive the non-PAR fee. The Medicare non-PAR fee is $57.00.

Medicare will pay 80% of the non-PAR fee ($57.00 × 0.80 = $45.60).

The patient will pay 20% of the non-PAR fee ($57.00 × 0.20 = $11.40).

Since the physician is accepting assignment on this claim, he cannot charge the patient any more than the 20% copayment. Therefore, the physician will receive $45.60 directly from Medicare.

93.   A

94.   A   Only one MS-DRG is assigned per inpatient hospitalization.

95.   A

96.   C

97.   A

98.   D

99.   A   The three relative value units are physician work, practice expense, and malpractice expense. These are adjusted by multiplying them by the geographical practice cost indices. Then, this total is multiplied by the national conversion factor.

100.   B   The participating physician agrees to accept Medicare's fee as payment in full; therefore, the physician would write off the difference between $700.00 and $450.00, which is 250.00.

101.   B

102.   B

103.   C

104.   A

105.   C

106.   D

107.   B

108.   D   Inpatient Rehabilitation Facilities (IRF) reports the HIPPS (Health Insurance Prospective Payment System) code on the claim. The HIPPS code is a five-digit CMG (Case Mix Group). Therefore, the HIPPS code for a patient with tier 1 comorbidity and a CMG of 0109 is B0109. Home Health Agencies (HHA) report the HIPPS code on the claim. The HIPPS code is a five-character alphanumeric code. The first character is the letter "H." The second, third, and fourth characters represent the HHRG (Home Health Resource Group). The fifth character represents what elements are computed or derived. Therefore, the HIPPS code for the HHRG C0F0S0 would be HAEJ1.

109.   D

110.   A   The malignant neoplasm was clearly present on admission, although it was not diagnosed until after the admission occurred.

111.   A   The atrial fibrillation developed prior to a written order for inpatient admission; therefore, it was present at the time of inpatient admission.

112.   B   The pulmonary embolism is an acute condition that was not present on admission because it developed after the patient was admitted and after the patient had surgery.

113.   C   Query the physician as to whether the decubitus ulcer was present on admission or developed after admission.

114.   A

ANSWER   EXPLANATION

115. C
116. D
117. A
118. B
119. D
120. A
121. D
122. C
123. D
124. D
125. B
126. A
127. C
128. D
129. C
130. D

REFERENCES

Abdelhak, M. and Hanken, M. (2016). *Health information management: Management of a strategic resource* (5th ed.). St. Louis, MO: Elsevier Saunders.

Bowie, M. J. and Green, M. A. (2016). *Essentials of health information management: Principles and practices* (3rd ed.). Clifton Park, NY: Cengage Learning.

Clack, C., Renfroe, L., and Rimmer, M. M. (2016). *Medical billing* 101 (2nd ed.). Clifton Park, NY: Cengage Learning.

Diamond, M. S. (2016). *Understanding hospital coding and billing: A worktext* (3rd ed.). Clifton Park, NY: Cengage Learning.

Green, M. A. (2016). *3-2-1-Code It!* (5th ed.). Clifton Park, NY: Cengage Learning.

Green, M. A. and Rowell, J. C. (2017). *Understanding health insurance: A guide to billing and reimbursement* (13th ed.). Clifton Park, NY: Cengage Learning.

Kuehn, L. (2016) *Procedural coding and reimbursement for physician services: Applying current procedural terminology and HCPCS 2016 Edition*. Chicago: American Health Information Association (AHIMA).

Oachs, P. and Watters, A. (2016). *Health information management: Concepts, principles, and practice* (5th ed). Chicago: American Health Information Management Association (AHIMA).

Sayles, N. and Gordon, L. (2016). *Health information management technology: An applied approach* (5th ed.). Chicago: American Health Information Management Association (AHIMA).

Schraffenberger, L. A. (2016). *Basic ICD-10-CM and ICD-10-PCS coding*. Chicago: American Health Information Management Association (AHIMA).

The following websites from the Centers for Medicare and Medicaid services provide links to pages containing official informational materials on the Medicare Fee-For-Service Payment:

- http://www.cms.hhs.gov/home/Medicare.asp
- https://www.cms.gov/Regulations-and-Guidance/Regulations-and-Guidance.html
- https://www.cms.gov/Outreach-and-Education/Medicare-Learning-Network-MLN/MLNProducts/downloads/MLNCatalog.pdf
- https://www.cms.gov/Medicare/Coding/NationalCorrectCodInitEd/index.html
- https://www.cms.gov/Medicare/Medicare-Fee-for-Service-Payment/ProspMedicareFeeSvcPmtGen/HIPPSCodes.html

Medical Billing and Reimbursement Systems Competencies

Questions	CCA Domain					
	1	2	3	4	5	6
1	X					
2		X				
3		X				
4		X				
5		X				
6		X				
7		X				
8		X				
9		X				
10		X				
11					X	
12					X	
13		X				
14		X				
15		X				
16		X				
17		X				
18		X				
19		X				
20		X				
21		X				
22		X				
23		X				
24						X
25				X		
26		X				
27		X				
28				X		
29	X					
30				X		
31	X					
32		X				
33		X				
34				X		
35	X					
36	X					
37		X				
38	X					
39	X					
40		X				
41		X				

Questions	CCA Domain					
	1	2	3	4	5	6
42		X				
43		X				
44		X				
45		X				
46		X				
47	X					
48	X					
49	X					
50		X				
51	X					
52		X				
53		X				
54		X				
55		X				
56		X				
57		X				
58		X				
59		X				
60				X		
61	X					
62	X					
63	X					
64	X					
65	X					
66	X					
67		X				
68	X					
69				X		
70		X				
71	X					
72	X					
73		X				
74	X					
75		X				
76	X					
77					X	
78					X	
79		X				
80		X				
81	X					
82					X	
83		X				

Questions	CCA Domain					
	1	2	3	4	5	6
84					X	
85		X				
86		X				
87		X				
88		X				
89		X				
90	X					
91		X				
92		X				
93		X				
94		X				
95	X					
96		X				
97	X					
98		X				
99		X				
100		X				
101		X				
102		X				
103		X				
104		X				
105		X				
106	X					
107	X					
108	X					
109	X					
110	X					
111	X					
112	X					
113	X					
114	X					
115		X				
116		X				
117		X				
118		X				
119		X				
120	X					
121		X				
122	X					
123			X			
124					X	
125		X				
126		X				

Questions	CCA Domain					
	1	2	3	4	5	6
127	X					
128		X				
129		X				
130	X					

IX. CCA Mock Quiz

CCA Quiz

1. Chronic otitis media with bilateral myringotomy and tube insertion using local anesthesia. (Code ICD-10-CM for diagnoses and CPT for procedures.)

H65.193	Other acute nonsuppurative otitis media, bilateral
H65.113	Acute and subacute allergic otitis media (mucoid) (sanguinous) (serous), bilateral
H66.93	Otitis media, unspecified, bilateral
69420	Myringotomy including aspiration and/or eustachian tube inflation
69433	Tympanostomy (requiring insertion of ventilating tube), local or topical anesthesia
-50	Bilateral Procedure

  A. H66.93, 69420-50   C. H65.113, 69420-50

  B. H66.93, 69433-50   D. H65.193, 69433-50

2. A coworker complained of the sudden onset of chest pain and was admitted to the hospital. A myocardial infarction was ruled out. You would code
   A. the myocardial infarction as if it were an established condition.
   B. both the infarction and the chest pain and sequence the infarction first.
   C. as an impending myocardial infarction.
   D. only the chest pain.

3. A 32-year-old female, known to be HIV positive, was admitted with lesions of the anterior trunk. Excisional diagnostic biopsies of the skin lesions were positive for Kaposi's sarcoma. Further examination revealed oral thrush. (Choose the correct ICD-10-CM diagnoses.)

B20	Human immunodeficiency virus [HIV] disease
Z21	Asymptomatic human immunodeficiency virus [HIV] infection status
C46.0	Kaposi's sarcoma, skin
L08.0	Pyoderma
B37.0	Candidiasis stomatitis (oral thrush)

  A. B20, L08.0   C. Z21, C46.0, K13.79

  B. B20, C46.0, B37.0   D. Z21, L08.0, K13.79

4. An 89-year-old male is admitted to a nursing home with confusion, hypotension, a temperature of 103.5, and obvious dehydration. Blood cultures were negative; however, urine culture was positive for *Escherichia coli*. The physician documents final diagnosis as septicemia, septic shock, UTI due to *E. coli*, and dehydration. (Code the ICD-10-CM diagnoses.)

A41.9	Septicemia, unspecified
A41.51	Sepsis due to *E. coli*
B96.20	Unspecified *E. coli* as the cause of diseases classified elsewhere
E86.0	Dehydration
F29	Psychosis, unspecified
I95.9	Hypotension, unspecified
N39.0	UTI, site not specified
R50.9	Fever, unspecified
R65.21	Severe sepsis with septic shock

  A. N39.0, I95.9, B96.20, R50.9, E86.0, F29

  B. A41.51, N39.0, B96.20, R65.21, E86.0

  C. N39.0, A41.9, B96.20, E86.0, R65.21, F29

  D. A41.9, E86.0, B96.20, R50.9, R65.21, F29

5. Mary is 6 weeks postmastectomy for carcinoma of the right breast. She is admitted for chemotherapy. What is the correct sequencing of the codes? (Code the ICD-10-CM diagnoses.)

C50.911	Malignant neoplasm of unspecified site of right female breast
Z85.3	Personal history of malignant neoplasm of the breast
Z51.11	Encounter for antineoplastic chemotherapy
Z08	Encounter for follow-up examination after completed treatment for malignant neoplasm

A. Z51.11, C50.911   C. Z08, Z51.11
B. Z51.11, Z85.3   D. Z85.3

6. Chip is 35 years old and has been previously diagnosed with lung cancer. He has been receiving chemotherapy and radiation. He develops seizures and is admitted. Workup revealed metastasis of the lung cancer to the brain. (Code the ICD-10-CM diagnoses.)

Z85.118	Personal history of other malignant neoplasm of the bronchus and lung
Z85.841	Personal history of malignant neoplasm of the brain
C34.90	Malignant neoplasm of unspecified part of unspecified bronchus or lung
C71.9	Malignant neoplasm of the brain, unspecified
C78.00	Secondary malignant neoplasm of unspecified lung
C79.31	Secondary malignant neoplasm of brain
G40.8	Other epilepsy and recurrent seizures
R56.9	Other convulsions (seizures, not otherwise specified)

A. R56.9, C34.90, C79.31   C. R56.9, Z85.118, Z85.841
B. R56.9, C79.31, C34.90   D. C79.31, C34.90, G40.8

7. Which of the following is coded as an adverse effect in ICD-10-CM?
   A. tinnitus due to allergic reaction after administration of ear drops
   B. mental retardation due to intracranial abscess
   C. rejection of transplanted kidney
   D. nonfunctioning pacemaker due to defective soldering

8. Mitch was diagnosed by his physician as having dehydration. Mitch has had gastroenteritis for several days, which has resulted in dehydration and requires intravenous hydration. Mitch also has chronic kidney disease and is at high risk for acute on chronic kidney failure. Two days following admission, Mitch develops acute renal failure. Mitch also has hypertension. (Code the ICD-10-CM diagnoses.)

E86.0	Dehydration
K52.9	Noninfective gastroenteritis and colitis, unspecified
I10	Essential hypertension
I12.9	Hypertensive chronic kidney disease with stage I through stage IV chronic kidney disease, or unspecified chronic kidney disease
I12.0	Hypertensive chronic kidney disease with stage V chronic kidney disease or end-stage renal disease
N17.9	Acute kidney failure, unspecified
N18.9	Chronic kidney disease, unspecified
N19	Renal failure, unspecified

A. N17.9, I12.9, E86.0   C. I12.0, E86.0
B. K52.9, E86.0, I12.9, N18.9, N17.9   D. E86.0, N19, N17.9, I10

9. Aunt Elsie is brought to the emergency room for increased confusion. She is subsequently diagnosed with Alzheimer's disease with dementia and cerebral atherosclerosis. She is also treated for hypertension and hypothyroidism. (Code the ICD-10-CM diagnoses.)

E03.9	Hypothyroidism, unspecified
F02.81	Dementia in other diseases classified elsewhere with behavioral disturbance
F02.80	Dementia in other diseases classified elsewhere without behavioral disturbance
F03.90	Unspecified dementia without behavioral disturbance
F03.91	Unspecified dementia with behavioral disturbance
G30.9	Alzheimer's disease, unspecified
I10	Essential hypertension
I67.2	Cerebral atherosclerosis

A. I67.2, F03.90, E03.9, I10

B. F03.90, I10, E03.9

C. G30.9, E03.9, I10, F03.91

D. G30.9, F02.80, I67.2, E03.9, I10

10. The patient presented to his physician's office due to increasingly severe pain in his right arm, shoulder, and neck for the past 6 weeks. MRI tests showed herniation of the C5–C6 disc. Patient was admitted and underwent an open cervical laminotomy and diskectomy of the C5–C6 disk. The patient is currently being treated for COPD and CAD with a history of PTCA. (Code the ICD-10-CM diagnoses and the procedures using ICD-10-PCS.)

M50.12	Cervical disc disorder with radiculopathy, mid-cervical region
M50.222	Other cervical disc displacement a C5-6 level
M50.02	Cervical disc disorder with myelopathy, mid-cervical region
J43.9	Emphysema, unspecified
J44.9	Chronic obstructive pulmonary disease, unspecified
I25.10	Atherosclerotic heart disease of native coronary artery without angina pectoris
Z98.61	Percutaneous transluminal coronary angioplasty status
0RB30ZZ	Excision of intervertebral disc
0PB30ZZ	Release, cervical spinal cord (decompression) (laminotomy)
0RT30ZZ	Resection, cervical vertebral disc, open approach

A. M50.12, J43.9, I25.10, Z98.61, 0RB30ZZ

B. M50.02, J44.9, I25.10, Z98.61, 0RB30ZZ

C. M50.02, J43.9, 0RB30ZZ

D. M50.222, J44.9, I25.10, Z98.61, 0PB30ZZ, 0RT30ZZ

11. Tom visits his physician because he has been feeling acute chest pain. Final diagnoses listed include acute pulmonary edema with congestive heart failure, subendocardial anterior wall myocardial infarction, hypertensive heart disease, and chronic obstructive pulmonary disease. (Code the ICD-10-CM diagnoses.)

I21.09	ST elevation (STEMI) myocardial infarction involving other coronary artery of anterior wall
I21.4	Non-ST elevation (NSTEMI) myocardial infarction
I11.9	Hypertensive heart disease, without heart failure
I11.0	Hypertensive heart disease, with heart failure
I50.9	Heart failure, unspecified
I50.1	Left ventricular heart failure, includes pulmonary edema with heart failure
J44.9	Chronic obstructive pulmonary disease, unspecified
J81.0	Acute edema of lung, unspecified

A. I21.4, I11.0, I50.1, J44.9

B. I21.09, I50.9. J81.0, I11.0, J44.9, I50.1

C. I21.4, I21.09, I11.0, J81.0, J44.9, I50.9

D. I21.09, I50.9. I11.9, J81.0, J44.9, I50.1

12. Patient was admitted from the nursing home with acute respiratory failure due to congestive heart failure. Chest X-rays also showed acute pulmonary edema. Patient was intubated and placed on mechanical ventilation for less than 24 hours and expired the day after admission.

I50.9	Heart failure, unspecified
I50.1	Left ventricular failure
J81.0	Acute edema of lung, unspecified
J96.00	Acute respiratory failure, unspecified whether with hypoxia or hypercapnia
J96.20	Acute and chronic respiratory failure, unspecified whether with hypoxia or hypercapnia
0BH17EZ	Insertion of endotrachial tube
5A1935Z	Continuous invasive mechanical ventilation for less than 24 consecutive hours

   A. I50.9, J96.20, J81.0, 0BH17EZ, 5A1935Z
   B. I50.9, J96.00, J81.0, 0BH17EZ, 5A1935Z
   C. J96.00, I50.1, 5A1935Z
   D. I50.9, J81.0, 0BH17EZ, 5A1935Z

13. Diverticulitis large bowel with ascending colon abscess was the diagnosis for a patient who was admitted with abdominal pain. Right hemicolectomy with colostomy performed. (Code the ICD-10-CM diagnoses and procedures using ICD-10-PCS.)

K57.20	Diverticulitis of large intestine with perforation and abscess without bleeding
K57.90	Diverticulosis of intestine, part unspecified, without perforation or abscess without bleeding
K57.92	Diverticulitis of intestine, part unspecified, without perforation or abscess without bleeding
K62.0	Anal polyp
0DTK0ZZ	Resection, ascending colon, open approach
0DTL0ZZ	Resection of transverse colon, open approach
0D1K0Z4	Bypass, ascending colon to cutaneous, open approach, no device

   A. K57.90, 0DTL0ZZ, 0D1K0Z4
   B. K57.92, 0DTK0ZZ, 0D1K0Z4
   C. K57.20, 0D1K0Z4
   D. K57.92, K62.0, 0DTL0ZZ

14. Patient has bilateral inguinal hernias; the left is indirect and the right is direct. He has open repairs of both hernias with flexible composite mesh prosthesis. (Code the ICD-10-CM diagnoses and procedures using ICD-10-PCS.)

K40.90	Unilateral inguinal hernia, without obstruction or gangrene, not specified as recurrent
K40.91	Unilateral inguinal hernia, without obstruction or gangrene, recurrent
K40.20	Bilateral inguinal hernia, without obstruction or gangrene, not specified as recurrent
0YQ50ZZ	Repair, inguinal region, right, open approach
0YQ60ZZ	Repair, inguinal region, left, open approach
0YUA0JZ	Supplement, inguinal region, bilateral, open, with synthetic substitute

   A. K40.91, K40.20, 0YUA0JZ
   B. K40.90, 0YQ50ZZ, 0YQ60ZZ
   C. K40.20, 0YUA0JZ
   D. K40.20, 0YQ50ZZ, 0YQ60ZZ

15. Vaginal delivery with episiotomy of full-term liveborn infant. Patient undergoes repair of delivery episiotomy and postdelivery elective vaginal endoscopic ligation of fallopian tubes bilaterally.

O80	Encounter for full-term uncomplicated delivery
Z30.2	Encounter for sterilization
Z37.0	Single liveborn
0UL74ZZ	Occlusion, bilateral fallopian tubes, percutaneous endoscopic approach, no device
10E0XZZ	Delivery of products of conception
0W8NXZZ	Division, perineum, female (episiotomy)

A. O80, Z37.0, Z30.2, 10E0XZZ, 0W8NXZZ, 0UL74ZZ
B. Z37.0, 0W8NXZZ, 0UL74ZZ
C. O80, Z37.0, 0UL74ZZ
D. O80, Z37.0, 10E0XZZ, 0UL74ZZ

16. Incomplete abortion complicated by excessive hemorrhage; dilation and curettage performed. (Code the ICD-10-CM diagnoses and procedures using ICD-10-PCS.)

D62	Acute posthemorrhagic anemia
O03.1	Delayed or excessive hemorrhage following incomplete spontaneous abortion
O03.4	Incomplete spontaneous abortion without complication
10D17ZZ	Extraction, retained products of conception, via natural opening
0UDB7ZZ	Extraction, endometrium, via natural opening

A. O03.1, 0UDB7ZZ
B. O03.1, D62, 0UDB7ZZ
C. O03.1, 10D17ZZ
D. O03.4, 10D17ZZ

17. John has chronic ulcers of the right calf and back. Both ulcers are excisionally debrided, and the ulcer of the back has a split-thickness skin graft, autologous. (Code the ICD-10-CM diagnoses and procedures using ICD-10-PCS.)

L97.219	Non-pressure chronic ulcer of right calf with unspecified severity
L98.429	Non-pressure chronic ulcer of back with unspecified severity
0HBKXZZ	Excisional debridement of skin, right lower leg
0HB6XZZ	Excisional debridement of skin, back
0HR6X74	Replacement, skin on the back, external, autologous tissue substitute, partial thickness

A. L97.219, L98.429, 0HBKXZZ, 0HB6XZZ, 0HR6X74
B. L97.219, L98.429, 0HBKXZZ
C. L98.429, 0HB6XZZ, 0HR6X74
D. L98.429, 0HBKXZZ, 0HB6XZZ, 0HR6X74

18. The physician has documented the final diagnoses as acute myocardial infarction, COPD, CHF, hypertension, atrial fibrillation, and status postcholecystectomy. The following conditions should be reported. (Code the ICD-10-CM diagnoses.)

I10	Essential hypertension
I11.0	Hypertensive heart disease, with heart failure
I21.3	ST elevation myocardial infarction (STEMI) of unspecified site
I48.91	Unspecified atrial fibrillation
I50.9	Heart failure, unspecified
J44.9	Chronic obstructive pulmonary disease, unspecified
Z90.49	Acquired absence of other specified parts of digestive tract

   A. I21.3, J44.9, I11.0, I48.91, Z90.49
   B. I21.3, J44.9, I50.9, I10, I48.91
   C. I21.3, J44.9, I50.9, I10, I48.91, Z90.49
   D. I21.3, J44.9, I10, I48.91

19. The autonomic nervous system has two divisions:
   A. the sympathetic system and the parasympathetic system.
   B. the sympathetic and the efferent peripheral system.
   C. the parasympathetic system and the peripheral nervous system.
   D. the afferent peripheral system and the somatic nervous system.

20. HPV or human papillomavirus is
   A. caused by the spirochete *Treponema pallidum*.
   B. a vaginal inflammation that is caused by a protozoan parasite.
   C. also known as genital warts.
   D. characterized by painful urination and an abnormal discharge.

21. A marked loss of bone density and increase in bone porosity is
   A. lumbago.   C. spondylitis.
   B. osteoarthritis.   D. osteoporosis.

22. The blood disorder in which red blood cells lack the normal ability to produce hemoglobin is called
   A. aplastic anemia.   C. pernicious anemia.
   B. hemolytic anemia.   D. thalassemia.

23. Which diagnostic technique records the patient's heart rates and rhythms over a 24-hour period?
   A. echocardiography   C. Holter monitor
   B. electrocardiography   D. angiocardiography

24. The physician's office note states: "Counseling visit, 15 minutes counseling in follow-up with a patient newly diagnosed with diabetes." If the physician reports code 99214, which piece of documentation is missing to substantiate this code?
   A. chief complaint   C. exam
   B. history   D. total length of visit

25. A patient initially consulted with Dr. Vasseur at the request of Dr. Meche, the patient's primary care physician. Dr. Vasseur examined the patient, prescribed medication, and ordered tests. Additional visits to Dr. Vasseur's office for continuing care would be assigned from which E/M section?
   A. Office and other outpatient services, new patient
   B. Office and other outpatient services, established patient
   C. Office or other outpatient consultations, new or established patient
   D. Confirmatory consultations, new or established patient

26. In order to correctly code a hernia repair, the coder needs to know all of the following EXCEPT
    A. the type of hernia.
    B. whether the hernia is strangulated or incarcerated.
    C. the age of the patient.
    D. whether the patient is obese or not.

27. According to CPT, a biopsy of the breast that involves removal of only a portion of the lesion for pathologic examination is
    A. percutaneous.
    B. incisional.
    C. excisional.
    D. punch.

28. A patient is seen in the emergency room following an accident. The physician documents that the wound required multiple layers and extensive undermining. According to CPT definitions, this type of repair would be classified as
    A. complex.
    B. intermediate.
    C. simple.
    D. advancement flap.

29. The emergency room discharge diagnosis for this ER encounter is "rule out myocardial infarction." The coder would assign
    A. a code for a myocardial infarction.
    B. a code for the patient's symptoms.
    C. a code for an impending myocardial infarction.
    D. no code for this condition.

30. _____ is a defect characterized by four anatomical abnormalities within the heart that results in poorly oxygenated blood being pumped to the body.
    A. Atrial septal defect
    B. Patent ductus arteriosus
    C. Tetralogy of Fallot
    D. Coarctation of the aorta

31. Urinary frequency, urgency, nocturia, incontinence, and hesitancy are all symptoms of
    A. BPH.
    B. end-stage kidney disease.
    C. salpingitis.
    D. genital prolapse.

32. Down's syndrome, Edwards' syndrome, and Patau syndrome are all examples of _____ defects.
    A. musculoskeletal
    B. chromosomal
    C. genitourinary tract
    D. digestive system

33. The type of anemia caused by a failure of the bone marrow to produce red blood cells is
    A. acute blood-loss anemia.
    B. sickle cell anemia.
    C. iron-deficiency anemia.
    D. aplastic anemia.

34. A patient has major surgery and sees the surgeon 10 days later for an unrelated E/M service. Indicate the modifier that should be attached to the E/M code for the service provided.
    A. -24
    B. -25
    C. -59
    D. -79

35. Patient presents to the hospital for a three-view X-ray of the right shoulder. The diagnosis is shoulder pain and the radiology report states the patient has a dislocated shoulder. What would be the correct codes to report to the insurance company?

M25.511	Pain in right shoulder
S43.004A	Unspecified dislocation of right shoulder joint, initial encounter
S43.014A	Anterior dislocation of right humerus, initial encounter
73020	Radiologic examination, shoulder; one view
73030	Radiologic examination, shoulder; complete, minimum of two views
73060	Radiologic examination; humerus, minimum of two views
RT	Right side

    A. S43.004A; 73060-RT
    B. M25.511; 73020-RT
    C. S43.014A; 73030-RT
    D. S43.004A; 73030-RT

CCA Mock Quiz Answer Key

ANSWER   EXPLANATION

1. B   CPT notes immediately following code 69433 instruct the coder to report 69433 with modifier -50 for a procedure performed bilaterally.

REFERENCE: AHA, p 219
Bowie (2017a), p 214
Bowie (2017b), p 215
Green, pp 713–714

2. D

REFERENCE: AHA, pp 57–58
Bowie (2017b), pp 50–54

3. B   The medical term for thrush is candidiasis.

REFERENCE: AHA, pp 156–157, 289
Bowie (2017b), p 83

4. B

REFERENCE: AHA, pp 150–155, 175, 260–261
Bowie (2017b), pp 70–71, 77, 171, 239, 320–321, 379–380

5. A   The cancer is coded as a current condition as long as the patient is receiving adjunct therapy.

REFERENCE: AHA, pp 442, 459–461, 465–466
Bowie (2017b), p 115, 450

6. A   Additional conditions that may not be routinely associated with a disease process should be coded when present. Seizures are not routinely associated with cancer; therefore, it is coded.

REFERENCE: AHA, pp 206, 448–451, 459–462
Bowie (2017b), pp 106–108, 387

7. A

REFERENCE: AHA, pp 514–518, 521–522
Bowie (2017b), p 409

8. B

REFERENCE: AHA, pp 263–265
Bowie (2017b), pp 157, 228, 318–319

9. D

REFERENCE: AHA, pp 173, 206
Bowie (2017b), pp 156–157, 188–189

10. D   When a patient has no known history of CABG and is diagnosed with coronary artery disease (CAD) with no mention of a specific vessel, it is appropriate to assign code I25.10 (coronary atherosclerosis of native coronary artery) since there is no history of prior bypass surgery.

REFERENCE: AHA, pp 230, 294–297, 392–393
Bowie (2017b), pp 230, 253, 302

11. A   Subendocardial MI takes precedence over anatomical site unless there were two separate acute MIs. Acute pulmonary edema is included in the code for congestive heart failure (CHF).

REFERENCE: AHA, pp 229–231, 386–389, 394–395, 403–405
Bowie (2017b), p 230

ANSWER   EXPLANATION

12. C   Acute pulmonary edema is included in the code for congestive heart failure (CHF). Insertion of endotracheal tube is included in the ventilation code.

REFERENCE: AHA, pp 233–235, 238–240, 395
Bowie (2017b), p 255

13. C

REFERENCE: AHA, pp 244–245, 247–248
Bowie (2017b), p 269

14. C

REFERENCE: AHA, p 253
Bowie (2017b), p 268

15. A

REFERENCE: AHA, pp 316, 319–320, 336, 338–339
Bowie (2017b), p 342

16. C

REFERENCE: AHA, pp 193, 346–347, 351–352
Bowie (2017b), p 342

17. A

REFERENCE: AHA, pp 286–287, 290
Bowie (2017b), p 286

18. B   Category Z90.49, acquired absence of other specified parts of digestive tract, is intended to be used for patient care where the absence of an organ affects treatment.

REFERENCE: AHA, pp 34–37, 229–230, 394–395, 403
Bowie (2017b), p 230

19. A

REFERENCE: Scott and Fong, p 172

20. C

REFERENCE: Scott and Fong, p 459

21. D

REFERENCE: Scott and Fong, pp 107–108

22. D

REFERENCE: Scott and Fong, p 244

23. C

REFERENCE: Scott and Fong, p 260

24. D   In order to use time as a factor in determining the appropriate E/M code, the total time spent with the patient, as well as the amount of time spent in counseling, must be recorded.

REFERENCE: Bowie (2017a), p 42
Johnson and Linker, p 133
Kuehn, pp 54–56

ANSWER   EXPLANATION

25. B Consultation codes can no longer be coded when the physician has taken an active part in the continued care of the patient.

REFERENCE: Bowie (2017a), pp 60–61
               Johnson and Linker, pp 114–115
               Keuhn, pp 60–61

26. D
REFERENCE: Bowie (2017a), 277
               Kuehn, pp 169–171

27. B

REFERENCE: Johnson and Linker, p 203
               Kuehn, pp 118–119

28. A

REFERENCE: Bowie (2017a), p 124
               Johnson and Linker, pp 209–211
               Kuehn, pp 112–113

29. B When a diagnosis is preceded by the phrase "rule out" in the outpatient setting, code condition(s) to the highest degree of certainty for that encounter/visit, such as symptoms, signs, abnormal test results, or other reasons for the visit.

REFERENCE: AHA, pp 57–58
               Bowie (2017b), pp 51–56

30. C

REFERENCE: Green, p 741

31. A

REFERENCE: Scott and Fong, p 456

32. B

REFERENCE: Scott and Fong, p 471

33. D

REFERENCE: Scott and Fong, p 244

34. A

REFERENCE: Bowie (2017a), p 19
               Green, p 364
               Keuhn, p 303

35. D

REFERENCE: AHA, pp 30–33
               AMA CPT (2017)
               Bowie (2017a), pp 497–498
               Bowie (2017b), p 404
               Kuehn, p 220

REFERENCES

American Hospital Association (AHA). (2016). *ICD-10-CM and ICD-10-PCS coding handbook 2017 (with Answers)*. Chicago: Nelly Leon-Chisen, RHIA Central Office on ICD-10-CM and ICD-10-PCS of the American Hospital Association (AHA).

American Medical Association (AMA). (2016). *Current procedural terminology (CPT) 2017 professional edition*. Chicago: Author.

Bowie, M. J. (2017a). *Understanding current procedural terminology and HCPCS coding systems* (5th ed.). Clifton Park, NY: Cengage Learning.

Bowie, M. J. (2017b). *Understanding ICD-10-CM and ICD-10-PCS: A worktext* (3rd ed.). Clifton Park, NY: Cengage Learning.

Green, M. A. (2016). *3-2-1 code it!* (5th ed.). Clifton Park, NY: Cengage Learning.

Johnson, S. L. and Linker, R. (2017). *Understanding medical coding: A comprehensive guide* (4th ed.). Clifton Park, NY: Cengage Learning.

Kuehn, L. (2016). *Procedural coding and reimbursement for physician services (2016): Applying Current Procedural Terminology and HCPCS*. Chicago: American Health Information Management Association (AHIMA).

Oachs, P. and Watters, A. (2016). *Health information management concepts: Principles and practice* (5th ed.). Chicago: American Health Information Management Association (AHIMA).

Scott, A. S. and Fong, P. E. (2017). *Body structures and functions* (13th ed.). Clifton Park, NY: Cengage Learning.

Competencies for the CCA Quiz	
Question	CCA Domain
1–35	1

X. CCA Mock Examination

CCA Mock Examination

1. Your organization is sending confidential patient information across the Internet using technology that will transform the original data into unintelligible code that can be re-created by authorized users. This technique is called
   A. a firewall.
   B. validity processing.
   C. a call-back process.
   D. data encryption.

2. As part of a concurrent record review, you need to locate the initial plan of action based on the attending physician's initial assessment of the patient. You can expect to find this documentation either within the body of the history and physical or in the
   A. doctor's admitting progress note.
   B. nurse's admit note.
   C. review of systems.
   D. discharge summary.

3. Employing the SOAP style of progress notes, choose the "assessment" statement from the following:
   A. Patient states low back pain with sciatica is as severe as it was on admission.
   B. Patient moving about very cautiously and appears to be in pain.
   C. Adjust pain medication; begin physical therapy tomorrow.
   D. Sciatica unimproved with hot pack therapy.

4. You have been hired to work with a computer-assisted coding initiative. The technology that you will be working with is
   A. electronic data interchange.
   B. intraoperability.
   C. message standards.
   D. natural language processing.

5. A final progress note is appropriate as a discharge summary for a hospitalization in which the patient
   A. dies within 24 hours of admission.
   B. has no comorbidities or complications during this episode of care.
   C. was admitted within 30 days with the same diagnosis.
   D. was an obstetric admission with a normal delivery and no complications.

6. In reviewing a medical record for coding purposes, the coder notes that the discharge summary has not yet been transcribed. In its absence, the best place to look for the patient's response to treatment and documentation of any complications that may have developed during this episode of care is in the
   A. doctors' progress note section.
   B. operative report.
   C. history and physical.
   D. doctors' orders.

7. You would expect to find documentation regarding the assessment of an obstetric patient's lochia, fundus, and perineum on the
   A. prenatal record.
   B. labor record.
   C. delivery room record.
   D. postpartum record.

8. A patient is admitted through the emergency department with diabetes mellitus. Three days after admission, the physician documents uncontrolled diabetes mellitus. What is the "present on admission" (POA) indicator for uncontrolled diabetes mellitus?
   A. N
   B. U
   C. W
   D. Y

SAMPLE MS-DRG REPORT		
MS-DRG IDENTIFIER	RELATIVE WEIGHT	NUMBER OF PATIENTS WITH THIS MS-DRG
A	1.234	12
B	3.122	10
C	2.165	19
D	5.118	16

9. Based on the preceding sample MS-DRG report, what is the case-mix index for this facility?
   A. 42.26275
   B. 2.965807
   C. 11.639
   D. 2.90975

10. The special form that plays the central role in planning and providing care at nursing, psychiatric, and rehabilitation facilities is the
    A. interdisciplinary patient care plan.
    B. medical history and review of systems.
    C. interval summary.
    D. problem list.

11. What legal term is used in describing sexual harassment in reference to unwelcome sexual advances, the request for sexual favors, and verbal or physical conduct of a sexual nature made in return for job benefits?
    A. res ipsa loquitur
    B. qui tam
    C. quid pro quo
    D. respondeat superior

12. Your facility would like to improve physician documentation in order to allow improved coding. As coding supervisor, you have found it very effective to provide the physicians with
    A. a copy of the facility coding guidelines, along with written information on improved documentation.
    B. the UHDDS and information on where each data element is collected and/or verified in your facility.
    C. regular in-service presentations on documentation, including its importance and tips for improvement.
    D. feedback on specific instances when improved documentation would improve coding.

		WATERSIDE HOSPITAL CODING PRODUCTIVITY WEEK ENDING JANUARY 2, 2017	
EMPLOYEE NUMBER	INPATIENT	OUTPATIENT PROCEDURE	OUTPATIENT OBSERVATION OR EMERGENCY RECORDS
425	120	35	16
426	48	89	95
427	80	92	4
428	65	109	16

13. The performance standard for coders is 28–33 workload units per day. Workload units are calculated as follows:

   Inpatient records = 1 workload unit

   Outpatient surgical procedure records = 0.75 workload units

   Outpatient observation/Emergency records = 0.50 workload units

   One week's productivity information is shown in the preceding table. What percentage of the coders is meeting the productivity standards?
   A. 100%
   B. 75%
   C. 50%
   D. 25%

14. Which of the following diagnoses or procedures would prevent the normal delivery code, O80, from being assigned?
   A. occiput presentation
   B. single liveborn
   C. episiotomy
   D. low forceps

15. Which of the following are considered late effects (sequelae) regardless of time?
   A. congenital defect
   B. nonunion
   C. nonhealing fracture
   D. poisoning

16. Patient is admitted for elective cholecystectomy for treatment of chronic cholecystitis with cholelithiasis. Prior to administration of general anesthesia, patient suffers cerebral thrombosis. Surgery is subsequently canceled. Code and sequence the coding from the following codes.

   I66.9   Occlusion and stenosis of unspecified cerebral artery
   K80.10 Calculus of gallbladder with chronic cholecystitis without obstruction
   Z53.09 Procedure and treatment not carried out because of other contraindication
   I97.821 Postprocedural cerebrovascular infarction following other surgery
   0FT40ZZ Resection of gallbladder, open approach (Cholecystectomy)

   A. I97.821, K80.10, 0FT40ZZ
   B. K80.10, I66.9, Z53.09
   C. I97.821, I66.9, Z53.09
   D. I66.9, Z53.09

17. Some ICD-10-CM codes are exempt from POA reporting because they
   A. represent circumstances regarding the health care encounter or factors influencing health status that do not represent a current disease or injury.
   B. are always present on admission.
   C. are always present on admission and represent circumstances regarding the health care encounter or factors influencing health status that do not represent a current disease or injury.
   D. represent external cause codes.

18. Which of these conditions are always considered "present on admission" (POA)?
    A. congenital conditions
    B. E codes
    C. acute conditions
    D. possible, probable, or suspected conditions

19. When coding multiple wound repairs in CPT,
    A. only the most complex repair is reported.
    B. only the least complex repair is reported.
    C. up to nine individual repair codes may be reported.
    D. all wound repairs are grouped and coded, with the most complex reported first.

20. Which of the following is vital for determining why the reimbursement from an insurance company is less than that which was expected?
    A. a CPT codebook
    B. the remittance advice
    C. talking to the patient
    D. knowledge of the individual insurance company's policies

21. Four people were seen in your Emergency Department yesterday. Which one will be coded as a poisoning?

    Robert: diagnosed with digitalis intoxication
    Gary: had an allergic reaction to a dye administered for a pyelogram
    David: developed syncope after taking Contac pills with a double scotch
    Brian: had an idiosyncratic reaction between two properly administered prescription drugs

    A. Robert   C. David
    B. Gary   D. Brian

22. Present on Admission (POA) indicators apply to
    A. inpatient reporting of diagnosis codes.
    B. outpatient reporting of procedure codes.
    C. inpatient reporting of diagnosis and procedure codes.
    D. outpatient reporting of diagnosis and procedure codes.

23. Using the ICD-10-CM code structure, which of the following would be used for "right upper quadrant abdominal tenderness"?
    A. R108.11   C. R10.811
    B. R10811.11   D. R1.0811

24. Which of the following scenarios identifies a pathologic fracture?
    A. greenstick fracture secondary to fall from a bed
    B. compression fracture of the skull after being hit with a baseball bat
    C. vertebral fracture with cord compression following a car accident
    D. compression fracture of the vertebrae as a result of bone metastasis

25. All of the following signs/symptoms suggest gram-negative pneumonia EXCEPT
    A. fever.   C. purulent sputum.
    B. patchy infiltrate.   D. decreased leukocyte count.

26. During her hospitalization for her third delivery, Janet had a sterilization procedure performed. When the record is coded, the code for sterilization, Z30.2, is
    A. not used.
    B. used and sequenced as the principal diagnosis.
    C. used and sequenced as a secondary diagnosis.
    D. the only code used.

27. Ensuring that data have been modified or accessed only by individuals who are authorized to do so is a function of data
    A. accuracy.   C. integrity.
    B. validity.   D. quality.

28. Which of the following statements is true?
    A. A surgical procedure may include one or more surgical operations.
    B. The terms *surgical operation* and *surgical procedure* are synonymous.
    C. A surgical operation may include one or more surgical procedures.
    D. The term *surgical procedure* is an incorrect term and should not be used.

29. Security devices that form barriers between routers of a public network and a private network to protect access by unauthorized users are called
    A. data translators.   C. data manipulation engines.
    B. passwords.   D. firewalls.

30. The Joint Commission requires that all medical records be completed within _____ following patient discharge.
    A. 30 days   C. 7 days
    B. 14 days   D. 90 days

31. You are conducting an educational session on benchmarking. You tell your audience that the key to benchmarking is to use the comparison to
    A. implement your QI process.
    B. make recommendations for improvement to the other department or organization.
    C. improve your department's processes.
    D. compare your department with another.

32. Which of the following procedures can be identified as "destruction" of lesions in CPT coding?
    A. removal of skin tags   C. laser removal of condylomata
    B. shaving of skin lesion   D. paring of hyperkeratotic lesion

33. A _____ is a collection of information or data that is organized in such a way that its contents can be queried and relationships created.
    A. database   C. record
    B. field   D. table

34. Staging
    A. refers to the monitoring of incidence and trends associated with a disease.
    B. is continued medical surveillance of a case.
    C. is a system for documenting the extent or spread of cancer.
    D. designates the degree of differentiation of cells.

35. Which diagnosis should be listed first when sequencing inpatient codes using the UHDDS?
    A. primary diagnosis   C. significant diagnosis
    B. principal diagnosis   D. admitting diagnosis

36. Which of the following would NOT require HCPCS/CPT codes?
    A. hospital ambulatory surgery visit   C. clinic visit
    B. hospital outpatient visit   D. hospital inpatient procedure

37. Patient was seen in the emergency department with lacerations on the left arm. Two lacerations, one 7 cm and one 9 cm, were closed with layered sutures.

12002	Simple repair of superficial wounds of scalp, neck, axillae, external genitalia, trunk and/or extremities (including hands and feet); 2.6 cm to 7.5 cm
12004	Simple repair of superficial wounds of scalp, neck, axillae, external genitalia, trunk, and/or extremities (including hands and feet); 7.6 cm to 12.5 cm
12035	Repair, intermediate, wounds of scalp, axillae, trunk, and/or extremities (excluding hands and feet); 12.6 cm to 20 cm
12045	Repair, intermediate, wounds of neck, hands, feet, and/or external genitalia; 12.6 cm to 20 cm

    A. 12045   C. 12002, 12004
    B. 12035   D. 12004

38. Patient was seen for excision of two interdigital neuromas from the left foot.

28080	Excision, interdigital (Morton's) neuroma, single, each
64774	Excision of neuroma; cutaneous nerve, surgically identifiable
64776	Excision of neuroma; digital nerve, one or both, same digit

    A. 64774   C. 28080
    B. 64776   D. 28080, 28080

39. Patient was seen today for regular hemodialysis. No problems reported; patient tolerated procedure well.

90935	Hemodialysis procedure with single physician evaluation
90937	Hemodialysis procedure requiring repeated evaluation(s) with or without substantial revision of dialysis prescription
90945	Dialysis procedure other than hemodialysis (e.g., peritoneal dialysis, hemofiltration, or other continuous renal replacement therapies), with single physician evaluation
+99354	Prolonged service in the office or other outpatient setting requiring direct (face-to-face) contact beyond the usual service, first hour (List separately in addition to code for office or other outpatient Evaluation and Management service.)

    A. 90937   C. 90945
    B. 99354   D. 90935

40. Office visit for 43-year-old male, new patient, with no complaints. Patient is applying for life insurance and requests a physical examination. A detailed health and family history was obtained, and a basic physical was done. Physician completed life insurance physical form at patient's request. Blood and urine were collected.

99381	Initial comprehensive preventive medicine evaluation and management of an individual including an age and gender appropriate history, examination, counseling/anticipatory guidance/risk factor reduction interventions, and the ordering of appropriate laboratory/diagnostic procedures, new patient; infant (age under 1 year)
99386	Initial comprehensive preventive medicine evaluation and management of an individual including an age and gender appropriate history examination, counseling/anticipatory guidance/risk factor reduction interventions, and the ordering of appropriate laboratory/diagnostic procedures, new patient; 40–64 years
99396	Periodic comprehensive preventive medicine reevaluation and management of an individual including an age and gender appropriate history, examination, counseling/anticipatory guidance/risk factor reduction interventions, and the ordering of appropriate laboratory/diagnostic procedures, established patient; 40–64 years
99450	Basic life and/or disability examination that includes completion of a medical history following a life insurance pro forma

A. 99450
B. 99386

C. 99396
D. 99381

41. Provide the CPT code for a quantitative drug assay that was performed for a patient to determine digoxin level.

80050	General health panel
80101	Drug screen, qualitative; single drug class method (e.g., immunoassay, enzyme assay), each drug class
80162	Digoxin (therapeutic drug assay, quantitative examination)
80166	Doxepin (therapeutic drug assay, quantitative examination)

A. 80101
B. 80050

C. 80166
D. 80162

42. Provide the CPT code for anesthesia services for the transvenous insertion of a pacemaker.

00530	Anesthesia for permanent transvenous pacemaker insertion
00560	Anesthesia for procedures on heart, pericardial sac, and great vessels of chest; without pump oxygenator
33202	Insertion of epicardial electrode(s); by open incision
33206	Insertion of new or replacement of permanent pacemaker with transvenous electrode(s); atrial

A. 00560
B. 33202, 00530

C. 00530
D. 33206, 00560

43. A 4-year-old had a repair of an incarcerated inguinal hernia. This is the first time this child has been treated for this condition.

49496	Repair initial inguinal hernia full-term infant, under age 6 months, or preterm infant over 50 weeks postconception age and under 6 months at the time of surgery with or without hydrocelectomy; incarcerated or strangulated
49501	Repair initial inguinal hernia, age 6 months to under 5 years, with or without hydrocelectomy; incarcerated or strangulated
49521	Repair recurrent inguinal hernia, any age; incarcerated or strangulated
49553	Repair initial femoral hernia, any age; incarcerated or strangulated

A. 49553
B. 49496

C. 49521
D. 49501

44. The patient had a thrombectomy, without catheter, of the peroneal artery, by leg incision.

34203	Embolectomy or thrombectomy, with or without catheter; popliteal-tibio-peroneal artery, by leg incision
35226	Repair blood vessel, direct; lower extremity
35302	Thromboendarterectomy, including patch graft, if performed, superficial femoral artery
37799	Unlisted procedure, vascular surgery

A. 34203
B. 37799

C. 35302
D. 35226

45. A patient with lung cancer and bone metastasis is seen for complex treatment planning by a radiation oncologist.

77263	Therapeutic radiology treatment planning; complex
77290	Therapeutic radiology simulation-aided field setting; complex
77315	Teletherapy, isodose plan (whether hand or computer calculated); complex (mantle or inverted Y, tangential ports, the use of wedges, compensators, complex blocking, rotational beam, or special beam considerations)
77334	Treatment devices, design and construction; complex (irregular blocks, special shields, compensators, wedges, molds, or casts)

A. 77315
B. 77263

C. 77290
D. 77334

46. An established patient was seen by physician in her office for DTaP-IPV/Hib.

90471	Immunization administration (includes percutaneous, intradermal, subcutaneous, or intramuscular injections); one vaccine (single or combination vaccine/toxoid)
90700	Diphtheria, tetanus toxoids, and acellular pertussis vaccine (DTaP), when administered to individuals younger than 7 years, for intramuscular use
90698	Diphtheria, tetanus toxoids and acellular pertussis vaccine (DTaP), Hemophilus influenza B vaccine, and poliovirus vaccine, inactivated, for intramuscular use
90748	Hepatitis B and Hemophilus influenza B vaccine (Hep B-Hib), for intramuscular use
99211	Office or other outpatient visit for the evaluation and management of an established patient, which may not require the presence of a physician. Usually, the presenting problem(s) are minimal. Typically, 5 minutes are spent performing or supervising these services

A. 90471
B. 90700, 90471

C. 90700, 90748, 99211
D. 90471, 90698

47. Which of the following procedures would NOT be coded to "resection" when using ICD-10-PCS?
   A. resection of the upper right lobe
   B. partial resection of upper left lobe
   C. excision of gallbladder
   D. excision of the sigmoid colon

48. If the same condition is described as both acute and chronic and separate subentries exist in the ICD-10-CM alphabetic index at the same indentation level,
   A. they should both be coded, acute sequenced first.
   B. they should both be coded, chronic sequenced first.
   C. only the acute condition should be coded.
   D. only the chronic condition should be coded.

49. A patient was sent to the surgeon's office as requested by the patient because the insurance company requires a second opinion regarding surgery. The patient has been complaining of lower back pain for over a year due to a herniated disk. The patient presents to the surgeon's office where a detailed history and physical examination was performed. Medical records from the primary care physician and the physical therapist were reviewed along with the tests performed in the office. Low medical decision making was made. A copy of the surgeon's reports was sent to the insurance company.
   A. 99242–32
   B. 99243

   C. 99253–32
   D. 99203–32

50. Patient arrives in the emergency room via a medical helicopter. The patient has sustained multiple life-threatening injuries due to a multiple car accident. The patient goes into cardiac arrest upon arrival. An hour and 30 minutes of critical care time is spent trying to stabilize the patient.

99282   Emergency department visit for the evaluation and management of a patient, which requires these three key components:
- An expanded problem focused history;
- An expanded problem focused examination; and
- Medical decision making of low complexity.

Counseling and/or coordination of care with other providers or agencies are provided consistent with the nature of the problem(s) and the patient's and/or family's needs.
Usually, the presenting problem(s) are of low to moderate severity.

99285   Emergency department visit for the evaluation and management of a patient, which requires these three key components within the constraints imposed by the urgency clinical condition and/or mental status:
- A comprehensive history;
- A comprehensive examination; and
- Medical decision making of high complexity.

Counseling and/or coordination of care with other providers or agencies are provided consistent with the nature of the problem(s) and the patient's and/or family's needs.
Usually, the presenting problem(s) are of high severity and pose an immediate significant threat to life or physiologic function.

99288   Physician direction of emergency medical systems (EMS) emergency care, advanced life support

99291   Critical care, evaluation and management of the critically ill or critically injured patient; first 30–74 minutes

+99292 Each additional 30 minutes (list separately in addition to code for primary service)

A. 99285, 99288, 99291
B. 99285, 99291, 99292
C. 99291, 99292, 99285
D. 99282

51. Patient presents with a diabetic ulcer that needs to be debrided. The patient was taken to the operating room where debridement of the muscle took place.

11011   Debridement including removal of foreign material at the site of an open fracture and/or an open dislocation; skin, subcutaneous tissue
11043   Debridement, muscle, and/or fascia (includes epidermis, dermis, and subcutaneous tissue, if performed); first 20 sq cm or less
11400   Excision, benign lesion including margins, except skin tag (unless listed elsewhere), trunk, arms or legs; excised diameter 0.5 cm or less
15999   Unlisted procedure, excision pressure ulcer (for free skin graft to close ulcer or donor site, see 15002 et seq)

A. 15999
B. 11400
C. 11011
D. 11043

52. Excision 2 cm subcutaneous soft tissue lipoma of the back. (Code for diagnoses using ICD-10-CM. Code for procedure using CPT.)

> D17.1   Benign lipomatous neoplasm of skin and subcutaneous tissue of trunk
> D17.30   Benign lipomatous neoplasm of skin and subcutaneous tissue of unspecified sites
> D23.5   Other benign neoplasm of skin of trunk
> D23.9   Other benign neoplasm of skin, unspecified
> 11600   Excision, malignant lesion, trunk, arms, or legs; excised diameter 0.5 cm or less
> 21556   Excision, tumor, soft tissue of neck or anterior thorax; subfascial (e.g., intramuscular); less than 5 cm
> 21925   Biopsy, soft tissue of back or flank; deep
> 21930   Excision, tumor, soft tissue of back or flank, subcutaneous; less than 3 cm

A.   D23.5, 11600   C.   D23.9, 21556
B.   D17.30, 21925   D.   D17.1, 21930

53. Patient undergoes a posterior L1-L5 spinal fusion for scoliosis with placement of a Harrington rod. Code using CPT.

> 22612   Arthrodesis, posterior or posteriorlateral technique, single level; lumbar (with lateral transverse technique, when performed
> 22800   Arthrodesis, posterior, for spinal deformity, with or without cast; up to 6 vertebral segments.
> +22840   Posterior nonsegmental instrumentation (e.g., Harrington rod technique, pedicle fixation across one interspace, atlantoaxial transarticular screw fixation, sublaminar wiring at C1, facet screw fixation) (list separately in addition to code for primary procedure)
> +22841   Internal spinal fixation by wiring spinous processes (list separately in addition to code for primary procedure)
> +22842   Posterior segmental instrumentation (e.g., pedicle fixation, dual rods with multiple hooks and sublaminar wires); 3–6 vertebral segments (list separately in addition to code for primary procedure)
> +22846   Anterior instrumentation; 4–7 vertebral segments (list separately in addition to code for primary procedure)

A.   22800, 22846   C.   22800, 22840
B.   22800, 22842   D.   22612, 22800, 22841

54. Patient has tear of the medial meniscus with loose bodies in the medial compartment of the left knee that was repaired by arthroscopic medial meniscectomy, shaving and trimming of meniscal rim, resection of synovium, and removal of the loose bodies. (Code using CPT procedure codes.)

27331	Arthrotomy, knee; including joint exploration, biopsy, or removal of loose or foreign bodies
27333	Arthrotomy, knee; medial and lateral
29800	Arthroscopy, temporomandibular joint, diagnostic, with or without synovial biopsy (separate procedure)
29804	Arthroscopy, temporomandibular joint, surgical; (for open procedures, use 21010)
29819	Arthroscopy, shoulder, surgical; with removal of loose body or foreign body (for open procedure, see 23040–23044, 23107)
29874	Arthroscopy, knee, surgical; for removal of loose body or foreign body (e.g., osteochondritis dissecans fragmentation, chondral fragmentation)
29881	Arthroscopy, knee, surgical; with meniscectomy (medial OR lateral, including any meniscal shaving)
LT	Left side

A. 29804, 29874-LT
B. 27333-LT, 27331-LT
C. 29800-LT, 29819-LT
D. 29881-LT

55. Single lung transplant without cardiopulmonary bypass. (Code for physician using CPT procedure codes only.)

32652	Thoracoscopy, surgical; with total pulmonary decortication, including intrapleural pneumonolysis
32850	Donor pneumonectomy(s) (including cold preservation), from cadaver donor
32851	Lung transplant, single; without cardiopulmonary bypass
32852	Lung transplant, single; with cardiopulmonary bypass

A. 32850
B. 32652
C. 32852
D. 32851

56. Patient has a year history of mitral valve regurgitation and now presents for a mitral valve replacement with bypass. (Code for physician using CPT procedure codes only.)

33425	Valvuloplasty, mitral valve, with cardiopulmonary bypass
33430	Replacement, mitral valve, with cardiopulmonary bypass
33460	Valvectomy, tricuspid valve, with cardiopulmonary bypass
35231	Repair blood vessel with vein graft; neck

A. 33430
B. 33460
C. 33425
D. 35231

57. Patient has breast carcinoma and is now undergoing complete axillary lymphadenectomy. (Code for physician using CPT procedure codes only.)

38525	Biopsy or excision of lymph nodes; open, deep axillary node(s)
38562	Limited lymphadenectomy for staging (separate procedure); pelvic and para-aortic
38740	Axillary lymphadenectomy; superficial
38745	Axillary lymphadenectomy; complete

A. 38525
B. 38740
C. 38562
D. 38745

58. Patient presents to the GI lab for a colonoscopy. During the colonoscopy, polyps were discovered in the ascending colon and in the transverse colon. Polyps in the ascending colon were removed via hot biopsy forceps, and the polyps in the transverse colon were removed by snare technique.

D12.2	Benign neoplasm of ascending colon
D12.3	Benign neoplasm of transverse colon
44392	Colonoscopy through stoma; with removal of polyps, hot biopsy forceps
44394	Colonoscopy through stoma; with removal of polyps, snare technique
45355	Colonoscopy, transabdominal via colotomy
45383	Colonoscopy, with ablation of polyps, not by hot biopsy forceps or snare technique
45384	Colonoscopy with removal of polyps, hot biopsy forceps
45385	Colonoscopy with removal of polyps, snare technique
-59	Distinct procedural service

A. D12.2, D12.3, 45355

B. D12.2, D12.3, 45384, 45385–59

C. D12.2, 44392, 44394–59

D. D12.3, 45355, 45383–59

59. Patient came to the hospital ambulatory surgical center for repair of incisional inguinal hernia. This is the second time the patient has developed this problem. The hernia was repaired with a Gore-Tex graft. Choose the appropriate ICD-10-CM and CPT codes.

K40.40	Unilateral inguinal hernia, with gangrene, not specified as recurrent
K40.90	Unilateral inguinal hernia, without obstruction or gangrene, not specified as recurrent
K43.9	Ventral hernia, without obstruction or gangrene
K40.91	Inguinal hernia, without obstruction or gangrene, recurrent
49520	Repair recurrent inguinal hernia, any age, reducible
49560	Repair initial incisional or ventral hernia, reducible
49565	Repair recurrent incisional or ventral hernia, reducible
+49568	Implantation of mesh or other prosthesis for incisional or ventral hernia repair or mesh for closure of debridement for necrotizing soft tissue infection. (List separately in addition to code for the incisional or ventral hernia repair.)

A. K40.91, 49565, 49568

B. K43.9, K40.90, 49520, 49568

C. K40.40, 49565

D. K40.40, K43.9, 49560, 49568

60. Female with 6 months of stress incontinence. Laparoscopic urethral suspension was completed. Choose the appropriate ICD-10-CM and CPT codes.

> N39.3 Stress incontinence (female) (male)
> N39.41 Urge incontinence
> N39.42 Incontinence without sensory awareness
> R32 Unspecified urinary incontinence
> 51840 Anterior vesicourethropexy or urethropexy (e.g., Marshall-Marchetti-Krantz, Burch); simple
> 51845 Abdominovaginal vesical neck suspension with or without endoscopic control
> 51990 Laparoscopy, surgical; urethral suspension for stress incontinence
> 51992 Laparoscopy, surgical; sling operation for stress incontinence

    A. N39.42, 51992   C. N39.41, 51840
    B. N39.3, 51990   D. R32, 51845

61. A patient is diagnosed with psychogenic paroxysmal tachycardia.
    A. I47.9   C. I47.8, F54
    B. F54   D. I47.9, F54

62. A patient is diagnosed with early onset Alzheimer's disease with dementia.
    A. G30.8, F02.81, Z91.83   C. G30.0, F02.80
    B. F02.81, G30.0, Z91.73   D. G30.0, Z91.73

63. A patient has end-stage kidney disease, which resulted from malignant hypertension.
    A. I12.0, N18.6   C. I13.11, N18.6
    B. I10, N18.6   D. I15.1, N18.6

64. A patient presents with dermatitis due to a prescription topical antibiotic cream used as directed by a physician.
    A. L08.89, T49.0x5   C. L02.91, T49.0x5
    B. L25.1, T49.0x5A   D. T49.0x5, L25.1

65. A patient presents with cervical spina bifida with hydrocephalus.
    A. Q76.0   C. Q05.0
    B. Q05   D. Q05.5

66. An infant has hypoglycemia and a mother with diabetes.
    A. P70.0   C. P70.1
    B. P70.2   D. P70.4

67. A woman has a Pap smear that detected cervical high-risk human papillomavirus (HPV). The DNA test was positive.
    A. R87.810   C. R87.820
    B. R87.811   D. R87.811

68. A patient suffered dizziness as a result of taking prescribed phenobarbital. The patient took his medication with beer.
    A. R42, T42.4x1A   C. T42.4x2A, R42
    B. R42, T42.3x1A   D. T42.3x1A, R42

69. The patient presents for a screening examination for lung cancer.
    A. Z03.89
    B. C78.00
    C. Z12.2
    D. C34.90

70. The diagnosis is as follows: "Carcinoma of axillary lymph nodes and lungs, metastatic from breast." Given this, which is (are) the primary cancer site(s)?
    A. axillary lymph nodes
    B. lungs
    C. breast
    D. both axillary lymph nodes and lungs

71. Robert Thompson was admitted with a chronic cough and the physician records "rule out lung cancer." What should be coded as the patient's diagnosis?
    A. chronic cough
    B. observation and evaluation without need for further medical care
    C. diagnosis of unknown etiology
    D. lung cancer

72. Which of the following is NOT related to diagnosing hypothyroidism?
    A. elevated liver enzymes and creatine
    B. a decrease in serum cholesterol and prolactin
    C. an increase in TSH
    D. an increase in serum cholesterol and prolactin

73. The use of radioactive sources placed into a tumor-bearing area to generate high-intensity radiation is termed
    A. stereotactic radiation treatment.
    B. proton beam treatment.
    C. brachytherapy.
    D. external beam radiation.

74. A patient has a total abdominal hysterectomy with bilateral salpingectomy. The coder selected the following codes:

58150	Total abdominal hysterectomy (corpus and cervix), with or without removal of tube(s) with or without removal of ovary(s)
58700	Salpingectomy, complete or partial unilateral or bilateral (separate procedure)

This type of coding is referred to as
    A. upcoding.
    B. unbundling.
    C. maximizing.
    D. optimization.

75. Which of the following is classified as a poisoning in ICD-10-CM?
    A. syncope due to Contac pills and a three-martini lunch
    B. digitalis intoxication
    C. reaction to dye administered for pyelogram
    D. idiosyncratic reaction between various drugs

76. CPT codes for a laparoscopic removal and replacement of both a gastric band and the subcutaneous port components.
    A. 43774, 43659
    B. 43659
    C. 43773
    D. 43848

77. CPT code(s) for a laryngoscopic submucosal removal of nonneoplastic lesion of the vocal cord with graft reconstruction. An operating microscope was used.
    A. 31546, 69990
    B. 31546, 20926
    C. 31546
    D. 31546, 20926-51

78. CPT code(s) for a laparoscopic takedown of the splenic flexure and a partial colectomy with anastomosis.
    A. 44140, 44213
    B. 44204
    C. 44213
    D. 44204, 44213

79. CPT code for a laparoscopic gastric restrictive procedure and placement of an adjustable gastric band.
    A. 43770
    B. 43800
    C. 43845
    D. 43846

80. CPT code for a high-energy ESW of the lateral humeral epicondyle using general anesthesia.
    A. 0019T
    B. 0101T
    C. 0102T
    D. 28890

81. A 32-year-old patient has a colonoscopy with removal of three polyps by snare. Moderate sedation was used and provided by the physician. The intraservice time was 30 minutes. (CPT coding)
    A. 45385, 45385-51, 45385-51
    B. 45385, 99151
    C. 45385, 99156, 99157
    D. 45385, 45385-51, 45385-51, 99156

82. Male patient has been diagnosed with benign prostatic hypertrophy and undergoes a transurethral destruction of the prostate by radiofrequency thermotherapy. (Code ICD-10-CM for diagnoses and CPT for procedures.)

N40.0	Enlarged prostate without lower urinary tract symptoms (LUTS)
52601	Transurethral electrosurgical resection of prostate including control of postoperative bleeding, complete (vasectomy, meatotomy, cystourethroscopy, urethral calibration and/or dilation, and internal urethrotomy are included)
52648	Laser vaporization of prostate, including control of postoperative bleeding, complete (vasectomy, meatotomy, cystourethroscopy, urethral calibration and/or dilation, internal urethrotomy, and transurethral transection of the prostate are included if performed)
53850	Transurethral destruction of prostate tissue; by microwave thermotherapy
53852	Transurethral destruction of prostate tissue; by radiofrequency thermotherapy

    A. N40.0, 52648
    B. N40.0, 53852
    C. N40.0, 52601
    D. N04.0, 53850

83. Hysteroscopy with D&C and polypectomy. (Code CPT for procedures.)

58100	Endometrial sampling (biopsy) with or without endocervical sampling (biopsy), without cervical dilation, any method (separate procedure)
58120	Dilation and curettage, diagnostic and/or therapeutic (nonobstetrical)
58555	Hysteroscopy, diagnostic (separate procedure)
58558	Hysteroscopy, surgical; with sampling (biopsy) of endometrium and/or polypectomy, with or without D&C
58563	Hysteroscopy, surgical; with endometrial ablation (e.g., endometrial resection, electrosurgical ablation, thermoablation)

    A. 58563
    B. 58558
    C. 58120, 58100, 58555
    D. 58558, 58120

84. Cesarean delivery with antepartum and postpartum care. (Code CPT for procedures.)

59400	Routine obstetric care, including antepartum care, vaginal delivery (with or without episiotomy and/or forceps), and postpartum care
59510	Routine obstetric care including antepartum care, cesarean delivery, and postpartum care
59514	Cesarean delivery only
59610	Routine obstetric care including antepartum care, vaginal delivery (with or without episiotomy and/or forceps) and postpartum care, after previous cesarean delivery

A. 59610
B. 59514
C. 59400
D. 59510

85. D&C for missed abortion, first trimester. (Code CPT for procedures.)

59820	Treatment of missed abortion, completed surgically; first trimester
59840	Induced abortion, by dilation and curettage
59850	Induced abortion, by one or more intra-amniotic injections (amniocentesis injections) including hospital admission and visits, delivery of fetus and secundines
59855	Induced abortion, by one or more vaginal suppositories (e.g., prostaglandin), with or without cervical dilation (e.g., laminaria), including hospital admission and visits, delivery of fetus and secundines

A. 59840
B. 59850
C. 59855
D. 59820

86. Total transcervical thymectomy. (Code CPT for procedures.)

60200	Excision of cyst or adenoma of thyroid, or transection of isthmus
60240	Thyroidectomy, total or complete
60520	Thymectomy, partial or total; transcervical approach (separate procedure)
60540	Adrenalectomy, partial or complete, or exploration of adrenal gland with or without biopsy, transabdominal, lumbar or dorsal (separate procedure)

A. 60520
B. 60540
C. 60240
D. 60200

87. Patient with carpal tunnel comes in for an open carpal tunnel release, right hand. (Code ICD-10-CM for diagnoses and CPT for procedures.)

G56.01	Carpal tunnel syndrome, right hand
64721	Neuroplasty and/or transposition; median nerve at carpal tunnel
64892	Nerve graft (includes obtaining graft), single strand, arm or leg; up to 4 cm length
64905	Nerve pedicle transfer; first stage
64999	Unlisted procedure, nervous system

A. G56.01, 64999
B. G56.01, 64721
C. G56.01, 64905
D. G56.01, 64892

88. Lumbar laminectomy (one segment) for decompression of spinal cord. (Code CPT for procedures.)

62263	Percutaneous lysis of epidural adhesions using solution injection (e.g., hypertonic saline, enzyme) or mechanical means (e.g., catheter) including radiologic localization (includes contrast when administered), multiple adhesiolysis sessions; 2 or more days
63005	Laminectomy, with exploration and/or decompression of spinal cord and/or cauda equina, without facetectomy, foraminotomy, or diskectomy (e.g., spinal stenosis), one or two vertebral segments; lumbar except for spondylolisthesis
63030	Laminotomy (hemilaminectomy), with decompression of nerve root(s), including partial facetectomy, foraminotomy, and/or excision of herniated intervertebral disk; one interspace, lumbar
63170	Laminectomy with myelotomy (e.g., Bischof or DREZ type), cervical, thoracic, or thoracolumbar

A. 63005
B. 62263
C. 63170
D. 63030

89. Phacoemulsification of left cataract with IOL implant and subconjunctival injection. (Code ICD-10-CM for diagnosis and CPT for procedures.)

H26.9	Unspecified cataract
66940	Removal of lens material; extracapsular
66983	Intracapsular cataract extraction with insertion of intraocular lens prosthesis (one-stage procedure)
66984	Extracapsular cataract removal with insertion of intraocular lens prosthesis (one-stage procedure) manual or mechanical technique (e.g., irrigation and aspiration or phacoemulsification)
68200	Subconjunctival injection

A. H26.9, 66940-LT
B. H26.9, 66983, 68200
C. H26.9, 66984-LT
D. H26.9, 66984-LT, 68200-LT

90. When a patient is admitted because of a primary neoplasm with metastasis and treatment is directed toward the secondary neoplasm only,
    A. code only the primary neoplasm as the principal diagnosis.
    B. the primary neoplasm is coded as the principal diagnosis and the secondary neoplasm is coded as an additional diagnosis.
    C. the secondary neoplasm is coded as the principal diagnosis, and the primary neoplasm is coded as an additional diagnosis.
    D. code only the secondary neoplasm as the principal diagnosis.

91. A document that acknowledges patient responsibility for payment if Medicare denies the claim is a(n)
    A. explanation of benefits.
    B. remittance advice.
    C. advance beneficiary notice.
    D. CMS-1500 claim form.

92. The _____ has the duty to adjust the MS-DRGs if necessary at the beginning of every fiscal year beginning _____.
    A. CMS, October 1
    B. IG, October 1
    C. CMS, January 1
    D. AHA, January 1

93. The purpose of the Correct Coding Initiative is to
    A. increase fines and penalties for bundling services into comprehensive CPT codes.
    B. restrict Medicare reimbursement to hospitals for ancillary services.
    C. teach coders how to unbundle codes.
    D. detect and prevent payment for improperly coded services.

94. CMS delegates its daily operations of the Medicare and Medicaid programs to
    A. the office of the Inspector General.
    B. the PRO in each state.
    C. the National Center for Vital and Health Statistics.
    D. the Medicare administrative contractor (MAC).

95. The _____ are the organizations that contract with Medicare to perform reviews of medical records with the corresponding Medicare claims to detect and correct improper payments.
    A. Atlas Systems
    B. medical outcomes study
    C. recovery audit contractors (RACs)
    D. adjusted clinical groups (ACGs) system

96. Which of the following could influence a facility's case mix?
    A. changes in DRG weights
    B. changes in the services offered by a facility
    C. accuracy of coding
    D. All answers apply.

97. The chargemaster relieves the coders from coding repetitive services that require little, if any, formal documentation analysis. This is called
    A. grouping.   C. soft coding.
    B. hard coding.   D. mapping.

98. The practice of using a code that results in a higher payment to the provider than the code that more accurately reflects the service provided is known as
    A. unbundling.   C. optimizing.
    B. upcoding.   D. downcoding.

99. The APC payment system is based on what coding system(s)?
    A. AMA's CPT codes
    B. CPT and ICD-10-CM diagnosis and procedure codes
    C. ICD-10-CM diagnosis and procedure codes
    D. CPT/HCPCS codes

100. Which of the following contains a list of coding edits developed by CMS in an effort to promote correct coding nationwide and to prevent the inappropriate unbundling of related services?
    A. National Coverage Determination (NCD)
    B. National Correct Coding Initiative (NCCI)
    C. CPT Assistant
    D. Healthcare Common Procedure Coding System (HCPCS)

CCA Mock Examination Answer Key

ANSWER   EXPLANATION

1. D

REFERENCE: Oachs and Watters, p 365
                     Sayles and Gordon, pp 265–266

2. A A clinical impression and an intended course of action are either entered in the physical examination or provided in the admission note. The admission note provides an overview of the patient and adds any relevant information that is not included in the history and physical examination.

REFERENCE: Oachs and Watters, pp 111–112
                     Sayles and Gordon, pp 90–94

3. D Progress note elements written in the acronym "SOAP" style are:
    S—subjective, records what the patient states is the problem
    O—objective, records what the practitioner identifies through the history, physical examination, and diagnostic tests
    A—assessment, combines the subjective and objective into a conclusion
    P—plan, what approach is going to be taken to resolve the problem

REFERENCE: Abdelhak and Hanken, p 113
                     Oachs and Watters, p 120
                     Sayles and Gordon, p 106

4. D

REFERENCE: Oachs and Watters, pp 348–350
                     Sayles and Gordon, pp 69, 293, 326, 462

5. D A final note may substitute for a discharge summary for patients admitted for less than 48 hours with minor problems, uncomplicated deliveries, and for normal neonates.

REFERENCE: Abdelhak and Hanken, p 110
                     Oachs and Watters, pp 114–115

6. A The physician releasing the patient should write a final note of summary of the patient's course of treatment, stating the patient's condition at discharge, and instructions for the patient's activity, diet, and medications as well as any follow-up appointments or instructions. If a patient expires, the final notes describe the circumstances regarding the death, the findings, the cause of death, and whether or not an autopsy was performed.

REFERENCE: Oachs and Watters, pp 111–112
                     Sayles and Gordon, pp 93–94

7. D The postpartum record contains information about the condition of the mother after delivery and includes an assessment of the lochia and conditions of the breasts, fundus, and perineum.

REFERENCE: Abdelhak and Hanken, p 108
                     Oachs and Watters, pp 100, 116
                     Sayles and Gordon, pp 99–100

ANSWER   EXPLANATION

8. D Not all of the components of the combination code for diabetes mellitus, uncontrolled, were present on admission. The diabetes mellitus was present on admission, but it was not "uncontrolled" until 3 days after admission.

        A. Y = yes, present on admission

        B. U = no information in the record

        C. W = clinically undetermined

        D. N = no, not present on admission

REFERENCE: Abdelhak and Hanken, pp 284–285
                       Sayles and Gordon, pp 437, 465

9. B CALCULATION:

     Step 1: Multiply each row (relative weight × number of patients).

     Step 2: Sum the totals of each row (169.051).

     Step 3: Divide the total relative weight sums (169.051) by the total number of patients (57)

$$\frac{169.051 \text{ total relative weight}}{57 \text{ total patients seen}} = 2.965807$$

REFERENCE: Oachs and Watters, p 225
                       Sayles and Gordon, pp 401, 441

10. A The interdisciplinary care plan is the foundation around which patient care is organized. It contains input from the unique perspective of each discipline involved. It includes an assessment, statement of goals, identification of specific activities, or strategies to achieve those goals and periodic assessments of goal attainment.

REFERENCE: Abdelhak and Hanken, p 104
                       Oachs and Watters, pp 118–119
                       Sayles and Gordon, pp 93–94

11. C

REFERENCE: Abdelhak and Hanken, p 596
                       McWay, pp 369, 519
                       Oachs and Watters, p 725

12. D

REFERENCE: Abdelhak and Hanken, pp 126–127
                       Oachs and Watters, pp 102, 272–275
                       Sayles and Gordon, pp 464–466

ANSWER   EXPLANATION

13. A Employee number 425: $120 + (35 \times 0.75) + (16 \times 0.5) = 154.25$
$154.25/5 = 30.85$ average work units per day

Employee number 426: $48 + (89 \times 0.75) + (95 \times 0.5) = 162.25$
$162.25/5 = 32.45$ average work units per day

Employee number 427: $80 + (92 \times 0.75) + (4 \times 0.5) = 151$
$151/5 = 30.2$ average work units per day

Employee number 428: $65 + (109 \times 0.75) + (16 \times 0.5) = 154.75$
$154.75/5 = 30.95$ average work units per day

REFERENCE: Abdelhak and Hanken, p 641

14. D

REFERENCE: AHA, pp 319–321
Bowie (2017b) pp 342–343
Schraffenberger (2016), p 499

15. B

REFERENCE: AHA, pp 15, 60–62, 501
Bowie (2017b), p 305
Green, pp 154–155, 249
Schraffenberger, pp 29–30, 633–634

16. B

REFERENCE: AHA, pp 126, 249–250, 398–401
Bowie (2017b), pp 237, 270–271, 452–453
Kuehn, p 38
Schraffenberger, pp 319–320, 376–378, 683

17. C

REFERENCE: AHA, pp 571–574
Green, p 1005
Schraffenberger, p 85

18. A

REFERENCE: AHA, pp 571–574
Green, p 1005
Schraffenberger, p 85

19. D

REFERENCE: Bowie (2017a), pp 123–125
Johnson and Linker, pp 209–211
Kuehn, pp 112–113

20. B

REFERENCE: Green, p 1030
Green and Rowell, pp 89–93
Johnson and Linker, p 514

ANSWER   EXPLANATION

21. C The condition should be coded as a poisoning when there is an interaction of an over-the-counter drug and alcohol. The other answer choices are adverse effects of a correctly administered prescription drug.

REFERENCE: AHA, pp 514–518
Bowie (2017b), pp 3, 409–411
Green, pp 208–211
Kuehn, pp 604–609

22. A

REFERENCE: AHA, pp 571–574
Green, p 1005
Schraffenberger, p 85

23. C All ICD-10-CM codes start with an alphabetic character. The basic code structure consists of three digits and then a decimal point. Most codes contain a maximum of six characters, with a few chapters having a seventh character.

REFERENCE: AHA, pp 12–16
Bowie (2017b), p 384
Green, pp 72–74, 308
Schraffenberger, pp 560–561

24. D

REFERENCE: AHA, pp 299–300, 462, 491
Bowie, (2017b), pp 305–306
Schraffenberger, pp 432–433, 577

25. D

REFERENCE: AHA, pp 224–226
Bowie (2017b), pp 251–252
Green, pp 134, 338–339
Schraffenberger, pp 341–344

26. C

REFERENCE: AHA, pp 338–339
Bowie (2017b), pp 449–450
Schraffenberger, p 662

27. C

REFERENCE: Sayles and Gordon, p 152

28. C A surgical operation is one or more surgical procedures performed at one time for one patient using a common approach or for a common purpose.

REFERENCE: Koch, p 190

29. D

REFERENCE: Oachs and Watters, p 366

30. A

REFERENCE: Oachs and Watters, p 126

ANSWER   EXPLANATION

31. C Benchmarking involves comparing your department to other departments or organizations known to be excellent in one or more areas. The success of benchmarking involves finding out how the other department functions and then incorporating their ideas into your department.

REFERENCE: Oachs and Watters, pp 171, 276, 631
               Sayles and Gordon, pp 465, 508, 587

32. C

REFERENCE: Bowie (2017a), pp 134–135
               Green, pp 667–668
               Johnson and Linker, pp 204–207
               Kuehn, p 117

33. A

REFERENCE: McWay, pp 261–263, 505
               Oachs and Watters, p 998

34. C *Staging* is a term used to refer for the progression of cancer. In accessing most types of cancer, a method (staging) is used to determine how far the cancer has progressed. The cancer is described in terms of how large the main tumor is, the degree to which it has invaded surrounding tissue, and the extent to which it has spread to lymph glands or other areas of the body. Staging not only helps to assess outlook but also the most appropriate treatment.

REFERENCE: Abdelhak and Hanken, pp 491–492
               Oachs and Watters, p 174
               Sayles and Gordon, pp 176–177

35. B According to the UHDDS, the principal diagnosis is to be sequenced first.

REFERENCE: AHA, pp 30–33
               Bowie (2017b), pp 56, 381
               Kuehn, p 30
               Schraffenberger, pp 93–98

36. D The hospital inpatient procedure would not be coded using HCPCS/CPT codes. Hospital inpatient procedures are coded using ICD-10-PCS codes.

REFERENCE: Bowie (2017b), p 1–4, 38–39, 465
               Green, p 392
               Johnson and Linker, p 10
               Oachs and Watters, pp 148–149
               Sayles and Gordon, pp 119–120, 122–124, 130
               Smith, pp 5–6

37. B The sizes of the layered wound repairs of the same body area are added together in order to select the correct CPT code.

REFERENCE: Bowie (2017a), p 124
               Green, pp 658–660
               Johnson and Linker, pp 80–81, 212–213
               Kuehn, pp 112–113
               Smith, pp 67–69

38. D Look up in CPT code book under foot, neuroma.

REFERENCE: AMA (2016)

ANSWER   EXPLANATION

39. D *Dialysis* is the main term to be referenced in the CPT manual index.

REFERENCE: Bowie (2017a), pp 438–439
              Green, pp 506, 952–953
              Johnson and Linker, pp 301, 403–404
              Kuehn, pp 264–265
              Smith, p 223

40. A The codes in this subsection are used to report evaluations for life or disability insurance baseline information.

REFERENCE: Bowie (2017a), p 82
              Green, p 582
              Johnson and Linker, p 147
              Kuehn, p 71

41. D

REFERENCE: Bowie (2017a), p 425
              Green, pp 924–925
              Johnson and Linker, pp 389–390
              Kuehn, pp 242–243

42. C

REFERENCE: Bowie (2017a), pp 94–95
              Green, pp 601–603, 617–618
              Johnson and Linker, pp 166–167
              Kuehn, pp 86–87, 144, 147

43. D

REFERENCE: Bowie (2017a), pp 227–228
              Green, pp 996–998
              Johnson and Linker, pp 176–177
              Kuehn, pp 169–174
              Smith, pp 125–126

44. A

REFERENCE: Bowie (2017a), p 216
              Green, p 746
              Johnson and Linker, 295–297

45. B

REFERENCE: Bowie (2017a), pp 414–415
              Green, pp 897–898
              Johnson and Linker, pp 374–375
              Smith, pp 170–171

ANSWER   EXPLANATION

46. D If immunization is the only service that the patient receives, then two codes are used to report the service: the immunization administration code is first, and then the code for the vaccine/toxoid.

REFERENCE: Bowie (2017a), pp 434–435
Green, pp 802–804
Johnson and Linker, p 400
Smith, p 220

47. B

REFERENCE: AHA, p 93
Bowie (2017b) p 487
Schraffenberger, pp 157, 197

48. A

REFERENCE: AHA, pp 58–59
Bowie (2017b), p 52
Schraffenberger, p 27

49. D

REFERENCE: Bowie (2017a), pp 41–43
Green, pp 517–526, 538–539
Johnson and Linker, pp 114–123
Schraffenberger, p 27
Smith, p 206

50. B

REFERENCE: Bowie (2017a), pp 116–117
Green, pp 573–575
Johnson and Linker, pp 138–140
Schraffenberger, p 63
Smith, p 209

51. D

REFERENCE: Bowie (2017a), pp 120, 155
Green, p 666
Johnson and Linker, pp 202–203

52. D Excision of lipomas code to excision of soft tissue.

REFERENCE: AHA, pp 442–444
Bowie (2017a), pp 154–155
Bowie (2017b), p 138
Green, p 557
Green and Rowell, pp 181–186
Smith, p 64

53. C

REFERENCE: Bowie (2017a), pp 154–155
Green, p 844
Johnson and Linker, pp 256–257

ANSWER   EXPLANATION

54. D If debridement or shaving of articular cartilage and a menisectomy are performed in the same compartment of the knee, then code only 29881.

REFERENCE: Bowie (2017a), pp 165–166
                 Green, p 703
                 Johnson and Linker, p 252
                 Schraffenberger, pp 130–131

55. D

REFERENCE: Bowie (2017a), p 193
                 Green, pp 736–737

56. A Valvuloplasty is a plastic repair of a valve.

REFERENCE: Bowie (2017a), pp 210–211
                 Green, pp 736–737
                 Johnson and Linker, pp 266, 293
                 Kuehn, p 148

57. D

REFERENCE: Bowie (2017a), p 238–239
                 Green, pp 763–764
                 Johnson and Linker, p 169

58. B According to CPT Assistant, when a colonoscopy with polypectomy is performed by two different techniques, both techniques are coded.

REFERENCE: AHA, p 442
                 Bowie (2017a), pp 272–273
                 Bowie (2017b) pp 97–103
                 Green, pp 790–793
                 Johnson and Linker, pp 172–173
                 Schraffenberger, pp 373–374
                 Smith, pp 119–121

59. A The mesh is reported as an additional code. The hernia is considered recurrent because this documentation states this is the second hernia.

REFERENCE: AHA, p 253
                 AMA (2016)
                 Bowie (2017a), pp 277–278
                 Bowie (2017b), pp 268–269
                 Green, pp 796–798
                 Johnson and Linker, pp 176–177
                 Smith, pp 125–126

60. B

REFERENCE: AHA, p 262
                 Bowie (2017a), p 298
                 Bowie (2017b) p 320
                 Green, p 806
                 Johnson and Linker, pp 178–180

ANSWER   EXPLANATION

61. D

REFERENCE: AHA, p 179
Bowie (2017b), pp 235–236
Schraffenberger, p 293

62. C

REFERENCE: AHA, pp 173, 206
Bowie (2017b), pp 167, 188–189

63. A

REFERENCE: AHA, pp 263–265
Bowie (2017b), pp 228–229, 318–319
Schraffenberger, pp 302–303

64. B

REFERENCE: AHA, pp 284–285
Bowie (2017b), pp 284, 409
Schraffenberger, pp 394, 556–557

65. C

REFERENCE: AHA, p 359
Bowie (2017b), pp 366–367
Schraffenberger, pp 532–533

66. C

REFERENCE: AHA, p 373
Bowie (2017b), pp 357–358
Schraffenberger, p 512

67. A

REFERENCE: AHA, p 142
Bowie (2017b), p 389
Schraffenberger, pp 556–557

68. B

REFERENCE: AHA, pp 516–518
Bowie (2017b), pp 385–386
Schraffenberger, pp 546–547

69. C

REFERENCE: AHA, p 132
Bowie (2017b), pp 444–446
Schraffenberger, p 669

70. C

REFERENCE: AHA, pp 449–451
Bowie (2017b), pp 106–110
Schraffenberger, pp 152–155

71. D

REFERENCE: AHA, pp 57–58
Bowie (2017b), p 58
Schraffenberger, p 100

ANSWER   EXPLANATION

72. B

REFERENCE: Bowie (2017b), p 150

73. C

REFERENCE: Bowie (2017a), p 414
              Johnson and Linker, pp 353, 375–376
              Kuehn, p 224
              Smith, p 172

74. B

REFERENCE: Bowie (2017a), pp 328–329
              Johnson and Linker, pp 361–362
              Schraffenberger, pp 104–105
              Smith, pp 55–57

75. A A reaction due to mixing drugs and alcohol is coded as a poisoning.

REFERENCE: AHA, pp 415–418
              Bowie (2017b), pp 119–120, 409–410
              Schraffenberger, pp 407–409

76. B

REFERENCE: Bowie (2017a), p 264
              Kuehn, p 163

77. C

REFERENCE: Bowie (2017a), pp 185–186
              Kuehn, pp 138–139

78. D

REFERENCE: Bowie (2017a), pp 185–186
              Kuehn, p 139

79. A

REFERENCE: Bowie (2017a), pp 185–186
              Kuehn, p 139

80. C

REFERENCE: Bowie (2017a), pp 95–96
              Green, p 807
              Kuehn, pp 86–87

81. C CPT designates certain procedures as including moderate sedation; therefore, moderate sedation is included in the code for the removal of polyps.

REFERENCE: Bowie (2017a), pp 272–273, 446

82. B

REFERENCE: AHA, pp 270–271
              Bowie (2017a), p 300
              Green, pp 507–508
              Kuehn, p 185

ANSWER   EXPLANATION

83. B

REFERENCE: Bowie (2017a), p 328
Green, pp 828–829
Johnson and Linker, pp 347–348, 354–355
Kuehn, pp 188–189

84. D

REFERENCE: Bowie (2017a), pp 340–341
Johnson and Linker, pp 319, 323–324
Kuehn, pp 190–191

85. D

REFERENCE: Bowie (2017a), p 343
Green, p 384
Johnson and Linker, pp 347–348, 354–355
Kuehn, p 192

86. A

REFERENCE: Bowie (2017a), p 353
Green, p 836
Kuehn, pp 194–197

87. B

REFERENCE: Bowie (2017a), p 370
Bowie (2017b), p 190
Green, p 848
Kuehn, p 202

88. A

REFERENCE: Bowie (2017a), pp 368–369
Green, p 843
Johnson and Linker, pp 256–257
Kuehn, p 200

89. C   Subconjunctival injections are included in 66984.

REFERENCE: AHA, pp 163, 216
AMA (2016)
Bowie (2017a), pp 379–381
Bowie (2017b), pp 202–203
Green, p 853
Johnson and Linker, pp 184–185
Kuehn, p 207

ANSWER   EXPLANATION

90. C

REFERENCE: AHA, p 459
               Bowie (2017b), pp 105–108

91. C

REFERENCE: Green and Rowell, pp 308, 383–384, 514–516
               Kuehn, p 329

92. A The CMS adjusts the MS-DRG list and reimbursement rates every fiscal year (October 1 through September 30).

REFERENCE: Kuehn, pp 700–702

93. D

REFERENCE: Green, pp 529–530

94. D Medicare administrative contractor is the new name for the previously termed carriers and fiscal intermediaries.

REFERENCE: Green, pp 30, 109

95. C

REFERENCE: Sayles and Gordon, pp 453–454

96. D

REFERENCE: Sayles and Gordon, pp 401–402, 441

97. B

REFERENCE: Sayles and Gordon, pp 424, 426

98. B

REFERENCE: Sayles and Gordon, pp 450–451

99. D

REFERENCE: Sayles and Gordon, pp 119, 130, 442

100. B

REFERENCE: Oachs and Watters, p 236

REFERENCES

Abdelhak, M. and Hanken, M. A. (2016). *Health information: Management of a strategic resource* (6th ed.). St. Louis, MO: Saunders Elsevier.

American Hospital Association (AHA). (2016). *ICD-10-CM and ICD-10-PCS coding handbook 2017 (with Answers)*. Chicago: Nelly Leon-Chisen, RHIA Central Office on ICD-10-CM and ICD-10-PCS of the American Hospital Association (AHA).

American Medical Association (AMA). (2016). *Physicians' current procedural terminology (CPT) 2017 professional edition*. Chicago: Author.

Bowie, M. (2017a). *Understanding current procedural terminology and HCPCS coding systems* (5th ed.). Clifton Park, NY: Cengage Learning.

Bowie, M. J. (2017b). *Understanding ICD-10-CM and ICD-10-PCS: A worktext* (3rd ed.). Clifton Park, NY: Cengage Learning

Green, M. (2016). *3-2-1 Code it!* (5th ed.). Clifton Park, NY: Cengage Learning.

Green, M. and Rowell, J. C. (2017). *Understanding health insurance: A guide to billing and reimbursement* (13th ed.). Clifton Park, NY: Learning.

Johnson, S. L. and Linker, R. (2017). *Understanding medical coding: A comprehensive guide* (4th ed.). Clifton Park, NY: Cengage Learning.

Koch, G. (2015). *Basic allied health statistics and analysis* (4th ed.). Clifton Park, NY: Cengage Learning.

Kuehn, L. (2016). *Procedural coding and reimbursement for physician services: Applying current procedural terminology and HCPCS 2017*. Chicago: American Health Information Management Association (AHIMA).

McWay, D. C. (2014). *Today's health information management: An integrated approach* (2nd ed.). Clifton Park, NY: Cengage Learning.

Oachs, P. and Watters, A. (2016), *Health information management concepts: Principles and practice* (5th ed.). Chicago: American Health Information Management Association (AHIMA).

Sayles, N. B. and Gordon, L. (2016). *Health information technology: An applied approach* (5th ed.). Chicago: American Health Information Management Association (AHIMA).

Smith, G. (2016). *Basic current procedural terminology and HCPCS coding, 2016*. Chicago: American Health Information Management Association (AHIMA).

Competencies for the CCA Mock Examination

Question	CCA Domain					
	1	2	3	4	5	6
1					X	
2			X			
3			X			
4					X	
5			X			
6			X			
7			X			
8	X					
9		X				
10			X			
11						X
12		X				
13			X			
14	X					
15	X					
16	X					
17	X					
18	X					
19	X					
20		X				
21	X					
22	X					
23	X					
24	X					
25	X					
26	X					
27						X
28	X					
29					X	
30			X			
31			X			
32	X					
33					X	
34	X					
35		X				
36	X					
37	X					
38	X					
39	X					
40	X					

Current Procedural Terminology © 2016 American Medical Association. All Rights Reserved.

Question	CCA Domain					
	1	2	3	4	5	6
41	X					
42	X					
43	X					
44	X					
45	X					
46	X					
47	X					
48	X					
49	X					
50	X					
51	X					
52	X					
53	X					
54	X					
55	X					
56	X					
57	X					
58	X					
59	X					
60	X					
61	X					
62	X					
63	X					
64	X					
65	X					
66	X					
67	X					
68	X					
69	X					
70	X					
71	X					
72	X					
73	X					
74	X					
75	X					
76	X					
77	X					
78	X					
79	X					

Question	CCA Domain					
	1	2	3	4	5	6
80	X					
81	X					
82	X					
83	X					
84	X					
85	X					
86	X					
87	X					
88	X					
89	X					
90	X					
91		X				
92		X				
93				X		
94				X		
95		X				
96		X				
97					X	
98		X				
99		X				
100		X				

APPENDIX A
PHARMACOLOGY

The most common prescription drugs with examples of diagnoses

Analgesics
acetaminophen w/codeine (Tylenol #2, #3, #4) mild to moderate pain
Advil (ibuprofen) mild to moderate pain
Aleve (naproxin) NSAID
aspirin, enteric coated (salicylate) reduces fever, relieves mild to moderate pain
Dilaudid (hydromorphine HCl) moderate to severe pain
Feldene (piroxicam) NSAID
hydrocodone w/APAP (Lortab 2.5) pain, moderate to severe; antitussives/expectorants, back pain
ibuprofen (Advil, Motrin) NSAID, arthritis, osteoarthritis; rheumatoid arthritis, dysmenorrhea; mild to moderate pain, fever; gout
Lortab (hydrocodone w/APAP) moderate to severe pain, expectorant
Motrin (ibuprofen) mild to moderate pain
naproxin (Aleve) NSAID
oxycodone pain
Oxycotin (oxycodone hydrochloride) opioid analgesic
Percocet (oxycodone APAP)
piroxicam (Feldene) NSAID
tramadol (Ultram) moderate to severe pain
Tylenol #2, #3, #4 (acetaminophen w/codeine) mild to moderate pain
Ultram (tramadol) short-term pain

Antibacterial
amoxicillin (AMOXIL) antibiotic; broad-spectrum antibacterial drug, urinary tract infections, strep throat
Amoxil (amoxicillin) antibiotic; broad-spectrum antibacterial drug
Augmentin (amoxicilln with clavulanate potassium) treats certain bacterial infections of the ears, lungs, sinus, skin, and urinary tract
Avelox (moxifloxacin hydrochloride) for susceptible strains of designated microorganisms
azithromycin (Zithromax) antibiotic
Bactrim (sulfamethoxazole and trimethoprim) antibiotic; treats ear, respiratory, and urinary tract infections as well as other infections caused by bacteria
Bactroban (mupirocin) topical antibiotic
cephalexin, USP (Keflex) antibiotic–antibacterial
ciprofloxacin (Cipro) antibacterial (drug-resistant bacteria)
Cipro (ciprofloxacin) antibacterial (drug-resistant bacteria)
clindamycin (Cleocin) antibacterial
doxycycline hyclate (Vibra-Tabs) antibacterial (drug-resistant bacteria)
erythromycin (Ery-Tab, Erythrocin) macrolide antibiotic
Flagyl (metronidazole) trichomoniasis
Keflex (cephalexin, USP) antibacterial antibiotic
levofloxacin (Levaquin) antibacterial (drug-resistant bacteria)
Levaquin (levofloxacin) antibacterial (drug-resistant bacteria), acute bacterial sinusitis
metronidazole tabs (Fagyl) trichomoniasis
minocycline (Solodyn) used to treat moderate to severe acne
mupirocin (Bactroban) topical antibiotic
Omnicef (cefdinir) drug-resistant bacteria
Penicillin VK infections

Antibacterial (continued)

Solodyn (minocycline HCl) used to treat moderate to severe acne
sulfamethoxazole and trimethoprim (Bactrim) antibiotic; treats ear, respiratory, and urinary tract infections as well as other infections caused by bacteria
tetracycline HCl (Sumycin, Panmycin) antibiotic
Vibra-Tabs (doxycycline hyclate, USP) antibacterial (drug-resistant bacteria)
Zithromax (azithromycin) antibiotic

Antifungal

Difucan (fluconazole) antifungal agent
fluconazole (Difucan) antifungal agent
Nystatin (Nystatin oral) antifungal agent
Nystatin (Nystop) topical antifungal cream

Anti-inflammatory

Anaprox (naproxen) relieves pain and swelling
Asacol (mesalamine) GI anti-inflammatory (5-aminosalicylic acid derivate)
Celebrex (celecoxib) osteoarthritis, rheumatoid arthritis
celecoxib (Celebrex) osteoarthritis and rheumatoid arthritis, adenomatous colorectal polyps
diclofenac (Voltaren) osteoarthritis, rheumatoid arthritis
Humira (adalimumab) rheumatoid arthritis, chronic plaque psoriasis, Crohn's disease, pain relief; reduces inflammation caused by a number of autoimmune diseases
Indocin (indomethacin) relieves pain, swelling, and joint stiffness
Lidoderm (lidocaine-transdermal) topical analgesic
Lortab (hydrocodone bitartrate and acetaminophen) relieves moderate to moderately severe pain
Medrol (methylprednisolone) reduces swelling and redness
methylprednisolone (Medrol) inflammatory disorders
Mobic (meloxicam) osteoarthritis and rheumatoid arthritis
Motrin (ibuprofen) relieves pain and swelling
Nalfon (fenoprofen calcium) reduces pain, swelling, and joint stiffness from arthritis
naproxen (Anaprox) NSAID, mild to moderate pain, osteoarthritis, rheumatoid arthritis, dysmenorrhea, gout, ankylosing spondylitis, fever
prednisone (Deltasone) inflammatory disorders, adrenal insufficiency, MS relapsing, pneumocystic pneumonia, asthma, inflammatory bowel disease
Ultram (tramadol hydrochloride) juvenile rheumatoid arthritis, rheumatoid arthritis, chronic fatigue syndrome
Voltaren (diclofenac) osteoarthritis, rheumatoid arthritis

Antineoplastic

Arimidex (anastrozole) treats breast cancer
anastrozole (Arimidex) treats breast cancer
Gleevec (imatinib mesylate) treats certain types of cancer (e.g., chronic myeloid leukemia, gastrointestinal stromal tumors, and myelodysplastic/myeloproliferative diseases). Stops or slows growth of cancer cells (tumors); causes cancer cells to die
imatinib (Gleevec) treats certain types of cancer (e.g., chronic myeloid leukemia, gastrointestinal stromal tumors, and myelodysplastic/myeloproliferative diseases). Stops or slows growth of cancer cells (tumors); causes cancer cells to die
Nolvadet (tamoxifen citrate) antineoplastic agent, SERM, estrogen receptor antagonist
tamoxifen citrate (Nolvadet) antineoplastic agent, SERM, estrogen receptor antagonist

Antiviral

acyclovir (Zovirax) decreases pain and speeds healing of sores or blisters from varicella (chickenpox), herpes zoster (shingles), and outbreaks of genital herpes
Afluria (influenza vaccine) active immunization against influenza disease
Atripla (evavirenz/emtricitabine/tenofovir disoproxil fumarate) HIV in adults
Norvir (ritonavir) anti-HIV medication
Reyataz (atazanavir) HIV protease inhibitors
Tamiflu (oseltamivir phosphate) antiviral
Truvada (emtricitabine and tenofovir) HIV treatment
Zostavax (shingle vaccine) herpes zoster (shingles) for age 50 and over

Cardiovascular

Accupril (quinapril) hypertension (HTN)
Aggrenox (aspirin and dypyridamole) reduces risk of strokes in patients who have had blood clots
Aldomet (methyldopa) HTN
Altace (ramipril) reduces risk of MI, stroke, HTN
Amodarone (cordarone, pacerone) antiarrhythmic
amlodipidine (Norvasc) angina, essential HTN (calcium channel blocker)
Atacand (candesartan cilexetil) antihypertensive
atenolol (Tenomin) angina pectoris, essential HTN, myocardial infarction
atorvastatin (Lipitor) hypercholesterolemia, hyperlipidemia; dysbetalipoproteinemia
Avalide (irbesartan-hydrochlorothiazide) HTN
Avapro (irbesartan) HTN
Azor (amlodipine and olmesartan medoxomil) HTN
benazepril (Lotensin) HTN, congestive heart failure (CHF)
Benicar (olmesartan medoxomil) HTN
Bystolic (nebivolol) beta-blocker HTN
Caduet (amlodipine besylate with atorvastatin) antihypertensive
Cardizen (diltiazem) calcium channel blocker treatment for chronic stable angina, HTN
Cardura (doxazosin) HTN
Catapres (clonidine HCl) HTN
Clonidine high blood pressure
clopidogrel bisulfate (Plavix) reduction of atherothrombotic events
Coreg (carvedilol) congestive heart failure
Coumadin (warfarin sodium) anticoagulant venous thrombosis, pulmonary embolism
Cozaar (losartan potassium) HTN
Crestor (rosuvastatin calcium) cholesterol
Digoxin (lanoxin) heart failure, irregular heartbeat (chronic atrial fibrillation)
Digitek heart failure
diltiazem (Cardizem) HTN, angina (calcium channel blocker)
Diovan (valsartan) hypertension, heart failure, postmyocardial infarction
doxazosin (Cardura) HTN, BPH
Dyazide (triamterene/HCTZ) diuretic, HTN
Effient (prasugrel) reduces risk of heart-related events or blood clots in stent
Enalapril maleate (Vasotec) hypertension
enalapril (Vasotec) HTN, CHF, acute MI, nephropathy, asymptomatic left ventricular dysfunction
Exforge (amlodipine and valsaran) HTN
furosemide (Lasix) diuretic, peripheral and pulmonary edema, hypercalcemia, kidney failure
Gemfibrozil high serum triglyceride
Hyzaar (losartan potassium-hydrochlorithiazide) HTN

Cardiovascular (continued)

Imdur (isosorbide mononitrate) angina
Inderal (propranolol HCl) beta-blocker, antihypertensive
isosorbide mononitrate (Imdur, ISMO) angina
ISMO (isosorbide mononitrate) angina
lanoxin (Digoxin) CHF, atrial fibrillation/flutter, paroxysmal atrial tachycardia
Lasix (furosemide) CHF, HTN, diuretic
Lipitor (atorvastatin) high cholesterol
lisinopril (Prinivil, Zestril) HTN, CHF, acute MI
Lopressor (metoprolol) HTN
Lotensin (benazepril) HTN
Lotrel (amlodipine besylate and benazepril HCl) HTN
lovastatin (Mevacor) cholesterol (statin)
Lovaza (omega-3-acid ethyl esters) antihyperlipidemic
metoprolol tartrate (Lopressor, Toprol XL) HTN, CHF, acute MI, angina
Mevacor (lovastatin) cholesterol-lowering agent
Miscardis HCT (telmisartan with hydrochlorothiazide)
Minipress (prazosin HCl) HTN
nebivolol (Bystolic) beta-blocker HTN
nifedipine ER (Procardia, Adalat) angina
Nitrostat (nitroglycerin) angina pectoris due to coronary artery disease
Norvasc (amlodipine besylate) HTN
Plavix (clopidogrel bisulfate) reduces risk of atherothrombotic events, heart attack, stroke, peripheral vascular disease
Pradaxa (dabigatran etexilae mesylate) blood thinner, reduces risk of strokes and blood clots in atrial fibrillation
Pravachol (pravastatin sodium) hypercholesterolemia, hyperlipidemia, dysbetalipoproteinemia
Prinivil (lisinopril) HTN
quinapril (Accupril) hypertension, CHF
ramipril (Altace) reduces risk of MI, stroke, hypertension
Ranexa (ranolazine) antianginal medication
simvastatin (Zocor) hypercholesterolemia, hypertriglyceridemia, dysbetalipoproteinemia
Tenormin (atenolol) Beta blocking agent
Toprol XL (metoprolol) HTN
triamterene/HCTZ (Dyazide) diuretic, hypertension, peripheral edema
Tricor (penofibrate) hypercholesterolemia
Trizac (diltiazem hydrochloride) hypertension
valsartan (Diovan) HTN
Vasotec (enalapril) HTN
verapamil angina, hypertension, supraventricular arrhythmia, atrial fibrillation/flutter, migraine prophylaxis
Vytorin (ezetimibe with simvastatin) cholesterol
warfarin (Coumadin) anticoagulation
Welchol (colsevelam Hcl) lowers cholesterol and A1C level
Xarelto (rivaroxaban) DVT and PE, aids with stroke prevention in atrial fibrillation
Zestril (lisinopril) HTN
Zetia (ezetimibe) primary hypercholesterolemia
Zocor (simvastatin) high cholesterol

Electrolytes

K-Dur (potassium chloride) hypokalemia, prevention of hypokalemia
Klor-Con (potassium chloride) hypokalemia, prevention of hypokalemia

Electrolytes (continued)

K-Tab (potassium)
potassium chloride (K-Dur, Klor-Con) hypokalemia, prevention of hypokalemia

Endocrinology

Actoplus Met, Actoplus Met XR (pioglitazone hydrochloride and metformin hydrochloride) DM type 2
Actos (pioglitazone hydrochloride) DM type 2
Aldactone (spironolactone) hyperaldosteronism
allopurinol (Zyloprim) gout
Armour (Thyroid) thyroid hormone
Byetta (exenatide) antidiabetic (incretin mimetic)
DiaBeta (glyburide) DM type 2
Estrace (estrogen) reduces menopausal symptoms
glipizide (Glucotrol XL) DM type 2
Glucophage XR (metformin hydrochloride) diabetes
Glucotrol XL (glipizide) DM type 2
glyburide (DiaBeta, Micronase) DM type 2
Humalog (insulin lispro, rDNA origin) diabetes
Humulin N (insulin isophane [rDNA origin]) DM
Janumet (sitagliptin/metaformin HCl) DM type 2
Januvia (sitagliptin) DM type 2
Lantus (insulin glargine [rDNA origin] injection) DM type 1
Levemir (insulin determir [rDNAorigin]) injection to control high blood sugar in DM
Levothroid (levothyroxine) hypothyroidism
levothyroxine (Levoxyl, Synthroid, Levothroid) hypothyroidism, myxedema coma, thyroid cancer
Levoxyl (levothyroxine sodium) hypothyroidism, pituitary TSH suppression
metformin (Glucophage) DM type 2
methylprednisolone endocrine disorders, rheumatic disorders
Micronase (glyburide) DM type 2
NovoLog (insulin) antidiabetic
Onglyza (saxagliptin) DM type 2
Synthroid (levothyroxine) hypothyroidism
thyroid (Armour) thyroid hormone
Trajenta (linagliptin) DM type 2
Uloric (febuxostat) lowers uric acid levels, gout
Victoza (liraglutide [rDNA origin] injection) adults with type 2 DM

Gastrointestinal

Aciphex (rabeprazole sodium) erosive or ulcerative GERD
Amitiza (lubiprosone) chronic idiopathic constipation (CIC)
Dexilant (dexlansoprazole) proton pump inhibitor GERD
esomeprazole magnesium (Nexium) GERD
Humira (adalimumab) injection, Crohn's disease
Lomotil (diphenoxylate) diarrhea
metoclopramide (Reglan) GERD
Nexium (esomeprazole magnesium) GERD
omeprazole (Prilosec) GERD, erosive esophagitis, gastric/duodenal ulcer, *H. pylori*
pantoprazole sodium (Protonix) GERD
Pepcid (famotidine) GERD, duodenal ulcer
Prevacid (lansoprazole) GERD
Prilosec (omeprazole) GERD

Gastrointestinal (continued)

Protonix (pantoprazole sodium) GERD, stomach ulcers, heartburn
Xantac (ranitidine HCl) duodenal ulcer, gastric ulcer

Genitourinary

allopurinol (Zyloprim) prophylaxis for gout, urate nephropathy, calcium oxalate calculi
AndroGel (testosterone gel) low testosterone
Aviane contraceptive
Avodart (dutasteride) prostate anti-inflammatory
azithromycin (Zithromax) chlamydia
Cialis (tadalifil) erectile dysfunction
conjugated estrogens (Premarin, Prempro) antineoplastics; cancer of breast and prostate, menopause; osteoporosis prevention; ovarian failure; primary atrophic vaginitis
Detrol (tolterodine tartrate) overactive bladder, urinary incontinence
Diflucan (fluconazole) vaginal yeast infections
Ditropan (oxybutynin chloride) urinary antispasmodic agent
Estrace (estradiol) reduces menopausal symptoms
estradiol (Estrace) vasomotor symptoms, atrophic vaginitis, osteoporosis prevention, palliative treatment for breast cancer and prostate cancer
Flomax (tamsulosin hydrochloride) benign prostatic hyperplasia
fluconazole (Diflucan) vaginal candidiasis, oropharyngeal and esophageal candidiasis, cryptococcal meningitis
Demadex (torsemide) loop diuretic
Levitra (vardenafil HCl) erectile dysfunction
Lo Loestrin Fe (norethindrone acetate and ethinyl estradiol) contraceptive
medroxyprogesterone (Provera) HRT, amenorrhea, dysfunctional uterine bleeding
norgestimate/ethinyl estradiol (Ortho Tri-Cyclen) oral contraceptive
Nuvaring (etonogestrel/ethinyl estradiol vaginal ring) contraceptive
Ortho Evra (norelgestromin/ethinyl estradiol) contraceptive
Ortho Tri-Cy Lo 28 (norgestimate/ethinyl estradiol) contraceptive
Premarin (conjugated estrogens) vasomotor symptoms and vaginal atrophy due to menopause, breast cancer, prostate cancer
Prempro (conjugated estrogens/medroxyprogesterone) reduces menopausal symptoms
Provera (medroxyprogesterone) restores normal menstrual periods
Pyridium (phenazopyridine HCl) urinary tract analgesic
Septra (trimethoprim/sulfametoxazole) antibacterial bladder infections
sildenafil citrate (Viagra) erectile dysfunction
trimethoprim/sulfametoxazole (Septra) antibacterial bladder infections
Trisprintec (Ortho Tri-Cyclen) (norgestimate/ethinyl estradiol) contraceptive
Valtrex (valacyclovir hydrochloride) herpes zoster, genital herpes
Vesicare (solifenacin succinate) anticholinergic agent (urinary bladder modifier)
Viagra (sildenafil citrate) erectile dysfunction
Yasmin (drospirenone and ethinyl estradiol) contraceptive
Zithromax (azithromycin) treat STD (chlamydia)
Zyloprim (allopurinol) gout, kidney stones

Immunology and Allergy

Adrenalin (epinephrine) allergies
Allegra (fexofenadine hydrochloride) allergies, hay fever
Astelin (azelastine hydrochloride) allergic rhinitis
CellCept (mycophenolate mofetil) lowers body's immune system, used to prevent body rejecting a kidney, liver, or heart transplant
Cetirizine (Zyrtec) allergies

Immunology and Allergy (continued)

Chlor-Trimeton (chloropheneramine maleate) allergies
Claritin (loratadine) allergies
Clarinex (desloratadine) seasonal allergic rhinitis
Dimetane (brompheniramine maleate) allergies
EpiPen (epinephrine) allergies
fexofenadine (Allegra) allergic rhinitis, chronic urticaria
Flonase (fluticasone propionate) allergic rhinitis, sleep apnea
fluticasone proprionate (Flonase) allergic rhinitis, sleep apnea
Humira Pen (aldalimumab injection) reduces pain and swelling due to arthritis, psoriasis, blocks a protein tumor necrosis factor (TNF)
loratadine (Claritin) allergies
momentasone nasal (Nasonex) seasonal and year-round allergy symptoms of the nose
mycophenolate mofetil (CellCept) lowers body's immune system, used to prevent body rejecting a kidney, liver, or heart transplant
Nasacort (triamcinolone acetonide, USP) seasonal and perennial allergic rhinitis
Nasonex (mometasone nasal) seasonal and year-round allergy symptoms of the nose
Rhinocort Aqua (budesonide nasal spray) antiallergy
Prograf (tacrolimus) lowers immune system to prevent rejection of transplanted organ
promethazine (Phenergan) allergic symptoms, nausea, motion sickness
Singular (montelukast sodium) allergic rhinitis
tacrolimus (Prograf) lowers immune system to prevent rejection of transplanted organ
Tussionex (chlorpheniramine with hydrocodone) antihistamine/antitussive
Zyrtec (cetirizine) allergic rhinitis, chronic urticaria

Musculoskeletal

Actonel (risedronate sodium) osteoporosis
alendronate (Fosamax) osteoporosis, Paget's disease
Baclofen (lioresal, kemstro) skeletal muscle relaxant
Boniva (ibandronate sodium) osteoporosis in postmenopausal women
carisoprodol (Soma) muscle spasm
cyclobenzaprine (Flexeril) muscle spasm
Evista (raloxifene hydrochloride) osteoporosis
Flexeril (cyclobenzaprine) muscle spasm, sciatica
Fosamax (alendronate sodium) osteoporosis
Skelaxin (metaxalone) acute, painful musculoskeletal conditions
Soma (carisoprodol) treats pain and discomfort from muscle injuries

Narcotic Cessation

Suboxone (buprenorphide and naloxone) treats narcotic (opiate) addiction

Neurological

Aricept (donepezil hydrochloride) mild to moderate dementias of the Alzheimer's type
benztropine mesylate (Cogentin) treats tremors, symptoms of Parkinson's disease
clonazepam (Klonopin) neuralgia, absence seizures, epilepsy, panic attacks
Depakote (divalproex) seizure disorders, psychiatric conditions, prevents migraines
Dilantin (phenytoin sodium) seizures
divalproex (Depakote) seizure disorder, mania, migraine prophylaxis
Exelon (rivastigmine tartrate) treats function and cognition in Alzheimer's patients
gabapentin (Neurontin) partial seizures, neuropathic pain, postherpetic neuralgia in adults, epilepsy
Imitrex (sumatriptan succinate) hemiplegic or basilar migraine
Keppra (levetiracetam) partial onset seizures due to epilepsy

Neurological (continued)

Klonopin (clonazepam) seizure disorders and panic attacks
Lamictal (lamotrigine) epilepsy
Lyrica (pregablalin) neurolopathic pain, postherpetic neuralgia, partial onset seizures, fibromyalgia
Mirapex (pramipexol dihydrochloride) anti-Parkinson's agent–dopamine agonist
Namenda (memantine HCl) agent for Alzheimer's dementia (NMDA receptor antagonist)
Neurontin (gabapentin) controls seizures, nerve pain
Requip (ropinirole HCl) anti-Parkinson's agent–dopamine agonist
Topamax (topiramate) epilepsy
Trileptal (oxcarbazepin) antiepileptic

Optical

Alphagan-P (brimonidine tartrate) glaucoma
Cosopt (dorzolamide hydrochloride and timolol maleate) reduces intraocular pressure in ocular hypertension, glaucoma
Combigan (brimonidine tartrate/timolol maleate) reduces intraocular pressure (IOP) in patients with glaucoma or ocular hypertension
Lotemax (loteprednol etabonate) internal and external inflammation of the eye
Lumigan (bimatoprost) glaucoma
Pataday (**Patanol**) (olopatadine) allergic conjunctivitis
TobraDex (tobramycin and dexamethasone) antibiotic ophthalmic corticosteroid
Travatan (travoprost) antiglaucoma agent (ophthalmic prostaglandin)
Vigamox (moxifloxacin hydrochloride) bacterial conjunctivitis
Xalatan (latanoprost) reduces intraocular pressure, glaucoma

Psychiatric

Abilify (aripiprazole) (amphetamine, dextroamphetamine) schizophrenia, bipolar conditions
Adderall ADHD
alprazolam (Xanax) anxiety, panic disorder
Ambien (zolpidem tartrate) sleep disorders, insomnia
amitriptyline (Elavil, Endep) depression, chronic pain
Aripiprazole (Abilify) schizophrenia, bipolar conditions
Ativan (lorazepam) anxiety
bupropion HCl (Wellbutrin SR) major depressive disorder
Budisol (butabarbital sodium) sedative or hypnotic, insomnia
Celexa (citalopram) depression
Citalopram (Celexa) depression
clonazepam (Klonopin) anti-anxiety
Concerta (methylphenidate HCl extended release) ADHD
Cymbalta (duloxetine hydrochloride) suicidal tendencies and depression
Desyrel (trazodone) depression
diazepam (Valium) anxiety, alcohol withdrawal stress, muscle spasm, seizure disorder, status epilepticus
Effexor XR (venlafaxine hydrochloride) major depressive disorder
Elavil (amitriptyline) depression, fibromyalgia
Endep (amitriptyline) depression
escitapropram oxalate (Lexapro) antidepressant
fluoxetine hydrochloride (Prozac) bulimia nervosa, depression, obsessive-compulsive disorder, social anxiety disorder
Focalin XR (dexmethylphenidate HCl) ADHD
Geodon (ziprasidone hydrochloride) antipsychotic schizophrenia, bipolar disorder
Haldol (haloperidol) treats mental/mood disorders

Psychiatric (continued)

hydroxyzine (Atarax) anxiety, psychoneurosis
Klonopin (clonazepam) anti-anxiety
Lexapro (escitapropram oxalate) antidepressant, anxiety
lisdexamfetamine (Vyvanse) ADHD
lorazepam (Ativan) anxiety, panic attacks, depression
Lunesta (eszopiclone) non-BZD (nonbenzodiazepines drug) hypnotic
modafinil (Provigil) sleep disorders
nortriptyline (Pamelor) depression
paroxetine (Paxil) anxiety, panic disorder, depression, obsessive-compulsive disorder
Paxil (paroxetine) panic attacks, depression, obsessive-compulsive disorder, post-traumatic stress disorder (PTSD)
Pristiq (desvenlafaxine) depression
Privigil (modafinil) sleep disorders
Prozac (fluoxetine) depression, obsessive-compulsive disorder, panic attacks, bulimia, premenstrual syndrome
Restoril (temazepam) insomnia
Risperdal (risperidone) schizophrenia
Seroquel (quetiapine fumarate) treatment of bipolar mania
sertraline (Zoloft) anxiety, panic disorder, depression, obsessive-compulsive disorder
Strattera (atomoxetine HCl) ADHD
trazodone (Desyrel) depression
Valium (diazepam) anxiety
venlafaxine (Effexor EX) depression, anxiety
Viibryd (vilazodone HCI) major depressive disorder (MDD)
Vyvanse (lisdexamfetamine) ADHD
Wellbutrin SR (bupropion HCl) major depressive disorder
Xanax (alprazolam) anxiety and panic disorders
ziprasidone hydrochloride (Geodon) antipsychotic schizophrenia, bipolar disorder
Zoloft (sertraline hydrochloride) depression, panic attacks, post-traumatic stress disorder
zolpidem (Ambien) insomnia
Zyprexa (olanzapine) dementia-related psychosis

Respiratory

Advair Diskus (fluticasone propionate) treatment of asthma
Advair HFA (fluticasone propionate and saleterol) asthma
albuterol (Proventil, Ventolin) asthma
Asmanex Twisthaler (mometasone furoate) maintenance treatment for asthma
Cheratussin AC (codeine and guaifenesin) cough suppressant and expectorant
Combivent Respimat (ipratropium bromide/albuterol) COPD
Dulera (mometasone furolate dehydrate) asthma control
Flovent HFA (fluticasone propionate) asthma
fluticasone propionate (Flovent) asthma
montelukast (Singular) asthma
Proair HFA (albuterol sulfate inhalation aerosol) asthma
Proventil HFA (albuterol) asthma
Singulair (montelukast) asthma
Spiriva (tiotropium bromide inhalation powder) bronchospasm associated with COPD
Symbicort (budesonide and formoterol) prevents bronchospasm in patients with asthma or COPD
Tussionex (pennkinetic) cough and upper respiratory symptoms with allergy or cold
Ventolin (albuterol) asthma
Xopenex (levalbuterol HCl) antiasthmatic (beta 2 agonist)

Smoking Cessation

Chantix (varenicline) aid to smoking cessation

Common Abbreviations

Always use with caution! Abbreviations may have multiple meanings.

a	before
aa	of each
ac, a.c.	before meals
AD	right ear
ad lib	as desired
alt dieb	alternate days
alt hr	alternate hours
alt noc	alternate nights
am, AM	morning
amt	amount
ante	before
APAP	acetaminophen
aq	aqueous (water)
AS	left ear
AU	both ears
Ba	barium
bid, b.i.d.	two times a day
bin	two times a night
BMR	basal metabolism rate
BP	blood pressure
C	100, Centigrade
c, w/	with
Ca	calcium
cap(s)	capsule(s)
cc	cubic centimeter
CHF	congestive heart failure
chol	cholesterol
Cl	chloride
cm	centimeter
c/o	complains of
comp	compounded of
CV	cardiovascular
d	day
D$_5$W	5% dextrose in water
D/C, dc	discontinue
dil	dilute
disp	dispense
DM	diabetes mellitus
dr	dram
dro(s)	drop(s)
Dx	diagnosis
EENT	eye, ear, nose, & throat
elix	elixir
emul	emulsion
et	and
EtOH	alcohol
exp	expired
ext	extract/external

FBS	fasting blood sugar
FDA	Food and Drug Administration
Fe	iron
Fl	fluid
fl oz	fluid ounce
G	gauge
g, GM, gm, gr	gram(s)
gal	gallon
gt, gtt	drop(s)
H	hour/hypodermic
HRT	hormone replacement therapy
Hs, h.s.	hour of sleep (bedtime)
HTN	hypertension
Hx	history
IM	intramuscular
inh	inhalation
Inj	injection
IPPV	intermittent positive pressure breathing
IU	international units
IV	intravenous
IVPB	IV piggyback (2nd line)
K	potassium
kg	kilogram
L	liter
lb	pound
Liq	liquid
mcg	microgram
MDI	metered dose inhaler
mg	milligram(s)
ml, mL	milliliter(s)
mm	millimeter
Na	sodium
NaCl 0.9%	normal saline
neg	negative
NKA	no known allergy
NKDA	no known drug allergy
no	number
noc, noct	night
non rep	do not repeat
NPO	nothing by mouth
NS	normal saline
NSAID	nonsteroidal anti-inflammatory drug(s)
O	pint
od	once day/daily
OD	right eye
ol	left eye

Common Abbreviations (continued)

om	every morning	R/O	rule out
os	left eye	Rx	prescription
OTC	over the counter	sat	saturated
ou	each eye	SC, sc, sq, subc, subq.	Subcutaneous
Oz, oz	ounce	Sig, sig	let be labeled as follows, directions
P	pulse, pint		
Pc, p.c.	after meals	SL	sublingual
PCA	patient-controlled analgesia, patient-controlled administration	SOB	shortness of breath
		stat	immediately
PCN	penicillin	susp	suspension
PDR	Physician's Desk Reference	T, tbsp	tablespoon
per	with	tab	tablet
PM, pm	evening	tid, t.i.d.	three times a day
PO, po, p.o.	by mouth	TO	telephone order
PRN, prn	as needed as necessary	Top, top	apply topically
		TPN	total parenteral nutrition
pt	pint, patient	tsp	teaspoon
pulv	powder	TX	treatment
Q, q	every	ut, diet, UD	as directed
q2h	every 2 hours	ud	as directed
qAM	every morning	UD	unit-dose package
qd, q.d.	every day	URI	upper respiratory infection
qh, q.h.	every hour	UTI	urinary tract infection
qh.s.	every bedtime	vag	vaginal
qid, q.i.d.	four times a day	VO	verbal order
qns	quantity not sufficient	vol	volume
qPM	every evening	VS	vital signs
qs, q.s.	as much as needed, sufficient quantity	wa	while awake
		wt	weight
qt	quart	x	times

BE ALERT FOR SOUNDALIKES

Drug names may be similar in sound as well as spelling. It is important to be alert when referring to drugs. For example:

Celebrex .... NSAID
 vs
Cerebyx .... anticonvulsant

DiaBeta....... oral hypoglycemic
 vs
Zebeta beta-adrenergic blocker

Paxil .... antidepressant
 vs
Taxol .... antineoplastic

REFERENCES FOR PHARMACOLOGY

Spratto, G. R. (2013). *Delmar health care drug handbook.* Clifton Park, NY: Cengage Learning.

Woodrow, R. (2015). *Essentials of pharmacology for health occupations* (7th ed.). Clifton Park, NY: Cengage Learning.

Websites for Pharmacology: http://www.rxlist.com/
http://www.epocrates.com/
http://www.fda.gov/drugs/
http://pdr.net/
http://mayoclinic.org/

HEMATOLOGY/COAGULATION

Complete Blood Count
Use: basic blood evaluation
AKA: CBC, CBC with differential
Note: usually includes Hct, Hgb, WBC counts and differential, platelet count, and often RBC count

Erythrocyte Count
AKA: RBC count (red blood cell)
High: acute hepatitis, acute MI, PID, rheumatoid arthritis
Low: anemias, leukemias, and following severe hemorrhage

Hematocrit
Use: determines the percent of whole blood composed of red blood cells
AKA: Hct, HCT, PVC
High: dehydration, Addison's disease, polycythemia due to dehydration, and shock
Low: anemia, severe hemorrhage

Hemoglobin
Use: measures Hgb in the blood
AKA: Hb, Hgb
High: dehydration, pernicious anemia, sickle cell anemia, thalassemia, polycythemia, obstructive pulmonary diseases, CHF
Low: excessive fluid intake, iron-deficiency anemia, pregnancy

Hemoglobin, Glycated
Use: monitors blood sugar control
AKA: HbA1C, GHb, DM control index
Note: Abnormal results over time indicate inadequate control

Leukocyte Count
AKA: WBC count (white blood cell)
High: acute infections, leukemias, acute hemorrhage
Low: chemotherapy, shock, cachexia

Partial Thromboplastin Time
Use: measures intrinsic clotting time
AKA: APTT, activated
High: cirrhosis, leukemia, vitamin K deficiency, hemophilia
Low: extensive ca, early stages of disseminated intravascular coagulation

Platelet Count
Use: dx a bleeding disorder or bone marrow disease
High: iron-deficiency anemia, postop patients, malignancies, polycythemia
Low: acute leukemia, aplastic anemia, thrombocytopenic purpura

Prothrombin Time
Use: monitors blood-thinning medications used to prevent blood clots
AKA: PT, Pro Time
Prolonged: severe liver damage, heparin use, low vitamin K diet, colitis, chronic diarrhea

Reticulocyte Count
Use: measures percent of reticulocytes (slightly immature red blood cells)
High: need for RBCs, hemolytic anemias, acute or severe bleeding
Low: bone marrow failure (toxicity, tumor, fibrosis, infection), cirrhosis, iron deficiency, radiation therapy

Sedimentation Rate
Use: monitors inflammatory and malignant diseases and acute MI
AKA: erythrocyte sedimentation rate, sed rate, ESR
High: pregnancy, menstruation, infectious diseases, tissue damage

SERUM ELECTROLYTES

AKA: "Lytes"
Note: essential to normal metabolism, exists as acids, bases, and salts

Calcium, Total
Use: blood test to screen/monitor diseases of bone or calcium regulation (diseases of parathyroid and kidneys)
AKA: Ca^{2+}, Ca^{2+}, serum calcium
High: metastatic ca of bone, lung, breast, Paget's disease, hyperparathyroidism, excess vitamin D
Low: severe pancreatitis, renal insufficiency, uremia, malabsorption, osteomalacia, hypoparathyroidism

SERUM ELECTROLYTES (continued)

Chloride
AKA: Cl
High: renal insufficiency, necrosis, dehydration, renal tubular acidosis, Cushing's syndrome, hyperventilation
Low: CHF, chronic renal failure, diabetic acidosis, diarrhea, excessive sweating, emphysema

Magnesium
AKA: Mg^{2+}
High: renal insufficiency, use of antacids with magnesium
Low: chronic alcoholism, chronic diarrhea, hepatic insufficiency

Phosphorus
AKA: PO4
High: renal insufficiency, healing fx, hypoparathyroidism, excess vitamin D
Low: chronic alcoholism, ketoacidosis, hyperalimentation, hyperparathyroidism

Potassium
AKA: K
High: renal insufficiency, adrenal insufficiency, Addison's disease, hypoventilation
Low: chronic diarrhea, vomiting or malabsorption syndrome, diabetic acidosis, chronic kidney disease, use of thiazide diuretics

Sodium
AKA: NA
High: (hypernatremia) excessive dietary intake, Cushing's disease, excessive sweating, diabetes insipidus
Low: (hyponatremia) ascites, CHF, insufficient intake, diarrhea, vomiting, SIADH (syndrome of inappropriate diuretic hormone), diuretic use, chronic renal insufficiency, excessive water intake, peripheral edema, pleural effusion

SERUM/URINE/STOOL

Acid Phosphatase
High: metastatic ca of bone, prostatic ca, some liver diseases, MI, pulmonary embolism, hepatobiliary diseases, hyperparathyroidism

Alanine Aminotransferase
Use: screens for liver disease
AKA: ALT, SGPT
High: acute hepatitis, liver necrosis

Albumin
Use: screens for liver or kidney disease or evaluates nutritional status
AKA: ALB
Note: Albumin is a protein
High: shock, dehydration, multiple myeloma
Low: malnutrition, malabsorption, acute or chronic glomerulonephritis, cancers, leukemia, hepatitis, cirrhosis, hepatocellular necrosis

Alkaline Phosphatase
Use: screens/monitors treatment for liver or bone disorders
AKA: ALP, alk phos
High: biliary duct obstruction, hyperparathyroidism, healing fx, rickets, osteomalacia, neoplastic bone disorders, liver diseases

Ammonia
AKA: NH^{4+}
Note: particularly toxic to the brain; can cause confusion and lethargy
High: CHF, liver failure, GI bleed, leukemia, pericarditis

Amylase
Use: blood test to diagnose/monitor pancreatic disease (blood)
Note: amylase is an enzyme that helps digest glycogen and starch
High: acute pancreatitis, ca of the pancreas, ovaries, or lungs, mumps, intestinal obstruction
Low: acute and chronic hepatitis, cirrhosis, toxemia of pregnancy

Anion Gap
Use: dx and tx of acidosis
High: lactic acidosis, diabetic ketoacidosis, alcoholic ketoacidosis, starvation, renal failure
Low: multiple myeloma, chronic vomiting, hyperaldosteronism

Arterial Blood Gases
AKA: ABGs
Abnormal Results: respiratory, metabolic or renal diseases, trauma

Aspartate Aminotransferase
Use: detects liver damage
AKA: AST, SGOT
High: acute MI, liver disease, diseases of skeletal muscles

SERUM/URINE/STOOL (continued)

Bilirubin, Total
Use: screens/monitors liver disorders
Note: bilirubin is a product of hemoglobin breakdown, causes jaundice
High: acute/chronic hepatitis, gallstones, toxic reaction to drugs/chemicals, infectious mononucleosis

Blood Urea Nitrogen
Use: evaluates kidney function and dialysis effectiveness
AKA: BUN
High: GI hemorrhage, dehydration, renal insufficiency
Low: hepatic failure, cachexia

Carbon Dioxide, Total
AKA: CO_2
High: respiratory diseases, vomiting, intestinal obstruction
Decreased: acidosis, nephritis, diarrhea

Carcinoembryonic Antigen
Use: dx cancer and monitor tx
AKA: CEA
High: colon, breast, lung, pancreatic, thyroid ca, also heavy smoking

Cholesterol, Total
Use: screens for heart disease
High: MI, uncontrolled DM, hypothyroidism, atherosclerosis, hypercholesterolemia, hyperlipidemia
Low: acute MI, pernicious anemia, malnutrition, liver disease, sepsis, malabsorption

Creatinine
Use: evaluates kidney function and tx
High: dehydration, diabetic nephropathy, kidney disease

Creatine (Phospho) Kinase
Use: evaluates muscle damage
AKA: CPK, CK
High: acute MI, muscular dystrophies, muscle injury, CNS trauma, stroke

Globulin
Use: protein evaluation
AKA: CPK, CK
High: hepatic disease, plasma cell neoplasms, lupus, malaria

Glucose
Use: diagnoses and manages DM
AKA: GTT glucose tolerance test
High: DM, IV therapy, hyperthyroidism, hyperpituitarism, liver diseases, nephritis
Low: hyperinsulinism, hyperthyroidism, Addison's disease

Iron
AKA: Fe
High: anemias, liver disease
Low: iron-deficiency anemia, excessive fluid intake, pregnancy

Lactose Dehydrogenase
AKA: LDH
High: acute MI, infectious hepatitis, malignant tumors and widespread ca, hemolytic and pernicious anemias, acute leukemias
Low: X-ray irradiation

Oxygen Saturation
AKA: oximetry, O_2
High: hyperventilation
Low: inadequate O_2 inspiration, hypoxic lung diseases, hypoxic cardiac diseases, severe hypoventilation

Prostate-Specific Antigen
AKA: PSA
High: BPH, prostate ca, prostatism

Stool Guaiac Test
Use: detects hidden blood in stool
AKA: hemoccult
Abnormal Results: NSAIDs, colon polyps, colon ca, GI tumors, esophagitis, gastritis, inflammatory bowel disease, peptic ulcer

Thyrotropin
AKA: THS
Abnormal Findings: hyperthyroidism, hypothyroidism, depression, acute starvation, pregnancy, old age

Thyroxine
AKA: T_4
High: Graves' disease, toxic thyroid adenoma, acute thyroiditis
Low: cretinism, myxedema, pituitary or iodine insufficiency, hypothalamic failure, renal failure, Cushing's disease, cirrhosis, advanced cancer

SERUM/URINE/STOOL (continued)

Triglycerides
AKA: TG
High: hyperlipidemias, hypothyroidism, poorly controlled DM, nephrotic syndrome, hypertension, alcoholic cirrhosis, pregnancy, MI
Low: malabsorption syndrome, malnutrition, hyperthyroidism

Uric Acid
High: gout, leukemia, renal insufficiency, polycythemia, pneumonia
Low: acute hepatitis

Viral Load
Use: severity of immune system damage, monitors HIV status and treatment
AKA: CD4 lymphocyte count
Low below 350 mL: herpes simplex, herpes zoster, TB
Low below 200 mL: pneumocystis carinii pneumonia
Low below 100 mL: AIDS dementia
Low below 50 mL: cytomegalovirus

COMMON ABBREVIATIONS

AKA	also known as
ca, Ca	cancer, calcium
CHF	congestive heart failure
DM	diabetes mellitus
Dx	diagnosis
fx	fracture
GI	gastrointestinal
HIV	human immunodeficiency virus
IV	intravenous
MI	myocardial infarction
NIDDM	non-insulin-dependent DM
NSAID	nonsteroidal anti-inflammatory
tx	treatment

REFERENCES FOR LAB TESTING

Please note that this is only a list of common laboratory tests, NOT a comprehensive list of laboratory tests. The references below provide extensive information on laboratory testing.

Daniels, R. (2015). *Delmar's guide to laboratory and diagnostic tests: Organized alphabetically* (3rd ed.). Clifton Park, NY: Cengage Learning.

Estridge, B. H. and Reynolds, A. P. (2012). *Basic clinical laboratory techniques* (6th ed.). Clifton Park, NY: Cengage Learning.

Ridley, J. (2011). *Essentials of clinical laboratory science.* Clifton Park, NY: Cengage Learning.

ONLINE RESOURCES:
Lab Tests Online
      http://www.labtestsonline.org/

Labcorp (Laboratory Corporation of America)
      https://www.labcorp.com/wps/portal/provider/testmenu/

Laboratory testing
      http://www.thedoctorsdoctor.com/laboratory_testing.htm

MedlinePlus
      http://www.nlm.nih.gov/medlineplus/laboratorytests.html

Test Reference
      http://www.testreference.net/

ICD-10-CM Official Guidelines for Coding and Reporting
FY 2017
(October 1, 2016 - September 30, 2017)

Narrative changes appear in bold text
Items <u>underlined</u> have been moved within the guidelines since the FY 2016 version
Italics **are used to indicate revisions to heading changes**

The Centers for Medicare and Medicaid Services (CMS) and the National Center for Health Statistics (NCHS), two departments within the U.S. Federal Government's Department of Health and Human Services (DHHS) provide the following guidelines for coding and reporting using the International Classification of Diseases, 10th Revision, Clinical Modification (ICD-10-CM). These guidelines should be used as a companion document to the official version of the ICD-10-CM as published on the NCHS website. The ICD-10-CM is a morbidity classification published by the United States for classifying diagnoses and reason for visits in all health care settings. The ICD-10-CM is based on the ICD-10, the statistical classification of disease published by the World Health Organization (WHO).

These guidelines have been approved by the four organizations that make up the Cooperating Parties for the ICD-10-CM: the American Hospital Association (AHA), the American Health Information Management Association (AHIMA), CMS, and NCHS.

These guidelines are a set of rules that have been developed to accompany and complement the official conventions and instructions provided within the ICD-10-CM itself. The instructions and conventions of the classification take precedence over guidelines. These guidelines are based on the coding and sequencing instructions in the Tabular List and Alphabetic Index of ICD-10-CM, but provide additional instruction. Adherence to these guidelines when assigning ICD-10-CM diagnosis codes is required under the Health Insurance Portability and Accountability Act (HIPAA). The diagnosis codes (Tabular List and Alphabetic Index) have been adopted under HIPAA for all healthcare settings. A joint effort between the healthcare provider and the coder is essential to achieve complete and accurate documentation, code assignment, and reporting of diagnoses and procedures. These guidelines have been developed to assist both the healthcare provider and the coder in identifying those diagnoses that are to be reported. The importance of consistent, complete documentation in the medical record cannot be overemphasized. Without such documentation accurate coding cannot be achieved. The entire record should be reviewed to determine the specific reason for the encounter and the conditions treated.

The term encounter is used for all settings, including hospital admissions. In the context of these guidelines, the term provider is used throughout the guidelines to mean physician or any qualified health care practitioner who is legally accountable for establishing the patient's diagnosis. Only this set of guidelines, approved by the Cooperating Parties, is official.

The guidelines are organized into sections. Section I includes the structure and conventions of the classification and general guidelines that apply to the entire classification, and chapter-specific guidelines that correspond to the chapters as they are arranged in the classification. Section II includes guidelines for selection of principal diagnosis for non-outpatient settings. Section III includes guidelines for reporting additional diagnoses in non-outpatient settings. Section IV is for outpatient coding and reporting. It is necessary to review all sections of the guidelines to fully understand all of the rules and instructions needed to code properly.

Section I. Conventions, general coding guidelines and chapter specific guidelines

The conventions, general guidelines and chapter-specific guidelines are applicable to all health care settings unless otherwise indicated. The conventions and instructions of the classification take precedence over guidelines.

A. Conventions for the ICD-10-CM

The conventions for the ICD-10-CM are the general rules for use of the classification independent of the guidelines. These conventions are incorporated within the Alphabetic Index and Tabular List of the ICD-10-CM as instructional notes.

1. The Alphabetic Index and Tabular List

The ICD-10-CM is divided into the Alphabetic Index, an alphabetical list of terms and their corresponding code, and the Tabular List, a structured list of codes divided into chapters based on body system or condition. The Alphabetic Index consists of the following parts: the Index of Diseases and Injury, the Index of External Causes of Injury, the Table of Neoplasms and the Table of Drugs and Chemicals.

See Section I.C2. General guidelines
See Section I.C.19. Adverse effects, poisoning, underdosing and toxic effects

2. Format and Structure:

The ICD-10-CM Tabular List contains categories, subcategories and codes. Characters for categories, subcategories and codes may be either a letter or a number. All categories are 3 characters. A three-character category that has no further subdivision is equivalent to a code. Subcategories are either 4 or 5 characters. Codes may be 3, 4, 5, 6 or 7 characters. That is, each level of subdivision after a category is a subcategory. The final level of subdivision is a code. Codes that have applicable 7th characters are still referred to as codes, not subcategories. A code that has an applicable 7th character is considered invalid without the 7th character.

The ICD-10-CM uses an indented format for ease in reference.

3. Use of codes for reporting purposes

For reporting purposes only codes are permissible, not categories or subcategories, and any applicable 7th character is required.

4. Placeholder character

The ICD-10-CM utilizes a placeholder character "X". The "X" is used as a placeholder at certain codes to allow for future expansion. An example of this is at the poisoning, adverse effect and underdosing codes, categories T36-T50.

Where a placeholder exists, the X must be used in order for the code to be considered a valid code.

5. 7th Characters

Certain ICD-10-CM categories have applicable 7th characters. The applicable 7th character is required for all codes within the category, or as the notes in the Tabular List instruct. The 7th character must always be the 7th character in the data field. If a code that requires a 7th character is not 6 characters, a placeholder X must be used to fill in the empty characters.

6. Abbreviations

a. Alphabetic Index abbreviations

NEC   "Not elsewhere classifiable"
This abbreviation in the Alphabetic Index represents "other specified." When a specific code is not available for a condition, the Alphabetic Index directs the coder to the "other specified" code in the Tabular List.

NOS   "Not otherwise specified"
This abbreviation is the equivalent of unspecified.

b. Tabular List abbreviations

NEC   "Not elsewhere classifiable"
This abbreviation in the Tabular List represents "other specified". When a specific code is not available for a condition, the Tabular List includes an NEC entry under a code to identify the code as the "other specified" code.

NOS   "Not otherwise specified"
This abbreviation is the equivalent of unspecified.

7. Punctuation

[ ]   Brackets are used in the Tabular List to enclose synonyms, alternative wording or explanatory phrases. Brackets are used in the Alphabetic Index to identify manifestation codes.

( )   Parentheses are used in both the Alphabetic Index and Tabular List to enclose supplementary words that may be present or absent in the statement of a disease or procedure without affecting the code number to which it is assigned. The terms within the parentheses are referred to as nonessential modifiers. The nonessential modifiers in the Alphabetic Index to Diseases apply to subterms following a main term except when a nonessential modifier and a subentry are mutually exclusive, the subentry takes precedence. For example, in the ICD-10-CM Alphabetic Index under the main term Enteritis, "acute" is a nonessential modifier and "chronic" is a subentry. In this case, the nonessential modifier "acute" does not apply to the subentry "chronic".

:   Colons are used in the Tabular List after an incomplete term which needs one or more of the modifiers following the colon to make it assignable to a given category.

8.   Use of "and".

See Section I.A.14. Use of the term "And"

9.   Other and Unspecified codes

a.   "Other" codes

Codes titled "other" or "other specified" are for use when the information in the medical record provides detail for which a specific code does not exist. Alphabetic Index entries with NEC in the line designate "other" codes in the Tabular List. These Alphabetic Index entries represent specific disease entities for which no specific code exists so the term is included within an "other" code.

b.   "Unspecified" codes

Codes titled "unspecified" are for use when the information in the medical record is insufficient to assign a more specific code. For those categories for which an unspecified code is not provided, the "other specified" code may represent both other and unspecified.

See Section I.B.18 Use of Signs/Symptom/Unspecified Codes

10.   Includes Notes

This note appears immediately under a three character code title to further define, or give examples of, the content of the category.

11.   Inclusion terms

List of terms is included under some codes. These terms are the conditions for which that code is to be used. The terms may be synonyms of the code title, or, in the case of "other specified" codes, the terms are a list of the various conditions assigned to that code. The inclusion terms are not necessarily exhaustive. Additional terms found only in the Alphabetic Index may also be assigned to a code.

12.   Excludes Notes

The ICD-10-CM has two types of excludes notes. Each type of note has a different definition for use but they are all similar in that they indicate that codes excluded from each other are independent of each other.

a. Excludes1

A type 1 Excludes note is a pure excludes note. It means "NOT CODED HERE!" An Excludes1 note indicates that the code excluded should never be used at the same time as the code above the Excludes1 note. An Excludes1 is used when two conditions cannot occur together, such as a congenital form versus an acquired form of the same condition.

An exception to the Excludes1 definition is the circumstance when the two conditions are unrelated to each other. If it is not clear whether the two conditions involving an Excludes1 note are related or not, query the provider. For example, code F45.8, Other somatoform disorders, has an Excludes1 note for "sleep related teeth grinding (G47.63)," because "teeth grinding" is an inclusion term under F45.8. Only one of these two codes should be assigned for teeth grinding. However psychogenic dysmenorrhea is also an inclusion term under F45.8, and a patient could have both this condition and sleep related teeth grinding. In this case, the two conditions are clearly unrelated to each other, and so it would be appropriate to report F45.8 and G47.63 together.

b. Excludes2

A type 2 Excludes note represents "Not included here." An excludes2 note indicates that the condition excluded is not part of the condition represented by the code, but a patient may have both conditions at the same time. When an Excludes2 note appears under a code, it is acceptable to use both the code and the excluded code together, when appropriate.

13. Etiology/manifestation convention ("code first", "use additional code" and "in diseases classified elsewhere" notes)

Certain conditions have both an underlying etiology and multiple body system manifestations due to the underlying etiology. For such conditions, the ICD-10-CM has a coding convention that requires the underlying condition be sequenced first, **if applicable,** followed by the manifestation. Wherever such a combination exists, there is a "use additional code" note at the etiology code, and a "code first" note at the manifestation code. These instructional notes indicate the proper sequencing order of the codes, etiology followed by manifestation.

In most cases the manifestation codes will have in the code title, "in diseases classified elsewhere." Codes with this title are a component of the etiology/ manifestation convention. The code title indicates that it is a manifestation code. "In diseases classified elsewhere" codes are never permitted to be used as first-listed or principal diagnosis codes. They must be used in conjunction with an underlying condition code and they must be listed following the underlying condition. See category F02, Dementia in other diseases classified elsewhere, for an example of this convention.

There are manifestation codes that do not have "in diseases classified elsewhere" in the title. For such codes, there is a "use additional code" note at the etiology code and a "code first" note at the manifestation code, and the rules for sequencing apply.

In addition to the notes in the Tabular List, these conditions also have a specific Alphabetic Index entry structure. In the Alphabetic Index both conditions are listed together with the etiology code first followed by the manifestation codes in brackets. The code in brackets is always to be sequenced second.

An example of the etiology/manifestation convention is dementia in Parkinson's disease. In the Alphabetic Index, code G20 is listed first, followed by code F02.80 or F02.81 in brackets. Code G20 represents the underlying etiology, Parkinson's disease, and must be sequenced first, whereas codes F02.80 and F02.81 represent the manifestation of dementia in diseases classified elsewhere, with or without behavioral disturbance.

"Code first" and "Use additional code" notes are also used as sequencing rules in the classification for certain codes that are not part of an etiology/ manifestation combination.

See Section I.B.7. Multiple coding for a single condition.

14. **"And"**

The word "and" should be interpreted to mean either "and" or "or" when it appears in a title.

For example, cases of "tuberculosis of bones", "tuberculosis of joints" and "tuberculosis of bones and joints" are classified to subcategory A18.0, Tuberculosis of bones and joints.

15. **"With"**

The word "with" should be interpreted to mean "associated with" or "due to" when it appears in a code title, the Alphabetic Index, or an instructional note in the Tabular List. **The classification presumes a causal relationship between the two conditions linked by these terms in the Alphabetic Index or Tabular List. These conditions should be coded as related even in the absence of provider documentation explicitly linking them, unless the documentation clearly states the conditions are unrelated. For conditions not specifically linked by these relational terms in the classification, provider documentation must link the conditions in order to code them as related.**

The word "with" in the Alphabetic Index is sequenced immediately following the main term, not in alphabetical order.

16. "See" and "See Also"

The "see" instruction following a main term in the Alphabetic Index indicates that another term should be referenced. It is necessary to go to the main term referenced with the "see" note to locate the correct code.

A "see also" instruction following a main term in the Alphabetic Index instructs that there is another main term that may also be referenced that may provide additional Alphabetic Index entries that may be useful. It is not necessary to follow the "see also" note when the original main term provides the necessary code.

17. "Code also" note

A "code also" note instructs that two codes may be required to fully describe a condition, but this note does not provide sequencing direction.

18. Default codes

A code listed next to a main term in the ICD-10-CM Alphabetic Index is referred to as a default code. The default code represents that condition that is most commonly associated with the main term, or is the unspecified code for the condition. If a condition is documented in a medical record (for example, appendicitis) without any additional information, such as acute or chronic, the default code should be assigned.

19. Code assignment and Clinical Criteria

The assignment of a diagnosis code is based on the provider's diagnostic statement that the condition exists. The provider's statement that the patient has a particular condition is sufficient. Code assignment is not based on clinical criteria used by the provider to establish the diagnosis.

B. General Coding Guidelines

1. Locating a code in the ICD-10-CM

To select a code in the classification that corresponds to a diagnosis or reason for visit documented in a medical record, first locate the term in the Alphabetic Index, and then verify the code in the Tabular List. Read and be guided by instructional notations that appear in both the Alphabetic Index and the Tabular List.

It is essential to use both the Alphabetic Index and Tabular List when locating and assigning a code. The Alphabetic Index does not always provide the full code. Selection of the full code, including laterality and any applicable 7th character can only be done in the Tabular List. A dash (-) at the end of an Alphabetic Index entry indicates that additional characters are required. Even if a dash is not included at the Alphabetic Index entry, it is necessary to refer to the Tabular List to verify that no 7th character is required.

2. Level of Detail in Coding

Diagnosis codes are to be used and reported at their highest number of characters available.

ICD-10-CM diagnosis codes are composed of codes with 3, 4, 5, 6 or 7 characters. Codes with three characters are included in ICD-10-CM as the heading of a category of codes that may be further subdivided by the use of fourth and/or fifth characters and/or sixth characters, which provide greater detail.

A three-character code is to be used only if it is not further subdivided. A code is invalid if it has not been coded to the full number of characters required for that code, including the 7th character, if applicable.

3. Code or codes from A00.0 through T88.9, Z00-Z99.8

The appropriate code or codes from A00.0 through T88.9, Z00-Z99.8 must be used to identify diagnoses, symptoms, conditions, problems, complaints or other reason(s) for the encounter/visit.

4. Signs and symptoms

Codes that describe symptoms and signs, as opposed to diagnoses, are acceptable for reporting purposes when a related definitive diagnosis has not been established (confirmed) by the provider. Chapter 18 of ICD-10-CM, Symptoms, Signs, and Abnormal Clinical and Laboratory Findings, Not Elsewhere Classified (codes R00.0 - R99) contains many, but not all, codes for symptoms.

See Section I.B.18 Use of Signs/Symptom/Unspecified Codes

5. Conditions that are an integral part of a disease process

Signs and symptoms that are associated routinely with a disease process should not be assigned as additional codes, unless otherwise instructed by the classification.

6. Conditions that are not an integral part of a disease process

Additional signs and symptoms that may not be associated routinely with a disease process should be coded when present.

7. Multiple coding for a single condition

In addition to the etiology/manifestation convention that requires two codes to fully describe a single condition that affects multiple body systems, there are other single conditions that also require more than one code. "Use additional code" notes are found in the Tabular List at codes that are not part of an

ICD-10-CM Official Guidelines for Coding and Reporting
FY 2017
Page 14 of 114
Courtesy of the Centers for Disease Control and Prevention, www.cdc.gov

etiology/manifestation pair where a secondary code is useful to fully describe a condition. The sequencing rule is the same as the etiology/manifestation pair, "use additional code" indicates that a secondary code should be added.

For example, for bacterial infections that are not included in chapter 1, a secondary code from category B95, Streptococcus, Staphylococcus, and Enterococcus, as the cause of diseases classified elsewhere, or B96, Other bacterial agents as the cause of diseases classified elsewhere, may be required to identify the bacterial organism causing the infection. A "use additional code" note will normally be found at the infectious disease code, indicating a need for the organism code to be added as a secondary code.

"Code first" notes are also under certain codes that are not specifically manifestation codes but may be due to an underlying cause. When there is a "code first" note and an underlying condition is present, the underlying condition should be sequenced first.

"Code, if applicable, any causal condition first" notes indicate that this code may be assigned as a principal diagnosis when the causal condition is unknown or not applicable. If a causal condition is known, then the code for that condition should be sequenced as the principal or first-listed diagnosis.

Multiple codes may be needed for sequela, complication codes and obstetric codes to more fully describe a condition. See the specific guidelines for these conditions for further instruction.

8. Acute and Chronic Conditions

If the same condition is described as both acute (subacute) and chronic, and separate subentries exist in the Alphabetic Index at the same indentation level, code both and sequence the acute (subacute) code first.

9. Combination Code

A combination code is a single code used to classify:
Two diagnoses, or
A diagnosis with an associated secondary process (manifestation)
A diagnosis with an associated complication

Combination codes are identified by referring to subterm entries in the Alphabetic Index and by reading the inclusion and exclusion notes in the Tabular List.

Assign only the combination code when that code fully identifies the diagnostic conditions involved or when the Alphabetic Index so directs. Multiple coding should not be used when the classification provides a combination code that clearly identifies all of the elements documented in the diagnosis. When the combination code lacks necessary specificity in describing the manifestation or complication, an additional code should be used as a secondary code.

10. Sequela (Late Effects)

A sequela is the residual effect (condition produced) after the acute phase of an illness or injury has terminated. There is no time limit on when a sequela code can be used. The residual may be apparent early, such as in cerebral infarction, or it may occur months or years later, such as that due to a previous injury. Examples of sequela include: scar formation resulting from a burn, deviated septum due to a nasal fracture, and infertility due to tubal occlusion from old tuberculosis. Coding of sequela generally requires two codes sequenced in the following order: the condition or nature of the sequela is sequenced first. The sequela code is sequenced second.

An exception to the above guidelines are those instances where the code for the sequela is followed by a manifestation code identified in the Tabular List and title, or the sequela code has been expanded (at the fourth, fifth or sixth character levels) to include the manifestation(s). The code for the acute phase of an illness or injury that led to the sequela is never used with a code for the late effect.

See Section I.C.9. Sequelae of cerebrovascular disease
See Section I.C.15. Sequelae of complication of pregnancy, childbirth and the puerperium
See Section I.C.19. Application of 7ᵗʰ characters for Chapter 19

11. Impending or Threatened Condition

Code any condition described at the time of discharge as "impending" or "threatened" as follows:

> If it did occur, code as confirmed diagnosis.
> If it did not occur, reference the Alphabetic Index to determine if the condition has a subentry term for "impending" or "threatened" and also reference main term entries for "Impending" and for "Threatened."
> If the subterms are listed, assign the given code.
> If the subterms are not listed, code the existing underlying condition(s) and not the condition described as impending or threatened.

12. Reporting Same Diagnosis Code More than Once

Each unique ICD-10-CM diagnosis code may be reported only once for an encounter. This applies to bilateral conditions when there are no distinct codes identifying laterality or two different conditions classified to the same ICD-10-CM diagnosis code.

13. Laterality

Some ICD-10-CM codes indicate laterality, specifying whether the condition occurs on the left, right or is bilateral. If no bilateral code is provided and the condition is bilateral, assign separate codes for both the left and right side. If the side is not identified in the medical record, assign the code for the unspecified side.

When a patient has a bilateral condition and each side is treated during separate encounters, assign the "bilateral" code (as the condition still exists on both sides), including for the encounter to treat the first side. For the second encounter for treatment after one side has previously been treated and the condition no longer exists on that side, assign the appropriate unilateral code for the side where the condition still exists (e.g., cataract surgery performed on each eye in separate encounters). The bilateral code would not be assigned for the subsequent encounter, as the patient no longer has the condition in the previously-treated site. If the treatment on the first side did not completely resolve the condition, then the bilateral code would still be appropriate.

14. **Documentation for BMI, *Depth of* Non-pressure ulcers, Pressure Ulcer Stages, Coma Scale, *and NIH Stroke Scale***

For the Body Mass Index (BMI), depth of non-pressure chronic ulcers, pressure ulcer stage, **coma scale, and NIH stroke scale (NIHSS) codes**, code assignment may be based on medical record documentation from clinicians who are not the patient's provider (i.e., physician or other qualified healthcare practitioner legally accountable for establishing the patient's diagnosis), since this information is typically documented by other clinicians involved in the care of the patient (e.g., a dietitian often documents the BMI, a nurse often documents the pressure ulcer stages, **and an emergency medical technician often documents the coma scale**). However, the associated diagnosis (such as overweight, obesity, **acute stroke,** or pressure ulcer) must be documented by the patient's provider. If there is conflicting medical record documentation, either from the same clinician or different clinicians, the patient's attending provider should be queried for clarification.

The BMI, **coma scale**, **and NIHSS** codes should only be reported as secondary diagnoses.

15. **Syndromes**

Follow the Alphabetic Index guidance when coding syndromes. In the absence of Alphabetic Index guidance, assign codes for the documented manifestations of the syndrome. Additional codes for manifestations that are not an integral part of the disease process may also be assigned when the condition does not have a unique code.

16. **Documentation of Complications of Care**

Code assignment is based on the provider's documentation of the relationship between the condition and the care or procedure, **unless otherwise instructed by the classification**. The guideline extends to any complications of care, regardless of the chapter the code is located in. It is important to note that not all conditions that occur during or following medical care or surgery are classified as complications. There must be a cause-and-effect relationship between the care provided and the condition, and an indication in the documentation that it is a complication. Query the provider for clarification, if the complication is not clearly documented.

17. Borderline Diagnosis

If the provider documents a "borderline" diagnosis at the time of discharge, the diagnosis is coded as confirmed, unless the classification provides a specific entry (e.g., borderline diabetes). If a borderline condition has a specific index entry in ICD-10-CM, it should be coded as such. Since borderline conditions are not uncertain diagnoses, no distinction is made between the care setting (inpatient versus outpatient). Whenever the documentation is unclear regarding a borderline condition, coders are encouraged to query for clarification.

18. Use of Sign/Symptom/Unspecified Codes

Sign/symptom and "unspecified" codes have acceptable, even necessary, uses. While specific diagnosis codes should be reported when they are supported by the available medical record documentation and clinical knowledge of the patient's health condition, there are instances when signs/symptoms or unspecified codes are the best choices for accurately reflecting the healthcare encounter. Each healthcare encounter should be coded to the level of certainty known for that encounter.

If a definitive diagnosis has not been established by the end of the encounter, it is appropriate to report codes for sign(s) and/or symptom(s) in lieu of a definitive diagnosis. When sufficient clinical information isn't known or available about a particular health condition to assign a more specific code, it is acceptable to report the appropriate "unspecified" code (e.g., a diagnosis of pneumonia has been determined, but not the specific type). Unspecified codes should be reported when they are the codes that most accurately reflect what is known about the patient's condition at the time of that particular encounter. It would be inappropriate to select a specific code that is not supported by the medical record documentation or conduct medically unnecessary diagnostic testing in order to determine a more specific code.

C. Chapter-Specific Coding Guidelines

In addition to general coding guidelines, there are guidelines for specific diagnoses and/or conditions in the classification. Unless otherwise indicated, these guidelines apply to all health care settings. Please refer to Section II for guidelines on the selection of principal diagnosis.

1. Chapter 1: Certain Infectious and Parasitic Diseases (A00-B99)

a. Human Immunodeficiency Virus (HIV) Infections

1) Code only confirmed cases

Code only confirmed cases of HIV infection/illness. This is an exception to the hospital inpatient guideline Section II, H.

In this context, "confirmation" does not require documentation of positive serology or culture for HIV; the provider's diagnostic statement that the patient is HIV positive, or has an HIV-related illness is sufficient.

2) Selection and sequencing of HIV codes

(a) Patient admitted for HIV-related condition

If a patient is admitted for an HIV-related condition, the principal diagnosis should be B20, Human immunodeficiency virus [HIV] disease followed by additional diagnosis codes for all reported HIV-related conditions.

(b) Patient with HIV disease admitted for unrelated condition

If a patient with HIV disease is admitted for an unrelated condition (such as a traumatic injury), the code for the unrelated condition (e.g., the nature of injury code) should be the principal diagnosis. Other diagnoses would be B20 followed by additional diagnosis codes for all reported HIV-related conditions.

(c) Whether the patient is newly diagnosed

Whether the patient is newly diagnosed or has had previous admissions/encounters for HIV conditions is irrelevant to the sequencing decision.

(d) Asymptomatic human immunodeficiency virus

Z21, Asymptomatic human immunodeficiency virus [HIV] infection status, is to be applied when the patient without any documentation of symptoms is listed as being "HIV positive," "known HIV," "HIV test positive," or similar terminology. Do not use this code if the term "AIDS" is used or if the patient is treated for any HIV-related illness or is described as having any condition(s) resulting from his/her HIV positive status; use B20 in these cases.

(e) **Patients with inconclusive HIV serology**

Patients with inconclusive HIV serology, but no definitive diagnosis or manifestations of the illness, may be assigned code R75, Inconclusive laboratory evidence of human immunodeficiency virus [HIV].

(f) **Previously diagnosed HIV-related illness**

Patients with any known prior diagnosis of an HIV-related illness should be coded to B20. Once a patient has developed an HIV-related illness, the patient should always be assigned code B20 on every subsequent admission/encounter. Patients previously diagnosed with any HIV illness (B20) should never be assigned to R75 or Z21, Asymptomatic human immunodeficiency virus [HIV] infection status.

(g) **HIV Infection in Pregnancy, Childbirth and the Puerperium**

During pregnancy, childbirth or the puerperium, a patient admitted (or presenting for a health care encounter) because of an HIV-related illness should receive a principal diagnosis code of O98.7-, Human immunodeficiency [HIV] disease complicating pregnancy, childbirth and the puerperium, followed by B20 and the code(s) for the HIV-related illness(es). Codes from Chapter 15 always take sequencing priority.

Patients with asymptomatic HIV infection status admitted (or presenting for a health care encounter) during pregnancy, childbirth, or the puerperium should receive codes of O98.7- and Z21.

(h) **Encounters for testing for HIV**

If a patient is being seen to determine his/her HIV status, use code Z11.4, Encounter for screening for human immunodeficiency virus [HIV]. Use additional codes for any associated high risk behavior.

If a patient with signs or symptoms is being seen for HIV testing, code the signs and symptoms. An additional counseling code Z71.7, Human immunodeficiency virus [HIV] counseling, may be used if counseling is provided during the encounter for the test.

When a patient returns to be informed of his/her HIV test results and the test result is negative, use code Z71.7, Human immunodeficiency virus [HIV] counseling.

If the results are positive, see previous guidelines and assign codes as appropriate.

b. Infectious agents as the cause of diseases classified to other chapters

Certain infections are classified in chapters other than Chapter 1 and no organism is identified as part of the infection code. In these instances, it is necessary to use an additional code from Chapter 1 to identify the organism. A code from category B95, Streptococcus, Staphylococcus, and Enterococcus as the cause of diseases classified to other chapters, B96, Other bacterial agents as the cause of diseases classified to other chapters, or B97, Viral agents as the cause of diseases classified to other chapters, is to be used as an additional code to identify the organism. An instructional note will be found at the infection code advising that an additional organism code is required.

c. Infections resistant to antibiotics

Many bacterial infections are resistant to current antibiotics. It is necessary to identify all infections documented as antibiotic resistant. Assign a code from category Z16, Resistance to antimicrobial drugs, following the infection code only if the infection code does not identify drug resistance.

d. Sepsis, Severe Sepsis, and Septic Shock

1) Coding of Sepsis and Severe Sepsis

(a) Sepsis

For a diagnosis of sepsis, assign the appropriate code for the underlying systemic infection. If the type of infection or causal organism is not further specified, assign code A41.9, Sepsis, unspecified organism.

A code from subcategory R65.2, Severe sepsis, should not be assigned unless severe sepsis or an associated acute organ dysfunction is documented.

(i) Negative or inconclusive blood cultures and sepsis

Negative or inconclusive blood cultures do not preclude a diagnosis of sepsis in patients with clinical evidence of the condition; however, the provider should be queried.

(ii) Urosepsis

The term urosepsis is a nonspecific term. It is not to be considered synonymous with sepsis. It has no default code in the Alphabetic Index. Should a provider use this term, he/she must be queried for clarification.

(iii)Sepsis with organ dysfunction

If a patient has sepsis and associated acute organ dysfunction or multiple organ dysfunction (MOD), follow the instructions for coding severe sepsis.

(iv)Acute organ dysfunction that is not clearly associated with the sepsis

If a patient has sepsis and an acute organ dysfunction, but the medical record documentation indicates that the acute organ dysfunction is related to a medical condition other than the sepsis, do not assign a code from subcategory R65.2, Severe sepsis. An acute organ dysfunction must be associated with the sepsis in order to assign the severe sepsis code. If the documentation is not clear as to whether an acute organ dysfunction is related to the sepsis or another medical condition, query the provider.

(b) **Severe sepsis**

The coding of severe sepsis requires a minimum of 2 codes: first a code for the underlying systemic infection, followed by a code from subcategory R65.2, Severe sepsis. If the causal organism is not documented, assign code A41.9, Sepsis, unspecified organism, for the infection. Additional code(s) for the associated acute organ dysfunction are also required.

Due to the complex nature of severe sepsis, some cases may require querying the provider prior to assignment of the codes.

2) Septic shock

(a) Septic shock generally refers to circulatory failure associated with severe sepsis, and therefore, it represents a type of acute organ dysfunction.

For cases of septic shock, the code for the systemic infection should be sequenced first, followed by code R65.21, Severe sepsis with septic shock or code T81.12, Postprocedural septic shock. Any additional codes for the other acute organ dysfunctions should also be assigned. As noted in the sequencing instructions in the Tabular List, the code for septic shock cannot be assigned as a principal diagnosis.

3) Sequencing of severe sepsis

If severe sepsis is present on admission, and meets the definition of principal diagnosis, the underlying systemic infection should be assigned as principal diagnosis followed by the appropriate code from subcategory R65.2 as required by the sequencing rules in the Tabular List. A code from subcategory R65.2 can never be assigned as a principal diagnosis.

When severe sepsis develops during an encounter (it was not present on admission), the underlying systemic infection and the appropriate code from subcategory R65.2 should be assigned as secondary diagnoses.

Severe sepsis may be present on admission, but the diagnosis may not be confirmed until sometime after admission. If the documentation is not clear whether severe sepsis was present on admission, the provider should be queried.

4) Sepsis and severe sepsis with a localized infection

If the reason for admission is both sepsis or severe sepsis and a localized infection, such as pneumonia or cellulitis, a code(s) for the underlying systemic infection should be assigned first and the code for the localized infection should be assigned as a secondary diagnosis. If the patient has severe sepsis, a code from subcategory R65.2 should also be assigned as a secondary diagnosis. If the patient is admitted with a localized infection, such as pneumonia, and sepsis/severe sepsis doesn't develop until after admission, the localized infection should be assigned first, followed by the appropriate sepsis/severe sepsis codes.

5)   Sepsis due to a postprocedural infection

(a)   **Documentation of causal relationship**

As with all postprocedural complications, code assignment is based on the provider's documentation of the relationship between the infection and the procedure.

(b)   **Sepsis due to a postprocedural infection**

For such cases, the postprocedural infection code, such as T80.2, Infections following infusion, transfusion, and therapeutic injection, T81.4, Infection following a procedure, T88.0, Infection following immunization, or O86.0, Infection of obstetric surgical wound, should be coded first, followed by the code for the specific infection. If the patient has severe sepsis, the appropriate code from subcategory R65.2 should also be assigned with the additional code(s) for any acute organ dysfunction.

(c)   **Postprocedural infection and postprocedural septic shock**

In cases where a postprocedural infection has occurred and has resulted in severe sepsis the code for the precipitating complication such as code T81.4, Infection following a procedure, or O86.0, Infection of obstetrical surgical wound should be coded first followed by code R65.20, Severe sepsis without septic shock. A code for the systemic infection should also be assigned.

If a postprocedural infection has resulted in postprocedural septic shock, the code for the precipitating complication such as code T81.4, Infection following a procedure, or O86.0, Infection of obstetrical surgical wound should be coded first followed by code T81.12-, Postprocedural septic shock. A code for the systemic infection should also be assigned.

6)   Sepsis and severe sepsis associated with a noninfectious process (condition)

In some cases a noninfectious process (condition), such as trauma, may lead to an infection which can result in sepsis or severe sepsis. If sepsis or severe sepsis is documented as associated with a noninfectious condition, such as a burn or serious injury, and this condition meets the definition for principal diagnosis, the code for the noninfectious condition should be sequenced first, followed by the code for the resulting infection. If severe sepsis is present, a code from subcategory

R65.2 should also be assigned with any associated organ dysfunction(s) codes. It is not necessary to assign a code from subcategory R65.1, Systemic inflammatory response syndrome (SIRS) of non-infectious origin, for these cases.

If the infection meets the definition of principal diagnosis, it should be sequenced before the non-infectious condition. When both the associated non-infectious condition and the infection meet the definition of principal diagnosis, either may be assigned as principal diagnosis.

Only one code from category R65, Symptoms and signs specifically associated with systemic inflammation and infection, should be assigned. Therefore, when a non-infectious condition leads to an infection resulting in severe sepsis, assign the appropriate code from subcategory R65.2, Severe sepsis. Do not additionally assign a code from subcategory R65.1, Systemic inflammatory response syndrome (SIRS) of non-infectious origin.

See Section I.C.18. SIRS due to non-infectious process

7) Sepsis and septic shock complicating abortion, pregnancy, childbirth, and the puerperium

See Section I.C.15. Sepsis and septic shock complicating abortion, pregnancy, childbirth and the puerperium

8) Newborn sepsis

See Section I.C.16. f. Bacterial sepsis of Newborn

e. Methicillin Resistant *Staphylococcus aureus* (MRSA) Conditions

1) Selection and sequencing of MRSA codes

(a) Combination codes for MRSA infection

When a patient is diagnosed with an infection that is due to methicillin resistant *Staphylococcus aureus* (MRSA), and that infection has a combination code that includes the causal organism (e.g., sepsis, pneumonia) assign the appropriate combination code for the condition (e.g., code A41.02, Sepsis due to Methicillin resistant Staphylococcus aureus or code J15.212, Pneumonia due to Methicillin resistant Staphylococcus aureus). Do not assign code B95.62, Methicillin resistant Staphylococcus aureus infection as the cause of diseases classified elsewhere, as an additional code, because the combination code includes the type of infection and the MRSA organism. Do not assign a code from subcategory Z16.11, Resistance to penicillins, as an additional diagnosis.

See Section C.1. for instructions on coding and sequencing of sepsis and severe sepsis.

(b) Other codes for MRSA infection

When there is documentation of a current infection (e.g., wound infection, stitch abscess, urinary tract infection) due to MRSA, and that infection does not have a combination code that includes the causal organism, assign the appropriate code to identify the condition along with code B95.62, Methicillin resistant Staphylococcus aureus infection as the cause of diseases classified elsewhere for the MRSA infection. Do not assign a code from subcategory Z16.11, Resistance to penicillins.

(c) Methicillin susceptible Staphylococcus aureus (MSSA) and MRSA colonization

The condition or state of being colonized or carrying MSSA or MRSA is called colonization or carriage, while an individual person is described as being colonized or being a carrier. Colonization means that MSSA or MSRA is present on or in the body without necessarily causing illness. A positive MRSA colonization test might be documented by the provider as "MRSA screen positive" or "MRSA nasal swab positive".

Assign code Z22.322, Carrier or suspected carrier of Methicillin resistant Staphylococcus aureus, for patients documented as having MRSA colonization. Assign code Z22.321, Carrier or suspected carrier of Methicillin susceptible Staphylococcus aureus, for patient documented as having MSSA colonization. Colonization is not necessarily indicative of a disease process or as the cause of a specific condition the patient may have unless documented as such by the provider.

(d) MRSA colonization and infection

If a patient is documented as having both MRSA colonization and infection during a hospital admission, code Z22.322, Carrier or suspected carrier of Methicillin resistant Staphylococcus aureus, and a code for the MRSA infection may both be assigned.

f. Zika virus infections

1) Code only confirmed cases

Code only a confirmed diagnosis of Zika virus (A92.5, Zika virus disease) as documented by the provider. This is an exception to the hospital inpatient guideline Section II, H.

In this context, "confirmation" does not require documentation of the type of test performed; the physician's diagnostic statement that the condition is confirmed is sufficient. This code should be assigned regardless of the stated mode of transmission.

If the provider documents "suspected", "possible" or "probable" Zika, do not assign code A92.5. Assign a code(s) explaining the reason for encounter (such as fever, rash, or joint pain) or Z20.828, Contact with and (suspected) exposure to other viral communicable diseases.

2. Chapter 2: Neoplasms (C00-D49)

General guidelines

Chapter 2 of the ICD-10-CM contains the codes for most benign and all malignant neoplasms. Certain benign neoplasms, such as prostatic adenomas, may be found in the specific body system chapters. To properly code a neoplasm it is necessary to determine from the record if the neoplasm is benign, in-situ, malignant, or of uncertain histologic behavior. If malignant, any secondary (metastatic) sites should also be determined.

Primary malignant neoplasms overlapping site boundaries

A primary malignant neoplasm that overlaps two or more contiguous (next to each other) sites should be classified to the subcategory/code .8 ('overlapping lesion'), unless the combination is specifically indexed elsewhere. For multiple neoplasms of the same site that are not contiguous such as tumors in different quadrants of the same breast, codes for each site should be assigned.

Malignant neoplasm of ectopic tissue

Malignant neoplasms of ectopic tissue are to be coded to the site of origin mentioned, e.g., ectopic pancreatic malignant neoplasms involving the stomach are coded to pancreas, unspecified (C25.9).

The neoplasm table in the Alphabetic Index should be referenced first. However, if the histological term is documented, that term should be referenced first, rather than going immediately to the Neoplasm Table, in order to determine which column in the Neoplasm Table is appropriate. For example, if the documentation indicates "adenoma," refer to the term in the Alphabetic Index to review the entries under this term and the instructional note to "see also neoplasm, by site, benign." The table provides the proper code based on the type of neoplasm and the site. It is important to select the proper column in the table that corresponds to the type of neoplasm. The Tabular List should then be referenced to verify that the correct code has been selected from the table and that a more specific site code does not exist. *See Section I.C.21. Factors influencing health status and contact with health services, Status, for information regarding Z15.0, codes for genetic susceptibility to cancer.*

a. Treatment directed at the malignancy

If the treatment is directed at the malignancy, designate the malignancy as the principal diagnosis.

The only exception to this guideline is if a patient admission/encounter is solely for the administration of chemotherapy, immunotherapy or radiation therapy, assign the appropriate Z51.-- code as the first-listed or principal diagnosis, and the diagnosis or problem for which the service is being performed as a secondary diagnosis.

b. Treatment of secondary site

When a patient is admitted because of a primary neoplasm with metastasis and treatment is directed toward the secondary site only, the secondary neoplasm is designated as the principal diagnosis even though the primary malignancy is still present.

c. Coding and sequencing of complications

Coding and sequencing of complications associated with the malignancies or with the therapy thereof are subject to the following guidelines:

1) Anemia associated with malignancy

When admission/encounter is for management of an anemia associated with the malignancy, and the treatment is only for anemia, the appropriate code for the malignancy is sequenced as the principal or first-listed diagnosis followed by the appropriate code for the anemia (such as code D63.0, Anemia in neoplastic disease).

2) Anemia associated with chemotherapy, immunotherapy and radiation therapy

When the admission/encounter is for management of an anemia associated with an adverse effect of the administration of chemotherapy or immunotherapy and the only treatment is for the anemia, the anemia code is sequenced first followed by the appropriate codes for the neoplasm and the adverse effect (T45.1X5, Adverse effect of antineoplastic and immunosuppressive drugs).

When the admission/encounter is for management of an anemia associated with an adverse effect of radiotherapy, the anemia code should be sequenced first, followed by the appropriate neoplasm code and code Y84.2, Radiological procedure and radiotherapy as the cause of abnormal reaction of the patient, or of later complication, without mention of misadventure at the time of the procedure.

3) Management of dehydration due to the malignancy

When the admission/encounter is for management of dehydration due to the malignancy and only the dehydration is being treated (intravenous rehydration), the dehydration is sequenced first, followed by the code(s) for the malignancy.

4) Treatment of a complication resulting from a surgical procedure

When the admission/encounter is for treatment of a complication resulting from a surgical procedure, designate the complication as the principal or first-listed diagnosis if treatment is directed at resolving the complication.

d. Primary malignancy previously excised

When a primary malignancy has been previously excised or eradicated from its site and there is no further treatment directed to that site and there is no evidence of any existing primary malignancy, a code from category Z85, Personal history of malignant neoplasm, should be used to indicate the former site of the malignancy. Any mention of extension, invasion, or metastasis to another site is coded as a secondary malignant neoplasm to that site. The secondary site may be the principal or first-listed with the Z85 code used as a secondary code.

e. Admissions/Encounters involving chemotherapy, immunotherapy and radiation therapy

1) Episode of care involves surgical removal of neoplasm

When an episode of care involves the surgical removal of a neoplasm, primary or secondary site, followed by adjunct chemotherapy or radiation treatment during the same episode of care, the code for the neoplasm should be assigned as principal or first-listed diagnosis.

2) Patient admission/encounter solely for administration of chemotherapy, immunotherapy and radiation therapy

If a patient admission/encounter is solely for the administration of chemotherapy, immunotherapy or radiation therapy assign code Z51.0, Encounter for antineoplastic radiation therapy, or Z51.11, Encounter for antineoplastic chemotherapy, or Z51.12, Encounter for antineoplastic immunotherapy as the first-listed or principal diagnosis. If a patient receives more than one of these therapies during the same admission more than one of these codes may be assigned, in any sequence.

The malignancy for which the therapy is being administered should be assigned as a secondary diagnosis.

3) Patient admitted for radiation therapy, chemotherapy or immunotherapy and develops complications

When a patient is admitted for the purpose of radiotherapy, immunotherapy or chemotherapy and develops complications such as uncontrolled nausea and vomiting or dehydration, the principal or first-listed diagnosis is Z51.0, Encounter for antineoplastic radiation therapy, or Z51.11, Encounter for antineoplastic chemotherapy, or Z51.12, Encounter for antineoplastic immunotherapy followed by any codes for the complications.

f. Admission/encounter to determine extent of malignancy

When the reason for admission/encounter is to determine the extent of the malignancy, or for a procedure such as paracentesis or thoracentesis, the primary malignancy or appropriate metastatic site is designated as the principal or first-listed diagnosis, even though chemotherapy or radiotherapy is administered.

g. Symptoms, signs, and abnormal findings listed in Chapter 18 associated with neoplasms

Symptoms, signs, and ill-defined conditions listed in Chapter 18 characteristic of, or associated with, an existing primary or secondary site malignancy cannot be used to replace the malignancy as principal or first-listed diagnosis, regardless of the number of admissions or encounters for treatment and care of the neoplasm.
See section I.C.21. Factors influencing health status and contact with health services, Encounter for prophylactic organ removal.

h. Admission/encounter for pain control/management

See Section I.C.6. for information on coding admission/encounter for pain control/management.

i. Malignancy in two or more noncontiguous sites

A patient may have more than one malignant tumor in the same organ. These tumors may represent different primaries or metastatic disease, depending on the site. Should the documentation be unclear, the provider should be queried as to the status of each tumor so that the correct codes can be assigned.

j. Disseminated malignant neoplasm, unspecified

Code C80.0, Disseminated malignant neoplasm, unspecified, is for use only in those cases where the patient has advanced metastatic disease and no known primary or secondary sites are specified. It should not be used in place of assigning codes for the primary site and all known secondary sites.

k. Malignant neoplasm without specification of site

Code C80.1, Malignant (primary) neoplasm, unspecified, equates to Cancer, unspecified. This code should only be used when no determination can be made as to the primary site of a malignancy. This code should rarely be used in the inpatient setting.

l. Sequencing of neoplasm codes

1) Encounter for treatment of primary malignancy

If the reason for the encounter is for treatment of a primary malignancy, assign the malignancy as the principal/first-listed diagnosis. The primary site is to be sequenced first, followed by any metastatic sites.

2) Encounter for treatment of secondary malignancy

When an encounter is for a primary malignancy with metastasis and treatment is directed toward the metastatic (secondary) site(s) only, the metastatic site(s) is designated as the principal/first-listed diagnosis. The primary malignancy is coded as an additional code.

3) Malignant neoplasm in a pregnant patient

When a pregnant woman has a malignant neoplasm, a code from subcategory O9A.1-, Malignant neoplasm complicating pregnancy, childbirth, and the puerperium, should be sequenced first, followed by the appropriate code from Chapter 2 to indicate the type of neoplasm.

4) Encounter for complication associated with a neoplasm

When an encounter is for management of a complication associated with a neoplasm, such as dehydration, and the treatment is only for the complication, the complication is coded first, followed by the appropriate code(s) for the neoplasm.

The exception to this guideline is anemia. When the admission/encounter is for management of an anemia associated with the malignancy, and the treatment is only for anemia, the appropriate code for the malignancy is sequenced as the principal or first-listed diagnosis followed by code D63.0, Anemia in neoplastic disease.

5) **Complication from surgical procedure for treatment of a neoplasm**

When an encounter is for treatment of a complication resulting from a surgical procedure performed for the treatment of the neoplasm, designate the complication as the principal/first-listed diagnosis. See guideline regarding the coding of a current malignancy versus personal history to determine if the code for the neoplasm should also be assigned.

6) **Pathologic fracture due to a neoplasm**

When an encounter is for a pathological fracture due to a neoplasm, and the focus of treatment is the fracture, a code from subcategory M84.5, Pathological fracture in neoplastic disease, should be sequenced first, followed by the code for the neoplasm.

If the focus of treatment is the neoplasm with an associated pathological fracture, the neoplasm code should be sequenced first, followed by a code from M84.5 for the pathological fracture.

m. Current malignancy versus personal history of malignancy

When a primary malignancy has been excised but further treatment, such as an additional surgery for the malignancy, radiation therapy or chemotherapy is directed to that site, the primary malignancy code should be used until treatment is completed.

When a primary malignancy has been previously excised or eradicated from its site, there is no further treatment (of the malignancy) directed to that site, and there is no evidence of any existing primary malignancy, a code from category Z85, Personal history of malignant neoplasm, should be used to indicate the former site of the malignancy.

See Section I.C.21. Factors influencing health status and contact with health services, History (of)

n. Leukemia, Multiple Myeloma, and Malignant Plasma Cell Neoplasms in remission versus personal history

The categories for leukemia, and category C90, Multiple myeloma and malignant plasma cell neoplasms, have codes indicating whether or not the leukemia has achieved remission. There are also codes Z85.6, Personal history of leukemia, and Z85.79, Personal history of other malignant neoplasms of lymphoid, hematopoietic and related tissues. If the documentation is unclear as to whether the leukemia has achieved remission, the provider should be queried.

See Section I.C.21. Factors influencing health status and contact with health services, History (of)

o. Aftercare following surgery for neoplasm

See Section I.C.21. Factors influencing health status and contact with health services, Aftercare

p. Follow-up care for completed treatment of a malignancy

See Section I.C.21. Factors influencing health status and contact with health services, Follow-up

q. Prophylactic organ removal for prevention of malignancy

See Section I.C. 21, Factors influencing health status and contact with health services, Prophylactic organ removal

r. Malignant neoplasm associated with transplanted organ

A malignant neoplasm of a transplanted organ should be coded as a transplant complication. Assign first the appropriate code from category T86.-, Complications of transplanted organs and tissue, followed by code C80.2, Malignant neoplasm associated with transplanted organ. Use an additional code for the specific malignancy.

3. Chapter 3: Disease of the blood and blood-forming organs and certain disorders involving the immune mechanism (D50-D89)

Reserved for future guideline expansion

4. Chapter 4: Endocrine, Nutritional, and Metabolic Diseases (E00-E89)

a. Diabetes mellitus

The diabetes mellitus codes are combination codes that include the type of diabetes mellitus, the body system affected, and the complications affecting that body system. As many codes within a particular category as are necessary to describe all of the complications of the disease may be used. They should be sequenced based on the reason for a particular encounter. Assign as many codes from categories E08 – E13 as needed to identify all of the associated conditions that the patient has.

1) **Type of diabetes**

The age of a patient is not the sole determining factor, though most type 1 diabetics develop the condition before reaching puberty. For this reason type 1 diabetes mellitus is also referred to as juvenile diabetes.

2) **Type of diabetes mellitus not documented**

If the type of diabetes mellitus is not documented in the medical record the default is E11.-, Type 2 diabetes mellitus.

3) **Diabetes mellitus and the use of insulin and oral hypoglycemics**

If the documentation in a medical record does not indicate the type of diabetes but does indicate that the patient uses insulin, code E11, Type 2 diabetes mellitus, should be assigned. Code Z79.4, Long-term (current) use of insulin, **or Z79.84, Long term (current) use of oral hypoglycemic drugs**, should also be assigned to indicate that the patient uses insulin **or hypoglycemic drugs**. Code Z79.4 should not be assigned if insulin is given temporarily to bring a type 2 patient's blood sugar under control during an encounter.

4) **Diabetes mellitus in pregnancy and gestational diabetes**

See Section I.C.15. Diabetes mellitus in pregnancy.
See Section I.C.15. Gestational (pregnancy induced) diabetes

5) **Complications due to insulin pump malfunction**

(a) **Underdose of insulin due to insulin pump failure**

An underdose of insulin due to an insulin pump failure should be assigned to a code from subcategory T85.6, Mechanical complication of other specified internal and external prosthetic devices, implants and grafts, that specifies the type of pump malfunction, as the principal or first-listed code, followed by code T38.3X6-, Underdosing of insulin and oral hypoglycemic [antidiabetic] drugs. Additional codes for the type of diabetes mellitus and any associated complications due to the underdosing should also be assigned.

(b) Overdose of insulin due to insulin pump failure

The principal or first-listed code for an encounter due to an insulin pump malfunction resulting in an overdose of insulin, should also be T85.6-, Mechanical complication of other specified internal and external prosthetic devices, implants and grafts, followed by code T38.3X1-, Poisoning by insulin and oral hypoglycemic [antidiabetic] drugs, accidental (unintentional).

6) Secondary diabetes mellitus

Codes under categories E08, Diabetes mellitus due to underlying condition, E09, Drug or chemical induced diabetes mellitus, and E13, Other specified diabetes mellitus, identify complications/manifestations associated with secondary diabetes mellitus. Secondary diabetes is always caused by another condition or event (e.g., cystic fibrosis, malignant neoplasm of pancreas, pancreatectomy, adverse effect of drug, or poisoning).

(a) Secondary diabetes mellitus and the use of insulin or hypoglycemic drugs

For patients who routinely use insulin **or hypoglycemic drugs,** code Z79.4, Long-term (current) use of insulin, **or Z79.84, Long term (current) use of oral hypoglycemic drugs** should also be assigned. Code Z79.4 should not be assigned if insulin is given temporarily to bring a patient's blood sugar under control during an encounter.

(b) Assigning and sequencing secondary diabetes codes and its causes

The sequencing of the secondary diabetes codes in relationship to codes for the cause of the diabetes is based on the Tabular List instructions for categories E08, E09 and E13.

(i) Secondary diabetes mellitus due to pancreatectomy

For postpancreatectomy diabetes mellitus (lack of insulin due to the surgical removal of all or part of the pancreas), assign code E89.1, Postprocedural hypoinsulinemia. Assign a code from category E13 and a code from subcategory Z90.41-, Acquired absence of pancreas, as additional codes.

(ii) Secondary diabetes due to drugs

Secondary diabetes may be caused by an adverse effect of correctly administered medications, poisoning or sequela of poisoning.

See section I.C.19.e for coding of adverse effects and poisoning, and section I.C.20 for external cause code reporting.

5. Chapter 5: Mental, Behavioral and Neurodevelopmental disorders (F01 – F99)

a. Pain disorders related to psychological factors

Assign code F45.41, for pain that is exclusively related to psychological disorders. As indicated by the Excludes 1 note under category G89, a code from category G89 should not be assigned with code F45.41.

Code F45.42, Pain disorders with related psychological factors, should be used with a code from category G89, Pain, not elsewhere classified, if there is documentation of a psychological component for a patient with acute or chronic pain.

See Section I.C.6. Pain

b. Mental and behavioral disorders due to psychoactive substance use

1) In Remission

Selection of codes for "in remission" for categories F10-F19, Mental and behavioral disorders due to psychoactive substance use (categories F10-F19 with -.21) requires the provider's clinical judgment. The appropriate codes for "in remission" are assigned only on the basis of provider documentation (as defined in the Official Guidelines for Coding and Reporting).

2) Psychoactive Substance Use, Abuse And Dependence

When the provider documentation refers to use, abuse and dependence of the same substance (e.g. alcohol, opioid, cannabis, etc.), only one code should be assigned to identify the pattern of use based on the following hierarchy:

- If both use and abuse are documented, assign only the code for abuse

- If both abuse and dependence are documented, assign only the code for dependence
- If use, abuse and dependence are all documented, assign only the code for dependence
- If both use and dependence are documented, assign only the code for dependence.

3) Psychoactive Substance Use

As with all other diagnoses, the codes for psychoactive substance use (F10.9-, F11.9-, F12.9-, F13.9-, F14.9-, F15.9-, F16.9-) should only be assigned based on provider documentation and when they meet the definition of a reportable diagnosis (see Section III, Reporting Additional Diagnoses). The codes are to be used only when the psychoactive substance use is associated with a mental or behavioral disorder, and such a relationship is documented by the provider.

6. Chapter 6: Diseases of the Nervous System (G00-G99)

a. Dominant/nondominant side

Codes from category G81, Hemiplegia and hemiparesis, and subcategories G83.1, Monoplegia of lower limb, G83.2, Monoplegia of upper limb, and G83.3, Monoplegia, unspecified, identify whether the dominant or nondominant side is affected. Should the affected side be documented, but not specified as dominant or nondominant, and the classification system does not indicate a default, code selection is as follows:
- For ambidextrous patients, the default should be dominant.
- If the left side is affected, the default is non-dominant.
- If the right side is affected, the default is dominant.

b. Pain - Category G89

1) General coding information

Codes in category G89, Pain, not elsewhere classified, may be used in conjunction with codes from other categories and chapters to provide more detail about acute or chronic pain and neoplasm-related pain, unless otherwise indicated below.

If the pain is not specified as acute or chronic, post-thoracotomy, postprocedural, or neoplasm-related, do not assign codes from category G89.

A code from category G89 should not be assigned if the underlying (definitive) diagnosis is known, unless the reason for the encounter is pain control/ management and not management of the underlying condition.

When an admission or encounter is for a procedure aimed at treating the underlying condition (e.g., spinal fusion, kyphoplasty), a code for the underlying condition (e.g., vertebral fracture, spinal stenosis) should be assigned as the principal diagnosis. No code from category G89 should be assigned.

(a) **Category G89 Codes as Principal or First-Listed Diagnosis**

Category G89 codes are acceptable as principal diagnosis or the first-listed code:

- When pain control or pain management is the reason for the admission/encounter (e.g., a patient with displaced intervertebral disc, nerve impingement and severe back pain presents for injection of steroid into the spinal canal). The underlying cause of the pain should be reported as an additional diagnosis, if known.

- When a patient is admitted for the insertion of a neurostimulator for pain control, assign the appropriate pain code as the principal or first-listed diagnosis. When an admission or encounter is for a procedure aimed at treating the underlying condition and a neurostimulator is inserted for pain control during the same admission/encounter, a code for the underlying condition should be assigned as the principal diagnosis and the appropriate pain code should be assigned as a secondary diagnosis.

(b) **Use of Category G89 Codes in Conjunction with Site Specific Pain Codes**

(i) **Assigning Category G89 and Site-Specific Pain Codes**

Codes from category G89 may be used in conjunction with codes that identify the site of pain (including codes from chapter 18) if the category G89 code provides additional information. For example, if the code describes the site of the pain, but does not fully describe whether the pain is acute or chronic, then both codes should be assigned.

(ii) Sequencing of Category G89 Codes with Site-Specific Pain Codes

The sequencing of category G89 codes with site-specific pain codes (including chapter 18 codes), is dependent on the circumstances of the encounter/admission as follows:

- If the encounter is for pain control or pain management, assign the code from category G89 followed by the code identifying the specific site of pain (e.g., encounter for pain management for acute neck pain from trauma is assigned code G89.11, Acute pain due to trauma, followed by code M54.2, Cervicalgia, to identify the site of pain).

- If the encounter is for any other reason except pain control or pain management, and a related definitive diagnosis has not been established (confirmed) by the provider, assign the code for the specific site of pain first, followed by the appropriate code from category G89.

2) Pain due to devices, implants and grafts

See Section I.C.19. Pain due to medical devices

3) Postoperative Pain

The provider's documentation should be used to guide the coding of postoperative pain, as well as *Section III. Reporting Additional Diagnoses* and *Section IV. Diagnostic Coding and Reporting in the Outpatient Setting.*

The default for post-thoracotomy and other postoperative pain not specified as acute or chronic is the code for the acute form.

Routine or expected postoperative pain immediately after surgery should not be coded.

(a) Postoperative pain not associated with specific postoperative complication

Postoperative pain not associated with a specific postoperative complication is assigned to the appropriate postoperative pain code in category G89.

(b) **Postoperative pain associated with specific postoperative complication**

Postoperative pain associated with a specific postoperative complication (such as painful wire sutures) is assigned to the appropriate code(s) found in Chapter 19, Injury, poisoning, and certain other consequences of external causes. If appropriate, use additional code(s) from category G89 to identify acute or chronic pain (G89.18 or G89.28).

4) **Chronic pain**

Chronic pain is classified to subcategory G89.2. There is no time frame defining when pain becomes chronic pain. The provider's documentation should be used to guide use of these codes.

5) **Neoplasm Related Pain**

Code G89.3 is assigned to pain documented as being related, associated or due to cancer, primary or secondary malignancy, or tumor. This code is assigned regardless of whether the pain is acute or chronic.

This code may be assigned as the principal or first-listed code when the stated reason for the admission/encounter is documented as pain control/pain management. The underlying neoplasm should be reported as an additional diagnosis.

When the reason for the admission/encounter is management of the neoplasm and the pain associated with the neoplasm is also documented, code G89.3 may be assigned as an additional diagnosis. It is not necessary to assign an additional code for the site of the pain.

See Section I.C.2 for instructions on the sequencing of neoplasms for all other stated reasons for the admission/encounter (except for pain control/pain management).

6) **Chronic pain syndrome**

Central pain syndrome (G89.0) and chronic pain syndrome (G89.4) are different than the term "chronic pain," and therefore codes should only be used when the provider has specifically documented this condition.

See Section I.C.5. Pain disorders related to psychological factors

7. Chapter 7: Diseases of the Eye and Adnexa (H00-H59)

a. Glaucoma

1) Assigning Glaucoma Codes

Assign as many codes from category H40, Glaucoma, as needed to identify the type of glaucoma, the affected eye, and the glaucoma stage.

2) Bilateral glaucoma with same type and stage

When a patient has bilateral glaucoma and both eyes are documented as being the same type and stage, and there is a code for bilateral glaucoma, report only the code for the type of glaucoma, bilateral, with the seventh character for the stage.

When a patient has bilateral glaucoma and both eyes are documented as being the same type and stage, and the classification does not provide a code for bilateral glaucoma (i.e. subcategories H40.10, H40.11 and H40.20) report only one code for the type of glaucoma with the appropriate seventh character for the stage.

3) Bilateral glaucoma stage with different types or stages

When a patient has bilateral glaucoma and each eye is documented as having a different type or stage, and the classification distinguishes laterality, assign the appropriate code for each eye rather than the code for bilateral glaucoma.

When a patient has bilateral glaucoma and each eye is documented as having a different type, and the classification does not distinguish laterality (i.e. subcategories H40.10, H40.11 and H40.20), assign one code for each type of glaucoma with the appropriate seventh character for the stage.

When a patient has bilateral glaucoma and each eye is documented as having the same type, but different stage, and the classification does not distinguish laterality (i.e. subcategories H40.10, H40.11 and H40.20), assign a code for the type of glaucoma for each eye with the seventh character for the specific glaucoma stage documented for each eye.

4) Patient admitted with glaucoma and stage evolves during the admission

If a patient is admitted with glaucoma and the stage progresses during the admission, assign the code for highest stage documented.

5) Indeterminate stage glaucoma

Assignment of the seventh character "4" for "indeterminate stage" should be based on the clinical documentation. The seventh character "4" is used for glaucomas whose stage cannot be clinically determined. This seventh character should not be confused with the seventh character "0", unspecified, which should be assigned when there is no documentation regarding the stage of the glaucoma.

8. Chapter 8: Diseases of the Ear and Mastoid Process (H60-H95)

Reserved for future guideline expansion

9. Chapter 9: Diseases of the Circulatory System (I00-I99)

a. Hypertension

The classification presumes a causal relationship between hypertension and heart involvement and between hypertension and kidney involvement, as the two conditions are linked by the term "with" in the Alphabetic Index. These conditions should be coded as related even in the absence of provider documentation explicitly linking them, unless the documentation clearly states the conditions are unrelated.

For hypertension and conditions not specifically linked by relational terms such as "with," "associated with" or "due to" in the classification, provider documentation must link the conditions in order to code them as related.

1) Hypertension with Heart Disease

Hypertension with heart conditions classified to I50.- or I51.4-I51.9, are assigned to a code from category I11, Hypertensive heart disease. Use an additional code from category I50, Heart failure, to identify the type of heart failure in those patients with heart failure.

The same heart conditions (I50.-, I51.4-I51.9) with hypertension are coded separately **if the provider has specifically documented a different cause.** Sequence according to the circumstances of the admission/encounter.

2) **Hypertensive Chronic Kidney Disease**

Assign codes from category I12, Hypertensive chronic kidney disease, when both hypertension and a condition classifiable to category N18, Chronic kidney disease (CKD), are present. **CKD should not be coded as hypertensive if the physician has specifically documented a different cause.**

The appropriate code from category N18 should be used as a secondary code with a code from category I12 to identify the stage of chronic kidney disease.

See Section I.C.14. Chronic kidney disease.

If a patient has hypertensive chronic kidney disease and acute renal failure, an additional code for the acute renal failure is required.

3) **Hypertensive Heart and Chronic Kidney Disease**

Assign codes from combination category I13, Hypertensive heart and chronic kidney disease, when **there is hypertension with both heart and kidney involvement.** If heart failure is present, assign an additional code from category I50 to identify the type of heart failure.

The appropriate code from category N18, Chronic kidney disease, should be used as a secondary code with a code from category I13 to identify the stage of chronic kidney disease.

See Section I.C.14. Chronic kidney disease.

The codes in category I13, Hypertensive heart and chronic kidney disease, are combination codes that include hypertension, heart disease and chronic kidney disease. The Includes note at I13 specifies that the conditions included at I11 and I12 are included together in I13. If a patient has hypertension, heart disease and chronic kidney disease, then a code from I13 should be used, not individual codes for hypertension, heart disease and chronic kidney disease, or codes from I11 or I12.

For patients with both acute renal failure and chronic kidney disease, an additional code for acute renal failure is required.

4) **Hypertensive Cerebrovascular Disease**

For hypertensive cerebrovascular disease, first assign the appropriate code from categories I60-I69, followed by the appropriate hypertension code.

5) **Hypertensive Retinopathy**

Subcategory H35.0, Background retinopathy and retinal vascular changes, should be used with a code from category I10 – I15, Hypertensive disease to include the systemic hypertension. The sequencing is based on the reason for the encounter.

6) **Hypertension, Secondary**

Secondary hypertension is due to an underlying condition. Two codes are required: one to identify the underlying etiology and one from category I15 to identify the hypertension. Sequencing of codes is determined by the reason for admission/encounter.

7) **Hypertension, Transient**

Assign code R03.0, Elevated blood pressure reading without diagnosis of hypertension, unless patient has an established diagnosis of hypertension. Assign code O13.-, Gestational [pregnancy-induced] hypertension without significant proteinuria, or O14.-, Pre-eclampsia, for transient hypertension of pregnancy.

8) **Hypertension, Controlled**

This diagnostic statement usually refers to an existing state of hypertension under control by therapy. Assign the appropriate code from categories I10-I15, Hypertensive diseases.

9) **Hypertension, Uncontrolled**

Uncontrolled hypertension may refer to untreated hypertension or hypertension not responding to current therapeutic regimen. In either case, assign the appropriate code from categories I10-I15, Hypertensive diseases.

10) **Hypertensive Crisis**
Assign a code from category I16, Hypertensive crisis, for documented hypertensive urgency, hypertensive emergency or unspecified hypertensive crisis. Code also any identified hypertensive disease (I10-I15). The sequencing is based on the reason for the encounter.

ICD-10-CM Official Guidelines for Coding and Reporting
FY 2017
Page 44 of 114
Courtesy of the Centers for Disease Control and Prevention, www.cdc.gov

b. Atherosclerotic Coronary Artery Disease and Angina

ICD-10-CM has combination codes for atherosclerotic heart disease with angina pectoris. The subcategories for these codes are I25.11, Atherosclerotic heart disease of native coronary artery with angina pectoris and I25.7, Atherosclerosis of coronary artery bypass graft(s) and coronary artery of transplanted heart with angina pectoris.

When using one of these combination codes it is not necessary to use an additional code for angina pectoris. A causal relationship can be assumed in a patient with both atherosclerosis and angina pectoris, unless the documentation indicates the angina is due to something other than the atherosclerosis.

If a patient with coronary artery disease is admitted due to an acute myocardial infarction (AMI), the AMI should be sequenced before the coronary artery disease.

See Section I.C.9. Acute myocardial infarction (AMI)

c. Intraoperative and Postprocedural Cerebrovascular Accident

Medical record documentation should clearly specify the cause- and-effect relationship between the medical intervention and the cerebrovascular accident in order to assign a code for intraoperative or postprocedural cerebrovascular accident.
Proper code assignment depends on whether it was an infarction or hemorrhage and whether it occurred intraoperatively or postoperatively. If it was a cerebral hemorrhage, code assignment depends on the type of procedure performed.

d. Sequelae of Cerebrovascular Disease

1) Category I69, Sequelae of Cerebrovascular disease

Category I69 is used to indicate conditions classifiable to categories I60-I67 as the causes of sequela (neurologic deficits), themselves classified elsewhere. These "late effects" include neurologic deficits that persist after initial onset of conditions classifiable to categories I60-I67. The neurologic deficits caused by cerebrovascular disease may be present from the onset or may arise at any time after the onset of the condition classifiable to categories I60-I67.

Codes from category I69, Sequelae of cerebrovascular disease, that specify hemiplegia, hemiparesis and monoplegia identify whether the dominant or nondominant side is affected. Should the affected side be documented, but not specified as dominant or nondominant, and the classification system does not indicate a default, code selection is as follows:

- For ambidextrous patients, the default should be dominant.
- If the left side is affected, the default is non-dominant.
- If the right side is affected, the default is dominant.

2) Codes from category I69 with codes from I60-I67

Codes from category I69 may be assigned on a health care record with codes from I60-I67, if the patient has a current cerebrovascular disease and deficits from an old cerebrovascular disease.

3) Codes from category I69 and Personal history of transient ischemic attack (TIA) and cerebral infarction (Z86.73)

Codes from category I69 should not be assigned if the patient does not have neurologic deficits.

See Section I.C.21. 4. History (of) for use of personal history codes

e. Acute myocardial infarction (AMI)

1) ST elevation myocardial infarction (STEMI) and non ST elevation myocardial infarction (NSTEMI)

The ICD-10-CM codes for acute myocardial infarction (AMI) identify the site, such as anterolateral wall or true posterior wall. Subcategories I21.0-I21.2 and code I21.3 are used for ST elevation myocardial infarction (STEMI). Code I21.4, Non-ST elevation (NSTEMI) myocardial infarction, is used for non ST elevation myocardial infarction (NSTEMI) and nontransmural MIs.

If NSTEMI evolves to STEMI, assign the STEMI code. If STEMI converts to NSTEMI due to thrombolytic therapy, it is still coded as STEMI.

For encounters occurring while the myocardial infarction is equal to, or less than, four weeks old, including transfers to another acute setting or a postacute setting, and the myocardial infarction **meets the definition for "other diagnoses" (see Section III, Reporting Additional Diagnoses)**, codes from category I21 may continue to be reported. For encounters after the 4 week time frame and the patient is still receiving care related to the myocardial infarction, the appropriate aftercare code should be assigned, rather than a code from category I21. For old or healed myocardial infarctions not requiring further care, code I25.2, Old myocardial infarction, may be assigned.

2) Acute myocardial infarction, unspecified

Code I21.3, ST elevation (STEMI) myocardial infarction of unspecified site, is the default for unspecified acute myocardial infarction. If only STEMI or transmural MI without the site is documented, assign code I21.3.

3) AMI documented as nontransmural or subendocardial but site provided

If an AMI is documented as nontransmural or subendocardial, but the site is provided, it is still coded as a subendocardial AMI.

See Section I.C.21.3 for information on coding status post administration of tPA in a different facility within the last 24 hours.

4) Subsequent acute myocardial infarction

A code from category I22, Subsequent ST elevation (STEMI) and non ST elevation (NSTEMI) myocardial infarction, is to be used when a patient who has suffered an AMI has a new AMI within the 4 week time frame of the initial AMI. A code from category I22 must be used in conjunction with a code from category I21. The sequencing of the I22 and I21 codes depends on the circumstances of the encounter.

10. Chapter 10: Diseases of the Respiratory System (J00-J99)

a. Chronic Obstructive Pulmonary Disease [COPD] and Asthma

1) Acute exacerbation of chronic obstructive bronchitis and asthma

The codes in categories J44 and J45 distinguish between uncomplicated cases and those in acute exacerbation. An acute exacerbation is a worsening or a decompensation of a chronic condition. An acute exacerbation is not equivalent to an infection superimposed on a chronic condition, though an exacerbation may be triggered by an infection.

b. Acute Respiratory Failure

1) Acute respiratory failure as principal diagnosis

A code from subcategory J96.0, Acute respiratory failure, or subcategory J96.2, Acute and chronic respiratory failure, may be assigned as a principal diagnosis when it is the condition established after study to be chiefly responsible for occasioning the admission to the hospital, and the selection is supported by the Alphabetic Index and Tabular List. However, chapter-specific coding guidelines (such as obstetrics, poisoning, HIV, newborn) that provide sequencing direction take precedence.

2) Acute respiratory failure as secondary diagnosis

Respiratory failure may be listed as a secondary diagnosis if it occurs after admission, or if it is present on admission, but does not meet the definition of principal diagnosis.

3) Sequencing of acute respiratory failure and another acute condition

When a patient is admitted with respiratory failure and another acute condition, (e.g., myocardial infarction, cerebrovascular accident, aspiration pneumonia), the principal diagnosis will not be the same in every situation. This applies whether the other acute condition is a respiratory or nonrespiratory condition. Selection of the principal diagnosis will be dependent on the circumstances of admission. If both the respiratory failure and the other acute condition are equally responsible for occasioning the admission to the hospital, and there are no chapter-specific sequencing rules, the guideline regarding two or more diagnoses that equally meet the definition for principal diagnosis *(Section II, C.)* may be applied in these situations.

If the documentation is not clear as to whether acute respiratory failure and another condition are equally responsible for occasioning the admission, query the provider for clarification.

c. Influenza due to certain identified influenza viruses

Code only confirmed cases of influenza due to certain identified influenza viruses (category J09), and due to other identified influenza virus (category J10). This is an exception to the hospital inpatient guideline Section II, H. (Uncertain Diagnosis).

In this context, "confirmation" does not require documentation of positive laboratory testing specific for avian or other novel influenza A or other identified influenza virus. However, coding should be based on the provider's diagnostic statement that the patient has avian influenza, or other novel influenza A, for category J09, or has another particular identified strain of influenza, such as H1N1 or H3N2, but not identified as novel or variant, for category J10.

If the provider records "suspected" or "possible" or "probable" avian influenza, or novel influenza, or other identified influenza, then the appropriate influenza code from category J11, Influenza due to unidentified influenza virus, should be assigned. A code from category J09, Influenza due to certain identified influenza viruses, should not be assigned nor should a code from category J10, Influenza due to other identified influenza virus.

d. Ventilator associated Pneumonia

1) Documentation of Ventilator associated Pneumonia

As with all procedural or postprocedural complications, code assignment is based on the provider's documentation of the relationship between the condition and the procedure.

Code J95.851, Ventilator associated pneumonia, should be assigned only when the provider has documented ventilator associated pneumonia (VAP). An additional code to identify the organism (e.g., Pseudomonas aeruginosa, code B96.5) should also be assigned. Do not assign an additional code from categories J12-J18 to identify the type of pneumonia.

Code J95.851 should not be assigned for cases where the patient has pneumonia and is on a mechanical ventilator and the provider has not specifically stated that the pneumonia is ventilator-associated pneumonia. If the documentation is unclear as to whether the patient has a pneumonia that is a complication attributable to the mechanical ventilator, query the provider.

2) Ventilator associated Pneumonia Develops after Admission

A patient may be admitted with one type of pneumonia (e.g., code J13, Pneumonia due to Streptococcus pneumonia) and subsequently develop VAP. In this instance, the principal diagnosis would be the appropriate code from categories J12-

J18 for the pneumonia diagnosed at the time of admission. Code J95.851, Ventilator associated pneumonia, would be assigned as an additional diagnosis when the provider has also documented the presence of ventilator associated pneumonia.

11. Chapter 11: Diseases of the Digestive System (K00-K95)

Reserved for future guideline expansion

12. Chapter 12: Diseases of the Skin and Subcutaneous Tissue (L00-L99)

a. Pressure ulcer stage codes

1) Pressure ulcer stages

Codes from category L89, Pressure ulcer, identify the site of the pressure ulcer as well as the stage of the ulcer.

The ICD-10-CM classifies pressure ulcer stages based on severity, which is designated by stages 1-4, unspecified stage and unstageable.

Assign as many codes from category L89 as needed to identify all the pressure ulcers the patient has, if applicable.

2) Unstageable pressure ulcers

Assignment of the code for unstageable pressure ulcer (L89.--0) should be based on the clinical documentation. These codes are used for pressure ulcers whose stage cannot be clinically determined (e.g., the ulcer is covered by eschar or has been treated with a skin or muscle graft) and pressure ulcers that are documented as deep tissue injury but not documented as due to trauma. This code should not be confused with the codes for unspecified stage (L89.--9). When there is no documentation regarding the stage of the pressure ulcer, assign the appropriate code for unspecified stage (L89.--9).

3) Documented pressure ulcer stage

Assignment of the pressure ulcer stage code should be guided by clinical documentation of the stage or documentation of the terms found in the Alphabetic Index. For clinical terms describing the stage that are not found in the Alphabetic Index, and there is no documentation of the stage, the provider should be queried.

4) Patients admitted with pressure ulcers documented as healed

No code is assigned if the documentation states that the pressure ulcer is completely healed.

5) Patients admitted with pressure ulcers documented as healing

Pressure ulcers described as healing should be assigned the appropriate pressure ulcer stage code based on the documentation in the medical record. If the documentation does not provide information about the stage of the healing pressure ulcer, assign the appropriate code for unspecified stage.

If the documentation is unclear as to whether the patient has a current (new) pressure ulcer or if the patient is being treated for a healing pressure ulcer, query the provider.

For ulcers that were present on admission but healed at the time of discharge, assign the code for the site and stage of the pressure ulcer at the time of admission.

6) Patient admitted with pressure ulcer evolving into another stage during the admission

If a patient is admitted with a pressure ulcer at one stage and it progresses to a higher stage, **two separate codes should be assigned: one code for the site and stage of the ulcer on admission and a second code for the same ulcer site and the highest stage reported during the stay.**

13. Chapter 13: Diseases of the Musculoskeletal System and Connective Tissue (M00-M99)

a. Site and laterality

Most of the codes within Chapter 13 have site and laterality designations. The site represents the bone, joint or the muscle involved. For some conditions where more than one bone, joint or muscle is usually involved, such as osteoarthritis, there is a "multiple sites" code available. For categories where no multiple site code is provided and more than one bone, joint or muscle is involved, multiple codes should be used to indicate the different sites involved.

1) Bone versus joint

For certain conditions, the bone may be affected at the upper or lower end, (e.g., avascular necrosis of bone, M87, Osteoporosis,

M80, M81). Though the portion of the bone affected may be at the joint, the site designation will be the bone, not the joint.

b. Acute traumatic versus chronic or recurrent musculoskeletal conditions

Many musculoskeletal conditions are a result of previous injury or trauma to a site, or are recurrent conditions. Bone, joint or muscle conditions that are the result of a healed injury are usually found in chapter 13. Recurrent bone, joint or muscle conditions are also usually found in chapter 13. Any current, acute injury should be coded to the appropriate injury code from chapter 19. Chronic or recurrent conditions should generally be coded with a code from chapter 13. If it is difficult to determine from the documentation in the record which code is best to describe a condition, query the provider.

c. Coding of Pathologic Fractures

7th character A is for use as long as the patient is receiving active treatment for the fracture. While the patient may be seen by a new or different provider over the course of treatment for a pathological fracture, assignment of the 7th character is based on whether the patient is undergoing active treatment and not whether the provider is seeing the patient for the first time.

7th character D is to be used for encounters after the patient has completed active treatment. The other 7th characters, listed under each subcategory in the Tabular List, are to be used for subsequent encounters for **routine care of fractures during the healing and recovery phase as well as** treatment of problems associated with the healing, such as malunions, nonunions, and sequelae.

Care for complications of surgical treatment for fracture repairs during the healing or recovery phase should be coded with the appropriate complication codes.

See Section I.C.19. Coding of traumatic fractures.

d. Osteoporosis

Osteoporosis is a systemic condition, meaning that all bones of the musculoskeletal system are affected. Therefore, site is not a component of the codes under category M81, Osteoporosis without current pathological fracture. The site codes under category M80, Osteoporosis with current pathological fracture, identify the site of the fracture, not the osteoporosis.

1) Osteoporosis without pathological fracture

Category M81, Osteoporosis without current pathological fracture, is for use for patients with osteoporosis who do not currently have a pathologic fracture due to the osteoporosis, even if they have had a fracture in the past. For patients with a history of osteoporosis fractures, status code Z87.310, Personal history of (healed) osteoporosis fracture, should follow the code from M81.

2) Osteoporosis with current pathological fracture

Category M80, Osteoporosis with current pathological fracture, is for patients who have a current pathologic fracture at the time of an encounter. The codes under M80 identify the site of the fracture. A code from category M80, not a traumatic fracture code, should be used for any patient with known osteoporosis who suffers a fracture, even if the patient had a minor fall or trauma, if that fall or trauma would not usually break a normal, healthy bone.

14. Chapter 14: Diseases of Genitourinary System (N00-N99)

a. Chronic kidney disease

1) Stages of chronic kidney disease (CKD)

The ICD-10-CM classifies CKD based on severity. The severity of CKD is designated by stages 1-5. Stage 2, code N18.2, equates to mild CKD; stage 3, code N18.3, equates to moderate CKD; and stage 4, code N18.4, equates to severe CKD. Code N18.6, End stage renal disease (ESRD), is assigned when the provider has documented end-stage-renal disease (ESRD).

If both a stage of CKD and ESRD are documented, assign code N18.6 only.

2) Chronic kidney disease and kidney transplant status

Patients who have undergone kidney transplant may still have some form of chronic kidney disease (CKD) because the kidney transplant may not fully restore kidney function. Therefore, the presence of CKD alone does not constitute a transplant complication. Assign the appropriate N18 code for the patient's stage of CKD and code Z94.0, Kidney transplant status. If a transplant complication such as failure or rejection or other transplant complication is documented, see section I.C.19.g for information on coding complications of a kidney transplant. If the documentation is unclear as to whether the patient has a complication of the transplant, query the provider.

3) Chronic kidney disease with other conditions

Patients with CKD may also suffer from other serious conditions, most commonly diabetes mellitus and hypertension. The sequencing of the CKD code in relationship to codes for other contributing conditions is based on the conventions in the Tabular List.

See I.C.9. Hypertensive chronic kidney disease.
See I.C.19. Chronic kidney disease and kidney transplant complications.

15. Chapter 15: Pregnancy, Childbirth, and the Puerperium (O00-O9A)

a. General Rules for Obstetric Cases

1) Codes from chapter 15 and sequencing priority

Obstetric cases require codes from chapter 15, codes in the range O00-O9A, Pregnancy, Childbirth, and the Puerperium. Chapter 15 codes have sequencing priority over codes from other chapters. Additional codes from other chapters may be used in conjunction with chapter 15 codes to further specify conditions. Should the provider document that the pregnancy is incidental to the encounter, then code Z33.1, Pregnant state, incidental, should be used in place of any chapter 15 codes. It is the provider's responsibility to state that the condition being treated is not affecting the pregnancy.

2) Chapter 15 codes used only on the maternal record

Chapter 15 codes are to be used only on the maternal record, never on the record of the newborn.

3) Final character for trimester

The majority of codes in Chapter 15 have a final character indicating the trimester of pregnancy. The timeframes for the trimesters are indicated at the beginning of the chapter. If trimester is not a component of a code, it is because the condition always occurs in a specific trimester, or the concept of trimester of pregnancy is not applicable. Certain codes have characters for only certain trimesters because the condition does not occur in all trimesters, but it may occur in more than just one.

Assignment of the final character for trimester should be based on the provider's documentation of the trimester (or number of weeks) for the current admission/encounter. This applies to the assignment of trimester for pre-existing conditions as well as those that develop during or are due to the pregnancy. The provider's documentation of the number of weeks may be used to assign the appropriate code identifying the trimester.

Whenever delivery occurs during the current admission, and there is an "in childbirth" option for the obstetric complication being coded, the "in childbirth" code should be assigned.

4) Selection of trimester for inpatient admissions that encompass more than one trimester

In instances when a patient is admitted to a hospital for complications of pregnancy during one trimester and remains in the hospital into a subsequent trimester, the trimester character for the antepartum complication code should be assigned on the basis of the trimester when the complication developed, not the trimester of the discharge. If the condition developed prior to the current admission/encounter or represents a pre-existing condition, the trimester character for the trimester at the time of the admission/encounter should be assigned.

5) Unspecified trimester

Each category that includes codes for trimester has a code for "unspecified trimester." The "unspecified trimester" code should rarely be used, such as when the documentation in the record is insufficient to determine the trimester and it is not possible to obtain clarification.

6) 7th character for Fetus Identification

Where applicable, a 7th character is to be assigned for certain categories (O31, O32, O33.3 - O33.6, O35, O36, O40, O41, O60.1, O60.2, O64, and O69) to identify the fetus for which the complication code applies.

Assign 7th character "0":
- For single gestations
- When the documentation in the record is insufficient to determine the fetus affected and it is not possible to obtain clarification.
- When it is not possible to clinically determine which fetus is affected.

b. Selection of OB Principal or First-listed Diagnosis

1) Routine outpatient prenatal visits

For routine outpatient prenatal visits when no complications are present, a code from category Z34, Encounter for supervision of normal pregnancy, should be used as the first-listed diagnosis. These codes should not be used in conjunction with chapter 15 codes.

2) *Supervision of High-Risk Pregnancy*

Codes from category O09, Supervision of high-risk pregnancy, are intended for use only during the prenatal period. For complications during the labor or delivery episode as a result of a high-risk pregnancy, assign the applicable complication codes from Chapter 15. If there are no complications during the labor or delivery episode, assign code O80, Encounter for full-term uncomplicated delivery.

For routine prenatal outpatient visits for patients with high-risk pregnancies, a code from category O09, Supervision of high-risk pregnancy, should be used as the first-listed diagnosis. Secondary chapter 15 codes may be used in conjunction with these codes if appropriate.

3) Episodes when no delivery occurs

In episodes when no delivery occurs, the principal diagnosis should correspond to the principal complication of the pregnancy which necessitated the encounter. Should more than one complication exist, all of which are treated or monitored, any of the complications codes may be sequenced first.

4) When a delivery occurs

When an obstetric patient is admitted and delivers during that admission, the condition that prompted the admission should be sequenced as the principal diagnosis. If multiple conditions prompted the admission, sequence the one most related to the delivery as the principal diagnosis. A code for any complication of the delivery should be assigned as an additional diagnosis. In cases of cesarean delivery, if the patient was admitted with a condition that resulted in the performance of a cesarean procedure, that condition should be selected as the principal diagnosis. If the reason for the admission was unrelated to the condition resulting in the cesarean delivery, the condition related to the reason for the admission should be selected as the principal diagnosis.

5) Outcome of delivery

A code from category Z37, Outcome of delivery, should be included on every maternal record when a delivery has occurred. These codes are not to be used on subsequent records or on the newborn record.

c. Pre-existing conditions versus conditions due to the pregnancy

Certain categories in Chapter 15 distinguish between conditions of the mother that existed prior to pregnancy (pre-existing) and those that are a direct result of pregnancy. When assigning codes from Chapter 15, it is important to assess if a condition was pre-existing prior to pregnancy or developed during or due to the pregnancy in order to assign the correct code.

Categories that do not distinguish between pre-existing and pregnancy-related conditions may be used for either. It is acceptable to use codes specifically for the puerperium with codes complicating pregnancy and childbirth if a condition arises postpartum during the delivery encounter.

d. Pre-existing hypertension in pregnancy

Category O10, Pre-existing hypertension complicating pregnancy, childbirth and the puerperium, includes codes for hypertensive heart and hypertensive chronic kidney disease. When assigning one of the O10 codes that includes hypertensive heart disease or hypertensive chronic kidney disease, it is necessary to add a secondary code from the appropriate hypertension category to specify the type of heart failure or chronic kidney disease.

See Section I.C.9. Hypertension.

e. Fetal Conditions Affecting the Management of the Mother

1) Codes from categories O35 and O36

Codes from categories O35, Maternal care for known or suspected fetal abnormality and damage, and O36, Maternal care for other fetal problems, are assigned only when the fetal condition is actually responsible for modifying the management of the mother, i.e., by requiring diagnostic studies, additional observation, special care, or termination of pregnancy. The fact that the fetal condition exists does not justify assigning a code from this series to the mother's record.

2) In utero surgery

In cases when surgery is performed on the fetus, a diagnosis code from category O35, Maternal care for known or suspected fetal abnormality and damage, should be assigned identifying the fetal condition. Assign the appropriate procedure code for the procedure performed.

No code from Chapter 16, the perinatal codes, should be used on the mother's record to identify fetal conditions. Surgery performed in utero on a fetus is still to be coded as an obstetric encounter.

f. HIV Infection in Pregnancy, Childbirth and the Puerperium

During pregnancy, childbirth or the puerperium, a patient admitted because of an HIV-related illness should receive a principal diagnosis from subcategory O98.7-, Human immunodeficiency [HIV] disease complicating pregnancy, childbirth and the puerperium, followed by the code(s) for the HIV-related illness(es).

Patients with asymptomatic HIV infection status admitted during pregnancy, childbirth, or the puerperium should receive codes of O98.7- and Z21, Asymptomatic human immunodeficiency virus [HIV] infection status.

g. Diabetes mellitus in pregnancy

Diabetes mellitus is a significant complicating factor in pregnancy. Pregnant women who are diabetic should be assigned a code from category O24, Diabetes mellitus in pregnancy, childbirth, and the puerperium, first, followed by the appropriate diabetes code(s) (E08-E13) from Chapter 4.

h. Long term use of insulin and oral hypoglycemics

Code Z79.4, Long-term (current) use of insulin, or **code Z79.84, Long-term (current) use of oral hypoglycemic drugs,** should also be assigned if the diabetes mellitus is being treated with insulin **or oral medications. If the patient is treated with both oral medications and insulin, only the code for insulin-controlled should be assigned.**

i. Gestational (pregnancy induced) diabetes

Gestational (pregnancy induced) diabetes can occur during the second and third trimester of pregnancy in women who were not diabetic prior to pregnancy. Gestational diabetes can cause complications in the pregnancy similar to those of pre-existing diabetes mellitus. It also puts the woman at greater risk of developing diabetes after the pregnancy. Codes for gestational diabetes are in subcategory O24.4, Gestational diabetes mellitus. No other code from category O24, Diabetes mellitus in pregnancy, childbirth, and the puerperium, should be used with a code from O24.4.

The codes under subcategory O24.4 include diet controlled, insulin controlled, **and controlled by oral hypoglycemic drugs**. If a patient with gestational diabetes is treated with both diet and insulin, only the code for insulin-controlled is required. **If a patient with gestational diabetes is treated with both diet and oral hypoglycemic medications, only the code for "controlled by oral hypoglycemic drugs" is required.** Code Z79.4, Long-term (current) use of insulin **or code Z79.84, Long-term (current) use of oral hypoglycemic drugs,** should not be assigned with codes from subcategory O24.4.

An abnormal glucose tolerance in pregnancy is assigned a code from subcategory O99.81, Abnormal glucose complicating pregnancy, childbirth, and the puerperium.

j. Sepsis and septic shock complicating abortion, pregnancy, childbirth and the puerperium

When assigning a chapter 15 code for sepsis complicating abortion, pregnancy, childbirth, and the puerperium, a code for the specific type of infection should be assigned as an additional diagnosis. If severe sepsis is present, a code from subcategory R65.2, Severe sepsis, and code(s) for associated organ dysfunction(s) should also be assigned as additional diagnoses.

k. Puerperal sepsis

Code O85, Puerperal sepsis, should be assigned with a secondary code to identify the causal organism (e.g., for a bacterial infection, assign a code from category B95-B96, Bacterial infections in conditions classified elsewhere). A code from category A40, Streptococcal sepsis, or A41, Other sepsis, should not be used for puerperal sepsis. If applicable, use additional codes to identify severe sepsis (R65.2-) and any associated acute organ dysfunction.

l. Alcohol and tobacco use during pregnancy, childbirth and the puerperium

1) Alcohol use during pregnancy, childbirth and the puerperium

Codes under subcategory O99.31, Alcohol use complicating pregnancy, childbirth, and the puerperium, should be assigned for any pregnancy case when a mother uses alcohol during the pregnancy or postpartum. A secondary code from category F10, Alcohol related disorders, should also be assigned to identify manifestations of the alcohol use.

2) Tobacco use during pregnancy, childbirth and the puerperium

Codes under subcategory O99.33, Smoking (tobacco) complicating pregnancy, childbirth, and the puerperium, should be assigned for any pregnancy case when a mother uses any type of tobacco product during the pregnancy or postpartum. A secondary code from category F17, Nicotine dependence, should also be assigned to identify the type of nicotine dependence.

m. Poisoning, toxic effects, adverse effects and underdosing in a pregnant patient

A code from subcategory O9A.2, Injury, poisoning and certain other consequences of external causes complicating pregnancy, childbirth, and the puerperium, should be sequenced first, followed by the appropriate injury, poisoning, toxic effect, adverse effect or underdosing code, and then the additional code(s) that specifies the condition caused by the poisoning, toxic effect, adverse effect or underdosing.

See Section I.C.19. Adverse effects, poisoning, underdosing and toxic effects.

n. Normal Delivery, Code O80

1) Encounter for full term uncomplicated delivery

Code O80 should be assigned when a woman is admitted for a full-term normal delivery and delivers a single, healthy infant without any complications antepartum, during the delivery, or postpartum during the delivery episode. Code O80 is always a principal diagnosis. It is not to be used if any other code from chapter 15 is needed to describe a current complication of the antenatal, delivery, or perinatal period. Additional codes from other chapters may be used with code O80 if they are not related to or are in any way complicating the pregnancy.

2) Uncomplicated delivery with resolved antepartum complication

Code O80 may be used if the patient had a complication at some point during the pregnancy, but the complication is not present at the time of the admission for delivery.

3) Outcome of delivery for O80

Z37.0, Single live birth, is the only outcome of delivery code appropriate for use with O80.

o. The Peripartum and Postpartum Periods

1) Peripartum and Postpartum periods

The postpartum period begins immediately after delivery and continues for six weeks following delivery. The peripartum period is defined as the last month of pregnancy to five months postpartum.

2) Peripartum and postpartum complication

A postpartum complication is any complication occurring within the six-week period.

3) Pregnancy-related complications after 6 week period

Chapter 15 codes may also be used to describe pregnancy-related complications after the peripartum or postpartum period if the provider documents that a condition is pregnancy related.

4) Admission for routine postpartum care following delivery outside hospital

When the mother delivers outside the hospital prior to admission and is admitted for routine postpartum care and no complications are noted, code Z39.0, Encounter for care and examination of mother immediately after delivery, should be assigned as the principal diagnosis.

5) Pregnancy associated cardiomyopathy

Pregnancy associated cardiomyopathy, code O90.3, is unique in that it may be diagnosed in the third trimester of pregnancy but may continue to progress months after delivery. For this reason, it is referred to as peripartum cardiomyopathy. Code O90.3 is only for use when the cardiomyopathy develops as a result of pregnancy in a woman who did not have pre-existing heart disease.

p. Code O94, Sequelae of complication of pregnancy, childbirth, and the puerperium

1) Code O94

Code O94, Sequelae of complication of pregnancy, childbirth, and the puerperium, is for use in those cases when an initial complication of a pregnancy develops a sequelae requiring care or treatment at a future date.

2) After the initial postpartum period

This code may be used at any time after the initial postpartum period.

3) Sequencing of Code O94

This code, like all sequela codes, is to be sequenced following the code describing the sequelae of the complication.

q. *Termination of Pregnancy and Spontaneous abortions*

1) Abortion with Liveborn Fetus

When an attempted termination of pregnancy results in a liveborn fetus, assign code Z33.2, Encounter for elective termination of pregnancy and a code from category Z37, Outcome of Delivery.

2) Retained Products of Conception following an abortion

Subsequent encounters for retained products of conception following a spontaneous abortion or elective termination of pregnancy are assigned the appropriate code from category O03, Spontaneous abortion, or codes O07.4, Failed attempted termination of pregnancy without complication and Z33.2, Encounter for elective termination of pregnancy. This advice is appropriate even when the patient was discharged previously with a discharge diagnosis of complete abortion.

3) Complications leading to abortion

Codes from Chapter 15 may be used as additional codes to identify any documented complications of the pregnancy in conjunction with codes in categories in O07 and O08.

r. Abuse in a pregnant patient

For suspected or confirmed cases of abuse of a pregnant patient, a code(s) from subcategories O9A.3, Physical abuse complicating pregnancy, childbirth, and the puerperium, O9A.4, Sexual abuse complicating pregnancy, childbirth, and the puerperium, and O9A.5, Psychological abuse complicating pregnancy, childbirth, and the puerperium, should be sequenced first, followed by the appropriate codes (if applicable) to identify any associated current injury due to physical abuse, sexual abuse, and the perpetrator of abuse.

See Section I.C.19. Adult and child abuse, neglect and other maltreatment.

16. Chapter 16: Certain Conditions Originating in the Perinatal Period (P00-P96)

For coding and reporting purposes the perinatal period is defined as before birth through the 28th day following birth. The following guidelines are provided for reporting purposes.

a. General Perinatal Rules

1) Use of Chapter 16 Codes

Codes in this chapter are <u>never</u> for use on the maternal record. Codes from Chapter 15, the obstetric chapter, are never permitted on the newborn record. Chapter 16 codes may be used throughout the life of the patient if the condition is still present.

2) Principal Diagnosis for Birth Record

When coding the birth episode in a newborn record, assign a code from category Z38, Liveborn infants according to place of birth and type of delivery, as the principal diagnosis. A code from category Z38 is assigned only once, to a newborn at the time of birth. If a newborn is transferred to another institution, a code from category Z38 should not be used at the receiving hospital.

A code from category Z38 is used only on the newborn record, not on the mother's record.

3) Use of Codes from other Chapters with Codes from Chapter 16

Codes from other chapters may be used with codes from chapter 16 if the codes from the other chapters provide more specific detail. Codes for signs and symptoms may be assigned when a definitive diagnosis has not been established. If the reason for the encounter is a perinatal condition, the code from chapter 16 should be sequenced first.

4) Use of Chapter 16 Codes after the Perinatal Period

Should a condition originate in the perinatal period, and continue throughout the life of the patient, the perinatal code should continue to be used regardless of the patient's age.

5) Birth process or community acquired conditions

If a newborn has a condition that may be either due to the birth process or community acquired and the documentation does not indicate which it is, the default is due to the birth process and the code from Chapter 16 should be used. If the condition is community-acquired, a code from Chapter 16 should not be assigned.

6) **Code all clinically significant conditions**

All clinically significant conditions noted on routine newborn examination should be coded. A condition is clinically significant if it requires:

- clinical evaluation; or
- therapeutic treatment; or
- diagnostic procedures; or
- extended length of hospital stay; or
- increased nursing care and/or monitoring; or
- has implications for future health care needs

Note: The perinatal guidelines listed above are the same as the general coding guidelines for "additional diagnoses", except for the final point regarding implications for future health care needs. Codes should be assigned for conditions that have been specified by the provider as having implications for future health care needs.

b. Observation and Evaluation of Newborns for Suspected Conditions not Found

1) **Assign a code from category Z05, Observation and evaluation of newborns and infants for suspected conditions ruled out, to identify those instances when a healthy newborn is evaluated for a suspected condition that is determined after study not to be present. Do not use a code from category Z05 when the patient has identified signs or symptoms of a suspected problem; in such cases code the sign or symptom.**

2) **A code from category Z05 may also be assigned as a principal or first-listed code for readmissions or encounters when the code from category Z38 code no longer applies. Codes from category Z05 are for use only for healthy newborns and infants for which no condition after study is found to be present.**

3) **Z05 on a birth record**

A code from category Z05 is to be used as a secondary code after the code from category Z38, Liveborn infants according to place of birth and type of delivery.

c. Coding Additional Perinatal Diagnoses

1) Assigning codes for conditions that require treatment

Assign codes for conditions that require treatment or further investigation, prolong the length of stay, or require resource utilization.

2) Codes for conditions specified as having implications for future health care needs

Assign codes for conditions that have been specified by the provider as having implications for future health care needs.

Note: This guideline should not be used for adult patients.

d. Prematurity and Fetal Growth Retardation

Providers utilize different criteria in determining prematurity. A code for prematurity should not be assigned unless it is documented. Assignment of codes in categories P05, Disorders of newborn related to slow fetal growth and fetal malnutrition, and P07, Disorders of newborn related to short gestation and low birth weight, not elsewhere classified, should be based on the recorded birth weight and estimated gestational age. Codes from category P05 should not be assigned with codes from category P07.

When both birth weight and gestational age are available, two codes from category P07 should be assigned, with the code for birth weight sequenced before the code for gestational age.

e. Low birth weight and immaturity status

Codes from category P07, Disorders of newborn related to short gestation and low birth weight, not elsewhere classified, are for use for a child or adult who was premature or had a low birth weight as a newborn and this is affecting the patient's current health status.

See Section I.C.21. Factors influencing health status and contact with health services, Status.

f. Bacterial Sepsis of Newborn

Category P36, Bacterial sepsis of newborn, includes congenital sepsis. If a perinate is documented as having sepsis without documentation of congenital or community acquired, the default is congenital and a code from category P36 should be assigned. If the P36 code includes the causal organism, an additional code from category B95, Streptococcus, Staphylococcus, and Enterococcus as the cause of diseases classified elsewhere, or B96, Other bacterial agents as the cause of diseases classified elsewhere, should not be assigned. If the P36 code does not include the causal organism, assign an additional code from category B96. If applicable, use additional codes to identify severe sepsis (R65.2-) and any associated acute organ dysfunction.

g. Stillbirth

Code P95, Stillbirth, is only for use in institutions that maintain separate records for stillbirths. No other code should be used with P95. Code P95 should not be used on the mother's record.

17. Chapter 17: Congenital malformations, deformations, and chromosomal abnormalities (Q00-Q99)

Assign an appropriate code(s) from categories Q00-Q99, Congenital malformations, deformations, and chromosomal abnormalities when a malformation/deformation or chromosomal abnormality is documented. A malformation/deformation/or chromosomal abnormality may be the principal/first-listed diagnosis on a record or a secondary diagnosis.

When a malformation/deformation or chromosomal abnormality does not have a unique code assignment, assign additional code(s) for any manifestations that may be present.

When the code assignment specifically identifies the malformation/deformation or chromosomal abnormality, manifestations that are an inherent component of the anomaly should not be coded separately. Additional codes should be assigned for manifestations that are not an inherent component.

Codes from Chapter 17 may be used throughout the life of the patient. If a congenital malformation or deformity has been corrected, a personal history code should be used to identify the history of the malformation or deformity. Although present at birth, malformation/deformation/or chromosomal abnormality may not be identified until later in life. Whenever the condition is diagnosed by the physician, it is appropriate to assign a code from codes Q00-Q99.For the birth admission, the appropriate code from category Z38, Liveborn infants, according to place of birth and type of delivery, should be sequenced as the principal diagnosis, followed by any congenital anomaly codes, Q00-Q99.

18. Chapter 18: Symptoms, signs, and abnormal clinical and laboratory findings, not elsewhere classified (R00-R99)

Chapter 18 includes symptoms, signs, abnormal results of clinical or other investigative procedures, and ill-defined conditions regarding which no diagnosis classifiable elsewhere is recorded. Signs and symptoms that point to a specific diagnosis have been assigned to a category in other chapters of the classification.

a. Use of symptom codes

Codes that describe symptoms and signs are acceptable for reporting purposes when a related definitive diagnosis has not been established (confirmed) by the provider.

b. Use of a symptom code with a definitive diagnosis code

Codes for signs and symptoms may be reported in addition to a related definitive diagnosis when the sign or symptom is not routinely associated with that diagnosis, such as the various signs and symptoms associated with complex syndromes. The definitive diagnosis code should be sequenced before the symptom code.

Signs or symptoms that are associated routinely with a disease process should not be assigned as additional codes, unless otherwise instructed by the classification.

c. Combination codes that include symptoms

ICD-10-CM contains a number of combination codes that identify both the definitive diagnosis and common symptoms of that diagnosis. When using one of these combination codes, an additional code should not be assigned for the symptom.

d. Repeated falls

Code R29.6, Repeated falls, is for use for encounters when a patient has recently fallen and the reason for the fall is being investigated.

Code Z91.81, History of falling, is for use when a patient has fallen in the past and is at risk for future falls. When appropriate, both codes R29.6 and Z91.81 may be assigned together.

e. Coma scale

The coma scale codes (R40.2-) can be used in conjunction with traumatic brain injury codes, acute cerebrovascular disease or sequelae of cerebrovascular disease codes. These codes are primarily for use by trauma registries, but they may be used in any setting where this information is collected. **The coma scale may also be used to assess the status of the central nervous system for other non-trauma conditions, such as monitoring patients in the intensive care unit**

regardless of medical condition. The coma scale codes should be sequenced after the diagnosis code(s).

These codes, one from each subcategory, are needed to complete the scale. The 7th character indicates when the scale was recorded. The 7th character should match for all three codes.

At a minimum, report the initial score documented on presentation at your facility. This may be a score from the emergency medicine technician (EMT) or in the emergency department. If desired, a facility may choose to capture multiple coma scale scores.

Assign code R40.24, Glasgow coma scale, total score, when only the total score is documented in the medical record and not the individual score(s).

f. Functional quadriplegia

Functional quadriplegia (code R53.2) is the lack of ability to use one's limbs or to ambulate due to extreme debility. It is not associated with neurologic deficit or injury, and code R53.2 should not be used for cases of neurologic quadriplegia. It should only be assigned if functional quadriplegia is specifically documented in the medical record.

g. SIRS due to Non-Infectious Process

The systemic inflammatory response syndrome (SIRS) can develop as a result of certain non-infectious disease processes, such as trauma, malignant neoplasm, or pancreatitis. When SIRS is documented with a noninfectious condition, and no subsequent infection is documented, the code for the underlying condition, such as an injury, should be assigned, followed by code R65.10, Systemic inflammatory response syndrome (SIRS) of non-infectious origin without acute organ dysfunction, or code R65.11, Systemic inflammatory response syndrome (SIRS) of non-infectious origin with acute organ dysfunction. If an associated acute organ dysfunction is documented, the appropriate code(s) for the specific type of organ dysfunction(s) should be assigned in addition to code R65.11. If acute organ dysfunction is documented, but it cannot be determined if the acute organ dysfunction is associated with SIRS or due to another condition (e.g., directly due to the trauma), the provider should be queried.

h. Death NOS

Code R99, Ill-defined and unknown cause of mortality, is only for use in the very limited circumstance when a patient who has already died is brought into an emergency department or other healthcare facility and is pronounced dead upon arrival. It does not represent the discharge disposition of death.

i. NIHSS Stroke Scale

The NIH stroke scale (NIHSS) codes (R29.7- -) can be used in conjunction with acute stroke codes (I63) to identify the patient's neurological status and the severity of the stroke. The stroke scale codes should be sequenced after the acute stroke diagnosis code(s).

At a minimum, report the initial score documented. If desired, a facility may choose to capture multiple stroke scale scores.

See Section I.B.14. for information concerning the medical record documentation that may be used for assignment of the NIHSS codes.

19. Chapter 19: Injury, poisoning, and certain other consequences of external causes (S00-T88)

a. Application of 7th Characters in Chapter 19

Most categories in chapter 19 have a 7th character requirement for each applicable code. Most categories in this chapter have three 7th character values (with the exception of fractures): A, initial encounter, D, subsequent encounter and S, sequela. Categories for traumatic fractures have additional 7th character values. While the patient may be seen by a new or different provider over the course of treatment for an injury, assignment of the 7th character is based on whether the patient is undergoing active treatment and not whether the provider is seeing the patient for the first time.

For complication codes, active treatment refers to treatment for the condition described by the code, even though it may be related to an earlier precipitating problem. For example, code T84.50XA, Infection and inflammatory reaction due to unspecified internal joint prosthesis, initial encounter, is used when active treatment is provided for the infection, even though the condition relates to the prosthetic device, implant or graft that was placed at a previous encounter.

7th character "A", initial encounter is used **for each encounter where** the patient is receiving active treatment for the condition.

7th character "D" subsequent encounter is used for encounters after the patient has **completed** active treatment of the condition and is receiving routine care for the condition during the healing or recovery phase.

The aftercare Z codes should not be used for aftercare for conditions such as injuries or poisonings, where 7th characters are provided to identify subsequent care. For example, for aftercare of an injury, assign the acute injury code with the 7th character "D" (subsequent encounter).

7th character "S", sequela, is for use for complications or conditions that arise as a direct result of a condition, such as scar formation after a burn. The scars are sequelae of the burn. When using 7th character "S", it is necessary to use both the injury code that precipitated the sequela and the code for the sequela itself. The "S" is added only to the injury code, not the sequela code. The 7th character "S" identifies the injury responsible for the sequela. The specific type of sequela (e.g. scar) is sequenced first, followed by the injury code.

See Section I.B.10 Sequelae, (Late Effects)

b. Coding of Injuries

When coding injuries, assign separate codes for each injury unless a combination code is provided, in which case the combination code is assigned. Code T07, Unspecified multiple injuries should not be assigned in the inpatient setting unless information for a more specific code is not available. Traumatic injury codes (S00-T14.9) are not to be used for normal, healing surgical wounds or to identify complications of surgical wounds.

The code for the most serious injury, as determined by the provider and the focus of treatment, is sequenced first.

1) Superficial injuries

Superficial injuries such as abrasions or contusions are not coded when associated with more severe injuries of the same site.

2) Primary injury with damage to nerves/blood vessels

When a primary injury results in minor damage to peripheral nerves or blood vessels, the primary injury is sequenced first with additional code(s) for injuries to nerves and spinal cord (such as category S04), and/or injury to blood vessels (such as category S15). When the primary injury is to the blood vessels or nerves, that injury should be sequenced first.

c. Coding of Traumatic Fractures

The principles of multiple coding of injuries should be followed in coding fractures. Fractures of specified sites are coded individually by site in accordance with both the provisions within categories S02, S12, S22, S32, S42, S49, S52, S59, S62, S72, S79, S82, S89, S92 and the level of detail furnished by medical record content.

A fracture not indicated as open or closed should be coded to closed. A fracture not indicated whether displaced or not displaced should be coded to displaced.

More specific guidelines are as follows:

1) **Initial vs. Subsequent Encounter for Fractures**

Traumatic fractures are coded using the appropriate 7th character for initial encounter (A, B, C) **for each encounter where** the patient is receiving active treatment for the fracture. The appropriate 7th character for initial encounter should also be assigned for a patient who delayed seeking treatment for the fracture or nonunion.

Fractures are coded using the appropriate 7th character for subsequent care for encounters after the patient has completed active treatment of the fracture and is receiving routine care for the fracture during the healing or recovery phase.

Care for complications of surgical treatment for fracture repairs during the healing or recovery phase should be coded with the appropriate complication codes.

Care of complications of fractures, such as malunion and nonunion, should be reported with the appropriate 7th character for subsequent care with nonunion (K, M, N,) or subsequent care with malunion (P, Q, R).

Malunion/nonunion: The appropriate 7th character for initial encounter should also be assigned for a patient who delayed seeking treatment for the fracture or nonunion.

The open fracture designations in the assignment of the 7th character for fractures of the forearm, femur and lower leg, including ankle are based on the Gustilo open fracture classification. When the Gustilo classification type is not specified for an open fracture, the 7th character for open fracture type I or II should be assigned (B, E, H, M, Q).

A code from category M80, not a traumatic fracture code, should be used for any patient with known osteoporosis who suffers a fracture, even if the patient had a minor fall or trauma, if that fall or trauma would not usually break a normal, healthy bone.
See Section I.C.13. Osteoporosis.

The aftercare Z codes should not be used for aftercare for traumatic fractures. For aftercare of a traumatic fracture, assign the acute fracture code with the appropriate 7th character.

2) Multiple fractures sequencing

Multiple fractures are sequenced in accordance with the severity of the fracture.

d. Coding of Burns and Corrosions

The ICD-10-CM makes a distinction between burns and corrosions. The burn codes are for thermal burns, except sunburns, that come from a heat source, such as a fire or hot appliance. The burn codes are also for burns resulting from electricity and radiation. Corrosions are burns due to chemicals. The guidelines are the same for burns and corrosions.

Current burns (T20-T25) are classified by depth, extent and by agent (X code). Burns are classified by depth as first degree (erythema), second degree (blistering), and third degree (full-thickness involvement). Burns of the eye and internal organs (T26-T28) are classified by site, but not by degree.

1) Sequencing of burn and related condition codes

Sequence first the code that reflects the highest degree of burn when more than one burn is present.

a. When the reason for the admission or encounter is for treatment of external multiple burns, sequence first the code that reflects the burn of the highest degree.

b. When a patient has both internal and external burns, the circumstances of admission govern the selection of the principal diagnosis or first-listed diagnosis.

c. When a patient is admitted for burn injuries and other related conditions such as smoke inhalation and/or respiratory failure, the circumstances of admission govern the selection of the principal or first-listed diagnosis.

2) Burns of the same local site

Classify burns of the same local site (three-character category level, T20-T28) but of different degrees to the subcategory identifying the highest degree recorded in the diagnosis.

3) Non-healing burns

Non-healing burns are coded as acute burns.

Necrosis of burned skin should be coded as a non-healed burn.

4) Infected Burn

For any documented infected burn site, use an additional code for the infection.

5) Assign separate codes for each burn site

When coding burns, assign separate codes for each burn site. Category T30, Burn and corrosion, body region unspecified is extremely vague and should rarely be used.

6) Burns and Corrosions Classified According to Extent of Body Surface Involved

Assign codes from category T31, Burns classified according to extent of body surface involved, or T32, Corrosions classified according to extent of body surface involved, when the site of the burn is not specified or when there is a need for additional data. It is advisable to use category T31 as additional coding when needed to provide data for evaluating burn mortality, such as that needed by burn units. It is also advisable to use category T31 as an additional code for reporting purposes when there is mention of a third-degree burn involving 20 percent or more of the body surface.

Categories T31 and T32 are based on the classic "rule of nines" in estimating body surface involved: head and neck are assigned nine percent, each arm nine percent, each leg 18 percent, the anterior trunk 18 percent, posterior trunk 18 percent, and genitalia one percent. Providers may change these percentage assignments where necessary to accommodate infants and children who have proportionately larger heads than adults, and patients who have large buttocks, thighs, or abdomen that involve burns.

7) Encounters for treatment of sequela of burns

Encounters for the treatment of the late effects of burns or corrosions (i.e., scars or joint contractures) should be coded with a burn or corrosion code with the 7th character "S" for sequela.

8) Sequelae with a late effect code and current burn

When appropriate, both a code for a current burn or corrosion with 7th character "A" or "D" and a burn or corrosion code with 7th character "S" may be assigned on the same record (when both a current burn and sequelae of an old burn exist). Burns and corrosions do not heal at the same rate and a current healing wound may still exist with sequela of a healed burn or corrosion.

See Section I.B.10 Sequela (Late Effects)

9) Use of an external cause code with burns and corrosions

An external cause code should be used with burns and corrosions to identify the source and intent of the burn, as well as the place where it occurred.

e. Adverse Effects, Poisoning, Underdosing and Toxic Effects

Codes in categories T36-T65 are combination codes that include the substance that was taken as well as the intent. No additional external cause code is required for poisonings, toxic effects, adverse effects and underdosing codes.

1) Do not code directly from the Table of Drugs

Do not code directly from the Table of Drugs and Chemicals. Always refer back to the Tabular List.

2) Use as many codes as necessary to describe

Use as many codes as necessary to describe completely all drugs, medicinal or biological substances.

3) If the same code would describe the causative agent

If the same code would describe the causative agent for more than one adverse reaction, poisoning, toxic effect or underdosing, assign the code only once.

4) If two or more drugs, medicinal or biological substances

If two or more drugs, medicinal or biological substances are reported, code each individually unless a combination code is listed in the Table of Drugs and Chemicals.

5) The occurrence of drug toxicity is classified in ICD-10-CM as follows:

(a) Adverse Effect

When coding an adverse effect of a drug that has been correctly prescribed and properly administered, assign the appropriate code for the nature of the adverse effect followed by the appropriate code for the adverse effect of the drug (T36-T50). The code for the drug should

have a 5th or 6th character "5" (for example T36.0X5-)
Examples of the nature of an adverse effect are tachycardia, delirium, gastrointestinal hemorrhaging, vomiting, hypokalemia, hepatitis, renal failure, or respiratory failure.

(b) **Poisoning**

When coding a poisoning or reaction to the improper use of a medication (e.g., overdose, wrong substance given or taken in error, wrong route of administration), first assign the appropriate code from categories T36-T50. The poisoning codes have an associated intent as their 5th or 6th character (accidental, intentional self-harm, assault and undetermined. **If the intent of the poisoning is unknown or unspecified, code the intent as accidental intent. The undetermined intent is only for use if the documentation in the record specifies that the intent cannot be determined.** Use additional code(s) for all manifestations of poisonings.

If there is also a diagnosis of abuse or dependence of the substance, the abuse or dependence is assigned as an additional code.

Examples of poisoning include:

(i) Error was made in drug prescription

Errors made in drug prescription or in the administration of the drug by provider, nurse, patient, or other person.

(ii) Overdose of a drug intentionally taken

If an overdose of a drug was intentionally taken or administered and resulted in drug toxicity, it would be coded as a poisoning.

(iii) Nonprescribed drug taken with correctly prescribed and properly administered drug

If a nonprescribed drug or medicinal agent was taken in combination with a correctly prescribed and properly administered drug, any drug toxicity or other reaction resulting from the interaction of the two drugs would be classified as a poisoning.

(iv) Interaction of drug(s) and alcohol

When a reaction results from the interaction of a drug(s) and alcohol, this would be classified as poisoning.

See Section I.C.4. if poisoning is the result of insulin pump malfunctions.

(c) Underdosing

Underdosing refers to taking less of a medication than is prescribed by a provider or a manufacturer's instruction. For underdosing, assign the code from categories T36-T50 (fifth or sixth character "6").

Codes for underdosing should never be assigned as principal or first-listed codes. If a patient has a relapse or exacerbation of the medical condition for which the drug is prescribed because of the reduction in dose, then the medical condition itself should be coded.

Noncompliance (Z91.12-, Z91.13-) or complication of care (Y63.6-Y63.9) codes are to be used with an underdosing code to indicate intent, if known.

(d) Toxic Effects

When a harmful substance is ingested or comes in contact with a person, this is classified as a toxic effect. The toxic effect codes are in categories T51-T65.

Toxic effect codes have an associated intent: accidental, intentional self-harm, assault and undetermined.

f. Adult and child abuse, neglect and other maltreatment

Sequence first the appropriate code from categories T74.- (Adult and child abuse, neglect and other maltreatment, confirmed) or T76.- (Adult and child abuse, neglect and other maltreatment, suspected) for abuse, neglect and other maltreatment, followed by any accompanying mental health or injury code(s).

If the documentation in the medical record states abuse or neglect it is coded as confirmed (T74.-). It is coded as suspected if it is documented as suspected (T76.-).

For cases of confirmed abuse or neglect an external cause code from the assault section (X92-**Y09)** should be added to identify the cause of any physical injuries. A perpetrator code (Y07) should be added when the perpetrator of the abuse is known. For suspected cases of abuse or neglect, do not report external cause or perpetrator code.

If a suspected case of abuse, neglect or mistreatment is ruled out during an encounter code Z04.71, Encounter for examination and observation following alleged physical adult abuse, ruled out, or code Z04.72, Encounter for examination and observation following alleged child physical abuse, ruled out, should be used, not a code from T76.

If a suspected case of alleged rape or sexual abuse is ruled out during an encounter code Z04.41, Encounter for examination and observation following alleged **adult rape** or code Z04.42, Encounter for examination and observation following alleged **child** rape, should be used, not a code from T76.
See Section I.C.15. Abuse in a pregnant patient.

g. Complications of care

1) General guidelines for complications of care

(a) Documentation of complications of care
See Section I.B.16. for information on documentation of complications of care.

2) Pain due to medical devices

Pain associated with devices, implants or grafts left in a surgical site (for example painful hip prosthesis) is assigned to the appropriate code(s) found in Chapter 19, Injury, poisoning, and certain other consequences of external causes. Specific codes for pain due to medical devices are found in the T code section of the ICD-10-CM. Use additional code(s) from category G89 to identify acute or chronic pain due to presence of the device, implant or graft (G89.18 or G89.28).

3) Transplant complications

(a) Transplant complications other than kidney
Codes under category T86, Complications of transplanted organs and tissues, are for use for both complications and rejection of transplanted organs. A transplant complication code is only assigned if the complication affects the function of the transplanted organ. Two codes are required to fully describe a transplant complication: the appropriate code from category T86 and a secondary code that identifies the complication.

Pre-existing conditions or conditions that develop after the transplant are not coded as complications unless they affect the function of the transplanted organs.

See I.C.21. for transplant organ removal status
See I.C.2. for malignant neoplasm associated with transplanted organ.

(b)   **Kidney transplant complications**

Patients who have undergone kidney transplant may still have some form of chronic kidney disease (CKD) because the kidney transplant may not fully restore kidney function. Code T86.1- should be assigned for documented complications of a kidney transplant, such as transplant failure or rejection or other transplant complication. Code T86.1- should not be assigned for post kidney transplant patients who have chronic kidney (CKD) unless a transplant complication such as transplant failure or rejection is documented. If the documentation is unclear as to whether the patient has a complication of the transplant, query the provider.

Conditions that affect the function of the transplanted kidney, other than CKD, should be assigned a code from subcategory T86.1, Complications of transplanted organ, Kidney, and a secondary code that identifies the complication.

For patients with CKD following a kidney transplant, but who do not have a complication such as failure or rejection, *see section I.C.14. Chronic kidney disease and kidney transplant status*.

4)   **Complication codes that include the external cause**

As with certain other T codes, some of the complications of care codes have the external cause included in the code. The code includes the nature of the complication as well as the type of procedure that caused the complication. No external cause code indicating the type of procedure is necessary for these codes.

5)   **Complications of care codes within the body system chapters**

Intraoperative and postprocedural complication codes are found within the body system chapters with codes specific to the organs and structures of that body system. These codes should be sequenced first, followed by a code(s) for the specific complication, if applicable.

20. Chapter 20: External Causes of Morbidity (V00-Y99)

The external causes of morbidity codes should never be sequenced as the first-listed or principal diagnosis.

External cause codes are intended to provide data for injury research and evaluation of injury prevention strategies. These codes capture how the injury or health condition happened (cause), the intent (unintentional or accidental; or intentional, such as suicide or assault), the place where the event occurred the activity of the patient at the time of the event, and the person's status (e.g., civilian, military).

There is no national requirement for mandatory ICD-10-CM external cause code reporting. Unless a provider is subject to a state-based external cause code reporting mandate or these codes are required by a particular payer, reporting of ICD-10-CM codes in Chapter 20, External Causes of Morbidity, is not required. In the absence of a mandatory reporting requirement, providers are encouraged to voluntarily report external cause codes, as they provide valuable data for injury research and evaluation of injury prevention strategies.

a. General External Cause Coding Guidelines

1) Used with any code in the range of A00.0-T88.9, Z00-Z99

An external cause code may be used with any code in the range of A00.0-T88.9, Z00-Z99, classification that is a health condition due to an external cause. Though they are most applicable to injuries, they are also valid for use with such things as infections or diseases due to an external source, and other health conditions, such as a heart attack that occurs during strenuous physical activity.

2) External cause code used for length of treatment

Assign the external cause code, with the appropriate 7th character (initial encounter, subsequent encounter or sequela) for each encounter for which the injury or condition is being treated.

Most categories in chapter 20 have a 7th character requirement for each applicable code. Most categories in this chapter have three 7th character values: A, initial encounter, D, subsequent encounter and S, sequela. While the patient may be seen by a new or different provider over the course of treatment for an injury or condition, assignment of the 7th character for external cause should match the 7th character of the code assigned for the associated injury or condition for the encounter.

3) Use the full range of external cause codes

Use the full range of external cause codes to completely describe the cause, the intent, the place of occurrence, and if applicable, the activity of the patient at the time of the event, and the patient's status, for all injuries, and other health conditions due to an external cause.

4) Assign as many external cause codes as necessary

Assign as many external cause codes as necessary to fully explain each cause. If only one external code can be recorded, assign the code most related to the principal diagnosis.

5) The selection of the appropriate external cause code

The selection of the appropriate external cause code is guided by the Alphabetic Index of External Causes and by Inclusion and Exclusion notes in the Tabular List.

6) External cause code can never be a principal diagnosis

An external cause code can never be a principal (first-listed) diagnosis.

7) Combination external cause codes

Certain of the external cause codes are combination codes that identify sequential events that result in an injury, such as a fall which results in striking against an object. The injury may be due to either event or both. The combination external cause code used should correspond to the sequence of events regardless of which caused the most serious injury.

8) No external cause code needed in certain circumstances

No external cause code from Chapter 20 is needed if the external cause and intent are included in a code from another chapter (e.g. T36.0X1- Poisoning by penicillins, accidental (unintentional)).

b. Place of Occurrence Guideline

Codes from category Y92, Place of occurrence of the external cause, are secondary codes for use after other external cause codes to identify the location of the patient at the time of injury or other condition.

Generally, a place of occurrence code is assigned only once, at the initial encounter for treatment. However, in the rare instance that a new injury occurs during hospitalization, an additional place of occurrence code may be assigned. No 7th characters are used for Y92.

Do not use place of occurrence code Y92.9 if the place is not stated or is not applicable.

c. Activity Code

Assign a code from category Y93, Activity code, to describe the activity of the patient at the time the injury or other health condition occurred.

An activity code is used only once, at the initial encounter for treatment. Only one code from Y93 should be recorded on a medical record.

The activity codes are not applicable to poisonings, adverse effects, misadventures or sequela.

Do not assign Y93.9, Unspecified activity, if the activity is not stated.

A code from category Y93 is appropriate for use with external cause and intent codes if identifying the activity provides additional information about the event.

d. Place of Occurrence, Activity, and Status Codes Used with other External Cause Code

When applicable, place of occurrence, activity, and external cause status codes are sequenced after the main external cause code(s). Regardless of the number of external cause codes assigned, generally there should be only one place of occurrence code, one activity code, and one external cause status code assigned to an encounter. However, in the rare instance that a new injury occurs during hospitalization, an additional place of occurrence code may be assigned.

e. If the Reporting Format Limits the Number of External Cause Codes

If the reporting format limits the number of external cause codes that can be used in reporting clinical data, report the code for the cause/intent most related to the principal diagnosis. If the format permits capture of additional external cause codes, the cause/intent, including medical misadventures, of the additional events should be reported rather than the codes for place, activity, or external status.

f. Multiple External Cause Coding Guidelines

More than one external cause code is required to fully describe the external cause of an illness or injury. The assignment of external cause codes should be sequenced in the following priority:

If two or more events cause separate injuries, an external cause code should be assigned for each cause. The first-listed external cause code will be selected in the following order:

External codes for child and adult abuse take priority over all other external cause codes.

See Section I.C.19., Child and Adult abuse guidelines.

External cause codes for terrorism events take priority over all other external cause codes except child and adult abuse.

External cause codes for cataclysmic events take priority over all other external cause codes except child and adult abuse and terrorism.

External cause codes for transport accidents take priority over all other external cause codes except cataclysmic events, child and adult abuse and terrorism.

Activity and external cause status codes are assigned following all causal (intent) external cause codes.

The first-listed external cause code should correspond to the cause of the most serious diagnosis due to an assault, accident, or self-harm, following the order of hierarchy listed above.

g. Child and Adult Abuse Guideline

Adult and child abuse, neglect and maltreatment are classified as assault. Any of the assault codes may be used to indicate the external cause of any injury resulting from the confirmed abuse.

For confirmed cases of abuse, neglect and maltreatment, when the perpetrator is known, a code from Y07, Perpetrator of maltreatment and neglect, should accompany any other assault codes.

See Section I.C.19. Adult and child abuse, neglect and other maltreatment

h. Unknown or Undetermined Intent Guideline

If the intent (accident, self-harm, assault) of the cause of an injury or other condition is unknown or unspecified, code the intent as accidental intent. All transport accident categories assume accidental intent.

1) Use of undetermined intent

External cause codes for events of undetermined intent are only for use if the documentation in the record specifies that the intent cannot be determined.

i. Sequelae (Late Effects) of External Cause Guidelines

1) Sequelae external cause codes

Sequela are reported using the external cause code with the 7th character "S" for sequela. These codes should be used with any report of a late effect or sequela resulting from a previous injury.

See Section I.B.10 Sequela (Late Effects)

2) Sequela external cause code with a related current injury

A sequela external cause code should never be used with a related current nature of injury code.

3) Use of sequela external cause codes for subsequent visits

Use a late effect external cause code for subsequent visits when a late effect of the initial injury is being treated. Do not use a late effect external cause code for subsequent visits for follow-up care (e.g., to assess healing, to receive rehabilitative therapy) of the injury when no late effect of the injury has been documented.

j. Terrorism Guidelines

1) Cause of injury identified by the Federal Government (FBI) as terrorism

When the cause of an injury is identified by the Federal Government (FBI) as terrorism, the first-listed external cause code should be a code from category Y38, Terrorism. The definition of terrorism employed by the FBI is found at the inclusion note at the beginning of category Y38. Use additional code for place of occurrence (Y92.-). More than one Y38 code may be assigned if the injury is the result of more than one mechanism of terrorism.

2) **Cause of an injury is suspected to be the result of terrorism**

When the cause of an injury is suspected to be the result of terrorism a code from category Y38 should not be assigned. Suspected cases should be classified as assault.

3) **Code Y38.9, Terrorism, secondary effects**

Assign code Y38.9, Terrorism, secondary effects, for conditions occurring subsequent to the terrorist event. This code should not be assigned for conditions that are due to the initial terrorist act.

It is acceptable to assign code Y38.9 with another code from Y38 if there is an injury due to the initial terrorist event and an injury that is a subsequent result of the terrorist event.

k. External cause status

A code from category Y99, External cause status, should be assigned whenever any other external cause code is assigned for an encounter, including an Activity code, except for the events noted below. Assign a code from category Y99, External cause status, to indicate the work status of the person at the time the event occurred. The status code indicates whether the event occurred during military activity, whether a non-military person was at work, whether an individual including a student or volunteer was involved in a non-work activity at the time of the causal event.

A code from Y99, External cause status, should be assigned, when applicable, with other external cause codes, such as transport accidents and falls. The external cause status codes are not applicable to poisonings, adverse effects, misadventures or late effects.
Do not assign a code from category Y99 if no other external cause codes (cause, activity) are applicable for the encounter.
An external cause status code is used only once, at the initial encounter for treatment. Only one code from Y99 should be recorded on a medical record.

Do not assign code Y99.9, Unspecified external cause status, if the status is not stated.

21. Chapter 21: Factors influencing health status and contact with health services (Z00-Z99)

Note: The chapter specific guidelines provide additional information about the use of Z codes for specified encounters.

a. Use of Z codes in any healthcare setting

Z codes are for use in any healthcare setting. Z codes may be used as either a first-listed (principal diagnosis code in the inpatient setting) or secondary code, depending on the circumstances of the encounter. Certain Z codes may only be used as first-listed or principal diagnosis.

b. Z Codes indicate a reason for an encounter

Z codes are not procedure codes. A corresponding procedure code must accompany a Z code to describe any procedure performed.

c. Categories of Z Codes

1) Contact/Exposure

Category Z20 indicates contact with, and suspected exposure to, communicable diseases. These codes are for patients who do not show any sign or symptom of a disease but are suspected to have been exposed to it by close personal contact with an infected individual or are in an area where a disease is epidemic.

Category Z77, Other contact with and (suspected) exposures hazardous to health, indicates contact with and suspected exposures hazardous to health.

Contact/exposure codes may be used as a first-listed code to explain an encounter for testing, or, more commonly, as a secondary code to identify a potential risk.

2) Inoculations and vaccinations

Code Z23 is for encounters for inoculations and vaccinations. It indicates that a patient is being seen to receive a prophylactic inoculation against a disease. Procedure codes are required to identify the actual administration of the injection and the type(s) of immunizations given. Code Z23 may be used as a secondary code if the inoculation is given as a routine part of preventive health care, such as a well-baby visit.

3) Status

Status codes indicate that a patient is either a carrier of a disease or has the sequelae or residual of a past disease or condition. This includes such things as the presence of prosthetic or mechanical devices resulting from past treatment. A status code is informative, because the status may affect the course of treatment and its outcome. A status code is distinct from a history code. The history code indicates that the patient no longer has the condition.

A status code should not be used with a diagnosis code from one of the body system chapters, if the diagnosis code includes the information provided by the status code. For example, code Z94.1, Heart transplant status, should not be used with a code from subcategory T86.2, Complications of heart transplant. The status code does not provide additional information. The complication code indicates that the patient is a heart transplant patient.

For encounters for weaning from a mechanical ventilator, assign a code from subcategory J96.1, Chronic respiratory failure, followed by code Z99.11, Dependence on respirator [ventilator] status.

The status Z codes/categories are:

Z14 Genetic carrier
Genetic carrier status indicates that a person carries a gene, associated with a particular disease, which may be passed to offspring who may develop that disease. The person does not have the disease and is not at risk of developing the disease.

Z15 Genetic susceptibility to disease
Genetic susceptibility indicates that a person has a gene that increases the risk of that person developing the disease.

Codes from category Z15 should not be used as principal or first-listed codes. If the patient has the condition to which he/she is susceptible, and that condition is the reason for the encounter, the code for the current condition should be sequenced first. If the patient is being seen for follow-up after completed treatment for this condition, and the condition no longer exists, a follow-up code should be sequenced first, followed by the appropriate personal history and genetic susceptibility codes. If the purpose of the encounter is genetic counseling associated with procreative management, code Z31.5, Encounter for genetic counseling, should be assigned as the first-listed code, followed by a code from category Z15. Additional codes should be assigned for any applicable family or personal history.

Z16 Resistance to antimicrobial drugs

This code indicates that a patient has a condition that is resistant to antimicrobial drug treatment. Sequence the infection code first.

Z17	Estrogen receptor status
Z18	Retained foreign body fragments
Z19	**Hormone sensitivity malignancy status**
Z21	Asymptomatic HIV infection status

This code indicates that a patient has tested positive for HIV but has manifested no signs or symptoms of the disease.

Z22	Carrier of infectious disease

Carrier status indicates that a person harbors the specific organisms of a disease without manifest symptoms and is capable of transmitting the infection.

Z28.3	Underimmunization status
Z33.1	Pregnant state, incidental

This code is a secondary code only for use when the pregnancy is in no way complicating the reason for visit. Otherwise, a code from the obstetric chapter is required.

Z66	Do not resuscitate

This code may be used when it is documented by the provider that a patient is on do not resuscitate status at any time during the stay.

Z67	Blood type
Z68	Body mass index (BMI)

As with all other secondary diagnosis codes, the BMI codes should only be assigned when they meet the definition of a reportable diagnosis (see Section III, Reporting Additional Diagnoses).

Z74.01	Bed confinement status
Z76.82	Awaiting organ transplant status
Z78	Other specified health status

Code Z78.1, Physical restraint status, may be used when it is documented by the provider that a patient has been put in restraints during the current encounter. Please note that this code should not be reported when it is documented by the provider that a patient is temporarily restrained during a procedure.

Z79	Long-term (current) drug therapy

Codes from this category indicate a patient's continuous use of a prescribed drug (including such things as aspirin therapy) for the long-term treatment of a condition or for prophylactic use. It is not for use for patients who have addictions to drugs. This subcategory is not for use of medications for detoxification or maintenance programs to prevent withdrawal symptoms in patients with drug dependence (e.g., methadone maintenance for opiate dependence). Assign the appropriate code for the drug dependence instead.

Assign a code from Z79 if the patient is receiving a medication for an extended period as a prophylactic measure (such as for the prevention of deep vein thrombosis) or as treatment of a chronic condition (such as arthritis) or a disease requiring a lengthy course of treatment (such as cancer). Do not assign a code from category Z79 for medication being administered for a brief period of time to treat an acute illness or injury (such as a course of antibiotics to treat acute bronchitis).

Z88   Allergy status to drugs, medicaments and biological substances
       Except: Z88.9, Allergy status to unspecified drugs, medicaments and biological substances status
Z89   Acquired absence of limb
Z90   Acquired absence of organs, not elsewhere classified
Z91.0- Allergy status, other than to drugs and biological substances
Z92.82 Status post administration of tPA (rtPA) in a different facility within the last 24 hours prior to admission to a current facility

Assign code Z92.82, Status post administration of tPA (rtPA) in a different facility within the last 24 hours prior to admission to current facility, as a secondary diagnosis when a patient is received by transfer into a facility and documentation indicates they were administered tissue plasminogen activator (tPA) within the last 24 hours prior to admission to the current facility.

This guideline applies even if the patient is still receiving the tPA at the time they are received into the current facility.

The appropriate code for the condition for which the tPA was administered (such as cerebrovascular disease or myocardial infarction) should be assigned first.

Code Z92.82 is only applicable to the receiving facility record and not to the transferring facility record.

Z93	Artificial opening status
Z94	Transplanted organ and tissue status
Z95	Presence of cardiac and vascular implants and grafts
Z96	Presence of other functional implants
Z97	Presence of other devices
Z98	Other postprocedural states

Assign code Z98.85, Transplanted organ removal status, to indicate that a transplanted organ has been previously removed. This code should not be assigned for the encounter in which the transplanted organ is removed. The complication necessitating removal of the transplant organ should be assigned for that encounter.

See section I.C19. for information on the coding of organ transplant complications.

Z99	Dependence on enabling machines and devices, not elsewhere classified

Note: Categories Z89-Z90 and Z93-Z99 are for use only if there are no complications or malfunctions of the organ or tissue replaced, the amputation site or the equipment on which the patient is dependent.

4) **History (of)**

There are two types of history Z codes, personal and family. Personal history codes explain a patient's past medical condition that no longer exists and is not receiving any treatment, but that has the potential for recurrence, and therefore may require continued monitoring.

Family history codes are for use when a patient has a family member(s) who has had a particular disease that causes the patient to be at higher risk of also contracting the disease.

Personal history codes may be used in conjunction with follow-up codes and family history codes may be used in conjunction with screening codes to explain the need for a test or procedure. History codes are also acceptable on any medical record regardless of the reason for visit. A history of an illness, even if no longer present, is important information that may alter the type of treatment ordered.

The history Z code categories are:

Z80   Family history of primary malignant neoplasm
Z81   Family history of mental and behavioral disorders
Z82   Family history of certain disabilities and chronic diseases (leading to disablement)
Z83   Family history of other specific disorders
Z84   Family history of other conditions
Z85   Personal history of malignant neoplasm
Z86   Personal history of certain other diseases
Z87   Personal history of other diseases and conditions
Z91.4-   Personal history of psychological trauma, not elsewhere classified
Z91.5   Personal history of self-harm
Z91.8-   Other specified personal risk factors, not elsewhere classified
Exception:
Z91.83, Wandering in diseases classified elsewhere
Z92   Personal history of medical treatment
Except: Z92.0, Personal history of contraception
Except: Z92.82, Status post administration of tPA (rtPA) in a different facility within the last 24 hours prior to admission to a current facility

5) Screening

Screening is the testing for disease or disease precursors in seemingly well individuals so that early detection and treatment can be provided for those who test positive for the disease (e.g., screening mammogram).

The testing of a person to rule out or confirm a suspected diagnosis because the patient has some sign or symptom is a diagnostic examination, not a screening. In these cases, the sign or symptom is used to explain the reason for the test.

A screening code may be a first-listed code if the reason for the visit is specifically the screening exam. It may also be used as an additional code if the screening is done during an office visit for other health problems. A screening code is not necessary if the screening is inherent to a routine examination, such as a pap smear done during a routine pelvic examination.

Should a condition be discovered during the screening then the code for the condition may be assigned as an additional diagnosis.

The Z code indicates that a screening exam is planned. A procedure code is required to confirm that the screening was performed.

The screening Z codes/categories:

Z11   Encounter for screening for infectious and parasitic diseases

Z12   Encounter for screening for malignant neoplasms

Z13   Encounter for screening for other diseases and disorders

            Except: Z13.9, Encounter for screening, unspecified

Z36   Encounter for antenatal screening for mother

6) Observation

There are **three** observation Z code categories. They are for use in very limited circumstances when a person is being observed for a suspected condition that is ruled out. The observation codes are not for use if an injury or illness or any signs or symptoms related to the suspected condition are present. In such cases the diagnosis/symptom code is used with the corresponding external cause code.

The observation codes are to be used as principal diagnosis only. **The only exception to this is when the principal diagnosis is required to be a code from category Z38, Liveborn infants according to place of birth and type of delivery. Then a code from category Z05, Encounter for observation and evaluation of newborn for suspected diseases and conditions ruled out, is sequenced after the Z38 code.** Additional codes may be used in addition to the observation code, but only if they are unrelated to the suspected condition being observed.

Codes from subcategory Z03.7, Encounter for suspected maternal and fetal conditions ruled out, may either be used as a first-listed or as an additional code assignment depending on the case. They are for use in very limited circumstances on a maternal record when an encounter is for a suspected maternal or fetal condition that is ruled out during that encounter (for example, a maternal or fetal condition may be suspected due to an abnormal test result). These codes should not be used when the condition is confirmed. In those cases, the confirmed condition should be coded. In addition, these codes are not for use if an illness or any signs or symptoms related to the suspected condition or problem are present. In such cases the diagnosis/symptom code is used.

Additional codes may be used in addition to the code from subcategory Z03.7, but only if they are unrelated to the suspected condition being evaluated.

Codes from subcategory Z03.7 may not be used for encounters for antenatal screening of mother. *See Section I.C.21. Screening.*

For encounters for suspected fetal condition that are inconclusive following testing and evaluation, assign the appropriate code from category O35, O36, O40 or O41.

The observation Z code categories:

Z03   Encounter for medical observation for suspected diseases and conditions ruled out

Z04   Encounter for examination and observation for other reasons
Except: Z04.9, Encounter for examination and observation for unspecified reason

Z05   Encounter for observation and evaluation of newborn for suspected diseases and conditions ruled out

7)   **Aftercare**

Aftercare visit codes cover situations when the initial treatment of a disease has been performed and the patient requires continued care during the healing or recovery phase, or for the long-term consequences of the disease. The aftercare Z code should not be used if treatment is directed at a current, acute disease. The diagnosis code is to be used in these cases. Exceptions to this rule are codes Z51.0, Encounter for antineoplastic radiation therapy, and codes from subcategory Z51.1, Encounter for antineoplastic chemotherapy and immunotherapy. These codes are to be first-listed, followed by the diagnosis code when a patient's encounter is solely to receive radiation therapy, chemotherapy, or immunotherapy for the treatment of a neoplasm. If the reason for the encounter is more than one type of antineoplastic therapy, code Z51.0 and a code from subcategory Z51.1 may be assigned together, in which case one of these codes would be reported as a secondary diagnosis.

The aftercare Z codes should also not be used for aftercare for injuries. For aftercare of an injury, assign the acute injury code with the appropriate 7th character (for subsequent encounter).

The aftercare codes are generally first-listed to explain the specific reason for the encounter. An aftercare code may be used as an additional code when some type of aftercare is provided in addition to the reason for admission and no diagnosis code is applicable. An example of this would be the closure of a colostomy during an encounter for treatment of another condition.

Aftercare codes should be used in conjunction with other aftercare codes or diagnosis codes to provide better detail on the specifics of an aftercare encounter visit, unless otherwise directed by the classification. Should a patient receive multiple types of antineoplastic therapy during the same encounter, code Z51.0, Encounter for antineoplastic radiation therapy, and codes from subcategory Z51.1, Encounter for antineoplastic chemotherapy and immunotherapy, may be used together on a record. The sequencing of multiple aftercare codes depends on the circumstances of the encounter.

Certain aftercare Z code categories need a secondary diagnosis code to describe the resolving condition or sequelae. For others, the condition is included in the code title.

Additional Z code aftercare category terms include fitting and adjustment, and attention to artificial openings.

Status Z codes may be used with aftercare Z codes to indicate the nature of the aftercare. For example code Z95.1, Presence of aortocoronary bypass graft, may be used with code Z48.812, Encounter for surgical aftercare following surgery on the circulatory system, to indicate the surgery for which the aftercare is being performed. A status code should not be used when the aftercare code indicates the type of status, such as using Z43.0, Encounter for attention to tracheostomy, with Z93.0, Tracheostomy status.

The aftercare Z category/codes:

Z42	Encounter for plastic and reconstructive surgery following medical procedure or healed injury
Z43	Encounter for attention to artificial openings
Z44	Encounter for fitting and adjustment of external prosthetic device
Z45	Encounter for adjustment and management of implanted device
Z46	Encounter for fitting and adjustment of other devices
Z47	Orthopedic aftercare

Z48	Encounter for other postprocedural aftercare
Z49	Encounter for care involving renal dialysis
Z51	Encounter for other aftercare **and medical care**

8) **Follow-up**

The follow-up codes are used to explain continuing surveillance following completed treatment of a disease, condition, or injury. They imply that the condition has been fully treated and no longer exists. They should not be confused with aftercare codes, or injury codes with a 7th character for subsequent encounter, that explain ongoing care of a healing condition or its sequelae. Follow-up codes may be used in conjunction with history codes to provide the full picture of the healed condition and its treatment. The follow-up code is sequenced first, followed by the history code.

A follow-up code may be used to explain multiple visits. Should a condition be found to have recurred on the follow-up visit, then the diagnosis code for the condition should be assigned in place of the follow-up code.

The follow-up Z code categories:
Z08	Encounter for follow-up examination after completed treatment for malignant neoplasm
Z09	Encounter for follow-up examination after completed treatment for conditions other than malignant neoplasm
Z39	Encounter for maternal postpartum care and examination

9) **Donor**

Codes in category Z52, Donors of organs and tissues, are used for living individuals who are donating blood or other body tissue. These codes are only for individuals donating for others, not for self-donations. They are not used to identify cadaveric donations.

10) **Counseling**

Counseling Z codes are used when a patient or family member receives assistance in the aftermath of an illness or injury, or when support is required in coping with family or social problems. They are not used in conjunction with a diagnosis code when the counseling component of care is considered integral to standard treatment.

The counseling Z codes/categories:

Z30.0-	Encounter for general counseling and advice on contraception
Z31.5	Encounter for genetic counseling
Z31.6-	Encounter for general counseling and advice on procreation
Z32.2	Encounter for childbirth instruction
Z32.3	Encounter for childcare instruction
Z69	Encounter for mental health services for victim and perpetrator of abuse
Z70	Counseling related to sexual attitude, behavior and orientation
Z71	Persons encountering health services for other counseling and medical advice, not elsewhere classified
Z76.81	Expectant mother prebirth pediatrician visit

11) **Encounters for Obstetrical and Reproductive Services**

See Section I.C.15. Pregnancy, Childbirth, and the Puerperium, for further instruction on the use of these codes.

Z codes for pregnancy are for use in those circumstances when none of the problems or complications included in the codes from the Obstetrics chapter exist (a routine prenatal visit or postpartum care). Codes in category Z34, Encounter for supervision of normal pregnancy, are always first-listed and are not to be used with any other code from the OB chapter.

Codes in category Z3A, Weeks of gestation, may be assigned to provide additional information about the pregnancy. **Category Z3A codes should not be assigned for pregnancies with abortive outcomes (categories O00-O08), elective termination of pregnancy (code Z33.32), nor for postpartum conditions, as category Z3A is not applicable to these conditions.** The date of the admission should be used to determine weeks of gestation for inpatient admissions that encompass more than one gestational week.

The outcome of delivery, category Z37, should be included on all maternal delivery records. It is always a secondary code. Codes in category Z37 should not be used on the newborn record.

Z codes for family planning (contraceptive) or procreative management and counseling should be included on an obstetric record either during the pregnancy or the postpartum stage, if applicable.

Z codes/categories for obstetrical and reproductive services:

Z30   Encounter for contraceptive management
Z31   Encounter for procreative management
Z32.2   Encounter for childbirth instruction
Z32.3   Encounter for childcare instruction
Z33   Pregnant state
Z34   Encounter for supervision of normal pregnancy
Z36   Encounter for antenatal screening of mother
Z3A   Weeks of gestation
Z37   Outcome of delivery
Z39   Encounter for maternal postpartum care and examination
Z76.81 Expectant mother prebirth pediatrician visit

12)   Newborns and Infants

See Section I.C.16. Newborn (Perinatal) Guidelines, for further instruction on the use of these codes.

Newborn Z codes/categories:

Z76.1 Encounter for health supervision and care of foundling
Z00.1- Encounter for routine child health examination
Z38   Liveborn infants according to place of birth and type of delivery

13)   Routine and administrative examinations

The Z codes allow for the description of encounters for routine examinations, such as, a general check-up, or, examinations for administrative purposes, such as, a pre-employment physical. The codes are not to be used if the examination is for diagnosis of a suspected condition or for treatment purposes. In such cases the diagnosis code is used. During a routine exam, should a diagnosis or condition be discovered, it should be coded as an additional code. Pre-existing and chronic conditions and history codes may also be included as additional codes as long as the examination is for administrative purposes and not focused on any particular condition.

Some of the codes for routine health examinations distinguish between "with" and "without" abnormal findings. Code assignment depends on the information that is known at the time the encounter is being coded. For example, if no abnormal findings were found during the examination, but the encounter is being coded before test results are back, it is acceptable to assign the code for "without abnormal findings." When assigning a code for "with abnormal findings," additional code(s) should be assigned to identify the specific abnormal finding(s).

Pre-operative examination and pre-procedural laboratory examination Z codes are for use only in those situations when a patient is being cleared for a procedure or surgery and no treatment is given.

The Z codes/categories for routine and administrative examinations:

Z00   Encounter for general examination without complaint, suspected or reported diagnosis

Z01   Encounter for other special examination without complaint, suspected or reported diagnosis

Z02   Encounter for administrative examination
           Except: Z02.9, Encounter for administrative examinations, unspecified

Z32.0-   Encounter for pregnancy test

14)   **Miscellaneous Z codes**

The miscellaneous Z codes capture a number of other health care encounters that do not fall into one of the other categories. Certain of these codes identify the reason for the encounter; others are for use as additional codes that provide useful information on circumstances that may affect a patient's care and treatment.

Prophylactic Organ Removal

For encounters specifically for prophylactic removal of an organ (such as prophylactic removal of breasts due to a genetic susceptibility to cancer or a family history of cancer), the principal or first-listed code should be a code from category Z40, Encounter for prophylactic surgery, followed by the appropriate codes to identify the associated risk factor (such as genetic susceptibility or family history).

If the patient has a malignancy of one site and is having prophylactic removal at another site to prevent either a new primary malignancy or metastatic disease, a code for the malignancy should also be assigned in addition to a code from subcategory Z40.0, Encounter for prophylactic surgery for risk factors related to malignant neoplasms. A Z40.0 code should not be assigned if the patient is having organ removal for treatment of a malignancy, such as the removal of the testes for the treatment of prostate cancer.

Miscellaneous Z codes/categories:

Z28	Immunization not carried out
	Except: Z28.3, Underimmunization status
Z29	**Encounter for other prophylactic measures**
Z40	Encounter for prophylactic surgery
Z41	Encounter for procedures for purposes other than remedying health state
	Except: Z41.9, Encounter for procedure for purposes other than remedying health state, unspecified
Z53	Persons encountering health services for specific procedures and treatment, not carried out
Z55	Problems related to education and literacy
Z56	Problems related to employment and unemployment
Z57	Occupational exposure to risk factors
Z58	Problems related to physical environment
Z59	Problems related to housing and economic circumstances
Z60	Problems related to social environment
Z62	Problems related to upbringing
Z63	Other problems related to primary support group, including family circumstances
Z64	Problems related to certain psychosocial circumstances
Z65	Problems related to other psychosocial circumstances
Z72	Problems related to lifestyle
	Note: These codes should be assigned only when the documentation specifies that the patient has an associated problem
Z73	Problems related to life management difficulty
Z74	Problems related to care provider dependency
	Except: Z74.01, Bed confinement status
Z75	Problems related to medical facilities and other health care
Z76.0	Encounter for issue of repeat prescription
Z76.3	Healthy person accompanying sick person
Z76.4	Other boarder to healthcare facility
Z76.5	Malingerer [conscious simulation]
Z91.1-	Patient's noncompliance with medical treatment and regimen
Z91.83	Wandering in diseases classified elsewhere
Z91.89	Other specified personal risk factors, not elsewhere classified

15) Nonspecific Z codes

Certain Z codes are so non-specific, or potentially redundant with other codes in the classification, that there can be little justification for their use in the inpatient setting. Their use in the outpatient setting should be limited to those instances when there is no further documentation to permit more precise coding. Otherwise, any sign or symptom or any other reason for visit that is captured in another code should be used.

Nonspecific Z codes/categories:

Z02.9   Encounter for administrative examinations, unspecified

Z04.9   Encounter for examination and observation for unspecified reason

Z13.9   Encounter for screening, unspecified

Z41.9   Encounter for procedure for purposes other than remedying health state, unspecified

Z52.9   Donor of unspecified organ or tissue

Z86.59   Personal history of other mental and behavioral disorders

Z88.9   Allergy status to unspecified drugs, medicaments and biological substances status

Z92.0   Personal history of contraception

16) Z Codes That May Only be Principal/First-Listed Diagnosis

The following Z codes/categories may only be reported as the principal/first-listed diagnosis, except when there are multiple encounters on the same day and the medical records for the encounters are combined:

Z00   Encounter for general examination without complaint, suspected or reported diagnosis
       Except: Z00.6

Z01   Encounter for other special examination without complaint, suspected or reported diagnosis

Z02   Encounter for administrative examination

Z03   Encounter for medical observation for suspected diseases and conditions ruled out

Z04   Encounter for examination and observation for other reasons

Z33.2 Encounter for elective termination of pregnancy

Z31.81 Encounter for male factor infertility in female patient

Z31.83 Encounter for assisted reproductive fertility procedure cycle

Z31.84 Encounter for fertility preservation procedure

Z34   Encounter for supervision of normal pregnancy

Z39   Encounter for maternal postpartum care and examination

Z38	Liveborn infants according to place of birth and type of delivery
Z42	Encounter for plastic and reconstructive surgery following medical procedure or healed injury
Z51.0	Encounter for antineoplastic radiation therapy
Z51.1-	Encounter for antineoplastic chemotherapy and immunotherapy
Z52	Donors of organs and tissues Except: Z52.9, Donor of unspecified organ or tissue
Z76.1	Encounter for health supervision and care of foundling
Z76.2	Encounter for health supervision and care of other healthy infant and child
Z99.12	Encounter for respirator [ventilator] dependence during power failure

Section II. Selection of Principal Diagnosis

The circumstances of inpatient admission always govern the selection of principal diagnosis. The principal diagnosis is defined in the Uniform Hospital Discharge Data Set (UHDDS) as "that condition established after study to be chiefly responsible for occasioning the admission of the patient to the hospital for care."

The UHDDS definitions are used by hospitals to report inpatient data elements in a standardized manner. These data elements and their definitions can be found in the July 31, 1985, Federal Register (Vol. 50, No, 147), pp. 31038-40.

Since that time the application of the UHDDS definitions has been expanded to include all non-outpatient settings (acute care, short term, long term care and psychiatric hospitals; home health agencies; rehab facilities; nursing homes, etc). **The UHDDS definitions also apply to hospice services (all levels of care).**

In determining principal diagnosis, coding conventions in the ICD-10-CM, the Tabular List and Alphabetic Index take precedence over these official coding guidelines.
(See Section I.A., Conventions for the ICD-10-CM)

The importance of consistent, complete documentation in the medical record cannot be overemphasized. Without such documentation the application of all coding guidelines is a difficult, if not impossible, task.

A. Codes for symptoms, signs, and ill-defined conditions

Codes for symptoms, signs, and ill-defined conditions from Chapter 18 are not to be used as principal diagnosis when a related definitive diagnosis has been established.

B. Two or more interrelated conditions, each potentially meeting the definition for principal diagnosis.

When there are two or more interrelated conditions (such as diseases in the same ICD-10-CM chapter or manifestations characteristically associated with a certain disease) potentially meeting the definition of principal diagnosis, either condition may be sequenced first, unless the circumstances of the admission, the therapy provided, the Tabular List, or the Alphabetic Index indicate otherwise.

C. Two or more diagnoses that equally meet the definition for principal diagnosis

In the unusual instance when two or more diagnoses equally meet the criteria for principal diagnosis as determined by the circumstances of admission, diagnostic workup and/or therapy provided, and the Alphabetic Index, Tabular List, or another coding guidelines does not provide sequencing direction, any one of the diagnoses may be sequenced first.

D. Two or more comparative or contrasting conditions

In those rare instances when two or more contrasting or comparative diagnoses are documented as "either/or" (or similar terminology), they are coded as if the diagnoses were confirmed and the diagnoses are sequenced according to the circumstances of the admission. If no further determination can be made as to which diagnosis should be principal, either diagnosis may be sequenced first.

E. A symptom(s) followed by contrasting/comparative diagnoses

GUIDELINE HAS BEEN DELETED EFFECTIVE OCTOBER 1, 2014

F. Original treatment plan not carried out

Sequence as the principal diagnosis the condition, which after study occasioned the admission to the hospital, even though treatment may not have been carried out due to unforeseen circumstances.

G. Complications of surgery and other medical care

When the admission is for treatment of a complication resulting from surgery or other medical care, the complication code is sequenced as the principal diagnosis. If the complication is classified to the T80-T88 series and the code lacks the necessary specificity in describing the complication, an additional code for the specific complication should be assigned.

H. Uncertain Diagnosis

If the diagnosis documented at the time of discharge is qualified as "probable", "suspected", "likely", "questionable", "possible", or "still to be ruled out", or other similar terms indicating uncertainty, code the condition as if it existed or was established. The bases for these guidelines are the diagnostic workup, arrangements for further workup or observation, and initial therapeutic approach that correspond most closely with the established diagnosis.

Note: This guideline is applicable only to inpatient admissions to short-term, acute, long-term care and psychiatric hospitals.

I. Admission from Observation Unit

1. Admission Following Medical Observation

When a patient is admitted to an observation unit for a medical condition, which either worsens or does not improve, and is subsequently admitted as an inpatient of the same hospital for this same medical condition, the principal diagnosis would be the medical condition which led to the hospital admission.

2. Admission Following Post-Operative Observation

When a patient is admitted to an observation unit to monitor a condition (or complication) that develops following outpatient surgery, and then is subsequently admitted as an inpatient of the same hospital, hospitals should apply the Uniform Hospital Discharge Data Set (UHDDS) definition of principal diagnosis as "that condition established after study to be chiefly responsible for occasioning the admission of the patient to the hospital for care."

J. Admission from Outpatient Surgery

When a patient receives surgery in the hospital's outpatient surgery department and is subsequently admitted for continuing inpatient care at the same hospital, the following guidelines should be followed in selecting the principal diagnosis for the inpatient admission:

- If the reason for the inpatient admission is a complication, assign the complication as the principal diagnosis.
- If no complication, or other condition, is documented as the reason for the inpatient admission, assign the reason for the outpatient surgery as the principal diagnosis.
- If the reason for the inpatient admission is another condition unrelated to the surgery, assign the unrelated condition as the principal diagnosis.

K. Admissions/Encounters for Rehabilitation

When the purpose for the admission/encounter is rehabilitation, sequence first the code for the condition for which the service is being performed. For example, for an admission/encounter for rehabilitation for right-sided dominant hemiplegia following a cerebrovascular infarction, report code I69.351, Hemiplegia and hemiparesis following cerebral infarction affecting right dominant side, as the first-listed or principal diagnosis.

If the condition for which the rehabilitation service is no longer present, report the appropriate aftercare code as the first-listed or principal diagnosis. For example, if a patient with severe degenerative osteoarthritis of the hip, underwent hip replacement and the current encounter/admission is for rehabilitation, report code Z47.1, Aftercare following joint replacement surgery, as the first-listed or principal diagnosis.

See Section I.C.21.c.7, Factors influencing health states and contact with health services, Aftercare.

Section III. Reporting Additional Diagnoses

GENERAL RULES FOR OTHER (ADDITIONAL) DIAGNOSES

For reporting purposes the definition for "other diagnoses" is interpreted as additional conditions that affect patient care in terms of requiring:

> clinical evaluation; or
> therapeutic treatment; or
> diagnostic procedures; or
> extended length of hospital stay; or
> increased nursing care and/or monitoring.

The UHDDS item #11-b defines Other Diagnoses as "all conditions that coexist at the time of admission, that develop subsequently, or that affect the treatment received and/or the length of stay. Diagnoses that relate to an earlier episode which have no bearing on the current hospital stay are to be excluded." UHDDS definitions apply to inpatients in acute care, short-term, long term care and psychiatric hospital setting. The UHDDS definitions are used by acute care short-term hospitals to report inpatient data elements in a standardized manner. These data elements and their definitions can be found in the July 31, 1985, Federal Register (Vol. 50, No, 147), pp. 31038-40.

Since that time the application of the UHDDS definitions has been expanded to include all non-outpatient settings (acute care, short term, long term care and psychiatric hospitals; home health agencies; rehab facilities; nursing homes, etc). **The UHDDS definitions also apply to hospice services (all levels of care).**

The following guidelines are to be applied in designating "other diagnoses" when neither the Alphabetic Index nor the Tabular List in ICD-10-CM provide direction. The listing of the diagnoses in the patient record is the responsibility of the attending provider.

A. Previous conditions

> If the provider has included a diagnosis in the final diagnostic statement, such as the discharge summary or the face sheet, it should ordinarily be coded. Some providers include in the diagnostic statement resolved conditions or diagnoses and status-post

procedures from previous admission that have no bearing on the current stay. Such conditions are not to be reported and are coded only if required by hospital policy.

However, history codes (categories Z80-Z87) may be used as secondary codes if the historical condition or family history has an impact on current care or influences treatment.

B. Abnormal findings

Abnormal findings (laboratory, x-ray, pathologic, and other diagnostic results) are not coded and reported unless the provider indicates their clinical significance. If the findings are outside the normal range and the attending provider has ordered other tests to evaluate the condition or prescribed treatment, it is appropriate to ask the provider whether the abnormal finding should be added.

Please note: This differs from the coding practices in the outpatient setting for coding encounters for diagnostic tests that have been interpreted by a provider.

C. Uncertain Diagnosis

If the diagnosis documented at the time of discharge is qualified as "probable", "suspected", "likely", "questionable", "possible", or "still to be ruled out" or other similar terms indicating uncertainty, code the condition as if it existed or was established. The bases for these guidelines are the diagnostic workup, arrangements for further workup or observation, and initial therapeutic approach that correspond most closely with the established diagnosis.

Note: This guideline is applicable only to inpatient admissions to short-term, acute, long-term care and psychiatric hospitals.

Section IV. Diagnostic Coding and Reporting Guidelines for Outpatient Services

These coding guidelines for outpatient diagnoses have been approved for use by hospitals/providers in coding and reporting hospital-based outpatient services and provider-based office visits. **Guidelines in Section I, Conventions, general coding guidelines and chapter-specific guidelines, should also be applied for outpatient services and office visits.**

Information about the use of certain abbreviations, punctuation, symbols, and other conventions used in the ICD-10-CM Tabular List (code numbers and titles), can be found in Section IA of these guidelines, under "Conventions Used in the Tabular List." Section I.B. contains general guidelines that apply to the entire classification. Section I.C. contains chapter-specific guidelines that correspond to the chapters as they are arranged in the classification. Information about the correct sequence to use in finding a code is also described in Section I.

The terms encounter and visit are often used interchangeably in describing outpatient service contacts and, therefore, appear together in these guidelines without distinguishing one from the other.

Though the conventions and general guidelines apply to all settings, coding guidelines for outpatient and provider reporting of diagnoses will vary in a number of instances from those for inpatient diagnoses, recognizing that:

The Uniform Hospital Discharge Data Set (UHDDS) definition of principal diagnosis **does not apply to hospital-based outpatient services and provider-based office visits**.

Coding guidelines for inconclusive diagnoses (probable, suspected, rule out, etc.) were developed for inpatient reporting and do not apply to outpatients.

A. Selection of first-listed condition

In the outpatient setting, the term first-listed diagnosis is used in lieu of principal diagnosis.

In determining the first-listed diagnosis the coding conventions of ICD-10-CM, as well as the general and disease specific guidelines take precedence over the outpatient guidelines.

Diagnoses often are not established at the time of the initial encounter/visit. It may take two or more visits before the diagnosis is confirmed.

The most critical rule involves beginning the search for the correct code assignment through the Alphabetic Index. Never begin searching initially in the Tabular List as this will lead to coding errors.

1. Outpatient Surgery

When a patient presents for outpatient surgery (same day surgery), code the reason for the surgery as the first-listed diagnosis (reason for the encounter), even if the surgery is not performed due to a contraindication.

2. Observation Stay

When a patient is admitted for observation for a medical condition, assign a code for the medical condition as the first-listed diagnosis.

When a patient presents for outpatient surgery and develops complications requiring admission to observation, code the reason for the surgery as the first reported diagnosis (reason for the encounter), followed by codes for the complications as secondary diagnoses.

B. Codes from A00.0 through T88.9, Z00-Z99

The appropriate code(s) from A00.0 through T88.9, Z00-Z99 must be used to identify diagnoses, symptoms, conditions, problems, complaints, or other reason(s) for the encounter/visit.

C. Accurate reporting of ICD-10-CM diagnosis codes

For accurate reporting of ICD-10-CM diagnosis codes, the documentation should describe the patient's condition, using terminology which includes specific diagnoses as well as symptoms, problems, or reasons for the encounter. There are ICD-10-CM codes to describe all of these.

D. Codes that describe symptoms and signs

Codes that describe symptoms and signs, as opposed to diagnoses, are acceptable for reporting purposes when a diagnosis has not been established (confirmed) by the provider. Chapter 18 of ICD-10-CM, Symptoms, Signs, and Abnormal Clinical and Laboratory Findings Not Elsewhere Classified (codes R00-R99) contain many, but not all codes for symptoms.

E. Encounters for circumstances other than a disease or injury

ICD-10-CM provides codes to deal with encounters for circumstances other than a disease or injury. The Factors Influencing Health Status and Contact with Health Services codes (Z00-Z99) are provided to deal with occasions when circumstances other than a disease or injury are recorded as diagnosis or problems.
See Section I.C.21. Factors influencing health status and contact with health services.

F. Level of Detail in Coding

1. ICD-10-CM codes with 3, 4, 5, 6 or 7 characters

ICD-10-CM is composed of codes with 3, 4, 5, 6 or 7 characters. Codes with three characters are included in ICD-10-CM as the heading of a category of codes that may be further subdivided by the use of fourth, fifth, sixth or seventh characters to provide greater specificity.

2. Use of full number of characters required for a code

A three-character code is to be used only if it is not further subdivided. A code is invalid if it has not been coded to the full number of characters required for that code, including the 7th character, if applicable.

G. ICD-10-CM code for the diagnosis, condition, problem, or other reason for encounter/visit

List first the ICD-10-CM code for the diagnosis, condition, problem, or other reason for encounter/visit shown in the medical record to be chiefly responsible for the services provided. List additional codes that describe any coexisting conditions. In some cases the first-listed diagnosis may be a symptom when a diagnosis has not been established (confirmed) by the physician.

H. Uncertain diagnosis

Do not code diagnoses documented as "probable", "suspected," "questionable," "rule out," or "working diagnosis" or other similar terms indicating uncertainty. Rather, code the condition(s) to the highest degree of certainty for that encounter/visit, such as symptoms, signs, abnormal test results, or other reason for the visit.

Please note: This differs from the coding practices used by short-term, acute care, long-term care and psychiatric hospitals.

I. Chronic diseases

Chronic diseases treated on an ongoing basis may be coded and reported as many times as the patient receives treatment and care for the condition(s)

J. Code all documented conditions that coexist

Code all documented conditions that coexist at the time of the encounter/visit, and require or affect patient care treatment or management. Do not code conditions that were previously treated and no longer exist. However, history codes (categories Z80-Z87) may be used as secondary codes if the historical condition or family history has an impact on current care or influences treatment.

K. Patients receiving diagnostic services only

For patients receiving diagnostic services only during an encounter/visit, sequence first the diagnosis, condition, problem, or other reason for encounter/visit shown in the medical record to be chiefly responsible for the outpatient services provided during the encounter/visit. Codes for other diagnoses (e.g., chronic conditions) may be sequenced as additional diagnoses.

For encounters for routine laboratory/radiology testing in the absence of any signs, symptoms, or associated diagnosis, assign Z01.89, Encounter for other specified special examinations. If routine testing is performed during the same encounter as a test to evaluate a sign, symptom, or diagnosis, it is appropriate to assign both the Z code and the code describing the reason for the non-routine test.

For outpatient encounters for diagnostic tests that have been interpreted by a physician, and the final report is available at the time of coding, code any confirmed or definitive diagnosis(es) documented in the interpretation. Do not code related signs and symptoms as additional diagnoses.

Please note: This differs from the coding practice in the hospital inpatient setting regarding abnormal findings on test results.

L. Patients receiving therapeutic services only

For patients receiving therapeutic services only during an encounter/visit, sequence first the diagnosis, condition, problem, or other reason for encounter/visit shown in the medical record to be chiefly responsible for the outpatient services provided during the encounter/visit. Codes for other diagnoses (e.g., chronic conditions) may be sequenced as additional diagnoses.

The only exception to this rule is that when the primary reason for the admission/encounter is chemotherapy or radiation therapy, the appropriate Z code for the service is listed first, and the diagnosis or problem for which the service is being performed listed second.

M. Patients receiving preoperative evaluations only

For patients receiving preoperative evaluations only, sequence first a code from subcategory Z01.81, Encounter for pre-procedural examinations, to describe the pre-op consultations. Assign a code for the condition to describe the reason for the surgery as an additional diagnosis. Code also any findings related to the pre-op evaluation.

N. Ambulatory surgery

For ambulatory surgery, code the diagnosis for which the surgery was performed. If the postoperative diagnosis is known to be different from the preoperative diagnosis at the time the diagnosis is confirmed, select the postoperative diagnosis for coding, since it is the most definitive.

O. Routine outpatient prenatal visits

See Section I.C.15. Routine outpatient prenatal visits.

P. Encounters for general medical examinations with abnormal findings

The subcategories for encounters for general medical examinations, Z00.0-, provide codes for with and without abnormal findings. Should a general medical examination result in an abnormal finding, the code for general medical examination with abnormal finding should be assigned as the first-listed diagnosis. **An examination with abnormal findings refers to a condition/diagnosis that is newly identified or a change in severity of a chronic condition (such as uncontrolled hypertension, or an acute exacerbation of chronic obstructive pulmonary disease) during a routine physical examination.** A secondary code for the abnormal finding should also be coded.

Q. Encounters for routine health screenings

See Section I.C.21. Factors influencing health status and contact with health services, Screening

Appendix I
Present on Admission Reporting Guidelines

Introduction

These guidelines are to be used as a supplement to the *ICD-10-CM Official Guidelines for Coding and Reporting* to facilitate the assignment of the Present on Admission (POA) indicator for each diagnosis and external cause of injury code reported on claim forms (UB-04 and 837 Institutional).

These guidelines are not intended to replace any guidelines in the main body of the *ICD-10-CM Official Guidelines for Coding and Reporting*. The POA guidelines are not intended to provide guidance on when a condition should be coded, but rather, how to apply the POA indicator to the final set of diagnosis codes that have been assigned in accordance with Sections I, II, and III of the official coding guidelines. Subsequent to the assignment of the ICD-10-CM codes, the POA indicator should then be assigned to those conditions that have been coded.

As stated in the Introduction to the ICD-10-CM Official Guidelines for Coding and Reporting, a joint effort between the healthcare provider and the coder is essential to achieve complete and accurate documentation, code assignment, and reporting of diagnoses and procedures. The importance of consistent, complete documentation in the medical record cannot be overemphasized. Medical record documentation from any provider involved in the care and treatment of the patient may be used to support the determination of whether a condition was present on admission or not. In the context of the official coding guidelines, the term "provider" means a physician or any qualified healthcare practitioner who is legally accountable for establishing the patient's diagnosis.

These guidelines are not a substitute for the provider's clinical judgment as to the determination of whether a condition was/was not present on admission. The provider should be queried regarding issues related to the linking of signs/symptoms, timing of test results, and the timing of findings.

Please see the CDC website for the detailed list of ICD-10-CM codes that do not require the use of a POA indicator (ftp://ftp.cdc.gov/pub/Health_Statistics/NCHS/Publications/ICD10CM/2017/). The conditions on this exempt list represent categories and/or codes for circumstances regarding the healthcare encounter or factors influencing health status that do not represent a current disease or injury or are always present on admission.

General Reporting Requirements

All claims involving inpatient admissions to general acute care hospitals or other facilities that are subject to a law or regulation mandating collection of present on admission information.

Present on admission is defined as present at the time the order for inpatient admission occurs -- conditions that develop during an outpatient encounter, including emergency department, observation, or outpatient surgery, are considered as present on admission.

POA indicator is assigned to principal and secondary diagnoses (as defined in Section II of the Official Guidelines for Coding and Reporting) and the external cause of injury codes.

Issues related to inconsistent, missing, conflicting or unclear documentation must still be resolved by the provider.

If a condition would not be coded and reported based on UHDDS definitions and current official coding guidelines, then the POA indicator would not be reported.

Reporting Options
    Y - Yes
    N - No
    U - Unknown
    W – Clinically undetermined
    Unreported/Not used – (Exempt from POA reporting)

Reporting Definitions
    Y = present at the time of inpatient admission
    N = not present at the time of inpatient admission
    U = documentation is insufficient to determine if condition is present on admission
    W = provider is unable to clinically determine whether condition was present on admission or not

Timeframe for POA Identification and Documentation

There is no required timeframe as to when a provider (per the definition of "provider" used in these guidelines) must identify or document a condition to be present on admission. In some clinical situations, it may not be possible for a provider to make a definitive diagnosis (or a condition may not be recognized or reported by the patient) for a period of time after admission. In some cases it may be several days before the provider arrives at a definitive diagnosis. This does not mean that the condition was not present on admission. Determination of whether the condition was present on admission or not will be based on the applicable POA guideline as identified in this document, or on the provider's best clinical judgment.

If at the time of code assignment the documentation is unclear as to whether a condition was present on admission or not, it is appropriate to query the provider for clarification.

Assigning the POA Indicator

Condition is on the "Exempt from Reporting" list
> Leave the "present on admission" field blank if the condition is on the list of ICD-10-CM codes for which this field is not applicable. This is the only circumstance in which the field may be left blank.

POA Explicitly Documented
> Assign Y for any condition the provider explicitly documents as being present on admission.

> Assign N for any condition the provider explicitly documents as not present at the time of admission.

Conditions diagnosed prior to inpatient admission
> Assign "Y" for conditions that were diagnosed prior to admission (example: hypertension, diabetes mellitus, asthma)

Conditions diagnosed during the admission but clearly present before admission
> Assign "Y" for conditions diagnosed during the admission that were clearly present but not diagnosed until after admission occurred.

> Diagnoses subsequently confirmed after admission are considered present on admission if at the time of admission they are documented as suspected, possible, rule out, differential diagnosis, or constitute an underlying cause of a symptom that is present at the time of admission.

Condition develops during outpatient encounter prior to inpatient admission
> Assign Y for any condition that develops during an outpatient encounter prior to a written order for inpatient admission.

Documentation does not indicate whether condition was present on admission
> Assign "U" when the medical record documentation is unclear as to whether the condition was present on admission. "U" should not be routinely assigned and used only in very limited circumstances. Coders are encouraged to query the providers when the documentation is unclear.

Documentation states that it cannot be determined whether the condition was or was not present on admission
> Assign "W" when the medical record documentation indicates that it cannot be clinically determined whether or not the condition was present on admission.

Chronic condition with acute exacerbation during the admission
> If a single code identifies both the chronic condition and the acute exacerbation, see POA guidelines pertaining to **codes that contain multiple clinical concepts**.

If a single code only identifies the chronic condition and not the acute exacerbation (e.g., acute exacerbation of chronic leukemia), assign "Y."

Conditions documented as possible, probable, suspected, or rule out at the time of discharge

If the final diagnosis contains a possible, probable, suspected, or rule out diagnosis, and this diagnosis was based on signs, symptoms or clinical findings suspected at the time of inpatient admission, assign "Y."

If the final diagnosis contains a possible, probable, suspected, or rule out diagnosis, and this diagnosis was based on signs, symptoms or clinical findings that were not present on admission, assign "N".

Conditions documented as impending or threatened at the time of discharge

If the final diagnosis contains an impending or threatened diagnosis, and this diagnosis is based on symptoms or clinical findings that were present on admission, assign "Y".

If the final diagnosis contains an impending or threatened diagnosis, and this diagnosis is based on symptoms or clinical findings that were not present on admission, assign "N".

Acute and Chronic Conditions

Assign "Y" for acute conditions that are present at time of admission and N for acute conditions that are not present at time of admission.

Assign "Y" for chronic conditions, even though the condition may not be diagnosed until after admission.

If a single code identifies both an acute and chronic condition, see the POA guidelines for codes **that contain multiple clinical concepts**.

Codes **That Contain Multiple Clinical Concepts**

Assign "N" if **at least one** of the **clinical concepts included in the** code was not present on admission (e.g., COPD with acute exacerbation and the exacerbation was not present on admission; gastric ulcer that does not start bleeding until after admission; asthma patient develops status asthmaticus after admission).

Assign "Y" if all of the **clinical concepts included in the code** were present on admission (e.g., **duodenal ulcer that perforates prior to admission**).

For infection codes that include the causal organism, assign "Y" if the infection (or signs of the infection) **were** present on admission, even though the culture results may not be known until after admission (e.g., patient is admitted with pneumonia and the provider documents Pseudomonas as the causal organism a few days later).

Same Diagnosis Code for Two or More Conditions

When the same ICD-10-CM diagnosis code applies to two or more conditions during the same encounter (e.g. two separate conditions classified to the same ICD-10-CM diagnosis code):
Assign "Y" if all conditions represented by the single ICD-10-CM code were present on admission (e.g. bilateral unspecified age-related cataracts).

Assign "N" if any of the conditions represented by the single ICD-10-CM code was not present on admission (e.g. traumatic secondary and recurrent hemorrhage and seroma is assigned to a single code T79.2, but only one of the conditions was present on admission).

Obstetrical conditions

Whether or not the patient delivers during the current hospitalization does not affect assignment of the POA indicator. The determining factor for POA assignment is whether the pregnancy complication or obstetrical condition described by the code was present at the time of admission or not.

If the pregnancy complication or obstetrical condition was present on admission (e.g., patient admitted in preterm labor), assign "Y".

If the pregnancy complication or obstetrical condition was not present on admission (e.g., 2nd degree laceration during delivery, postpartum hemorrhage that occurred during current hospitalization, fetal distress develops after admission), assign "N".

If the obstetrical code includes more than one diagnosis and any of the diagnoses identified by the code were not present on admission assign "N".
(e.g., Category O11, Pre-existing hypertension with pre-eclampsia)

Perinatal conditions

Newborns are not considered to be admitted until after birth. Therefore, any condition present at birth or that developed in utero is considered present at admission and should be assigned "Y". This includes conditions that occur during delivery (e.g., injury during delivery, meconium aspiration, exposure to streptococcus B in the vaginal canal).

Congenital conditions and anomalies

Assign "Y" for congenital conditions and anomalies except for categories Q00-Q99, Congenital anomalies, which are on the exempt list. Congenital conditions are always considered present on admission.

External cause of injury codes

Assign "Y" for any external cause code representing an external cause of morbidity that occurred prior to inpatient admission (e.g., patient fell out of bed at home, patient fell out of bed in emergency room prior to admission)

Assign "N" for any external cause code representing an external cause of morbidity that occurred during inpatient hospitalization (e.g., patient fell out of hospital bed during hospital stay, patient experienced an adverse reaction to a medication administered after inpatient admission)